BORN to LEAD
WALLABY TEST CAPTAINS

Born to Lead
WALLABY TEST CAPTAINS

MAX HOWELL

WITH DR. LINGYU XIE

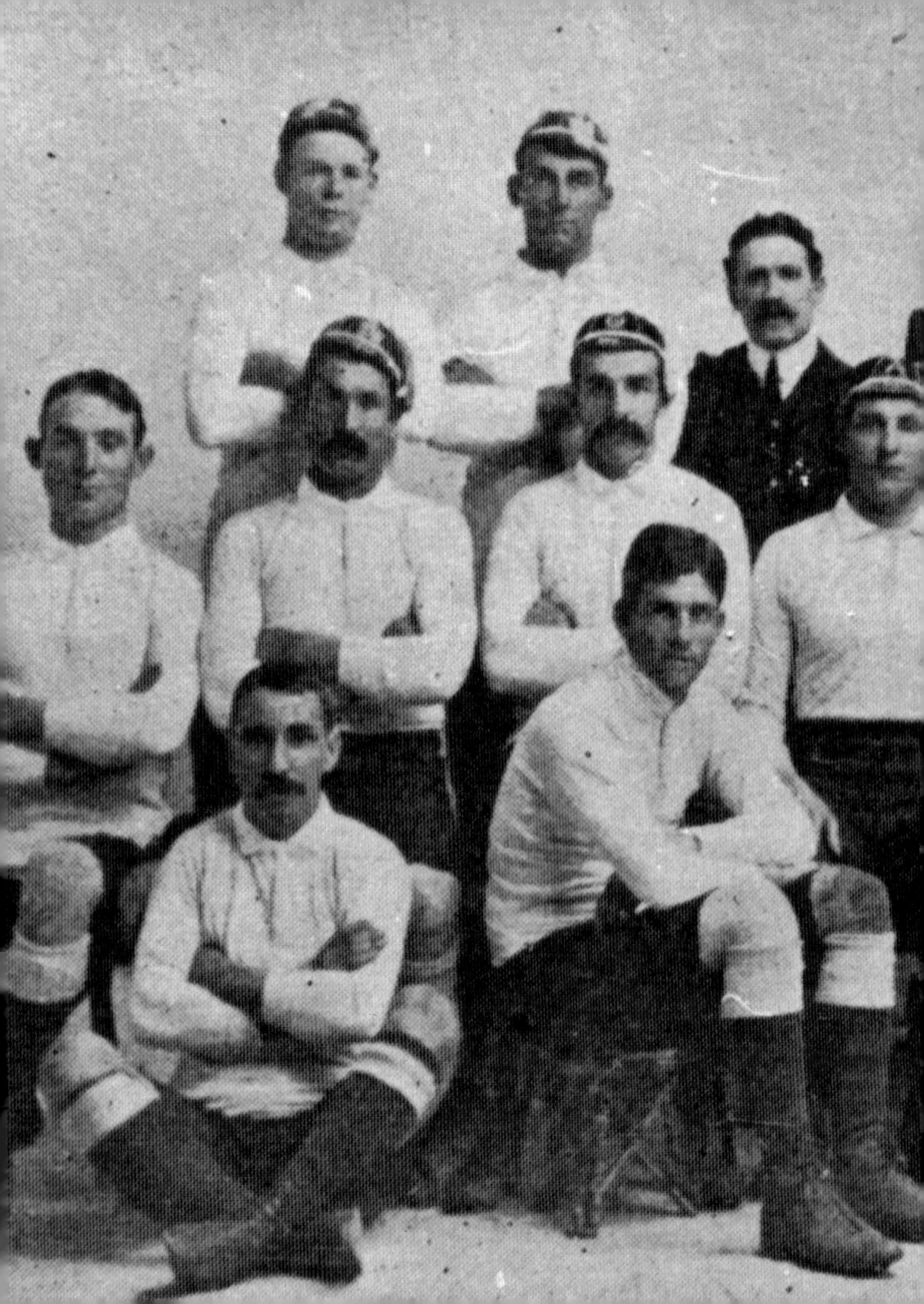

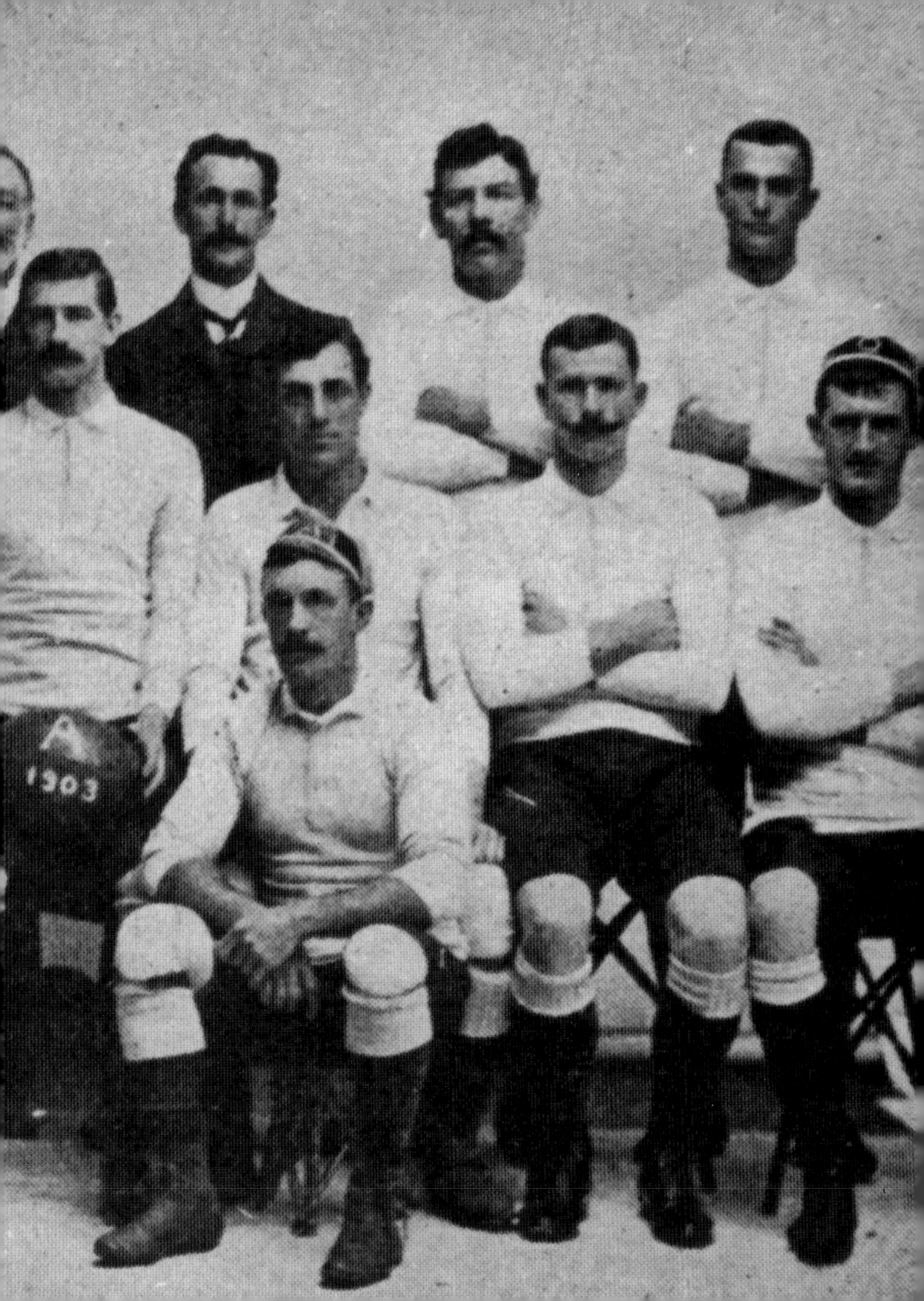
1903

ISBN 1-877252-18-2
Published in 2005 by Celebrity Books
Private Box 302 750
North Harbour, Auckland
New Zealand

Cover Design, book design and production by Dexter Fry
Printed in China through Bookbuilders, Hong Kong

Celebrity Books is the imprint of the Celebrity Book Company Limited.
160 Bush Road
Albany, North Shore City
New Zealand

'The photographs used in this book are supplied by The Max Howell Family Collection and Col Whelan of Action Photographics. We have made every effort to identify each and every photo from the Max Howell Family collections for origination'.

CONTENTS

Acknowledgements 8
Rugby prior to test captaincy 9
What makes a captain 11
Captains of Australia 16
1 FRANK ROW 17
2 BOB McCOWAN 19
3 STAN WICKHAM 21
4 FRANK NICHOLSON 24
5 PETER BURGE 26
6 ALLEN OXLADE 28
7 HERBERT MORAN 32
8 CHRIS McKIVAT 39
9 SYD MIDDLETON 45
10 WARD PRENTICE 48
11 TED FAHEY 51
12 LARRY DWYER 54
13 FRED WOOD 58
14 JIMMY FLYNN 64
15 WILLIAM WATSON 68
16 ARTHUR WALKER 71
17 DARBY LOUDON 74
18 WALTER FRIEND 76
19 BILLY SHEEHAN 78
20 TED THORN 82
21 CHARLIE FOX 85
22 TOM LAWTON 88
23 JOHNNY WALLACE 92
24 SYD MALCOLM 95
25 BOB LOUDON 98
26 JIMMY CLARK 100
27 DAVE COWPER 102
28 ALEX ROSS 105
29 RON WALDEN 110
30 CYRIL TOWERS 113
31 VAY WILSON 117
32 BILL McLEAN 120
33 PHIL HARDCASTLE 124
34 TREVOR ALLAN 127
35 NEV COTTRELL 130
36 KEITH WINNING 133
37 COL WINDON 135
38 JOHN SOLOMON 140
39 NICHOLAS SHEHADIE 145
40 ALAN CAMERON 149
41 DICK TOOTH 152
42 BOB DAVIDSON 155
43 DES CONNOR 159
44 CHARLES WILSON 162
45 PETER FENWICKE 166
46 KEN CATCHPOLE 169
47 PETER JOHNSON 174
48 JIM LENEHAN 178
49 JOHN THORNETT 182
50 GREG DAVIS 186
51 PETER SULLIVAN 190
52 JOHN HIPWELL 194
53 GEOFF SHAW 198
54 TONY SHAW 202
55 MARK LOANE 208
56 PAUL McLEAN 213
57 MARK ELLA 217
58 ANDREW SLACK 221
59 STEVE WILLIAMS 226
60 SIMON POIDEVIN 230
61 DAVID CODEY 235
62 MICHAEL LYNAGH 238
63 NICK FARR-JONES 244
64 PHIL KEARNS 252
65 ROD McCALL 259
66 JOHN EALES 263
67 TIM HORAN 271
68 DAVID WILSON 276
69 JASON LITTLE 281
70 GEORGE GREGAN 285
71 CHRIS WHITAKER 290
72 NATHAN SHARPE 293
Australian test summary 296

ACKNOWLEDGEMENTS

The following contributors are acknowledged: first to my wife Dr. Lingyu Xie, who did much of the research in this volume and whose charming personality made the writing as a delight; to Teejay Haar for his fine contribution on the schools of Wallabies; to the Jamieson family, Anne, Ray and Thomas for their friendship and professionalism in preparation of the manuscript; to Bensley Wilkes, my co-author on other projects, for his outstanding diligence in finally completing a list of games Wallabies played for Australia that were not tests; to Steve Johnson for his work on matches people have played for NSW; to Dexter Fry and Paul Neazor for their editorial association; to Colin and Naomi Whelan of Action Photographics, for their understanding, professionalism and superb images; and to the publisher, Bill Honeybone, one of my close friends for life.

RUGBY PRIOR TO TEST CAPTAINCY

There was much action on the rugby front by touring teams before 1899 when Australia's first captain emerged.

The first international tour was by New South Wales to New Zealand in 1882. A Southern Rugby Union [later the NSWRU] concept, the original idea was to bring a New Zealand team to Australia, but it had a luke-warm reception in the Canterbury and Otago Unions. Instead, it was suggested that a New South Wales side should tour New Zealand. There was no national body in either country at this point in time.

There was a trial match in Australia against a Queensland team, and then players were asked to put their names up for consideration. How times have changed. Eventually 16 were selected, and they sailed on 31st August 1882 on the *Rotomahana*. Sixteen players on a 7-match tour was an unenviable task, but the New South Welshmen won four and lost three, a creditable record.

This was the first international tour by any country.

There were some illustrious players on this NSW team, none of whom was ever to become a Test player. There was forward Ted Raper, player, manager and captain, forward Bob Thallon, who also acted as secretary, Harold Baylis, 'Jumbo' Walker and H.B. Fligg. Six came from the University Club (Sydney), three from each of the Wallaroo, Redfern and Balmain clubs, and a single representative from St. Leonards. Eleven of the team played in every match.

Rugby history, and particularly Australian rugby history, was made by this tour.

In 1884 New Zealand reciprocated, sending 19 players to NSW under captain William Millton and manager Sam Sleigh. Joe Warbrick missed the steamer to Wellington from Auckland and therefore had to travel to Sydney on his own, and James O'Donnell was arrested prior to departure because of monies owing various creditors, but the creditors did not show up in court and O'Donnell made the tour. It is little wonder that he decided to stay in Australia. The team, minus Joe Warbrick, sailed on the *Hauroto*.

This excursion was a sign of things to come, as eight matches were played in NSW and eight were won, the points for being 167 against a mere 17.

Among the NSW pioneers was captain Harold Baylis, L.E.F Neill and H. Tange.

The NZ 'Natives' team was next to tour. Some 28 players embarked on an unbelievable 107 match tour. It started in New Zealand in the winter of 1888, they played in Australia on the way to Britain (where 74 matches were played, up to four a week), then back to Australia in 1889. They also played a number of Australian Rules matches. Some five 'whites' were part of the 28-member team, so 'Natives' was somewhat of a misnomer. One Australian-born player was in the mix, Mac McCausland. There were five Warbricks in the team, a wonderful rugby-playing family who later would have a big influence on Australian rugby.

Some of the Australians to stand out against the 'Natives' in 1889 were Percy Colquhoun, Herbert Read, James McMahon, John Shaw and the Belbridge brothers in NSW, and Harry Abbott, Harry Speakman and 'Bull' Peirson in Queensland.

The first British tour to Australia was in 1888. Run on the same lines as cricket tours, this excursion was arranged by cricketers Alfred Shaw, Arthur Shrewsbury and James Lilywhite. It was a 22-member party, and they played 16 games, winning 14, losing none and drawing two. A tragedy beset this group as the captain, Bob Seddon, drowned while sculling on the Hunter River not long after arrival. Andrew Stoddart, an international cricketer, took over the captaincy and was arguably the team's finest player.

Players to shine in Australia at this time were Harry Braddon, an ex-New Zealander, Percy Colquhoun, Charles Tange and John Shaw (NSW) as well as Jimmy Orr, Frank Baynes, 'Jumbo' Peirson and Bill Eason (Queensland).

As the British tour of 1888 was an entrepreneurial one aiming to make money, the British played 19 Australian Rules Games as well (surprisingly winning seven and losing 12).

A particularly historic tour was the 1893 tour by New Zealand, as it was the first tour under the NZRFU banner, as the NZRFU had been formed in 1892. Three Unions had not affiliated, however, Canterbury, Otago and Southland, hence their players were not included. The team played in both states, playing 10 games and losing one, against NSW.

No tests were played, though many Australians such as Walter Cobb, Harry Abbott, Bill Galloway and Fred Henlen (NSW) were outstanding, as well as Bob McCowan, Harry Luya, Dan Allman and Fred O'Rourke (Queensland).

In 1894 NSW toured New Zealand once more, 26 players engaging in 12 matches. They were captained by ex-New Zealander Frank Surman. The player/manager was James McMahon.

A New Zealand team played just once against the 'Cornstalks', as NSW was named, and despite losing its first six games this one was won by 8–6. Only four games were won by NSW, so the victory against New Zealand became all the more special.

Some of the most outstanding players at this time were Walter Cobb, James McMahon, Frank Surman, Bill Galloway, Jumbo Carson and Fred Henlen.

In 1896 Queensland toured New Zealand. The captain was Sam Cockroft, the 1893/94 New Zealand representative, who had taken up work in Brisbane in 1895.

Only six matches were played, one against New Zealand, and Queensland lost all six. There were some fine players on the Queensland team such as future Australian captain Bob McCowan, 'Poley' Evans, W.H. Tanner and A.S. Gralton.

The following year, 1897, New Zealand came to Australia under Alf Bayly. Tom Pauling and Bill Hardcastle were on this team, and they were to contribute to Australia's rugby prowess in later years. Hardcastle would later switch codes and play rugby league with the Kangaroos on their tour to England 1908-09.

Harold Abbott, Stan Wickham, Bill Galloway, Fred Henlen, James Carson, Alf Braund and Alf Hanna shone for NSW, and Bob McCowan, Poley Evans, Ernie Currie, Dan Allman and Bill Tanner for Queensland.

The pity is that no player from 1882 to 1897 gained test status for his efforts, and similarly no-one could ever claim to captain Australia. Test rugby and test captaincy would occur in the year 1899.

WHAT MAKES A CAPTAIN?

The whole question of captaincy is an intriguing one. What makes a good captain, a leader? There are some basic concepts that immediately come to mind, but more often than not they are misconceptions. The simple fact is there are more types of captains than there are players on a rugby field. Put into a nutshell, there is no such thing as a captaincy or leadership profile that can be stated with any certainty. There have been small captains, tall captains, quiet captains, noisy captains, introvert and extrovert captains, forward captains, back captains, 'mad dog' captains, weak captains, strong captains, 'into the valley of death' captains, lucky captains, unlucky captains, high-principled captains, articulate captains, non-articulate captains, stuttering captains, theoretical captains and non-theoretical captains. What is for certain is that there have never been unpatriotic captains, or gutless captains. No-one in Australia's rugby history has dishonoured the position.

The point is that captaincy and leadership are not constants. They are variables and any one of the categories mentioned previously can result in a successful or unsuccessful captain. The leader may be a fullback, lock or hooker. We have seen them all.

Let us look at the position analysis first. Syd Malcolm, Ken Catchpole, Nick Farr-Jones, Chris Whitaker, Des Connor, Chris McKivat, George Gregan and Fred Wood were all half-backs, and captaining from that position makes a lot of sense because of the close link between the forwards and the backs. It is a central and control position, one close to the action.

Then there are fly halves who were captains, such as Paul McLean, Mark Ella, Michael Lynagh, Dick Tooth, John Solomon and Tom Lawton. Again, it is a control or central position.

As for centres, there have been Andrew Slack, Tim Horan, Jason Little, Trevor Allan, John Solomon, Geoff Shaw, Stan Wickham, Ward Prentice, Billy Sheehan, Johnny Wallace, Dave Cowper and Cyril Towers. Some have been phenomenally successful. Just away from the main action, the position is close enough and yet far enough to allow for some contemplation and analysis.

What about wingers? They are a rarity, perhaps because they are considered too far from the action. A few played there occasionally and became captains like Jason Little and Dave Cowper, but the moral of the story seems to be that if you are a wing and you want to captain Australia change positions.

Fullback is also not common for captaincy, but Alex Ross, one of the greatest, and Jim Lenehan captained Australia. The position certainly allows for an overview and an analysis of strategy, but distance from the action precludes the position from captaincy except in rare instances. It is tough to lead from behind.

In theory a hooker would seem to be the worst position for captaining, as the hooker has no view of the overall situation with his head in a scrummage. But there have been outstanding captains who were hookers, such as Peter Johnson, Phil Kearns and Nev Cottrell. Life on the field is not solely in the scrum, and a hooker is certainly in the action. But what can he advise the backs?

What about props? There have not been many, but Bob Davidson, Ron Walden, Nick Shehadie, John Thornett and Allen Oxlade made it as captains and were highly successful.

The locks have provided quite a few captains, such as Phil Hardcastle, John Eales, Alan Cameron, Peter Burge, Syd Middleton, Steve Williams, Rod McCall and Nathan Sharpe. Again, close to the action they certainly are, so as well as being in central they are also in control positions.

In the number eight position there has been Mark Loane, one of the finest, and he always regarded the position as the centre of the universe, the very best control position. A captain as number eight makes a lot of sense, as it is both a central and control position, but played correctly there is an opportunity to look over the strategy of the opponents, and yet they can view success or non-success in the scrum and the lineout, in particular.

When it comes to flankers, the field opens up. There has been Paddy Moran, Bill McLean, Keith Winning, Colin Windon, Charles Wilson, Greg Davis, Peter Sullivan, Tony Shaw, Simon Poidevin, David Codey and David Wilson. They lead the forays, back up the backs and so on, so a player as captain here makes a great deal of sense.

What has to be evident, however, is that captaincy has nothing to do with one's position on the field. It is possible to captain Australia successfully from any position on the field, though it is reasonably obvious that the chances are better if the player is a halfback, five-eighth, centre, prop, lock or flanker.

Selections, it can be seen, are not generally made on the basis of position, but rather are made with respect to an individual person, certain qualities that he possesses that are considered at that moment in time as suggesting leadership.

What, then, are the definitive characteristics of an Australian captain? There have been 'baby' captains, like Trevor Allan and Ken Catchpole, and older captains, like Phil Hardcastle and Bill McLean.

There have been quiet captains, like Alex Ross, Trevor Allan, Michael Lynagh, John Eales, Jason Little, Andrew Slack, Paul McLean, and vocal captains, like Bill McLean and Tony Shaw.

There have been 'mad dog', 'into the valley of death' and 'no retreat' captains, like Bill McLean, Greg Davis and Tony Shaw.

There have been knowledgeable, theoretical and intellectual captains, chief among them Johnny Wallace and Cyril Towers, Mark Loane and Paddy Moran.

There has only been one stuttering captain in history, Phil Hardcastle, who gave the greatest dinner address ever heard on a Wallaby tour: 'W-w-w-words f-f-f-fail m-m-m-me!'

There was at least one cunning, full of guile captain, Colin Windon, who seemed to know the angles or possibilities in a game, and how to exploit them.

As for articulate captains, there have been Johnny Wallace, Nick Farr-Jones, Andrew Slack and Mark Loane. They could exhort with the best of them in a logical and thought-out manner.

There have been working class captains, like Trevor Allan, Col Windon, Nick Shehadie, Dick Tooth, Bob Davidson, Peter Burge, John Hipwell, Syd Malcolm, Chris McKivat, and Bob Davidson, and on the other hand a whole host from the private schools, or middle and upper class captains. They are too numerous to mention.

There have been country lads, like Jason Little, Tim Horan, Geoff Shaw, Peter Fenwicke, Mark Loane, Jim Lenehan, Simon Poidevin and Larry Dwyer.

There have been two Rhodes Scholars, Tommy Lawton Sr and Johnny Wallace, 'Rock of Gibraltar' captains like Alex Ross and Mark Loane; bald-headed captains like Tony Shaw, George Gregan and Nathan Sharpe, prolific point-scoring captains, like Michael Lynagh, Paul McLean and Mark Ella, and there has even been a delegatory captain in Michael Lynagh who did not like to make the dressing room oration. There have also been players of sheer genius. Ken Catchpole, Mark Ella, John Eales and Paul McLean come easily to mind. They often led by their superb, unique deeds.

Many have been 'engine room' types: John Thornett, Peter Johnson, Steve Williams, Rod McCall, Phil Hardcastle, Nick Shehadie, Alan Cameron, Charlie Fox, Willie Watson, Ron Waldren, Nev Cottrell, Vay Wilson. Some were speed burners, like Dave Cowper, Johnny Wallace, Trevor Allan, Jason Little and Tim Horan. At the same time there was a plodder or two, Phil Hardcastle coming quickly to mind.

There were 'service to the game' captains, who were usually awarded a captaincy perhaps only once because of their sterling and continuous performances over the years, such as Rod McCall, Chris Whitaker, Jason Little, Nathan Sharpe and Tim Horan. There were 'lucky' captains, Keith Winning and Bob Davidson coming to mind, and unlucky ones, like 'Dooney' Hayes who captained a tour but never a test, Vay Wilson and Bill McLean.

A particular note should be made of those who captained Australia in non-test matches but never a test. The author feels strongly about this group, as recognition of them is well overdue. As any Wallaby knows, it is an honour to lead one's country out on the field. It is an unforgettable experience. These individuals should have their rightful place in history identified, just like test captains.

Some who captained Australia but not in a test are cited. The list is not necessarily complete, and the authors would appreciate hearing of names missed.

Viv Dunn (1 match 1921)
Owen Humphreys (1 match 1921)
Tom Davis (2 matches 1921)
Jock Blackwood (1 match 1925)
Dinny Love (2 matches 1933)
Gordon Sturtridge (1 match 1933)
'Dooney' Hayes (3 matches 1936)
Keith Windon (1 match 1936)
'Bernie' Schulte (2 matches 1946)
'Mick' Cremin (4 matches 1946-47)
Arthur Buchan (1 match 1946)
Eddie Broad (1 match 1948)
John Blomley (1 match 1953)
Tony Miller (2 matches 1953-58)
Rod Phelps (1 match 1957)
Ron Harvey (1 match 1958)
Keith Ellis (2 matches 1958)
Beres Ellwood (1 match 1962)
John Freedman (4 matches 1963)
Peter Crittle (2 matches 1963-66)
Jim Miller (1 match 1967)
Phil Smith (1 match 1969)
John Ballesty (3 matches 1969)
Rupert Rosenblum (1 match 1969)
Roy Prosser (1 match 1969)
Geoff Richardson (1 match 1971)
Dick Cocks (1 match 1973)
Stuart MacDougall (1 match 1975)
Dick L'Estrange (2 matches 1975)
Reg Smith (2 matches 1975-76)
Ron Graham (1 match 1976)

Gary Pearse (2 matches 1978)
Mick Mathers (2 matches 1981)
Michael Hawker (5 matches 1982-87)
Phil Clements (1 match 1982)
Duncan Hall (3 matches 1983)
Bill Calcraft (3 matches 1984-86)
Chris Roche (2 matches 1984)
Roger Gould (1 match 1984)
Glen Ella (1 match 1986)
Ross Reynolds (1 match 1986)
Bill Campbell (8 matches 1988-90)
David Campese (1 match 1988)
Brad Burke (1 match 1988)
Tom Lawton Jnr (4 matches 1989)
Greg Martin (1 match 1991)
Peter Slattery (3 matches 1992)
David Nucifora (1 match 1992)
Troy Coker (2 matches 1992)
Tim Gavin (1 match 1993)
Tim Kava (2 matches 1993)

Australians should doff their hats to the above list. They are unsung heroes in the history of Australian rugby.

What is also of interest are the schools captains came from. It is often argued that rugby union is the game of the upper classes. This is not borne out in the following analysis. Some 22 captains came from state schools. This number would assuredly be enlarged if the individuals whose school is not known are analysed: Peter Burge, Syd Malcolm, Chris McKivat, Syd Middleton and Ward Prentice. Burge, Malcolm, McKivat and Middleton were definitely from the working class.

Sixteen captains came from Catholic Schools. Most people would think there might be more, and arguments about Catholic preferences in selections cannot be upheld, at least with respect to captaincy. Also, it has to be acknowledged that these schools have fees, but nowhere near those of private schools, particularly in past years. The status of the Catholic Schools is an intermediate one between the state schools and private schools.

Some 27 captains came from private or GPS Schools, a figure by no means dominant. If the unknown players are included as state school boys, there have been approximately the same number of Wallaby captains from state and private schools.

The two schools which have produced the most Wallaby captains are Sydney Grammar, with six, and Brisbane Grammar, with five.

Only 23 of the 72 Wallaby captains have come from Queensland.

STATE SCHOOLS (22)

North Sydney Technical High School: Trevor Allan

Ashgrove (Q): Des Connor, John Eales

Petrie Terrace High School (Q): Allen Oxlade

Newcastle Technical High School: Bob Davidson

Wallsend High School: John Hipwell

Matraville High School: Mark Ella

Randwick Boys' High School: Col Windon (also Sydney Grammar)

Sydney Boys' High School: Peter Johnson, John Thornett, Chris Whitaker, Stan Wickham (also Parramatta Marist Brothers), Frank Row

Brisbane State High School: Bill McLean, David Wilson (also Ipswich Grammar)

Fort Street High School: Frank Row

Cleveland Street Public School: Nick Shehadie (also Crown Street Public School)

Chatswood High School: Peter Sullivan

Manly High School: Ted Thorn

Newcastle Boys' High School: Dick Tooth

Dubbo High School: Ron Walden

Gympie High School (Q): Vay Wilson

CATHOLIC SCHOOLS (16)

Gregory Terrace (Q): Jimmy Clark, Jimmy

Flynn, Michael Lynagh, Tony Shaw

St Laurence (Q): Nev Cottrell

Patrician Brothers, Orange: Larry Dwyer

Joeys: Ted Fahey, 'Paddy' Moran (also St Aloysius), Steve Williams

St Edmunds, ACT: George Gregan

Nudgee (Q): Mark Loane (also Gympie Christian Brothers), Paul McLean (also St Edmunds CBC)

St Columbans (Q): Rod McCall

St Patricks, Goulburn: Simon Poidevin

Villanova College (Q): Andrew Slack

Waverley College: Cyril Towers (also Roma High School, Qld, and Randwick Boys' High School)

PRIVATE SCHOOLS (27)

Newington: Alan Cameron, Dave Cowper, Nick Farr-Jones, Phil Kearns

Scots: Ken Catchpole, Phil Hardcastle, John Solomon

Shore: David Codey

Kings: Peter Fenwicke, Watty Friend, Billy Sheehan

Downlands (Q): Tim Horan

Sydney Grammar: Charlie Fox, Bob Loudon, Bob McCowan, Alex Ross, Arthur Walker, Johnnie Wallace

Brisbane Grammar (Q): Tom Lawton, Dick Marks, Frank Nicholson, 'Chilla' Wilson, Keith Winning

Riverview: Jim Lenehan

Toowoomba Grammar (Q): Jason Little

Southport (Q): Nathan Sharpe

Edmund Rice College: Geoff Shaw

NEW ZEALAND EDUCATED (3)

New Zealand Schools: Greg Davis, Darby Loudon, Willie Watson

SCHOOLS NOT KNOWN (5)

Peter Burge, Syd Malcolm, Chris McKivat, Syd Middleton, Ward Prentice.

The main point that seems to come out of this exercise is that captaincy does not fit one particular category, nor does leadership. Obviously Australia's captains have all been men of strong mettle, giving their all for their country. Nothing less would be expected of them. There have been successful and unsuccessful captains, but never once has there been a personal failure. The position is held in reverence by all those who run out first for their country. No matter how deserved a person was to be called upon to captain the Wallabies, he was lucky, fortunate to be provided with the opportunity when others equally well qualified might have been but were not called upon.

Taking John Eales, Nick Farr-Jones, John Thornett and George Gregan as examples, our longest-serving captains, they were so exceptional that rarely would others in their team be provided with the opportunity, that great honour, of getting the call to captain their country. That is the luck of the draw. Others have made it because it was in a period when there was no enduring captain, and many were tried.

The captains of Australia are a proud and now an honoured group, and that is how it should be. Surely every player has the dream to captain his country. From 1899 to 2004 approximatey 800 players have represented Australia, but only 72 have captained the Wallabies. No wonder this group can hold its head high and shoulders back.

This book is also a plea, as noted beforehand, for the well-overdue recognition of those who led out Australia in non-test matches, for this honour was performed with equal commitment and idealism.

Captions Of Australia

Ever since the year of 1899
Wallabies have run out in line.
The first to appear was the captain of the day
Determined to hold up in the heat of the fray.

The responsibility is ever enormous,
Hopes of all of a victory glorious.
Wins and losses have dotted the years,
A victory of substance bringing all to tears.

Gregan, Ella, Farr-Jones and Connor
Have handled their roles with honour.
Lynagh, Hipwell, Tony and Geoff Shaw
Have asked their teams to fight once more.

Loane, Thornett, Poidevin and Slack
All united in exhorting the pack
To absorb the pressure and never give in
For only then could Australia win.

All knew that defence was the key,
And called for a big hit for all to see.
They yelled at the lineout to jump even higher,
Particularly when all seemed so dire.

At times you need a man like McCall
To knock a few heads and watch them fall.
A captain's role is to hold the line
To tell the team that all will be fine.

The reality is it's wins that bring cheers,
While losing may occasion jeers.
What lonelier abode than a loser's room,
The air all fraught with gloom and doom.

'Tis the captain that has to meet the press
When indeed he may be under duress.
So the question needs to be asked,
Is it worth it when it does not last?

The honour it is to lead the green and gold
Is more than most mortals can ever behold.
Wherever they go and whatever they do.
They're Wallaby captains through and through.

Maxwell L. Howell

FRANK ROW

Australia's First Rugby Captain

AUSTRALIA'S TEST HISTORY began in 1899 when a second entrepreneurial team arrived from Great Britain, led by the Rev. Mathew Mullineux. He was to be immortalised by 'Banjo' Paterson in his bush ballad, "*The Reverend Mullineux*":

I'd reckon his weight at eight-stun-eight,
And his height at five-foot-two,
With a face as plain as an eight-day clock
And a walk as brisk as a bantam cock-
Game as a bantam, too.
Hard and wiry and full of steam,
That's the boss of the English Team,
Reverend Mullineux.

The first match of the Great Britain tour was against Goulburn, and the second was against a strong New South Wales team. Frank ('Banger') Row was the fullback in that game for the home side and lived up to his nickname with many telling tackles. He appeared as centre for Metropolis in the third encounter, and converted the only try by his team.

History was made on June 24 1899 when Australia's first test was played and Frank Row became Australia's first test captain. Only five of the team were from Queensland. Australia played in sky blue jerseys with the Australian coat of arms.

Frank Row: Australia's first test captain.

Born on January 28, 1877 at Dalby, Queensland, Row died on that very day in 1950, thus being 73 years of age. His father was William Row, an Englishman who came to Queensland to farm in 1864. The family moved to Sydney, and Row played for Manly Federals, Wallaroos and North Sydney. He transferred to New Zealand in the early 1900s, and captained Wellington in 1902. His brother Norman, a flanker, played six tests for Australia.

Jack Pollard has this to say about 'Banger' Row in *Australian Rugby*: "Frank Row enjoyed telling how he, and his brother Norman, took their father to watch his first rugby match. They looked up from the field at halftime and were surprised to see his seat empty. When they arrived home after the game they asked him why he had left early and their father said: 'Never seen such a lot of ruffians."'

Things were markedly different in those far-off days. When the team initially got together they elected the captain. Thus Frank Row, Queensland-born but a New South Wales resident, became Australia's first test captain. Australia won this first test by 13–3, Row inspiring his team with a brilliant display.

The twelfth match of the tour marked the second test at Bowen Park Exhibition Ground, Queensland. In those days players were invited to play, and Sydney experts were outraged when the skipper was not one of those asked. It appeared to be a cost-saving exercise, and only six players were nominated from the southern state. Great Britain emerged victorious in the second test by 11–0.

Frank Row went up against the British once more in their 15th match, against New South Wales, and he also fronted up for Metropolis in the following match. The 17th match was the third test, once more at the Sydney Cricket Ground, and again Row was elected captain. His defence in the game was once again solid, and he marked one of the game's immortals, the Welshman, Gwyn Nicholls. Britain won narrowly 11–10.

Row also captained Australia in the final test in Sydney, won convincingly by Britain by 13–0. Thus Row became part of Australia's rugby history, being its first test captain and being at the helm in three of the four tests played by his country.

FRANK ROW
(New South Wales)
CAPTAIN: 3 matches (3 tests) (v Great Britain 1899)
BORN: Dalby, Queensland, 28 January 1877
DIED: 28 January 1950
SCHOOL: Sydney Boys High School
NEW SOUTH WALES REPRESENTATION: 10 matches (1896–1902)
AUSTRALIAN REPRESENTATION: 3 matches (3 tests) 1899

BOB McCOWAN

A Fall From Grace

AUSTRALIA'S SECOND TEST was played in Brisbane in 1899, and was won by Britain 11–0. Because of money concerns, only six from New South Wales were included – Lonnie Spragg, Peter Ward, Bob Challoner, Charlie Ellis and Hyam Marks, but there was no place for first test captain Frank Row, so Australia's second test captain was Queensland's Bob McCowan. He played at fullback in two of the 1899 tests, and wing three-quarter in the final test. This was his complete test career. Like Row, he was elected to the captaincy by the players. Australia wore a maroon jersey with the Australian coat of arms.

Bob McCowan was the first Queenslander to captain Australia.

Born in Renfrewshire, Scotland, on February 1875, McCowan died at Murwillumbah, New South Wales, in 1944. He played for Brisbane Grammar while at school and Past Grammar following graduation. He captained his school team, and three others in that school team faced the British in Brisbane: 'Poley' Evans, Albert Henry and Charlie Graham. Jack Davis described McCowan as "short, remarkably quick and good in any era." Considered the "finest produced in Queensland", he was said to be "fast, clever in handling, kicking and passing the ball, and tackles well... Indeed, he possessed in high degree the essentials of a crack three-quarter."

McCowan played 24 times for the northern state from 1893 to 1900 and was captain in seven of these state matches. As well as going up against Great Britain, he played against New Zealand in 1893, 1896 and 1897.

George Smith told *The Cynic*, comparing Queensland and New South Wales after the 1897 New Zealand visit: "I think the Sydney men are far in front of those in Brisbane whom we played against. The backs up there seemed to lack combination altogether. If it had not been for McCowan's fine play, we would have put up much bigger scores than we did. He is the best fullback we have seen over here – kicks with either foot and is a very sure tackler – I know it."

The second Australian test team at Brisbane 1899. Back row: P. Carew, A. C. Corfe, H. Marks, C. Ellis; Second row: C. Hill, C. Graham, A. Henry, N. Street, A. G. Challoner, A.S. Spragg, H. Nelson; Front row: P. Ward, T. Ward, W. H. Tanner, R. McCowan (Capt.), E. Currie, W. Evans.

McCowan captained Queensland in an upset victory over the 1899 British team. A press report noted: "For the Queensland team McCowan at fullback had not much to do, but what he had he did well. He tackled in fine style, and in this respect he saved his side on several occasions. He also kicked well, making good use of the touch-line."

It would appear as if McCowan had the world at his feet, captaining his state and his country, and with a successful law practice, but his life was to have a sad ending. It began with an unsuccessful plunge on Phar Lap for the 1929 Melbourne Cup, and culminated in a gaol sentence of 14 years for fraudulently misappropriating £15,000 from a trust fund. After his release he moved to New South Wales and worked as a bar-room cleaner.

BOB McCOWAN
(Queensland)
CAPTAIN: 1 match (1test) (v Britain, 1899)
BORN: Renfrewshire, Scotland 28 February 1875
DIED: 1941
SCHOOL: Brisbane Grammar School
CLUBS: Past Grammar
QUEENSLAND REPRESENTATION: 1893–1900
AUSTRALIAN REPRESENTATION: 3 matches (3 tests)

STAN WICKHAM

Australia's First Touring Captain

WHATEVER ELSE Stan Wickham did in his long representative career, he will go down in history as Australia's first touring captain. Teams from New South Wales and Queensland had toured before, but this was Australia's first tour, to New Zealand in 1905.

There were 23 players on that initial tour, 14 from New South Wales and nine from Queensland. James Henderson, who also managed the 1901 New South Wales team to New Zealand, was the manager. There were some famous names on the Australian team, and they all became part of Australia's rugby history. There was Phil Carmichael from Queensland at fullback who played with his cap on. The three-quarters were Doug McLean, the scion of the famous Queensland rugby family, Arthur Penman, Charlie ('Boxer') Russell, Frank Bede Smith, L.M. Smith, and Stan Wickham, the five-eighths were Ernie Anlezark and Mick Dore, and the halfback was Fred Wood, who later captained his country.

The forwards were Alex Burdon, whose broken collar-bone was the prime cause of the rugby league split, Peter Burge, another captain to be, ex-New Zealander Jimmy Clarken, Tom Colton, Bill Hirschberg, Fred Nicholson, Ned O'Brien, 'Butcher' Oxlade, 'Billy' Richards and former British player Blair Swannell.

In those days tourists went by ship, the voyage from Sydney to Wellington being on the *Warrimoo*. This tour looked like easy pickings for the Australian team, as most had played against New Zealand in Australia a few weeks earlier, and the top New Zealand players were already on their way to England. It was a disappointing tour considering these facts, with Australia playing seven games and winning only three, these being the last three games against Manawatu-Hawkes Bay, Wanganui-Taranaki and Auckland. Stan Wickham played every match on tour and was top scorer with 18 points, with two penalty goals and three goals from marks.

A prolific point scorer, perhaps Wickham's finest representative appearance was for New South Wales against the 1897 New Zealand tourists. He scored two tries and a conversion in a thrilling and rare 22–8 victory.

Wickham's representative career began for New South Wales against Queensland in 1895 at the tender age of 19. He last played for New South Wales in 1906, so his career at the top spanned 11 years. Twenty-four of his representative games were against Queensland.

Born at Parramatta in 1877, he went to school at the Parramatta Marist Brothers, where he learned the game. He played for the Parramatta Club in 1893 and 1894, then for the powerful Wallaroo side in 1895 and 1896. It was then off

The moustached Stan Wickham, Australia's first touring captain. He would later be assistant manager of the 1908 Wallabies to the British Isles.

to the central west, where he represented Lucknow and played in Country versus City games from 1896 to 1899. In 1900 he was back in Sydney playing for Western Suburbs. He logged 87 first-grade games for his club.

Peter Sharpham, in *The First Wallabies*, said this of Stan Wickham: "A dashing centre three-quarter or fullback who was renowned for his exaggerated sidestep and swerve, and an accomplished coach."

When the team to tour the British Isles in 1908–09 was announced, only the manager, Captain James McMahon, was named to accompany the team. There were also two Official Visitors, E.S. Marks and Frank Roberts. There was a public furore over Wickham's omission, and a vehement public campaign led to his later inclusion as assistant manager.

Coaches were frowned upon in those days, and the assistant manager could not have been labelled as the coach by the amateur moguls in the British Isles. All coaching was supposed to be done by the captain, who in this case was Herbert ('Paddy') Moran. The fine point of the tour agreement was ignored, and Stan Wickham acted unofficially as the coach. The manager was also a recent player so the First Wallabies were well looked after in the coaching department.

A significant figure in Australia's early rugby, Wickham captained his country in four of his five test matches. Strangely, though, he never had the satisfaction of captaining or playing in a winning test side.

STAN WICKHAM

CAPTAIN: 10 matches (4 tests) (1 New Zealand 1903, 2 Great Britain 1904, 1 New Zealand 1905)
BORN: Lucknow (New South Wales), 1 January 1876)
DIED: March 1960
SCHOOL: Parramatta Marist Brothers'
CLUBS: Parramatta, Wallaroo (Sydney), Central West, Western Suburbs
NEW SOUTH WALES REPRESENTATION: 37 matches (1895–1906)
AUSTRALIAN REPRESENTATION: 11 matches (5 tests) (1903–05)

FRANK NICHOLSON

First Queenslander To Captain An Australian Team in Sydney

FRANK NICHOLSON had a relatively short career, although he played 13 games for Queensland from 1900 to 1904. All but two of these were against New South Wales. His career was interrupted by his enlistment in the Boer War, as happened with other rugby-playing Queenslanders Sine Boland, Arthur Corfe, Bill Galloway and Bill Hodgkinson.

Queensland rugby was very strong prior to and during Nicholson's hey-day, much of this due to the influence of intentional Harry Speakman, who migrated to Australia after playing on the 1888 British tour, and the Maori brothers Billy and Fred Warbrick, who excelled on the field and in the coaching ranks in Queensland. Then there was also the footballing legacy of Bob McCowan, 'Poley' Evans, 'Doey' Tanner, 'Paddy' Carew, Sine Boland, and 'Ginger' and 'Puddin' Colton.

Nicholson's major break-through at the top level came in 1903 with the visit of the New Zealand team, which many old-timers claim was the finest team ever to leave its shores. Led by veteran Jimmy Duncan, there were outstanding players like Billy Wallace, Opai Asher, Duncan McGregor, Dave Gallaher, Billy Stead and George Nicholson. They played 10 matches and won all of them.

Frank Nicholson's first jaunt into the big-time was at the Brisbane Exhibition Ground for

Frank Nicholson: Second Brisbane Grammar player to captain Australia and first Queenslander to captain Australia in Sydney.

Queensland on 1 August 1903 against this super-charged New Zealand team. He was not the captain, Lew Dixon was, but there were fine players on his side like ex-New Zealander Charlie Redwood, Doug McLean, Mick Dore, Austin Gralton, Charters Towers' Billy Richards and Allen ('Butcher') Oxlade.

Oxlade's nickname came about as his fans thought he cut up his opponents. Queensland was over-run by New Zealand to the tune of 17–0. Nicholson played in the second Queensland game as well, the locals going down by an even greater score, 28–0. Queensland did not manage a single point against the rampaging tourists.

Nicholson's efforts were rewarded, however, as he and four other Queenslanders – Charlie Redwood, Lew Evans, Austin Gralton and Sine Boland – were selected to play in the test in Sydney. Australia was trounced by 22–3.

In 1904 Frank Nicholson became the second captain of Australia to come from Brisbane Grammar School, and the first Queenslander to captain his country in a Sydney test. He had captained Queensland in the inter-state series, Queensland winning the second encounter by 11–7. His brother Fred scored a try in that game, and three weeks after Frank captained Australia, Fred made the team for his sole test.

There were seven Queenslanders in the first test against 'Darkie' Bedell-Sivright's Great Britain team: Charlie Redwood, Jack Hindmarsh, Lew Evans, Edgie Dore, Frank Nicholson, Billy Richards and Tom Colton. Frank was elected captain ahead of Stan Wickham, but Australia was downed by 17–0.

Frank Nicholson went to New Zealand with Australia's 1905 team, but he did not play a single game, presumably suffering an injury.

So his test captaincy in 1904 was his last big match. He then departed Australian shores, going to Philadelphia to study dentistry.

On his return, in 1911 he became both a Queensland selector and its coach.

FRANK NICHOLSON
CAPTAIN: 1 match (1 test) (v Britain 1904)
BORN: Villeneuva (Qld) 15 October 1878
DIED: 1970
SCHOOL: Brisbane Grammar School
CLUBS: Toombul (Qld)
QUEENSLAND REPRESENTATION:
1900–04: 13 games
AUSTRALIAN REPRESENTATION:
2 matches 1903–04 (2 tests)

PETER BURGE

The Tourist from Hell

PETER BURGE was called 'Emu', doubtless because of the thin legs and prancing walk of the 6–footer. Born in 1884, he died at 72 years of age.

Burge has one record that he doubtless wished he never had. He was on two rugby union tours, to New Zealand with the first full Australian team in 1905, and the then 'tour of tours' to the British Isles, Canada and the United States in 1908–09, the first such venture. In both trips Peter Burge only played one game, his injuries ruling out any further appearances. Peter made his first big-time appearance in 1904, playing for Metropolis against Great Britain. The British were led by a tough character in David Bedell-Sivright. The team included Pat McEvedy, who later became President of the NZRFU, and immortal Welsh players Rhys Gabe, Willie Llewellyn, Tommy Vile, who became President of the Welsh Rugby Union, and Percy Bush. The experience was a good one for the 20–year-old Burge, though the team lost by 6–19.

Peter Burge: nicknamed 'Emu', misfortune followed him around.

The 1905 New Zealand team under captain Jimmy Hunter came to Australia as a prelude to their tour to Britain, and only played three games. Peter Burge appeared in all of them, one for the Metropolitan Union (lost 3–22) and two for New South Wales (lost 0–19 and a surprising 8–8 draw in the last game).

Peter Burge toured New Zealand that same year, but as mentioned played only one game. However he was part of history, as this was the first tour overseas by an Australian team.

In 1906 Burge was involved in a bitter incident. Jack Pollard described it in *The Game and The Players*: "[For New South Wales] Peter Burge jumped in the air and kicked Phil Carmichael, the high-scoring Queensland fullback, on the chest. The referee took one look at Carmichael writhing on the ground but ordered off the wrong player, Harold Judd.

"An amazing scene developed, when New South Wales players, including 'Paddy' Moran, grouped around the referee, to support the alibi of the innocent Judd, while the real culprit hid silent in the background. In the end, Judd stayed on the field, but he did not relieve Queensland's intense bitterness when he demanded an apology. The crowd continued to shout insults at the New South Wales side for the rest of the game..."

N.S.W. won these brutal encounters 11–9 and 8–6.

By 1907 Burge was at the peak of his powers, playing four games against New Zealand, one for New South Wales and three for Australia. He was Australian captain in two of the tests, recording one draw and a loss. In 1908 he played in two matches for New South Wales against the touring Anglo-Welsh.

Then came the ill-fated 1908–09 tour, when he broke his tibia in the first match against Devon. Peter Flanagan from Queensland also had his leg broken while acting as a touch-judge in the third match, and at 22 never played again. Burge and Flanagan hobbled around with crutches the rest of the tour. Replacements were sent over, one being his brother, 'Son' Burge, and Ken Gavin, great-uncle of the modern international, Tim.

When the 1908–09 Wallabies returned to Australia, fourteen of them defected to rugby league. A shock-wave went through rugby union circles, and it was many years before the game's popularity was restored. Peter Burge was one of the new professionals, and he signed for 100 pounds. The others were Chris McKivat, Charles Russell, Arthur McCabe, John Barnett, Ken Gavin, Charles McMurtrie, William Dix, Edward McIntyre and Ed Mandible. It was a severe body blow to the amateur code. Burge later toured with Chris McKivat's 1911–12 Kangaroos.

PETER BURGE
CAPTAIN : 2 matches (2 tests) (v New Zealand 1907)
BORN: Penrith, 14 February 1884
DIED: July, 1956
SCHOOL: not known
CLUBS: South Sydney
NEW SOUTH WALES REPRESENTATION: 3 matches (1907–08)
AUSTRALIAN REPRESENTATION: 4 matches, 3 tests (1907-08)

ALLEN OXLADE

The 'Butcher' Who Became An Alderman

IN *VIEWLESS WINDS*, Herbert Moran said of Allen Oxlade: "In the front row [of Queensland] was a small, tough little player named Oxlade, nick-named 'Butcher'. He was very combative and very courageous, holding his own with men three, four, and five stone heavier. In later life he became as broad as he was long, and died a city alderman of Brisbane." One reporter said he was build like a pony, but was a strong as a horse, another called him "Terror Forward."

Allen Oxlade: Fiercely competitive on a rugby field.

His son, Boyd, played in the last three tests for Australia prior to World War II, in 1938. He was also a member of the ill-fated 1939 tour to the British Isles that did not play a game because of the outbreak of the war.

'Butcher' started his rugby career in Sydney with Norths in 1900, but went back to Queensland and played for Norths there for six successive seasons from 1902, and again in 1912. Among the Norths (Queensland) players when Oxlade joined them were such greats as Lonnie Spragg, Austin Gralton, Edgie Dore, Charlie Freestone and Bertie St John, the remarkable one-armed athlete from Rockhampton, who was also Queensland champion in tennis.

Toombul and Norths, in the Brisbane competition, always seemed to have rough games and Ian Diem wrote in *Red! Red! Red*: "Team mate Harry Green wrote Allen Oxlade will 'take as much as you can give and don't forget he will pay back.' Known as 'Butcher' because he carved up his opponents, he was punched by Toombul centre Fred Cleeve, whereupon Oxlade kicked him and was sent off by Charles Campbell. Oxlade was subsequently suspended and missed the southern tour."

His career reached its peak between 1904 and 1907. His first appearance against an international team was for Queensland in 1903 against New Zealand. There were other famous Queenslanders in the team: Charlie Redwood, Doug McLean, Mick Dore, Lew Evans, Austin Gralton, Billy Richards and Frank Nicholson among them. The New Zealanders had more than their share of legends on tour, including Billy Wallace, Opai Asher, Jimmy Duncan, Billy Stead, Duncan McGregor, George Nicholson and Dave Gallaher. New Zealand was much too strong in the match, beating the locals by 17–0.

In 1904 'Butcher' came into his own, and despite his small size he became an indispensable part of Queensland and Australian teams. This was the year of 'Darkie' Bedell-Sivright's Great Britain side, which included some all-time Welsh greats such as Percy Bush, Rhys Gabe, Willie Llewellyn and Tommy Vile. Blair Swannell, who was on the 1899 tour, was the only British player to repeat tours, and he stayed on and played in and for Australia.

Herbert Moran did not mix words when speaking of Swannell. In *Viewless Winds* he said Swannell "was, for a number of years, a bad influence in Sydney football... His conception of Rugby was one of trained violence." It must have been something when Oxlade and Swannell faced one another in following years.

In 1904 Oxlade played twice for Queensland and twice for Australia. His play made him a certainty for Australia's first-ever tour of New Zealand in 1905. Some Queenslanders on that tour felt that they were discriminated against by the selectors, but Oxlade was one of only five who played in every match.

No team came to Australia in 1906, so Oxlade had to wait until Jimmy Hunter's team from New Zealand came to resume his international career. He was not picked in the first test at the Sydney Cricket Ground, and only three Queenslanders – Phil Carmichael, George Watson and Peter Flanagan – were selected. In a crazy selection procedure Australia had two selectors, James McMahon of Sydney and 'Poley' Evans of Brisbane, and the local man had the casting vote.

Hence when the Brisbane test team was announced there were seven Queenslanders selected, and 'Butcher' Oxlade was captain. The current Queensland captain was Billy Richards, who was also picked, but Oxlade led the team. New Zealand won by 14 points to 5, despite the presence of luminaries such as Dally Messenger, 'Boxer' Russell, Peter Burge and Peter Flanagan.

This was the end of Oxlade's footballing days, as he travelled for Hofnungs in the north of Queensland for four years and then joined Oxlade Brothers in Brisbane, a family painting firm.

Rugby ended in Queensland out of respect for the first World War, and was not renewed in the north to 1929. This 1929 team was called "The Revivalists". A New Zealand team captained by the immortal Cliff Porter came that year and the second test was held in Brisbane.

Ian Diehm reported in *Red! Red! Red!*: "The match attracted giants of other days. Among the crowd were Bob McCowan, Phil Carmichael, Tom Welsby, 'Poley' Evans, 'Doey' Tanner, Jack Walsh, Jimmy Flynn, Charlie Redwood, 'Bluey' Thompson, Fred Lea and Alderman Allen Oxlade, known as the 'Terror forward'. When the All Black forward Reuben McWilliams buried little Australian halfback Sydney Malcolm, the hugely rotund Oxlade burst forth with, 'I'd have got McWilliams for that!'"

'Butcher' Oxlade was the third Queenslander to captain his country.

ALLEN OXLADE

CAPTAIN: 1 match (1 test) (v New Zealand 1907)

BORN: 1932

SCHOOL: Petrie Terrace State School, Brisbane

CLUBS: Norths (Sydney), Norths (Brisbane), Past Grammar

QUEENSLAND REPRESENTATION: 28 matches (1902–12)

AUSTRALIAN REPRESENTATION: 10 matches (4 tests) (1905–07)

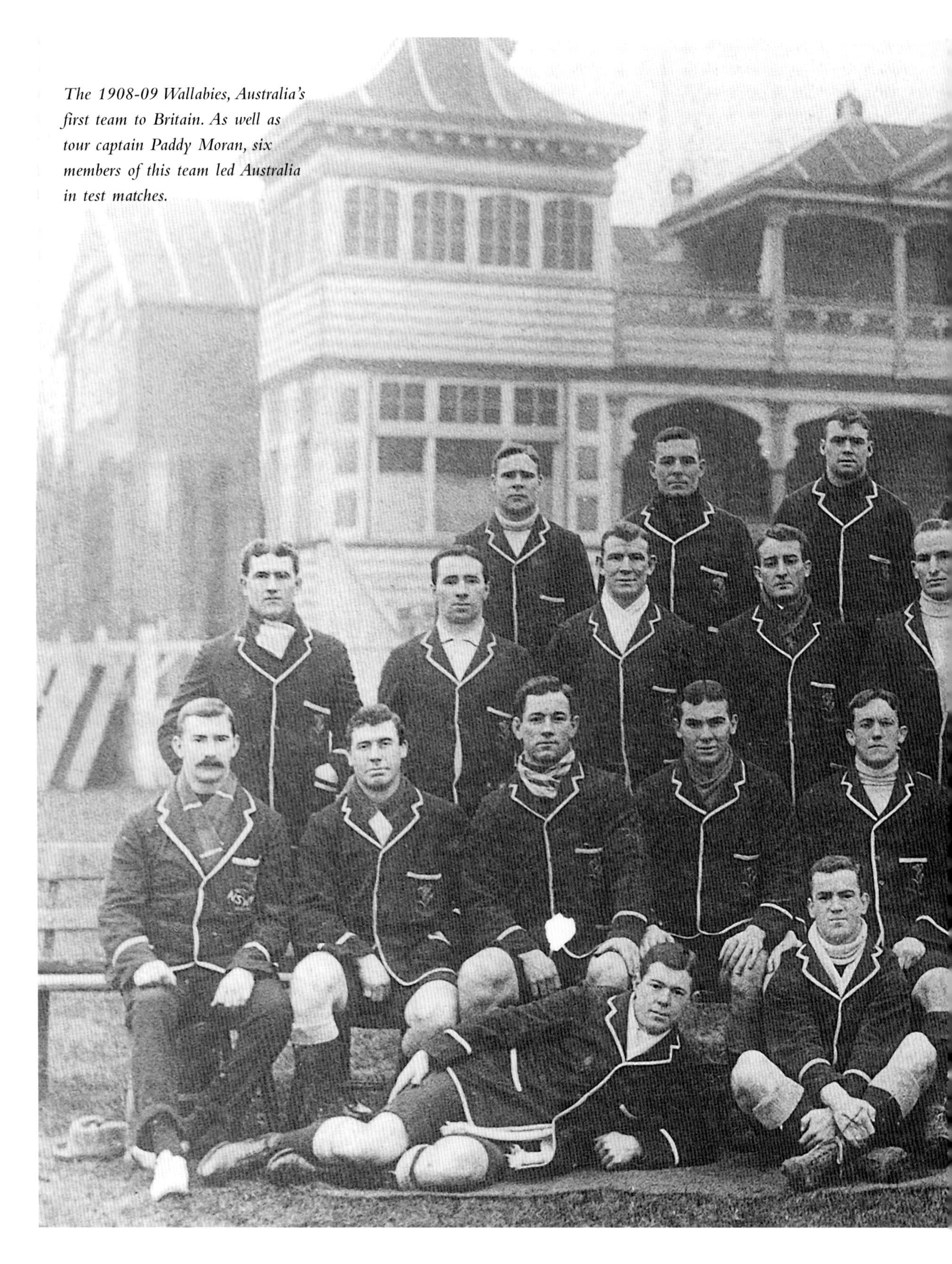

The 1908-09 Wallabies, Australia's first team to Britain. As well as tour captain Paddy Moran, six members of this team led Australia in test matches.

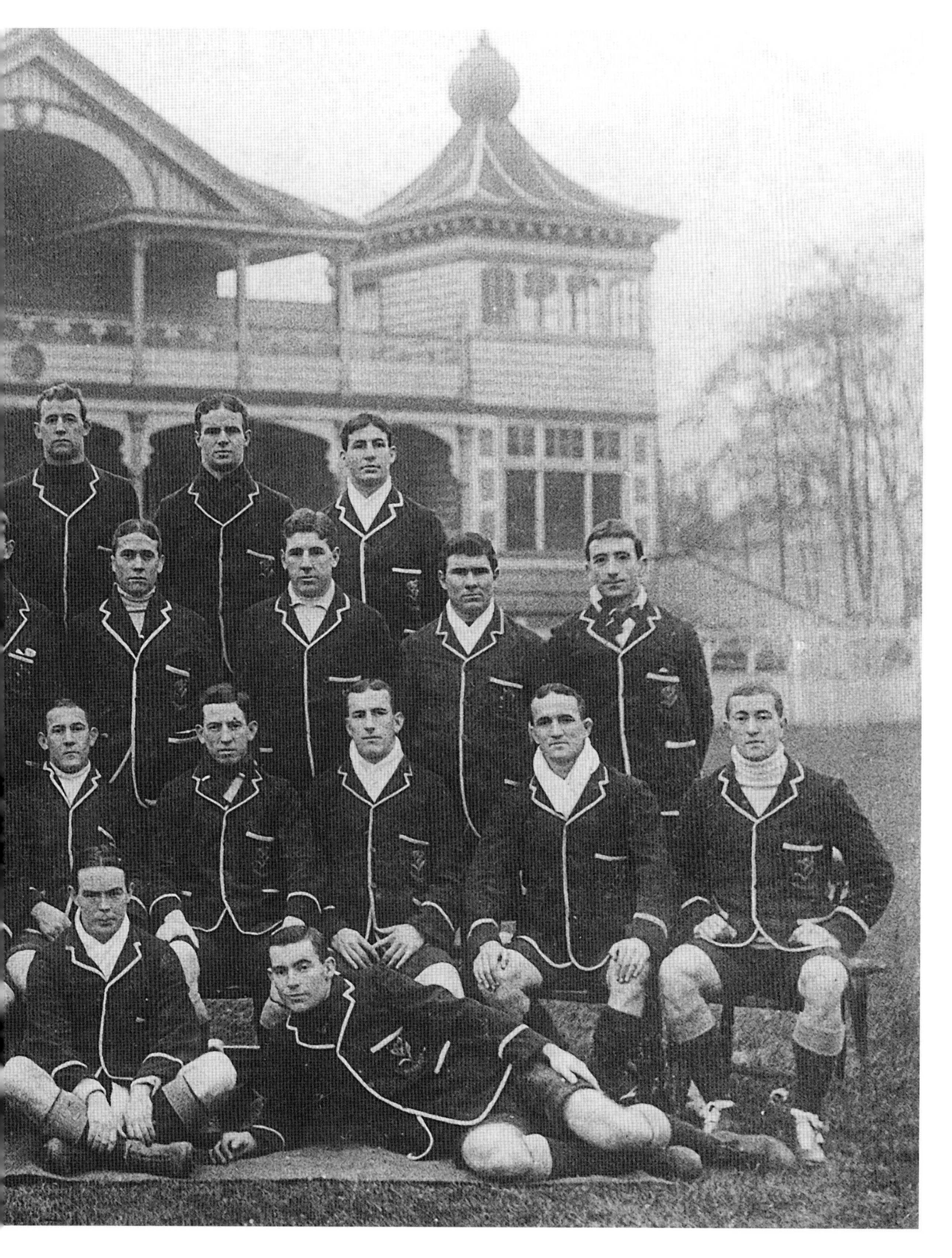

HERBERT ('PADDY') MORAN

Captain of the First Wallabies

In hindsight it is difficult to understand how 'Paddy' Moran was selected as captain of Australia's first 'Wallaby' tour to the British Isles and North America. He had never played for Australia, his limited captaincy experience was of the Sydney University team in 1907 and a Newcastle team which beat Metropolitan (Sydney) in 1908 at the Sydney Cricket Ground. He reportedly played little in 1907, yet the records of Sydney University show he received 'Blues' in 1905, 1906 and 1907. He did not make himself available for the Sydney University tour of New Zealand in 1907.

It is necessary to look at the state and Australian captains from 1905 to 1908 to consider the various candidates. The only Australian tour overseas in this time period was to New Zealand in 1905, when Stan Wickham was captain. He had run his athletic course by 1908, and accompanied the 1908–09 team as assistant manager: in actual fact, though not in name, he was Australia's coach.

In 1907 New Zealand came to Australia. Cecil Murnin captained New South Wales, Billy Richards from Charters Towers captained Queensland, and 'Butcher' Oxlade and Peter Burge captained Australia. James Hughes and Fred Wood captained New South Wales and Skeet Ahearn led Queensland against the 1908 Anglo-Welsh team. The Anglo-Welsh did not play a test. So logically the candidates should have been Oxlade, Hughes, Burge, Richards, Ahearn and Murnin. Billy Richards, like Wickham, was at the tail end of his career, and like Ahearn and Oxlade was not picked for the tour. So that leaves Burge, Hughes, Wood and Murnin as outstanding choices. Hughes was selected on the tour but declined because of his medical studies. Dare it be suggested that the others were eliminated because they were all definitely of the working class?

The selection of Moran, as it turned out, was somewhat fortuitous, as Murnin took ill and returned to Australia without playing a game. Burge broke a leg in the first match and did not play again on tour, and Wood gave indifferent displays for most of the tour because of lumbago.

Moran himself was of working class origins, being the son of Roman Catholic Irish parents. His mother died in childbirth when he was five

Dr. Herbert ('Paddy') Moran looked more the scholar than the rugby player.

years of age. His father was a baker who struggled in the early years, but as time went on he expanded his business and made his fortune. Herbert went first to Darlington Superior Public School then to St Aloysius in Surry Hills, a rough area, and then St Joseph's College, all good Catholic institutions which did not have the financial back-up of places like The Kings School or Riverview.

A scholarly type, he looked more like an Oxford don than a representative flanker. He came into the game somewhat reluctantly, playing first for the Rose Bay club as a prop in his third year at University. He cut down a pair of pants, and nailed some leather bars and sprigs on the bottom of his ordinary shoes. In his next year at University, where he was studying medicine, he was invited to turn out for the University second team, again as a prop. A rather intelligent young man, somewhat introspective, he went to University at 15 years of age and was now 19.

Moran certainly did not consider himself as one of the working class, as it appears by this time his father's bakery business had expanded and the family was very well off. In *Viewless Winds* he noted, following the first wave of professionalism in 1907: "For the students of Sydney University the establishment of professionalism in sport meant serious loss. In my time the undergraduates were in danger of all being stamped into a single mould. They were being given one uniform pattern in their prejudices and preferences. Sport provided an extra-mural course in a totally different discipline. We tussled with factory hands and firemen, with miners, wharf-labourers and carters. These players might have rougher manners, but in many of the elementary virtues of life they were our superiors. Above all they had a hard edge to their characters, and a robuster humour. By contact with them we [so he obviously did not think of himself as the working class] gained immeasurably more than they. When professionalism came, University players were shut out from friendships with men in ranks called lower and their education suffered by it."

He was asked at the age of 19 to tour the lower Northern Rivers in New South Wales. One senses that Moran was socially naive at this time, certainly not worldly, and enjoyed the camaraderie of the male rugby world. He told the story of one of his team-mates, Bill, who always drank five or six pints of beer before playing, believing that it improved his vigour and speed, and during a ruck emerged with the ball and ran eighty yards before diving across the goal-line for a glorious try – over his own line.

At the post-mortem poor Bill justified his mistake by saying "the jerseys of the two sides were very alike," but this did not fully explain Bill ignoring the frantic calls of his full-back, "Billy, you silly b.......!" Perhaps the five or six pints taken before his game might have been offered as an excuse, but this was never considered by the afore-mentioned Bill.

At the next country town the Mayor addressed the team. After the normal 'bonds of Empire' speech and reference to the town's performance at the last Butter Show, he went on: "You may beat us," he said, in an eloquent and moving peroration, "you may beat our country lads tomorrow" and he emphasised tomorrow (cheers) "but from what I hears of your doin's down at Taree, the day will come when on this ground, and beside this river, we'll be beatin' you city fellows with your own prodigy" (prolonged applause). Clayton (one of the players), who as befits a lawyer could always interpret the mind of a deponent, said that he meant this last word to be progeny.

It would appear that Moran became the prime candidate for Australian captaincy when he brought a Newcastle team to Sydney and they defeated a strong Metropolitan team. This may be the case, but in many ways Moran still remains a surprise choice.

Biographies, short or long, have glossed over Moran. Peter Sharpham in his excellent *The First Wallabies* describes his on-the-field style: "Moran's philosophy was to endeavour to be the first forward to a breakdown in play and ensure his side's possession of the ball, the turn-of-the-century equivalent of Chris Roche or Simon Poidevin. He was tireless in cover defence and did not shirk the middle of the rucks and mauls. He drove his players on with the words 'Australia, boys!' and taught many of his charges their table manners and how to dress for formal occasions. If he did not leave the field of play in a state of complete exhaustion at the end of the game Moran considered he had not fulfilled his role as captain of Australia."

There is no doubt that he applied himself diligently as captain of the first Wallabies. He captained Australia in the first eight games in the British Isles, only one of which, against Llanelly, was lost. Ever since the words of 'Sospan Fach' have spewed out of Welsh lips: "We beat the Wallabies in 1908."

In the eighth game, against London, he showed the force of his character. As described by Peter Sharpham in *The First Wallabies*: "the main feature during the second half was an extraordinary display of courage by Herbert Moran. He dislocated his left shoulder late in the first half but played on with his left arm strapped to his side and led his team by example. On three occasions he fielded the ball with his right hand and dashed through to the last line of defence before offloading to his supports. More than once he dived on the rolling ball as the London pack rampaged in a dribbling rush towards the Australian line."

Understandably his injury placed him on the sidelines, and his next match was against Cambridge University, won by the Wallabies 11–9. His injury meant, among other things, that he could not play against Cornwall in the gold medal match at the Olympic Games. He actually missed six matches, and after Cambridge felt his shoulder was too tender to play against Oxford in the following match, as well as Yorkshire and Lancashire.

His comeback was against Somerset, won by Australia, and then he missed Combined Midlands and East Midlands Counties. He was back as captain in a 24–0 victory over the Anglo-Welsh, and was considered sufficiently fit to lead the Wallabies against Wales. Wales won by 9–6, there being some controversial decisions which did not aid Australia. The *News of the World* reported: "...Moran was the best forward."

Moran was rested against Glamorgan League, but was back at the helm at Newport (won 5–3), Abertillery (3–3), Swansea (lost 0–6) and Cardiff (lost 8–24).

The team was supposed to play a test in France, but it was cancelled due to the inclement weather. Then disaster struck as, prior to the English international, on New Year's Eve 1909, Moran slipped on the ice while walking with his team and sprained his Achilles tendon. As a consequence he had to withdraw on the morning of the English test. It was a severe personal blow for Moran. Australia won the match by 9–3.

Two days later Moran left his team to take up medical studies in Edinburgh, thus missing the final two games in England against Bristol and Clifton and Plymouth, as well as the North American section of the tour, which was an additional five games.

Some comment needs to be made about Moran leaving the team. As a member of the 1947–48 9–month Wallaby tour, this author finds it quite incredible that the tour organisers and Moran himself would have contemplated such a departure. I believe it should not have been permitted.

It is interesting to weigh the words of Moran in *Viewless Winds*: "The last match of the tour was against England. We were all tired by that time of the whole business." Tired everyone might have been, but the England international was simply not the end of the tour. Australia had to play two more games in England as part of their tour, though admittedly these games were not on the original official itinerary but became commitments, and five more in Canada and the United States. The captain, in the opinion of the author with the experience of a similar tour at his disposal, should have travelled with his team until the complete tour was over. Could one imagine this happening with a New Zealand or a South African captain? It would never be contemplated or condoned.

Herbert Moran's record shows that he captained Australia 16 times, all on this tour, but in only one test, against Wales.

It needs to be stated that Herbert Moran was a complex, at times strange individual, as his three books reveal: *Viewless Winds, In My Fashion* and *Beyond the Hill Lies China*. He was certainly an idealist, espousing the credo of the true amateur and castigating those who transgressed ethical boundaries during a game. As he said himself, he "disliked getting too far involved in a life of athleticism," and refused to play after he left the Wallabies.

After finishing his fellowship at Edinburgh, he returned to Sydney at the end of 1910. He worked at the only teaching hospital, Prince Alfred, and set up his first practice in an industrial, working class suburb, and he found himself often at odds with his colleagues.

When the First World War started he sailed to London and offered his services, being made a lieutenant in the RAMC. He was sent to Gallipoli and contracted amoebic dysentery, was sent to Mesopotamia to become ill again, was repatriated to India and thence Australia.

More and more he became interested in cancer, so three years after the war he went to Paris to study the use of radium, and then to the United States to take in the latest research there. He was a true pioneer, being the first of his profession to use radium needles or radium tubes in the treatment of cancer in Australia. He went to France again in 1926 working at the Cancer Clinic of Villejeuf.

Perhaps too introverted and intellectual for his own good, he retired in 1935 from medical practice, a mere 50 years of age. He had become disillusioned with many in his profession, inertia in his own country, anti-Irish sentiment and inroads into rigorous standards within Catholicism. A disturbed person in many respects, he said: "I could not find peace."

He turned once more to Europe, searching for a new vision, where there was hope for mankind. He roamed through France, Italy, Germany and England, pursued by phantoms within his own mind.

He came under the spell of Italy and became fluent in the language, and in fact did much to initiate the teaching of Italian in Australia at the University level. He had four audiences with Mussolini, and for a time seemed under his spell. He acted as a one-man legation to argue for continued good relations between the two countries, despite the invasion of Abyssinia.

Moran even got permission to go to Abyssinia in 1936 as a freelance doctor.

As with most things, eventually he became disillusioned with Rome and went to live elsewhere in Europe, staying there for a year to learn German. So he was certainly an uncommon rugby player, fluent in French, Italian and German.

He went back to Australia in November 1937, arriving the day of the Melbourne Cup, and when he stated that the world would soon be at war again he was ignored. He returned to Rome, then to Paris, and was at Antwerp when war broke out.

Moran immediately went to England to volunteer his services, and was initially made a full lieutenant in the British Forces, but was transferred at his own request to the Australian Military Forces. He became a lieutenant-colonel; but he never lost his hyper-critical manner, being "a traditionalist, by temperament and faith."

In February 1945 he noticed the deteriorating irregular shape of a mole on his own stomach, which he had excised. He soon realised he was doomed with cancer, but reflected: "There was nothing to do but carry on."

He was released from the Army on April 14, 1945, now being racked with pain. In May 1945 the War ended. He died on November 20 1945 in the Hope House Nursing Home, Cambridge. The 1947–48 Wallabies visited his grave.

His last words are a reflection of the man: "But the call has sounded and I must go. I must go forth after the long wander of my faith, into the darkness; into the darkness and beyond, hesitant still a little.

"Suddenly a road pierces the dark uncertainty of my doubt; and I see the way bright and clear before me. The air is gentle to the listening trees

Caricatures of leading players were common in Paddy Moran's day.

which bird-song perfumes and so, with joyous step, submissive to the Will, I take the road."

Herbert Moran abhorred the aboriginal war-cry that the Australian team gave during his tour. He refused to lead it, and "regularly hid myself among the team, a conscientious objection." This war-cry eventually died a natural death but one thing did not, with Australian teams being the called the Wallabies from this point on.

In *Viewless Winds*, Moran stated: "When we arrived at Plymouth a pack of journalists fell upon us. They were very anxious to give us some distinctive name, but their first suggestion of 'Rabbits' we indignantly rejected. It really was going a little too far to palm off on us the name of a pest their ancestors had foisted on our country! Ultimately we became the 'Wallabies', although we wore for emblem on our jerseys not the figure of this marsupial but the floral design of a waratah."

Whatever the origins of the name, Herbert Moran was the first captain of the 'Wallabies'.

HERBERT ('PADDY') MORAN

CAPTAIN: 1 test (v Wales 1908), 15 other matches
BORN: Rose Bay 29 April 1885
DIED: 20 November 1945
SCHOOL: St Aloysius College, St Joseph's College (Sydney)
CLUBS: Rose Bay, University of Sydney, Newcastle
NEW SOUTH WALES REPRESENTATION: 6 matches (1906-08)
AUSTRALIAN REPRESENTATION: 16 matches (1 test) (1909–09)

CHRIS McKIVAT

The First Dual Captain: Rugby Union & Rugby League

As the years roll on we increasingly lose any memory of past great players, and this is certainly the case with Christopher Hobart McKivat. Peter Sharpham states unequivocally in *The First Wallabies*: "Chris McKivat is considered by many students of both codes to be possibly the greatest Australian test football skipper of all time, ranking with the likes of Andrew Slack, Nick Farr-Jones, John Thornett, Cyril Towers, Trevor Allen [sic], Clive Churchill, Arthur Summons and Mal Meninga."

What do some of the experts say of Chris McKivat? Malcolm Andrews, wrote in *ABC Rugby League*: "Not only was Chris McKivat one of Australia's greatest halfbacks, but he was also one of his country's finest captains."

Johnny Quinlan, quoted in Ian Heads' *The Kangaroos*: "Chris McKivat was the ideal captain. Chris was one of those commendable generals who do not expect his men to make sacrifices they themselves are not prepared and willing to take. His was a genial disposition which, assisted by extraordinary tact and judgement, but balanced by quick and unhesitating decision, made him a natural leader. He always set an example in conduct and training."

Ian Heads, *True Blue*: "Imbued with striking leadership qualities, Chris McKivat – known variously as 'The boy from the bush' and 'The hairy bloke' – was a towering figure in rugby league in New South Wales."

Jack Pollard, *The Australian Game*: "McKivat, cool and composed under the heaviest pressure, developed into a masterful tactician, partly because he was coached early by the New Zealand rugby star Bob Whiteside, and because he was observant, thoughtful and studious."

Peter Sharpham, *The First Wallabies*: "He was a tough and crafty scrum-half or five-eighth who could read the game superbly."

Chris McKivat was born on 27 November 1882 at Cumnock, a small town between Orange and Dubbo in central New South Wales. A boy from the bush, he first came to the notice of rugby pundits when he appeared for Western New South Wales against Great Britain in their 1904 tour of Australia. There were a number of very fine players in the country team, notably Machattie Smith, Frank Bede Smith, George Anlezark, Norm Street and Ken Gavin. Though the team was beaten 21–6, enough people were impressed with the 22-year-old that he was inveigled into going to

Sydney, and playing for Glebe. The Glebe club was star-studded in those days, with such players as Alex Burdon, Jimmy Clarken, Charlie Hedley, Fred Wood, Tom Griffin, Darb Hickey and Syd Middleton. The only problem at Glebe, and it persevered throughout the British tour, was that the resident halfback was Wood and so McKivat more often than not was forced to play five-eighth.

Of solid build, 5ft 8in and 12st, McKivat came to the fore on the national scene in 1907 during the visit to Australia of the All Blacks. The time period is interesting as word was circulating that a professional rugby league team, the 'All Golds' as they were to be known, would tour Australia and the British Isles. This rumour became a reality, and 'Dally' Messenger, arguably Australia's best rugby player of the day, was signed up by them. Eight All Blacks were in the All Golds party. This was the first wave of professionalism to hit Australia, rugby league clubs were formed the next year and competition began.

McKivat's entry into the big-time was in the second New South Wales match against the 1907 All Blacks. There were some mighty players on the state team: Billy Dix, Messenger, 'Boxer' Russell, Frank Bede Smith, Ed Mandible, Fred Wood, Tom Griffin, Paddy McCue, Peter Burge and Norm Row. The strength of New South Wales was demonstrated by their 14–0 victory.

McKivat played five-eighth to Wood, and this was repeated in his first test at the Sydney Cricket Ground, Australia going down 6–26. He was not in the test team for the second encounter, but was in the centre for the third test, a hard-fought draw.

With a tour to the British Isles, France and North America in the offing, players endeavoured to impress the selection against an Anglo-Welsh team. McKivat made the New South Wales team (as five-eighth), but no tests were played.

Chris McKivat was selected for the grand tour, the first to the northern hemisphere ever taken by Australia. 'Paddy' Moran was the captain, and halfback Fred Wood the vice-captain. There was also another halfback on tour, Joshua Stevenson. McKivat was picked as a five-eighth, along with Ward Prentice. Stevenson was injured near the end of his only match on tour, against Penycraig.

The general legend that has been passed down to the modern aficionado is that Wood, the vice-captain, kept McKivat out of his preferred halfback position. This was reinforced by Moran in *Viewless Winds*: "I took care, however, though captain and a selector, never to pick myself. When it came to selecting the back row I left the room, after stating my own preferences... The vice-captain [Fred Wood] was a great little player who never found his form in England. It used to be unpleasant for us when, in the face of this, he insisted for a long time on his own selection. We did not want unfriendliness, but for nine matches in succession he kept McKivatt [sic] out of his proper position."

In the opinion of the author these comments with respect to Wood are grossly unfair. The simple fact is that McKivat was picked for the tour as a five-eighth. The selected halves were Wood and Stephenson. In club rugby for Glebe Wood was the halfback and McKivat the five-eighth, and McKivat was five-eighth and centre

Chris McKivat captained Australia in both rugby union and rugby league.

Chris McKivat: At halfback or five-eighth, he was the best of his generation.

in his only two games for Australia, and he was five-eighth and Wood halfback for the New South Wales game against the Anglo-Welsh. McKivat had not played halfback in club or representative rugby.

In unravelling this intriguing piece of rugby folklore, there is no doubt that Wood was not at his best on the tour. As Sharpham put it in *The First Wallabies*: "For most of the 1908–09 tour he [Wood] played with the extreme pain of recurrent lumbago caused by his hip injury of 1906, which explains his indifferent form early in the tour."

Coming to an analysis of the 1908–09 tour, one sees that the teams were picked logically with Wood at halfback and McKivat five-eighth. This was the Wallaby line-up against Devon, Gloucestershire, Cornwall, Glamorgan County, Neath & Aberavon, Llanelly and London. It should be noted that Australia won all but one of those games, against Llanelly. It is also true that Australia won its next twelve games following the Llanelly loss without Wood, who was injured. As both halves were injured, McKivat moved into the halfback position and he was sensational.

As the captain Moran was also injured, McKivat was given the captaincy and the half-back position against Cornwall by default, and in so doing he received a gold medal as this was part of the Olympic rugby tournament.

McKivat was also captain and halfback in the following matches: Combined Army and Navy, Durham, Northumberland and Cumberland, Cheshire and London. Moran was back to captain the side against Cambridge University (in which McKivat played), but McKivat captained against Oxford University, Yorkshire,

Lancashire, and Moran against Somerset. Wood returned from injury to captain the team against Combined Midlands and East Midlands Counties (McKivat playing five-eighth), and then McKivat was rested against the Anglo-Welsh. He had played 18 of 20 games to that stage, an enormous physical challenge. McKivat was back at halfback against Wales, and then five-eighth against Glamorgan League, Newport, Abertillery, Swansea and Cardiff.

The next match was against England. The captain Moran was injured, and while Wood had been playing well the selectors had also been impressed with McKivat. Sharpham in *The First Wallabies* reported: "Arthur McCabe went to five-eighth and Chris McKivat moved back to scrum-half, ousting Fred Wood. Although Wood had played splendidly in Wales it was considered by Moran, McMahon and Wickham [the selectors along with Wood] that the combination of McKivat and McCabe was superior to a Wood-McKivat partnership and Wood had little option but to gracefully accede to his fellow selectors' wishes."

With this decision, Chris McKivat entered an exclusive club. Although he only captained the test team once, it happened on Monday 9 January 1909 and he led them brilliantly to a 9–3 victory.

The tour did not end there. McKivat captained the team against Bristol and Clifton and played five-eighth against Plymouth. Then the team departed for Canada and California. McKivat captained the team against the University of California, did not play against Stanford and was at five-eighth against All-California, Vancouver and Victoria.

In an incredible performance, the boy from the bush played in 33 out of 36 matches on tour. He was outstanding as a five-eighth and halfback, but was considered better in the latter position. Equally important is that he captained his country on 15 occasions, one of them being the England test.

Not many amusing stories have been remembered about him, but Moran tells one in *Viewless Winds*. It happened in the Abertillery game: "About this time the newspapers had nosed out the fact that we were in receipt of three shillings a day, out-of-pocket expenses, and they were trying to make a great scandal out of it... In the midst then of my vehement exhortations to the players to throw themselves resolutely down on the ball, McKivatt [sic] looked up with an Irish twinkle in his eyes and exclaimed: 'Blimey, doctor, it don't work out to be a penny a ruck'."

In 1909 the rugby world was changed forever when 14 of the Wallabies turned professional: McKivat, McCabe, McCue, Barnett, the Burge brothers, McMurtrie, McIntyre, Gavin, Dix, Mandible, Hickey, Craig and Russell. The player who got the most money was Chris McKivat, who was signed up for £200.

McKivat captained the 1911–12 Kangaroos to England and his durability became evident once more, as he played 30 consecutive games. Glebe entered the Sydney rugby league competition and he played for them from 1910 to 1914. After retirement he coached Glebe then switched to North Sydney, steering them through their legendary premiership years of 1921–22.

Ian Heads, in *The Kangaroos*, has this to say of McKivat: "Skipper McKivat was the driving, inspirational force of the whole campaign. There is a famous tour story of a Coventry outfitter putting up a prize of an overcoat to the first Colonial player to score a try in England. 'I knew that overcoat would be mine', McKivat would say, a twinkle in his eye when he told the story in later years. In his first chance in that first match of the tour, McKivat dummied and scored – and won the coat. English critics glowingly praised him for his leadership and the quality of his play. One story told was of a Kangaroo prop fighting for a loose head which was not rightly his in the scrum. Twice McKivat called 'out' to his man, demanding that he pack down correctly. The enthusiastic scrummager persisted. McKivat did not call again, he kicked the front rower, sharply – and when the astonished forward wheeled around McKivat said simply: 'Get in behind, man.' McKivat was a quiet man off the field, but on it he never let up. From start to finish he snapped out staccato commands, urging his men to greater efforts. He was an unselfish player, and a splendid supporter of the man with the ball, playing a part in many tries on tour."

His was a superb career. In rugby union he played in 34 games for Australia, which included four tests. He won a gold medal in Olympic rugby in 1908, and captained the Wallabies against England. He won an Ashes league series in Britain 1911–12, and became the first man to captain Australia in both codes.

CHRIS McKIVAT

CAPTAIN: 15 matches (1 test) (v England, 1909)

BORN: 27 November 1882 at Cumnock, New South Wales

DIED: May 1941

SCHOOL: not known

CLUBS: Central West New South Wales, Glebe

NEW SOUTH WALES REPRESENTATION: 16 matches (1905–09)

AUSTRALIAN REPRESENTATION: 34 matches (4 tests) (1907–09)

SYD MIDDLETON

An Olympian In Two Sports

SYD MIDDLETON is unique as he competed for Australia in two different Olympic sports, rugby union in 1908, when he won a gold medal, and rowing in 1912 as a member of the eight, who were beaten in the quarter final.

Born in Glebe, Sydney, on 24 February 1884, Syd Middleton first of all made his mark at the top level in rugby union. He played for the suburb of his birth and came to the attention of the Australian selectors when playing for New South Wales against Queensland and the Anglo-Welsh touring team of 1908, the latter resulting in a nail-biting, 0–3 loss.

His timing was perfect as it was that season that Australia was sending its first national rugby union team to the northern hemisphere. It was when they got to London by boat that they received the appellation the 'Wallabies'. The name stuck. Middleton was a rangy backrow forward in a team captained by Herbert 'Paddy' Moran, and the vice-captain was Fred Wood, also from the Glebe club. This team is called 'The First Wallabies'. For a long period of time a team was only considered a Wallaby one if it undertook the northern hemisphere tour. Thus the 1939 Australian team was designated 'The Second Wallabies', though war broke out and they did not play a game. The 1947–48 Australians were called 'The Third Wallabies', and so on.

Syd Middleton: Test rugby captain, Olympic rower, decorated war hero.

In recent times these early distinctions have been waived, and any person who represents Australia in rugby union is now a considered a Wallaby.

Syd Middleton was the second tallest player

on the 1908–09 tour at 6ft 1in, exceeded only by Cecil Murnin, who did not play a game and returned home. This made Middleton invaluable in the lineout. He and Paddy McCue were the heaviest, at 14st.

Jack Pollard says of him, in *Australian Rugby*: "A robust back row forward from the powerful Glebe Club in Sydney with a long lineout reach, whose vigour helped develop Australian forward play in the early years of international rugby. He was a noted oarsman, an impressive physical specimen, and an incredibly tireless player. His general manner and sportsmanship won him many admirers."

There is certainly no doubt about his physical condition. He played in every one of the first 18 tour games, an incredible feat. He was obviously considered an indispensable part of the Wallaby pack.

One game was an historic one, though the Wallabies did not at the time realise its significance. The Olympic Games of 1908 were held in London, and rugby was placed on the programme. Cornwall was the county champion, and they were selected to represent England, and Australia was the opponent. No other country participated. Scotland, Ireland and France, in particular, were disputing many matters with the English Rugby Union. They ignored the invitations. Why Wales did not compete is a mystery. Neither the captain nor the vice-captain of the Wallabies played.

Moran wrote of the match in *Viewless Winds*: "We had already defeated this team [i.e. Cornwall, 18 to 5] in our third match, but our opponents were hopeful of turning the tables because, in the meantime, they had been reinforced by two internationals who had been absent in Australia [with the Anglo-Welsh tourists]. It was the first match after my injury [a dislocated shoulder] and I was, for the first time, an onlooker. Our team played magnificent football, chiefly due to the fact that McKivatt [sic] was at last in his proper position at half and McCabe was at five-eights [sic]. We were leading easily when an important official came to me to lay a complaint that our men were using running spikes; at half-time they had found some scratches on the body of one of the players. This was the comble! ... I insisted at once on an examination of the boots of all the players as they came off the field at full-time ... on the whole the boots of the Cornish players were in the worse condition. There was not the trace of a spike!"

It was the easiest game of their tour to this point, the Wallabies racing away to the tune of 32–3. Middleton was dominant, particularly in the lineout. Each Wallaby in that match was thereafter an Olympic gold medallist. The team on that historic day was Phil Carmichael, 'Boxer' Russell, John Hickey, Frank Bede Smith, Dan Carroll, Chris McKivat (capt), Arthur McCabe, Tom Richards, Malcolm McArthur, Bob Craig, Syd Middleton, Paddy McCue, Charles McMurtrie, Tom Griffin and John Barnett.

In his sixteenth successive match, against Oxford University, Middleton got his marching orders. The captain, Moran, described the occasion in *Viewless Winds*: "I was sitting in the pavilion with G.V. Portus, for I was still nursing a shoulder that had been dislocated at Richmond, when suddenly on a line-out I saw one of our biggest forwards swing a blow that hit an opposing forward. A.O. Jones promptly sent our man off; what else could he do? Jones was an admirable referee.

"The man who committed this offence was a magnificent athlete, rower, boxer and footballer, and actually a very good sportsman, but irritable and hot-headed. I followed him into the dressing-room with murder in my heart for one who was and is still a firm friend. But when I saw his bowed head I said nothing and walked out. He is still paying for that indiscretion. It has pursued him for thirty years. It followed him to the war and it still pops up, every now and again, when the striker and the struck meet socially in London, where they both live."

Strangely, Middleton was picked for the next two games, against Yorkshire and Lancashire, presumably awaiting a decision on his case. He then missed the next five games, including his chance of a first test, against Wales.

His re-entry onto the playing field was against Newport and he played in all remaining 13 games of the tour, including his first test against England. Thus he played in 31 of the Wallabies' 36 matches.

On his return to Australia 14 of the Wallabies defected to rugby league, but Middleton was not interested. In 1910 his faith in the amateur code was rewarded when he captained New South Wales in two matches against the All Blacks and two matches against New Zealand Maori. He led Australia in the three tests against New Zealand that year, one of which was won.

Syd Middleton played 33 games for Australia in his career including four tests, and he led the team in three of them. An inspiration, he rose above his minor indiscretion against Oxford through his own force of character.

From this point on Middleton concentrated on rowing, and completed a rare double when he represented Australasia, Australia and New Zealand having a combined team at this time, in the eights competition at the 1912 Stockholm Olympics. The team was John Ryrie, Simon Fraser, Hugh Ward, Thomas Parker, Henry Hauenstein, Sydney Middleton, Harry Ross-Boden, Robert Fitzhardinge (stroke) and Robert Waley (cox). The team won its heat, but lost in the final to the Leander Club from England, which went on to win the gold medal.

Peter Sharpham, in his excellent book *The First Wallabies*, stated: "In 1920 he was a member of the Australian eight which carried all before them at the Henley Regatta in England, including the Leander eight who went on to take the silver medal at the subsequent Antwerp Olympics. He represented Australia at Antwerp, but last-minute changes to the crew deprived the team of a medal." This latter assertion is debatable, as the AOC's official history, *Australia at the Olympic Games* by Harry Gordon, and Howell and Howell's *Aussie Gold: The Story of Australia at the Olympic Games* do not list any rowing representation at the 1920 Antwerp Games. Middleton represented at the 1912 Games, as Sharpham noted.

Syd Middleton enlisted in World War I, serving at Gallipoli and France, and was awarded the Distinguished Service Order (DSO) for bravery in action.

A bachelor for most of his life, he married in England and lived there. He died in London at 63 years of age.

SYD MIDDLETON
CAPTAIN: 3 matches (3 tests) (v New Zealand 1910)
BORN: Glebe, Sydney, 24 February 1884
DIED: London, 1945
SCHOOL: not known
CLUBS: Glebe
NEW SOUTH WALES REPRESENTATION: 12 matches (1908–11)
AUSTRALIAN REPRESENTATION: 33 matches (4 tests) (1908–10)

WARD PRENTICE

Captain of the First-Ever Tour to the USA & Canada

WARD PRENTICE played 32 times for Australia, including six tests, and he was captain in one of those tests, against the United States of America in 1912. His contribution to rugby union was particularly significant as he undertook two overseas tours. In his second tour, to the United States and Canada, Prentice led Australia's first-ever tour there.

A Western Suburbs (Sydney) man through and through, he had four other brothers who played first grade at various times, and two others who competed in the lower grades. Ward represented and captained Australia, while brother Clarrie was selected for one test, against New Zealand in 1914. Ward played 129 first grade games for Wests and Clarrie 59. Clarrie later turned professional and toured with the 1921–22 Kangaroos, thus becoming a dual international as he played in the three tests and 25 of the 36 tour games.

Ward Prentice was a popular tourist, as he had a fine singing voice and gave many a rendition on ship and shore.

He first came to notice for New South Wales against the Anglo-Welsh in 1908, and his performance was good enough to force his selection as a five-eighth on the 1908–09 tour of the British Isles and North America. The other five-eighth was Chris McKivat, arguably the best Australian back on the tour, and Prentice therefore had to bide his time to get a chance.

There was a tug-of-war going on which affected Prentice's appearances. Fred Wood, the vice-captain, was determined to play halfback, and yet did not strike form early on. Then everyone became increasingly aware that the superior halfback was McKivat. The Wood-McKivat combination dominated, however, and Prentice's opportunities were often in the centres, particularly inside centre. He was versatile enough to take it all in his stride. In the first 15 games, he only played in three.

Against Oxford University he was placed in his preferred position, five-eighth, with McKivat at halfback. This was the match where Syd Middleton was sent off the field for throwing a punch, and the Wallabies played a man short most of the game. Australia, despite this, won 19–3. Prentice impressed with his dodging runs and smooth play. Against Yorkshire McKivat and Prentice teamed up again.

Peter Sharpham wrote in *The First Wallabies* that knee injuries were also a factor in his limited appearances but noted that throughout the tour he "distinguished himself by his unselfish team play and clever cross-kicking for his loose forwards and wingers," and that he "was a very

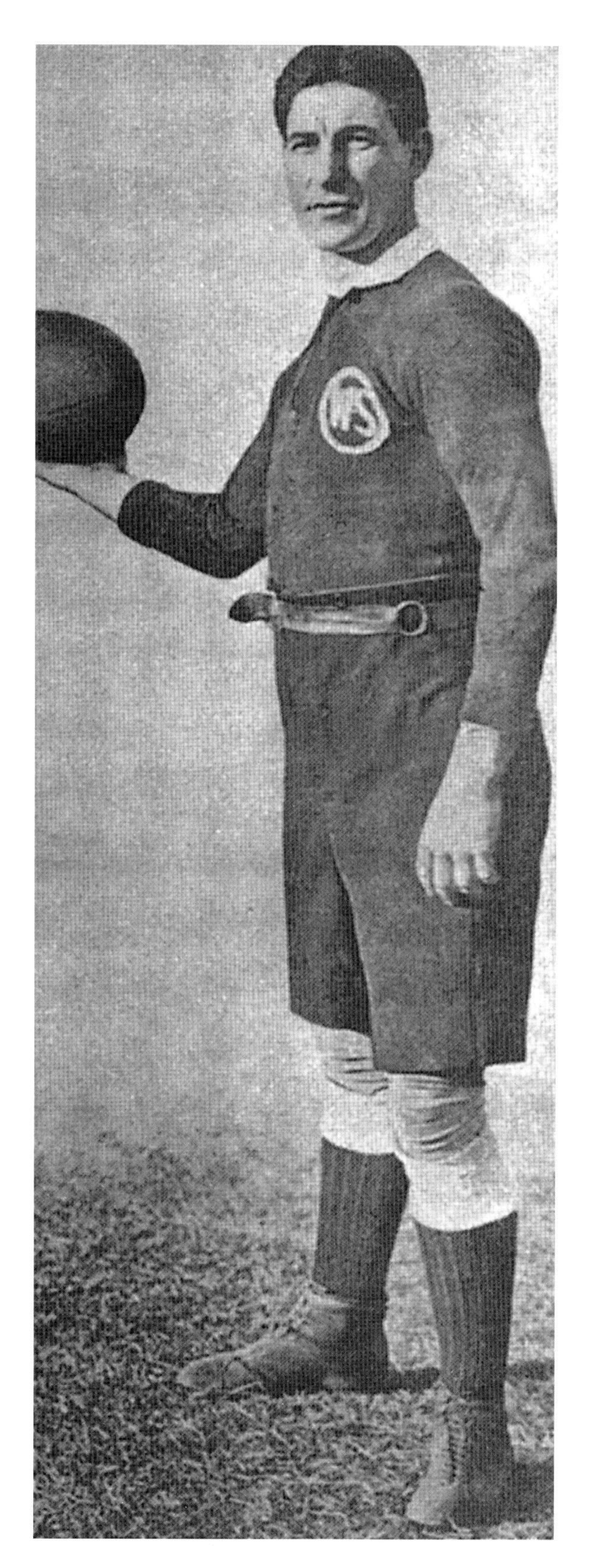

astute cover-defender and on numerous occasions on tour saved certain tries by launching himself at opposition wingers when they were set to score." Pollard, in *Australian Rugby* observed that he "had exceptional handling ability."

The match prior to the first international against Wales was against the Anglo-Welsh, and this time he partnered the vice-captain, Fred Wood. In scoring the 'try of the match' Prentice side-stepped through almost the whole team and touched down in the corner.

In what must have been a tense meeting of the selectors, Chris McKivat was selected as halfback for the test over the vice-captain Fred Wood, and Prentice was slotted into five-eighth.

In the emotion-charged test, Prentice's first, he set up Australia's first try by flanker Tom Richards and impressed once more with his dodging runs and solid defence. However he had to go off the field for a time as twice he was kicked in the mouth during the first half and had to have stitches inserted after the game.

Australia lost the match 6–9, the manager James McMahon stating: "The fastest game I ever saw, and I suppose, considering the [slippery] nature of the ground, the Australians played remarkably well." Prentice proved himself of test standard and was not awed by the occasion.

The extent of the injury to his mouth was such that he missed the following five matches, yet he was picked in the test against England as a centre. McKivat and Arthur McCabe were the halfback-five-eighth selection. Australia won a hard-fought match 9–3. Prentice was injured during the match at Blackheath, but never shirked his duties on the field. He did not play in the final two matches of the British

Ward Prentice in the colours of his beloved Western Suburbs club.

section of the tour. He had only played in eight of 30 matches, but two of them were the most important in the calendar, the tests against Wales and England.

There were five matches on the Canada/USA section of the tour and Prentice played in all of them, thus increasing his games to 13 of 35. When the Wallabies returned home he fronted up against New South Wales, in the centre.

The greatest moments of his career were undoubtedly his captaincy of the 1912 Australian team to the USA and Canada. It was not an easy tour, as players were placed in various fraternity houses and discipline was virtually impossible to administer. The American Universities had come to Australia in 1910, playing against university and country teams and the touring New Zealand Maoris. That visit was disappointing, but it was felt by the New South Wales authorities that the potential in America was unlimited and they agreed to the 1912 tour. Prentice was captain, and Dr Otto Bohrsmann the manager. The secretary of the New South Wales RU, W.W. Hill, toured with the team and refereed some of the games.

Alhough nominally an Australian team, only four of the 24 were from Queensland, five if Queensland-born Tom Richards, now a resident in New South Wales, was included. The jersey was the New South Wales light blue one including the Waratah emblem, with the word Australia under the waratah.

It was not a successful tour. Some 16 matches were played, and only 11 were won. The Australians were beaten by Stanford University, University of California at Berkeley, and the three Canadian teams, Vancouver, British Columbia and Victoria. There was one test only, against the USA, which Australia won narrowly 11–8. Prentice captained Australia in the test, played in the centre and kicked a penalty goal near the end.

On tour Prentice never spared himself, playing in 15 of the 16 tour games. This tour was his swan-song in international rugby.

A fine sportsman, Ward Prentice was one of the few to represent his state in both rugby and cricket. He was badly wounded in World War I, but lived to the ripe old age of 82.

WARD PRENTICE

CAPTAIN: 15 matches (1 test) (v USA, 1912)
BORN: 30 July 1886 at Homebush, Sydney
DIED: 1969
SCHOOL: not known
CLUBS: 129 games (Western Suburbs, Sydney), 2 (Eastern Suburbs)
NEW SOUTH WALES REPRESENTATION: 25 matches (1908–12)
AUSTRALIAN REPRESENTATION: 32 matches (6 tests) (1908–12)

TED FAHEY

Captain by Default

A LOCK FORWARD from Eastern Suburbs who was to captain Australia and New South Wales in his career, Ted Fahey was an imposing figure at 6ft and 14st. By modern standards his size is unremarkable but he was a big man in his era.

A product of Sydney's St Joseph's College, he came under the influence of Blair Swannell there. Swannell was a former international, coming to Australia with the Great Britain side in 1899 and 1904, and remaining there after the latter tour. A hard-nosed, controversial man, Herbert Moran wrote of him in *Viewless Winds*: "Blair Swannell was, for a number of years, a bad influence in Sydney football... His conception of Rugby was one of trained violence.... he had no enlightened ideas about sport and used to teach schoolboys all sorts of tricks and tactics which were highly objectionable." Swannell played for Australia, thus becoming a dual international, and lost his life at Gallipoli, one rumour having it that he was shot by his own men.

Maybe Fahey learned a trick or two from Swannell, and if so it seemed to pay off, as he was to captain St. Joseph's to the GPS premiership and then led the Combined GPS team in 1907.

Fahey went to the Eastern Suburbs Club in 1908 and he played 73 matches for them in first grade. In those days a residential restriction applied and one could only play for clubs defined in specific boundaries. In the 1914 season the rugby authorities re-defined its boundaries, meaning Fahey was obliged to switch clubs. Because of this Fahey, Bill Cody, Ron Bolden and Harold Baker went from Eastern Suburbs to Randwick and Jimmy Clarken transferred from Glebe. Fahey captained Randwick in 1914 and played 11 games for them.

Fahey was in active service during the war. When rugby competitions resumed in 1919 after they had been cancelled for the duration, Fahey returned to and captained Easts in a most difficult season for rugby union, as rugby league competitions had continued throughout the war and taken over public interest.

As Fahey began club rugby in 1908, one year out of school, he had little chance of making the 1908–09 Wallaby tour of the British Isles and North America.

It was in 1910 that he had his opportunity at the higher levels, being selected on the New South Wales team against New Zealand twice and New Zealand Maori twice. There were no tours to or from Australia in 1911, so Fahey was limited to two games for the state against Queensland, New South Wales winning handily by 34–14 and 35–14.

In 1912 a team was selected to tour the USA and Canada, and three from Easts made the

team: ASB ('Wakka') Walker, a 19–year-old, Harald George and Ted Fahey. They went by ship to the USA on the *Moana* and Ted was one of those to 'feed the fishes' as he departed the Heads, while he and Walker were two of the four 'sickies' who could not leave their cabin for a full four days. They played two matches two and three days after their arrival, winning against the Barbarians 29–8 (Fahey scoring a try) and then Santa Clara College 20–8 (Fahey kicking one of six conversion attempts).

It was not a successful tour, Australia winning only 11 of 16 games. Fortunately they won the only test against the USA 12–8, and this was to be his first test. Australia was behind most of the game, scoring 12 points in the last 18 minutes to win.

Some 24 players, under captain Ward Prentice and managed by Dr. Otto Bohrsmann and assisted by W.W. (Billy) Hill, were on the trip, and Ted Fahey played 15 of the 16 games. The three matches in Canada, against Vancouver, British Columbia and Canada, were lost.

One major problem was that the team was housed in fraternity houses, and no external discipline could be imposed on them. Bob Adamson, a Sydney University player, was asked to give his verdict after the tour had ended. "We were never in bed. That was the trouble. I never had such a time in my life."

Fahey was one whose reputation remained intact, and he captained Eastern Suburbs to a premiership win in 1913, and played for New South Wales against Queensland and twice against the visiting New Zealand Maori team.

That same year Australia toured New Zealand under fullback Larry Dwyer, with Ted Fahey as vice-captain. Fahey played in six of the nine games. Dwyer was injured against Wanganui in

Ted Fahey: One of the leading forwards of his day.

the third match, so the burden of captaincy of Australia fell to Fahey, who captained Australia in the first two tests as well as in the 'minor' game against Southland. Fahey himself was injured against South Canterbury and missed the final two games, including one test.

In 1914 New Zealand came to Australia, and this was the 'Declaration of War' tour, the war breaking out midway through its tour. Fahey played for New South Wales (twice) and Metropolitan against the tourists, before playing the final test.

After his active service, Fahey returned to Eastern Suburbs in 1919. He captained New South Wales and Australia against the AIF team that year.

Ted Fahey's is a name not remembered to any extent these days, but he was a stalwart for his club Eastern Suburbs and played 25 matches for his country, of which four were tests. He made two tours with Australia, to the USA and Canada in 1912 and New Zealand in 1913. A loyal team man, he gave of his best in every match he played.

TED FAHEY

CAPTAIN: 7 matches (2 tests) (v New Zealand 1913)
BORN: July 7 1888
DIED: 1950
SCHOOL: St Josephs College (Sydney)
CLUBS: Eastern Suburbs (73), Randwick (11)
NEW SOUTH WALES REPRESENTATION: 39 matches (1910–19)
AUSTRALIAN REPRESENTATION: 25 matches (4 tests) (1912–14)

LARRY DWYER

The Captain from the Bush

THE LARRY DWYER story is an unusual one, in that he was the son of poor Irish immigrants and was born and bred in the bush, in Orange, New South Wales. Yet he rose to captain his country despite his adversities.

Pollard, in *Australian Rugby*, said of him: "He first played football at the Orange Patrician Brothers School wearing street shoes because football boots were a luxury few boys at the school could afford. He left school at 12 and worked as a clerk in a solicitor's office, and began to play rugby for the Orange Waratahs. He scrounged footballs from his club, and retired alone to the paddock to teach himself to kick with both feet."

He certainly honed his skills. As Chester and McMillan described him in *The Visitors*: "The captain, Larry Dwyer, rates among the great Australian fullbacks for his ability to kick a ball the length of the field, his uncanny handling skills, his prowess at punching holes in the defence and his deadly tackling."

It was obviously a disadvantage to come from a country centre and represent his state and his country. When he played for any teams that required him to be away from Orange, he would ask for leave from his employers, but was therefore required to work late at night before catching a train to Sydney. He would stay up all night, and then return to Orange as soon as he could after a match. It was this desire and motivation that eventually got him to the top.

As for his handling skills, when he was not on the rugby field he was playing handball, and won national championships in the sport. Larry Dwyer was a superb athlete and very well conditioned.

When Larry Dwyer started coming into his own, rugby was at somewhat of a low-point. The New Zealand 'All Golds' rugby league team came to Australia in 1907, played games and signed 'Dally' Messenger. Rugby league teams were formed, and a team was sent to England in 1908, being there at the same time as Moran's touring 1908–09 Wallabies.

Rugby union appeared to be getting the upper hand, when the code was shocked by the defection of 14 of the Wallaby team to the British Isles. It was a severe body-blow, and with most of the top players in the rugby league code, public interest shifted to their games.

Larry Dwyer appeared on the scene at a difficult time for the amateur code. He first came to public notice playing for the Western Districts team of New South Wales in 1908, and impressed with his coolness under pressure. It was in 1910 when he was openly recognised, playing for New South Wales twice against a touring New Zealand team, led by Fred ('General') Roberts. The All Black fullback was

Larry Dwyer: A poor boy from the country with unparalleled determination

Joe O'Leary, who gained immediate fame for being the only All Black to front up for every meal on a particularly rough ship crossing. Some other New Zealand greats on the team were Simon Mynott, Frank Mitchinson, 'Bolla' Francis and 'Ranji' Wilson. Among the best-known New South Wales players were Ward Prentice, Syd Middleton, Ted Fahey, Fred Wood, Jimmy Clarken and Tom Griffin. The 'Blues' were beaten in both matches, by 8–21 and 11–17.

Dwyer's performances put him into his first test team, captained by Syd Middleton. New Zealand won a close encounter 6–0, and Dwyer was adjudged the outstanding Australian player. He was an automatic selection for the second test, played only two days later. Australia won by 11–0, in a sensational upset, and as Howell, *et al* report in *They Came To Conquer*: "All the home team played with distinction, but none was better than Dwyer, whose defensive work was of the highest standard."

With the series tied 1–1, Dwyer was retained for the third test, and though he personally played well New Zealand crushed Australia to the tune of 28–13.

The American Universities toured in 1910 and Larry Dwyer played for Central-Western against them, the home team being narrowly defeated by 9–11.

The New Zealand Maori team was also in Australia in 1910, and although there was no test, Dwyer was first choice for both New South Wales games, New South Wales winning both 11–0 and 27–13. In the first encounter Howell, *et al* state: "Dwyer was in terrific form at fullback, saving try after try in the first spell."

In 1911 there were no tours in or out of the country, but in 1912 a team was picked to tour the USA and Canada under captain Ward Prentice, and Larry Dwyer was selected.

The 1912 tour was a disappointing one, as only 11 matches were won in 16 matches, including losses in all three Canadian matches. Dwyer had picked up an injury and missed the first two games, but finished up playing in 12 of the matches, against Stanford University (twice), University of California at Berkeley (three times), the Olympic Club, St. Mary's College, University of Nevada, Santa Clara College, the USA in the only test, British Columbia and Victoria, Canada. It did not help that players were distributed around various fraternity houses during their stay, as discipline was almost impossible to exert. What the Australians lacked on the playing field they made up for on the social side, Bob Adamson asserting that they hardly went to bed on tour. For the 28-year-old Dwyer, it all seemed a long way from Orange, New South Wales.

In 1913 the New Zealand Maori came back to Australia on an 8–match tour, during which no tests were played. Larry Dwyer was captain in the two New South Wales games (won 15–3 and 16–5), and for Western Districts at Bathurst (lost 8–11). Dwyer was in the three-quarter line in these three games. In the Western Districts game, he scored an excellent try which he converted.

It was little wonder then that the 'boy from the bush' captained Australia on its 1913 tour of New Zealand. Dwyer played in six of the nine matches. He played against Auckland, Taranaki and Wanganui, but was injured in the latter game and therefore missed the first two tests and the match against Southland. The vice-captain, Ted Fahey, took over in his absence. Dwyer was back into action against South Canterbury (won 16–3), New Zealand (won 16–5) and Marlborough (30–3). Although the tour was not successful, Australia winning four and losing five, one test had been won and Dwyer was acclaimed by all the New Zealand experts as one of the finest they had ever seen.

In 1914 New Zealand toured Australia in what has been called the 'Declaration of War Tour', as World War I was declared halfway through the tour, taking much of the gloss off it. Larry Dwyer represented New South Wales against them, and despite being under considerable pressure from the All Blacks he was picked out for special mention through his performance, in particular for his defensive work.

He captained Central-Western Districts four days later, and was picked in the first test; Australia, captained by Fred Wood, lost narrowly by 0–5. Dwyer was also selected for the Brisbane test (lost 0–17), New South Wales (lost 10–25) and Australia as a centre in the third test (lost 7–22).

The war caused rugby union to cease in Australia, and a great fillip to the game when peace was declared was the visit of the AIF team to Australia. Highly trained, and having competed in the AIF Inter-Service matches in Europe, the AIF team was too good for Australian teams. It had been five years since Dwyer had played top rugby, but he was on the New South Wales team against them (losing 14–42), then Australia (an 18–25 loss), the *Sydney Morning Herald* noting that in the New South Wales game: "The side was well served in many positions, notably at fullback, where Dwyer showed out."

This match for Australia was the final one Larry Dwyer played at the top level. He was 35 years of age and had done more than he could ever have hoped. He played 24 matches for his country, eight of them tests. He captained his country in tests to an impeccable record, winning one and losing none. He also captained Australia in five mid-week games.

Larry Dwyer is a wonderful example of determination taking a person to the top. Poor in material wealth, he was rich in the experiences he gained, going on two tours for Australia, one of them as captain of the Wallabies. He came a long way for a boy from the bush who could not afford football boots.

LARRY DWYER

CAPTAIN: 6 matches (1 test) (v New Zealand 1913)
BORN: 2 February 1884
DIED: 1964
SCHOOL: Orange Patrician Brothers, Orange, New South Wales
CLUBS: Orange Waratahs, New South Wales Country
NEW SOUTH WALES REPRESENTATION: 31 matches (1909–19)
AUSTRALIAN REPRESENTATION: 24 matches (8 tests) (1910–14)

FRED WOOD

A Player's Player

FRED ('POSSUM') WOOD, born in England, was a giant in the rugby union code when its very edifices seemed to be falling down. He was one who held firm when he could easily have turned professional. His career ran from 1905 to 1914, so it encompassed two waves of professionalism, the visit of the New Zealand 'All Golds' in 1907, the subsequent signing of 'Dally' Messenger and the formation of rugby league clubs, and the startling defection of 14 of the 1908–09 Wallabies after their return to Australia.

Wood, in these very troubling years for rugby union, captained his club Glebe, New South Wales and his country. He toured New Zealand in 1905 and 1913, and the British Isles and North America in 1908–09. His career span at the top level lasted from 1905 to 1914 and despite occasional rebuffs he stood tall, despite being a mere 5ft 2in in height. He was squat and solid, though he weighed only 10st 7lb on the 1908–09 tour.

Peter Sharpham, in *The First Wallabies*, called him "a fearless scrum-half." Jack Pollard in *Australian Rugby* says of him that he "was a very solid, reliable performer behind the Australian scrum ... Wood was stocky with powerful legs and shoulders, and in bruising matches against big forwards had the ability to absorb punishment."

He first attracted notice at the higher level against the touring 1905 New Zealand team, captained by Jimmy Hunter, with notables such as George Gillett, 'Massa' Johnston, George Nicholson, Simon Mynott, George Smith and Billy Wallace. The All Blacks were using Australia as a warm-up for their impending tour of Britain and scheduled three matches, two against New South Wales and one against the Metropolitan Union. Wood missed the first state game, but impressed for the Metropolitan Union and was selected for the second New South Wales match, the latter resulting in a draw. Some of the outstanding players on the 'Blues' were 'Boxer' Russell, Ernie Anlezark, Cecil Murnin, Blair Swannell, Peter Burge, Harold Judd, Jimmy Clarken and Alex Burdon.

A full Australian team, the first national side ever selected to tour overseas, was announced the day after the second state game. Stan Wickham was the skipper, and the 21–year-old Fred Wood was officially the sole halfback,

Fred ('Possum') Wood was an inspiration at a time when the professional movement made serious inroads into the union code.

although Queensland's Mick Dore also had experience in the position. Dore was selected for the first match, so Wood's first appearance for Australia was against Marlborough-Nelson-Buller-West Coast. Chester and McMillan, in *The Visitors*, wrote that "Anlezark, Wood, Wickham and McLean stood out among the backs."

Dore was selected for the match against Canterbury-South Canterbury, as well as the test against New Zealand. Wood played in the final three matches, once as five-eighth, and therefore had played in four of the seven matches. It was a solid beginning to a long career.

There were no tours in or out of Australia in 1906, but in 1907 the All Blacks were back to test Australia's mettle. Wood appeared in their first match, playing for New South Wales. 'Dally' Messenger, a key figure in rugby league later on, was on the wing. New South Wales lost 3–11. In the next match, surprisingly won by the 'Blues' 14–0, his five-eighth partner was also from Glebe, Chris McKivat. They were the automatic selections for their first test, but Australia was thoroughly drubbed at 6–26.

The second test was in Brisbane, and in a selectorial farce the two selectors, James McMahon of Sydney and Poley Evans of Brisbane, agreed that the local man had the casting vote. The captain was therefore Allen Oxlade from Brisbane, and in all there were seven Queenslanders in the team. Fred Wood held his position, though Chris McKivat was replaced by Eric Mandible. New Zealand again won, 14–5.

In the final test, McKivat was recalled, but at centre, the halves being Wood and Mandible.

The Anglo-Welsh toured in 1908 and Fred Wood played in the two main New South Wales games, captaining his state in the first game, played in terrible conditions. Players from each team could not be differentiated. Howell, *et al*, in *They Came To Conquer* reported: "The New South Wales captain, Fred Wood, played magnificently." The Anglo-Welsh won both games, 3–0 and 8–0. It is of interest, based on later developments, that McKivat played five-eighth in the first encounter, but was dropped for the second.

The big news that enveloped all the rugby players of Australia was the possibility of an eight-month long tour of the British Isles and North America. It was Australia's first excursion to the northern hemisphere and was rightly hailed as the tour of a lifetime.

The tour is brilliantly analysed by Peter Sharpham in *The First Wallabies*. The team was captained by Herbert ('Paddy') Moran, with Fred Wood selected as the vice-captain. It is of interest that Wood and Newcastle's Joshua Stevenson were the selected halfbacks. Stevenson played in only one match, at Penycraig. He was injured and was a passenger from that time on. How different things might have been if he had been healthy. It forced the selectors to look elsewhere for a back-up half-back, and the choice fell to Chris McKivat, Wood's partner at Glebe.

McKivat was a brilliant and versatile player, and given the chance through circumstance showed more initiative and break-through possibilities than Wood. What exacerbated Wood's problem was that he had physical problems allegedly due to the damp English winter. He suffered from rheumatism or lumbago from a previously injured hip and his form was affected. However he had his own personal pride, and he was not only vice-captain but also a tour selector.

The problem is revealed in captain Moran's book, *Viewless Winds*: "Our team [against

Cornwall] the gold medal Olympic game played magnificent football, chiefly due to the fact that McKivatt [sic] was at last in his proper position at half and MacCabe [sic] at five-eights [sic]." Though this may have been the case, in actual fact Wood had been seriously injured, and missed the matches against Cambridge, Oxford, Yorkshire, Lancashire and Somerset. This allowed McKivat to shine. His re-appearance was against a Combined Midlands and East Midlands Counties, and Sharpham noted: "Wood, returning from a long injury, seemed slow and hesitant around the scrum-base and second-phase play."

The next match was against Wales, the first international, and the selectors picked McKivat at halfback and Ward Prentice at five-eighth. Wales won a close and emotional match by 9–0.

Wood next fronted up, as captain, against Glamorgan League. Sharpham wrote "... the whole team, more than capably lead by Fred Wood, played superbly in the abysmal conditions." Opinions are consistent that Wood's form improved in the latter stages of the tour, but McKivat was still superior.

In what this author regards as an incorrect assessment, Moran states in *Viewless Winds*: "The vice-captain was a great little player who never found his form in England. It used to be unpleasant for us when, in the face of this, he insisted for a long time on his own selection. We did not want unfriendliness, but for nine matches in succession he kept McKivatt [sic] out of his proper position."

These comments by Moran presumably allude to the opening matches, in which Wood played in seven, not nine matches before being injured. After all, McKivat had played five-eighth for his club, New South Wales and Australia before the team left. Wood was selected as a halfback and McKivat five-eighth. It must have been difficult for Wood himself to accept what was becoming a reality.

This author's reading is that increasingly Wood accepted the reality of the situation and instead concentrated on improving his own game. What is for certain is that after his return to the field in the British Isles, Wood played 13 games, seven of them as captain. He missed both internationals and the gold medal game against Cornwall in the 1908 Olympic Games. Only one game was lost when he was captain, so he did his best. He played 20 games on tour.

McKivat, as it turned out, was one of 14 Wallabies who defected after the tour, got the highest fee and then he captained the 1911–12 Kangaroos to Britain, when they won the Ashes. McKivat was a brilliant player, and there was no disgrace in Wood eventually playing second fiddle to him on this tour.

In 1910 New Zealand toured Australia, and Wood played against them twice for New South Wales and in the three tests. The first was won by New Zealand 6–0, the second by Australia 11–0 and the tie-breaker by New Zealand 28–13.

The second test represented the first test won over New Zealand in seven meetings (one match had been drawn) and the first time Australia had held an opponent scoreless. Howell, *et al* state in *They Came To Conquer*: "At a time of turmoil for the game, Australia's second test win was a real fillip ... Wood was a terrier around the field."

The same year, 1910, the New Zealand Maori toured, and Wood played in the two games for New South Wales, which the 'Blues' won. There were no tests.

In 1911 and 1912 there was no international rugby, but in 1913 a starved rugby-union fraternity in Australia gloried in a visit from the New Zealand Maori. Fred Wood scored a try and a penalty goal in the first 15–3 New South Wales victory. He also played in the second New South Wales match, again won by the locals, 16–5.

That same year, 1913, Australia embarked on a 9–match tour of New Zealand under captain Larry Dwyer. Chester and McMillan said of Wood in *The Visitors*: "Fred Wood, generally known as 'Possum', played 12 tests for Australia and 38 [sic–45] games for New South Wales. Short and chunky, he could stand up to the biggest forwards and was highly rated among rugby halfbacks of his time."

The team was not overly successful, winning

The Australian team of 1907: Fred Wood holds the ball, the captain Allen Oxlade is behind him and 'Dally' Messenger sits on Oxlade's left.

four and losing five, but Fred Wood played in eight of the nine games. He played in all three tests. In the second test, Chester and McMillan wrote: "Wood turned on his best game of the tour and was the outstanding back on the field." After the third test, they said: "Wood was again the outstanding back on the field, his passing and control of the game being quite magnificent."

Now 30 years of age, the curtain rang down on his career after the visit of the 1914 All Blacks. He captained New South Wales against them in both matches and captained Australia in the first and third tests. It was a fitting end to his career. War broke out late in the tour, and all minds were on what might happen. Harald George and Fred Thompson were both killed at Gallipoli and Bill Tasker severely injured. They had all played in the final test.

One has the feeling that but for the War Fred Wood would have still been tossing balls out from the scrum base for many years to come, and still prepared to go down courageously in front of rampaging packs.

This author has great admiration for the diminutive Wood. He was a player's player, captaining his club, his state and his country. In all he played 39 matches for Australia, 12 of them tests. In the test arena he captained Australia twice, but in addition led the team in four midweek games. What he lacked in size he made up for in heart. He was one of the rocks on which the foundation of Australian rugby was re-built. He never gave up on the game.

The words of Moran in *Viewless Winds* come to mind when thinking of Fred Wood: "For Rugby is a great game, not ending with the blown whistle. Years after we see again the rift in the opposing defences. We get ready to break through with a sudden flash of speed. Long after the events we still stretch ourselves full length barely to reach the heels of a flying three-quarter, drag them to ourselves and him to the ground. We leap, once more, higher than the others on a long line-out, gather the ball on our finger-tips, marvellously, and head the rush onward. We sink at the feet of dribbling forwards and gather the ball as the attacking force tumbles pell-mell upon us; the situation is saved. We feel the joyous rapture of massed forwards taking it on in a fierce irruption, or of centre-threes swerving through and just reaching the white line as they hit the green turf. The earth trembles, but a try has been scored."

Fred Wood lived to only 40 years of age, and would have had such dreams. He died during the season of 1924, and the NSWRU organised a fund for his wife and children.

FRED WOOD

CAPTAIN: 6 matches (2 tests) (1 v New Zealand 1910, 1 v New Zealand 1914),
BORN: Staffordshire, England 21 January 1884
DIED: 1924
SCHOOL: Educated in the U.K.
CLUBS: Glebe (112 first grade games)
NEW SOUTH WALES REPRESENTATION: 45 matches (1905–14)
AUSTRALIAN REPRESENTATION: 39 matches (12 tests) (1907–14)

JIMMY FLYNN

The Youngest Captain of Australia

JIMMY FLYNN was a teenage phenomenon. He learned his rugby at St Joseph's Christian Brothers College (Brisbane), one of the great nurseries for the sport in Australia and similar to its counterpart in New South Wales, and played and captained Brothers Rugby Club. Only Randwick has produced more rugby internationals than Brothers.

His was an instantly recognisable talent, and he was selected to play for his state one day before his 18th birthday which is a superb achievement, accomplished by but a few. Primarily a halfback, he showed his versatility by also playing in the centre at the top level. He also became Australia's youngest-ever captain, at 20 years and seven months. The pity is the First World War broke out soon afterwards, and therefore Flynn was unable to play during what one would conjecture would be his peak years.

Flynn was 17 years of age when first selected to play for Queensland, his home state. Some of the players with him on that occasion were Herb McCabe and Lou Meibusch, two outstanding wingers, 'Copper' Kent, Allen ('Butcher') Oxlade, Billy Richards and Pat Murphy. In their first match against New South Wales, at the Exhibition Ground, Queensland defeated the southerners in a thrilling match by 18–15. In the return match in Queensland, the 'Reds' repeated the dose, winning 23–8. This remained a rare feat for many years. Bob Willocks scored 11 points in the game, beating Lonnie Spragg's record set ten years previously. His record, in turn, would stand for 20 years. Oxlade was the captain in these glorious victories. Austin Gralton, a famous Queensland halfback, was the coach. Queensland won dual home victories for the first time since 1901.

The Blues were thirsting for revenge and in terrible conditions eked out a 12–3 victory in Sydney. The second encounter acted as a selection trial for the 1912 Australian tour of Canada and the USA. With the score 6–4 in favour of New South Wales, Oxlade was seriously injured. This turned out to be his 28th and last game for his state. The Queensland coach, Austin Gralton, requested a replacement, which was the practice of the day, but the New South Wales captain refused, contrary to the spirit of the time. New South Wales then ran away with the match by 29–4.

The selectors chose Tom Richards, a Queenslander then residing in Sydney, Bob Willocks, Lou Meibusch, Jimmy Flynn and

Peter Cunning, all from Queensland for this overseas tour. Willocks withdrew, thus vacating his place in rugby history, Bill Murphy being added. Flynn was still 18 years of age as he went on the tour, as was Lou Meibusch.

The 1912 tour was more of a continuous party than a serious series of games, the team being astonished at the level of social activity in Canada and the United States. Bob Adamson, on his return to Australia said that the team hardly slept and this appears to have been the case. A good time was certainly had by all, but only 11 victories out of 16 games came the way of the Australians. The captain was Ward Prentice and the manager Dr. Otto Bohrsmann.

Fortunately Australia won the sole test by 12–8, coming from behind to eke out a sensational victory. Jimmy Flynn was not selected for the test. 'Bobs', writing for the San Francisco Chronicle, said: "If ever a team looked to be hopelessly outclassed the Waratahs [sic] did yesterday in the first half and for twenty minutes' play after the interval."

Flynn played ten games on the tour, against the Barbarians, Olympic Club, University of California (three times), St. Mary's, University of Nevada, Santa Clara College, Vancouver and British Columbia.

It would not have been designated as a successful tour by Jimmy on the field, as in a rare instance in Australian rugby he was ordered off the field by the referee for abusing him in the match against a Combined Vancouver-Victoria team. It was doubtless frustration on his part, but there can be no excuse over what happened. Two forwards were sent off on the 1908 tour, so Flynn has the questionable but certainly historic distinction of being the first back.

Jimmy Flynn: Teen-age phenomenon.

Jimmy Flynn came into his own in 1913 and 1914. Although still 19 years of age, he first of all went up against a powerful New Zealand Maori team. There were 10,000 at the game and the 'Reds' won decisively, by 19–9. In the return encounter in the middle of the week, the Maori came out on top by 11–0.

Queensland went up next against a powerful New South Wales team, but Flynn was unable to play through a smallpox vaccination that floored quite a few on the team. Queensland, led by Bob Willocks, clawed its way to a 13–3 victory. Willocks, a mighty player and captain, was unable to travel south and, in fact, this

The Australian team of 1930, captained by Tom Lawton (with ball). Selector Jimmy Flynn in suit behind him.

proved to be his last game for the state. Flynn, despite his age, was appointed captain for the southern tour. Queensland lost the opening encounter by 6–26.

The return fixture at Sydney University Oval was later declared by Flynn to be his most exciting game ever. New South Wales was in the lead by 21–17 with time nearly gone when Queensland scored a try. Norman Roe wrote in *Maroon*: "With the result depending on his effort, Flynn took the kick at goal. The ball hit the crossbar, bounced up, fell back behind the bar, the referee signalled a goal, the full time bell rang and Queensland had won, 22–21."

"This kick has passed into folk lore. It is said that after it struck the bar the ball deflated, leading to the legend that Queensland won with a burst ball!

"Jimmy Flynn recalled years later: 'My heart nearly stopped while that ball seemed to hang there before it came down on the far side of the bar. To me it seemed like half an hour.'

"Apart from the decisive and dramatic goal kick his contribution to this success was considerable, as he converted two tries, and kicked a penalty goal and a goal from a mark."

Flynn played four games against the All Blacks in 1914, two for Queensland, in which he was the captain, and two tests for Australia. It was in the match on August 1, 1914, that he was elevated to the captaincy of his country, thus became Australia's youngest-ever captain. He was invited to play in the third test in Sydney, but had to decline.

The First World War interrupted this precocious player's career, and one can only wonder as to the heights he might have reached in the game. He appeared in two games for Australia against the brilliant AIF team in 1919.

Flynn's contribution to rugby did not end with his playing career. Rugby Union went into demise in Queensland from 1919 to 1929, but he played a big role in its revival in the northern state. He became both a Queensland and Australian selector, the latter in 1929 and 1930. He was on the selection panel which picked the Australian teams which won all three tests against the 1929 All Blacks and then beat the British Lions in 1930.

Jimmy Flynn's record as the youngest-ever captain of Australia will in all probability never be broken. As for his career, one wonders what might have been if the War had not interrupted such a phenomenal talent.

JIMMY FLYNN
CAPTAIN: 1 match (1 test) (1914 v New Zealand)
BORN: 23 June 1894
DIED: 1965
SCHOOL: St Joseph's Christian Brothers College (Brisbane)
CLUB: Brothers (Brisbane)
QUEENSLAND REPRESENTATION: 17 matches (1912–19)
AUSTRALIAN REPRESENTATION: 16 matches (2 tests) (1912-14)

WILLIAM ('WILLIE') WATSON

The New Zealander Who Became a Wallaby

THERE HAVE BEEN many New Zealanders who have played for Australia, John Carson, Jimmy Clarken, Arthur Corfe, John Cornes, Greg Davis, Keith Gudsell, John Hammon, Bill Hardcastle, Mark Harding, Wilf Hemingway, Ernest Hills, Rod Kellaher, Darby and Bob Loudon, Barry McDonald, Charlie Redwood, Sid Riley, James Sampson, Owen Stephens, Bob Thompson, Pat Walsh, Peter Ward, Bill Webb, Bob Westfield, Larry Wogan and Willie Watson among them.

Willie Watson was a superb soldier and a distinguished rugby player.

Only four have captained Australia. The first to be so honoured was Willie Watson, followed by brothers Darby and Bob Loudon, and then Greg Davis.

Australian-born players who played for New Zealand were Reg Bell (1922), Des Connor (1961–64), Ru Cooke (1903), Alf Eckhold (1907), Maurice Graham (1960), Evan Jessep (1931–32), Artie Lambourn (1934–35), Bill Mackrell (1905–06), Scott McLeod (1996–97), Bill Mitchell (1910), Syd Orchard (1896–97), Eddie Stapleton (1960), Snowy Svenson (1922–26), Tuna Swain (1928), Fred Tilyard (1923), Jim Tilyard (1913, 1920) and Francis Young (1896)

Only three Australians have played for both Australia and the All Blacks, Evan Jessep, Des Connor and Eddie Stapleton. The Stapleton case is interesting as the New Zealanders wanted to field two teams in a trial game on the way to South Africa, and Eddie Stapleton was ready and willing. This one cameo appearance made him an All Black forever.

Willie Watson was born in Nelson, New Zealand, November 10 1887. He came to Australia in 1911 and made an immediate impact as a front row forward with Newtown.

No touring teams came to Australia in 1911 and 1912, but he made a strong impression on his debut for New South Wales in 1912 and was selected on the 1912 tour of the United States and Canada. The team was overwhelmed with hospitality and lacked strong management. They generally stayed in fraternity houses in the United States, and revelled in the social life and undergraduate antics of the college lads. Training was secondary, the enjoyment of the tour was primary. In what must be the worst record of any

Australian touring team, particularly considering the opposition, the Australians lost all of their Canadian matches among five defeats. There was one test against the United States, which Watson played in, and it was won narrowly after the locals had led most of the game.

Willie Watson was one of the successes of the tour, and played in 11 of the 16 games.

The New Zealand Maori team arrived in 1913, and Watson played in both New South Wales games against them, with the Blues recording two victories (15–3 and 16–5). Australian rugby union had been struggling since the defection of 14 of the Wallabies in 1909, and doubtless would have died out if there had not been the continual Maori and New Zealand tours.

A Wallaby team was selected to go to New Zealand in 1913 under Larry Dwyer, the first tour to the land of the long white cloud since 1905. Watson was not the sole New Zealand-born member of the team, the other being Larry Wogan. Five of this team later died in the First World War, five-eighth 'Twit' Tasker, forwards 'Doss' Wallach, Harald George and Fred Thompson, and back Hubert Jones.

The tour was not overly successful, Australia winning only four of the nine games, but Watson was hailed as one of the best players on the tour and played in eight of the games, including all three tests. The same front row played in each test, with David Williams and Willie Watson as props and Harald George as hooker.

New Zealand came to Australia in what Howell, *et al* in *They Came To Conquer* have called the 'Declaration of War' Tour, as war broke out during the All Black tour. Watson played in the first match for New South Wales, at which sixty former Blues attended. New Zealand won handily, 17–6. He also played in the first test at the Sydney Cricket Ground, a close encounter won by the All Blacks 5–0. Watson was not selected in the second test at Brisbane, eight Queenslanders being selected, as was the custom of the time. He did, however, play for the Metropolitan Union against the visitors before an injury precluded his selection in the following state and Australian games.

Rugby union players flocked to join up in the war, all Sydney clubs being decimated because of it, and the authorities decided it was unpatriotic to hold competitions during the War. This was to have serious consequences, as the rugby league continued their competitions.

During the war, Watson won the DCM and the MC and bar serving with the Australian Imperial Forces. He later served in the Second World War as well, being given command of the Papuan Infantry Battalion with the rank of major, and was awarded the DSO.

When World War I ended on November 11 1918, there were some 250,000 troops awaiting a return to Australia. In order to alleviate the problems of keeping such a large group reasonably happy, a system of non-military employment was introduced, as well as a programme encompassing a wide variety of sports.

There was the Inter-Allied Games held in Pershing Stadium in Paris from 22 June to 6 July 1919, and this included sports like boxing, baseball, basketball, football (rugby, American football and soccer), quoits and track and field athletics. Some 65 Australians competed, but not in rugby.

The AIF rugby team was engaged elsewhere. King George V gave a Cup (the King's Cup) for competition in rugby among nations represented in the allied armies. Some 16 matches were played, the teams being the Imperial Army (called the 'Mother Country'), Australia, Canada, New Zealand, the Royal Air Force and South Africa.

When the serious competition began for the King's Cup, Lieutenant Willie Watson was the captain. The internationals were Watson, Jimmy Clarken, 'Bill' Cody, Dudley Suttor, Fred Thompson, Jackie Beith, Dan Carroll and Darb Hickey.

They played 16 matches in all, winning 12, although only five of them were in the King's Cup competition. The AIF team lost to the Royal Air Force and the 'Mother Country', but defeated New Zealand, who won the Cup.

It was decided that the AIF would play eight games in Australia. Beith stayed in the British Isles for medical studies, Dan Carroll went to the USA to settle, and Darb Hickey went back to rugby league.

This tour is designated by Howell *et al* in *They Came To Conquer* as 'The Saviours of the Game', as they brought Rugby Union back to rugby union followers who had missed out because of the war. The AIF team won all of its games, scoring 268 to 78 points and beating in turn New South Wales, Australia, New England, Queensland, Queensland AIF, Australia, North-West Union and Australia. Watson played in five of the eight games, all as captain.

The *Sydney Morning Herald* commented: "The disabandonment of the team will cause some regret, for the side has given Rugby Union football a great impetus in Sydney. The forwards in particular revived a phase of the game that was gradually weakening from the old standard, and when these players are merged into the different clubs an improvement should be noted.

"It was a very fine performance on the part of Major Walter Mathews [manager] and Lieutenant W. Watson to organise such a team from scattered sources, and in some instances to choose soldiers, practically unknown in football, but whose selection was more than justified by results."

Despite these efforts it was not until 1929 that rugby union was revived in Queensland, and consequently New South Wales matches against touring teams were, much later, designated as tests by the ARU. After all, the New South Wales team constituted the best rugby players in Australia at the time.

The 32–year-old Watson, now playing for Glebe-Balmain, was picked as captain of New South Wales in 1920 and thus he became a test skipper, though he was not aware of such in his lifetime. He was, indeed, captain in all three New South Wales matches.

In total, Watson played 46 club games for Newtown, 13 for Glebe-Balmain and 20 matches for New South Wales. He played 24 matches for his country (including the three New South Wales games in 1920 when he captained the side), and won eight caps in all.

A distinguished man in every respect, a war hero, a leader of men, he was a tough front row forward who never shirked his duties, grafting away unspectacularly and bravely for his adopted country. His leadership and example did much to restore Union's image after the war.

He was made Australian Consul-General in New York, and died there in 1961.

WILLIE WATSON

CAPTAIN: 3 matches (3 tests) (New South Wales v New Zealand, 1920)
BORN: November 10 1887 (Nelson)
DIED: September 9 1961 (New York)
SCHOOL: Born and educated in New Zealand
CLUB: Newtown, First AIF, Glebe-Balmain (46 Newtown, 13 Glebe-Balmain)
NEW SOUTH WALES REPRESENTATION: 22 matches (1912–20)
AUSTRALIAN REPRESENTATION: 24 matches (8 tests) (1912–20)

ARTHUR ('WAKKA') WALKER

Twelve Years at the Top

'WAKKA' WALKER is one of the few who played for his country before his state, being the second youngest at 19 years of age to tour California and British Columbia with the Australian team in 1912. Despite his age he played in nine of the games, twice as a substitute.

Eddie Kann had this to say of 'Wakka' Walker in *Easts Rugby Story*: "Toughest of tough half backs, A.S.B. Walker was known as 'Wakka' by all and sundry in Rugby in which he ranks as one of Easts most Homeric footballers. No one at Easts, not even his contemporaries, could tell the author 'Wakka's' Christian names which he himself probably wanted to forget, as A.S.B. stood for Arthur Stanley Billingsgate.

"'Arthur' might have been acceptable because characteristics of his play were speed, quick thinking and a bewildering side-step. He could zig-zag through a loose ruck like forked lightning! Arthur Murray's dancers no doubt would have been amazed by 'Wakka's' footwork.

"Walker also was noted for his 'dummy'. One young half, promoted to first grade, was told 'to watch Walker's hands.' Reports of Easts matches continually told the story how Walker darted round the scrum or ruck, feinted and dodged through the bewildered defence for a try.

"Walker also was a smashing tackler. In games in which the opposition hammered Easts goal line the former would always be to the fore in keeping them out. 'Wakka' was foremost a master of dazzling attacking rugby and a master tactician. He was classed as a half back in the same bracket as the famous Chris McKivat and other illustrious predecessors as scrum workers.

"Walker was good company as well as a most unselfish footballer."

Wakka 'was a great practical joker', said Larry Wogan who toured both America and New Zealand with him. After Walker had been made a state selector and team manager, later New South Wales players, while housed at a Coogee hotel to undergo training to meet the All Blacks, also enjoyed their association with 'Wakka'... and his 'nieces'. Walker was a Sydney Grammar School Old Boy who played representative rugby from 1912 to 1924. The war took a big slice out of his career.

In 1912, when he first played for Australia on the North American tour, he was not only a mere 19 years of age, but a diminutive 5ft 6in and 11st 6lb.

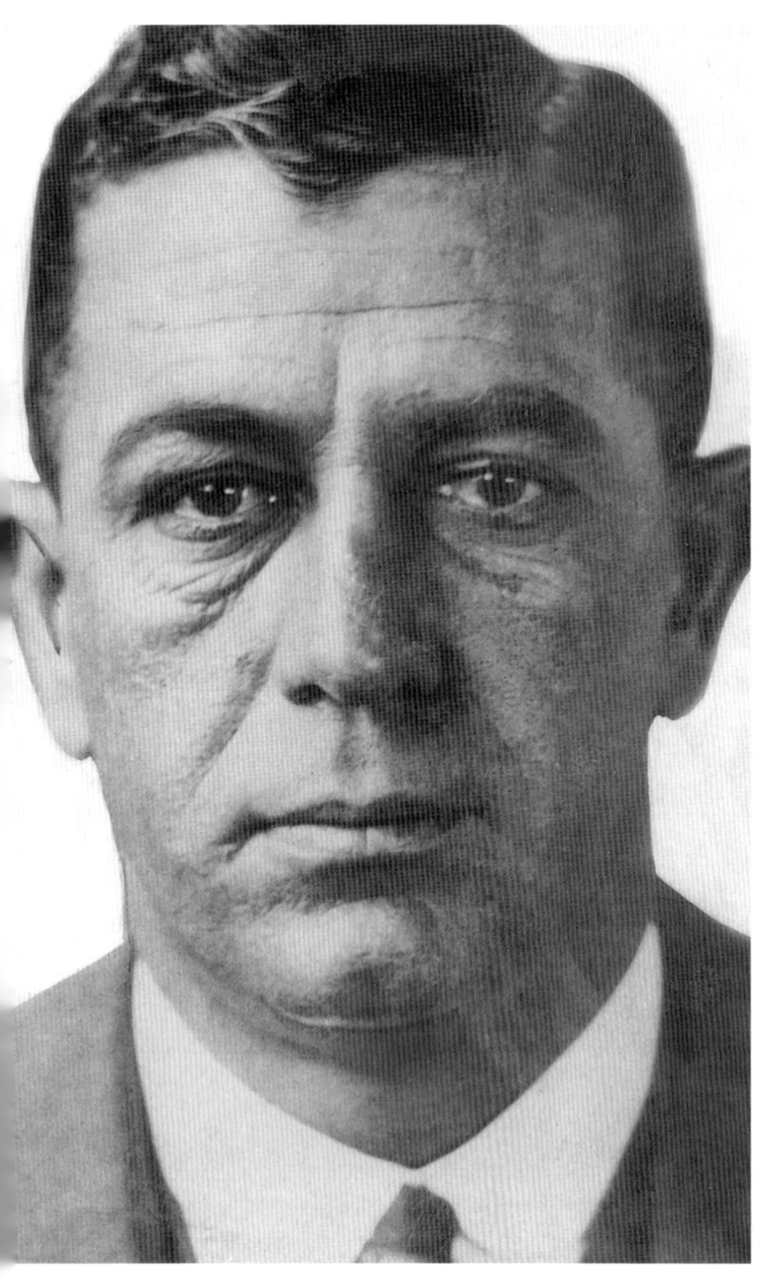

'Wakka' Walker was the toughest of tough halfbacks.

He was not selected in either the Metropolitan or New South Wales sides against the visiting Maori team in 1913 and he also missed selection for the 1913 tour of New Zealand, 'Twit' Tasker, who also played five-eighth, and the experienced Fred Wood getting the nod. These selections also held up on the 1914 'Declaration of War' tour by New Zealand. So Walker had not represented his country since the 1912 tour.

During the war 'Wakka' was with the Light Horse and after the armistice played in the Empire Expeditionary Forces Rugby competition at Cairo. He did not have an opportunity to make the AIF team for the King's Cup and tour with Australia because of his Egyptian posting.

After the war, and following his return to Australia, Walker captained Easts, and then played for Australia against the AIF team that toured Australia. This tour was a considerable fillip for the Union code after the war and Walker took part in the first and third matches against the AIF team.

New Zealand toured in 1920, and 'Wakka' played in two of the three New South Wales teams against them. These are now considered tests as Queensland had disbanded, not coming back into the national scene until 1929.

When the 1921 season came around, Willie Watson had departed for the USA and Walker took over the captaincy of New South Wales from him. His main competition, as Fred Wood had retired, was Manly's Norman Mingay.

South Africa made their first visit to Australia in 1921, led by Theo Pienaar, although the test captain was 'Boy' Morkel. Incredibly, there were five members of the Morkel family in the team.

In the first match against New South Wales (now a test), Walker was captain, the home team losing to the mighty 'Boks by 10–25. He captained the locals in the second and third matches as well, New South Wales losing by 11–16 and 9–28. In the final clash, The *Sydney Morning Herald* reporter noted: "Among the New South Wales players, A.S. Walker at half-back, showed sterling form... But his forwards let him down badly."

That same year, 1921, New South Wales

toured New Zealand, playing 10 games. 'Wakka' Walker was the captain and played in eight games, which included one test (won 17–0). Though New South Wales played against many of the minor unions, this was the best tour any team from Australia had ever had, New South Wales winning nine and losing only the game against Wellington. Some of the New South Wales players who would leave an indelible record in Australian rugby were Johnny Wallace, 'Pup' Raymond, 'Slip' Carr, Otto Nothling (who played cricket for Australia when Don Bradman was dropped for the only time in his career), and Charlie Fox. The tour was a triumph for Walker.

In 1922 Walker was 28 years of age and he continued to captain New South Wales in the first and third matches versus the Maori, and then fronted up against the All Blacks in the three New South Wales matches against them, two of which New South Wales won. Against the Maori in the first match he received a large gash on his head early in the game but he showed his courage by playing on.

He was still at it in 1923, playing two games against the Maori, but he had been superseded as captain by 'Watty' Friend. He did not go on the 1923 tour to New Zealand, the halfback positions going to Norm Mingay, Wally Meagher and Jack Duncan.

Incredibly he was back in 1924, captaining New South Wales twice against the All Blacks. He also played in the third game, but Ted Thorn was the new captain.

Walker enjoyed some career at the top level, lasting from 1912 to 1924. In all he captained New South Wales 18 times in his 24 state appearances and he played 77 times for his beloved Easts. On his retirement he became a State selector for a number of years. He died at Forster in September 1958, aged 65. He had been in poor health for some time.

Arthur Walker captained New South Wales in what is now regarded as tests in Australia some 11 times. This was a record at the time.

A fun-loving man, he was a sturdy player with lots of heart. He was lightning fast on attack and tireless on defence. He was tough, and his opponents knew it. He was a veritable legend in his day.

ARTHUR WALKER

CAPTAIN: 15 matches (11 tests) (1922-24)
BORN: Sydney, 1893
DIED: September, 1958 (Forster)
SCHOOL: Sydney Grammar
CLUB: Eastern Suburbs (77 club matches)
NEW SOUTH WALES REPRESENTATION: 32 matches (1912-24)
AUSTRALIAN REPRESENTATION: 33 matches (16 tests) (1912-24)

DR DARBY LOUDON

One of Two Brothers to Captain Australia

DARBY LOUDON, if he were alive today, would be very surprised at where he stands in the history of Australian Rugby Union. First, he would be taken aback that all the games he played for New South Wales against international teams are now regarded as tests. This decision was made, and rightly so, by the ARU 23 years after he had passed away. After all, Queensland had discontinued rugby and the New South Wales players were the best in Australia at that time.

Darby Loudon captained Australia once in a short career.

Second, he would be delighted to know that he captained Australia (New South Wales) in one test, against New Zealand Maori on June 26 1922.

Third, he would be disappointed that one of rugby's most authoritative tomes, by Rod Chester, Ron Palenski and Chester McMillan, *The Encyclopedia of New Zealand Rugby*, has not recognised this feat. Even allowing for the fact that New Zealand does not recognise Maori or New South Wales games as tests despite Australia's decisions with regard to this, he does at the very least deserve a mention.

Another New Zealand-born player, Darby was born in Leeston (Canterbury). There is no exact record of when he arrived in Australia, but he did attend Sydney Grammar School for a time. Then he went to Sydney University to study medicine, which he completed there.

The New South Wales union recommenced competitions after the First World War in 1919, and Sydney University immediately came to the fore. University won the competition easily, losing only one game to Glebe-Balmain 17–18. This fine record occurred despite the fact that the University was closed until 5 May 1919 because of the raging influenza epidemic.

The captain of that first post-war University team was Darby Loudon. There were some fine players on the team, including 'Pup' Raymond, who became a Rhodes Scholar in 1922, Fred Gwynne, A.E. Gregg, Otto Nothling (who played cricket once for Australia when Bradman was dropped) and E.M. Sheppard. The official team photo shows a motley-looking lot, with football jerseys of variegated colours, and a complete lack of consistency with respect to socks.

The team reversed the earlier result against Glebe-Balmain in the final round, beating them in a high-scoring game 39–25. The *Sydney Morning Herald* noted: "University by defeating Glebe-Balmain, increased its lead in the competition by six points. The rules state that a final should be played, but with such a margin University is in an unassailable position, and a further game would be unnecessary and uninteresting." Thus it remained.

Darby Loudon was awarded a University Blue that year. They were hard to come by, with only Nothling, Raymond, Satterthwaite, Shephard and Slegar getting 'Blues' in 1919.

The AIF team played throughout Australia in 1919 and did much to revitalise the Union code. Sydney University was represented in the team by pre-war University players Dr Bruce Beith and team manager Captain Wally Mathews. Loudon's first big-game experience was against the AIF team, playing for New South Wales in their first match in Australia.

Loudon did not play against the visiting New Zealand team in 1920, perhaps due to his medical work, but he must have been honoured when he was selected in the 1921 New South Wales tour to the land of his birth. There were 27 players on the team. The captain was 'Wakka' Walker, and the manager the outstanding referee T.H. Bosward. In *The Encyclopedia of New Zealand Rugby* the spelling of Loudon's first name is given as Derby, and one other source has it that way. Jack Pollard has it as Darby.

Some of the other outstanding players on the team were Johnny Wallace, 'Slip' Carr, Nothling, Charlie Fox, 'Chook' Fowles, Raymond and the veteran Larry Wogan.

There were 10 games and New South Wales won nine of them. This was the best record of any Australian touring team up to this time. In fairness it must be stated that the Springboks were on tour at this time and New South Wales played most of their games against weaker Unions. It might also be noted that the 1908 aboriginal war-cry was given by the visitors prior to games.

Darby Loudon was one of the successes of the tour. He played in nine of the 10 games and was second-highest scorer, with two tries, nine conversions and four penalty goals for 36 points.

His appointment with history came when the 1922 Maori team came to Australia. He played in the three New South Wales games against them, and in the second, on 26 June 1922, he was the captain. As these are now considered tests, Dr Darby Loudon was an Australian captain. Only for one test, but who would not have desired to do the same?

A backrower, Darby Loudon was an intelligent player, solid in attack and defence. He was also a fine kicker.

His brother Bob also became an Australian captain. They are the only brother combination to achieve this feat in Australia's long history. While several sets of brothers have played for their country, the Loudons are the only pair to both captain test teams.

DR DARBY LOUDON

CAPTAIN: 1 test (v New Zealand Maori 1922)
BORN: March 12, 1897 (Leeston, New Zealand)
DIED: 1963
SCHOOL: Early education New Zealand, Sydney Grammar School, Sydney University
CLUBS: Sydney University, North Sydney and GPS Old Boys
NEW SOUTH WALES REPRESENTATION: 16 matches (1919–22)
AUSTRALIAN REPRESENTATION: 12 matches (4 tests) (1919–22)

WALTER ('WATTY') FRIEND

The Captain Who Never Lost

King's School in Sydney has produced some great rugby players over the years.

In 1888 King's School Past and Present played the touring British side. The British did not lose a game on tour, but this was one of their two draws, finishing up at 10–10. Three masters at the school played, including New South Wales players Harold Baylis, Greg Wade and J. Rice.

The School was smart enough not to front up against the visiting New Zealand tourists in 1893 and 1897, but when the British team arrived in 1899 they played a match against the Great Public Schools, A.G.H. Gardiner being one we know of as coming from King's School.

Watty Friend: New South Wales was always stronger when he took the field.

Watty Friend, after leaving school, played for Glebe-Balmain, and he played 56 games for the club. His elder brother, R.M., played for New South Wales against the AIF and Queensland.

Watty was a forward, and a tough one at that. When he dropped out of the tour to New Zealand in 1923, *The Visitors* noted: "The absence of W.S. Friend, the outstanding forward who had played against the All Blacks in 1920 and 1922 and had captained New South Wales against New Zealand Maoris in 1923, weakened the side considerably." For Friend to be so lauded by a New Zealand publication attests to his outstanding ability. We are unaware of why he did not tour New Zealand, and for that matter why he never went overseas during his career, but it was not uncommon in those days for firms to deny leave for sporting tours.

Watty's first flirtation with the big time was for a New South Wales 2nd XV against New Zealand in 1920. Watty impressed in the 18–31 loss, scoring two fine tries, and was selected for the following New South Wales team (now regarded as a test) and the Metropolitan Union against the All Blacks. He played three games against them in seven days. The New Zealand captain was Jimmy Tilyard, and some of the top players were Ces Badeley, 'Moke' Belliss, Billy Duncan, Teddy Roberts, Jack Steel and Alf West. Watty had survived his baptism by fire.

In 1921 the mighty Springboks came on their first trip to Australia. There were five of the Morkel family in the team. An anomaly concerned the captain, Theo Pienaar, who seemed to have been selected for diplomatic rather than playing reasons. He did not play a test and his deputy, Boy Morkel, captained the team.

Watty played in the three tests against them and was cited in each game as being among the Waratahs' top players. In the second New South Wales game, won by the Springboks 16–11, the *Sydney Morning Herald* reporter noted: "Yet against this formidable-looking combination in the African front line the New South Wales forwards acquitted themselves remarkably well, frequently bursting through the ponderous opposition with ball at toe, and carrying it on with those dribbling rushes which are the very essence of Rugby."

In 1922 the All Blacks came, and Watty played in the three matches against them. 'Moke' Belliss was the New Zealand captain and they were formidable, none more so than the mighty Maurice Brownlie, a man of commanding physical presence, immense strength and indomitable will. Another was Harold Masters, who later on made a considerable contribution to Australian coaching at Easts, and he would become an Australian selector.

In the first New South Wales match, Howell *et al* in *They Came To Conquer* state: "Tom Davis, Watty Fiend and Fox [were] the best for New South Wales." The second game was won by New South Wales 14–8; this was the All Blacks' first loss in Australia since 1910 and their first to New South Wales since 1907.

The third match was won by New South Wales 8–6, Tom Davis, Bill Marrott and Watty standing out in a determined home effort. This was New Zealand's first series loss in its proud history, and was a credit to both players and administrators in New South Wales in bringing the game back to its former glory.

Watty Friend was elevated to the captaincy of New South Wales in 1923. He led New South Wales in what are now regarded as tests against New Zealand Maori and thus he is a test captain. As captain he had a 100 percent winning record, since New South Wales won the series 3–0. Watty led his team from the front, showing superb leadership qualities.

WALTER 'WATTY' FRIEND

CAPTAIN: 3 tests (v New Zealand Maori 1923)
BORN: September 19 1898
DIED: 1983
SCHOOL: King's School
CLUB: 56 matches (Glebe-Balmain)
NEW SOUTH WALES REPRESENTATION: 10 matches (1920–23)
AUSTRALIAN REPRESENTATION: 10 matches (10 tests) (1920–23)

BILLY SHEEHAN

Rhodes Scholar and Waratah

IN 1923, for the second time in a row, a King's School graduate became a Waratah (Australian) captain. This time it was a rather lightweight back under 11st, but one who could scamper with the best of them from five-eighth to wing. An exciting player, it is rightly or wrongly understood that he lost some of his spice and side-stepping ability on heavy grounds.

Billy Sheehan rose to prominence early on in his career. He was only 18 years of age when he made his big-time debut against a Springbok team making its first trip to Australia in 1921. He was in the three-quarters with some outstanding players, 'Pup' Raymond, Larry Wogan and Edwin Carr, and they went up against four highly talented 'Boks, Wally Clarkson, Attie van Heerden, Jackie Weepner and Charlie du Meyer. Raymond, a medico, was awarded a Rhodes Scholarship, an Oxford Blue and an OBE in recognition of his contribution to various walks of life.

In the third match of three, all won by the tourists, Sheehan scored a try, the *Sydney Morning Herald* noting: "Sheehan ..., so far as he was allowed, played excellently."

While playing for Sydney University he received five Blues in 1921, 1923, 1924, 1926 and 1927, a rare occurrence. Under his captaincy, University won the Shute Shield back-to-back in 1923 and 1924. The Shute Shield was established after a University front row forward, Robert Shute, collapsed in a game and died from a cerebral haemorrhage. From 1923 the shield was awarded to the Sydney First Grade Premiership winner.

Some of the players in 1923–24 University teams were Duncan ('Chook') Fowles, Otto Nothling, Alex Ross, 'Bot' Stanley and Arthur Erby. The team was coached by Dr 'Paddy' Moran, the captain of the 1908 Wallabies. Sheehan still captained University until 1927, after which Alex Ross took over.

In 1922 New Zealand toured Australia under 'Moke' Belliss, and the now 19–year-old with the flashing feet and decisive side-step had to go up against players like the legendary All Black Mark Nicholls. To everyone's surprise, after getting a fair hiding in the first match, New South Wales bounced back with two victories over the All Blacks, by 14–8 and 8–6. This was New Zealand's first loss in any series, and the studious Sheehan's reputation went up a notch.

In 1923 Sheehan was in two New South Wales victories over the New Zealand Maori team in Australia, though an injury in the second match prevented him from playing in the final encounter. However his performances and his captaincy of Sydney University brought him the honour of leading the New South

Wales team on its 1923 tour of New Zealand.

Unfortunately some ten of the Blues' top players declared themselves unable to tour, among them 'Watty' Friend, 'Wakka' Walker, 'Pup' Raymond, Pym, Johnny Wallace (who had taken up a Rhodes Scholarship at Oxford) and Larry Wogan. The New South Wales team to tour in 1923 was young, inexperienced and light. It was a pity as the 1921 New South Wales tour to New Zealand was highly successful and New South Wales had won two out of three matches in 1922.

The 1923 New South Wales team played 10 matches in all, winning two and losing eight. In a rarity for a touring party the visitors were heavily outscored, only registering 119 points to the locals' 245. Sheehan did everything he could to prevent the slaughter, playing in seven of the 10 games and each of the three tests, but to no avail. The Blues lost to New Zealand by scores of 9–19, 6–34 and 11–38.

When 1924 came around, he had lost the captaincy to halfback 'Wakka' Walker, Sheehan being at five-eighth. New South Wales surprisingly won the first match 20–16, but the All Blacks rebounded in the second by 21–5. Sheehan was not picked in the third and deciding match, won convincingly by New Zealand 38–8.

In 1925 he did not appear in any representative games through his studies, but stormed back in 1926 against the Cliff Porter-captained All Blacks. In the first match against the visitors Sheehan teamed up with Randwick's legendary Wally Meagher. The home team fielded a mighty backline, with Syd King and Cyril Towers in the centres, the brilliant Owen Crossman and Allen ('Sheik') Bowers on the wing, and the formidable Alex Ross as fullback. The All Blacks were stunned as New South

Billy Sheehan: a brilliant three-quarter.

Wales rolled them 26–20, Sheehan scoring a fine try that was set up by Crossman.

As so often, the All Blacks retrenched and won the next three games, 11–6, 14–0 and 28–21. What was certain was that the standard of New South Wales had risen again.

The prospect of the 1927–28 Waratah tour was one that held the attention of all state players. It had been almost 20 years since a team had left Australian shores, and stories of the 1908 Wallaby tour had been told and re-told. It was a 9–month tour that involved a circumnavigation of the globe. This tour changed the nature of rugby in Australia forever, as the Waratah style of open rugby became the credo of all Australian teams in the future.

What players they were! The captain was Johnny Wallace, who while studying in the British Isles had played for Scotland. Tom Lawton, another Rhodes Scholar, Cyril Towers, Charlie Fox, 'Jock' Blackwood, 'Jack' Ford, Wally Meagher, Syd Malcolm and Eric Ford were only the brightest stars in a talented team.

Peter Fenton, writer and poet, penned this piece on the Waratahs in his excellent book *For The Sake Of The Game.*

THE WARATAHS

The Waratahs who packed their bags in nineteen twenty-seven
And sailed away to play the running game,
Spent six weeks on the high seas as they made their way to Devon
With neither thought of riches nor of fame.

But they were meant for greatness, it was somehow pre-ordained,
They thrilled the crowds at every rugby ground,
They played the game with passion and the glory they attained
Is tribute to the legends that abound.

For here were people playing for the magic of the sport
The simple thrill of running with the ball,
No thought of breaking records, no immortal claims were sought,
The game was all that mattered to them all.

And twice a week they gave their all and never cried 'enough.'
In rain and sleet, in weather foul and fair,
As always with a smile that said; we know you boys are tough
Come match us as we give the ball some air.

Their names will live forever when the greatest deeds are done
Like Lawton, Wallace, Ross and big Jack Ford, and Breckenridge,
The iron man, who spoiled the half-backs' fun,
And Towers who so many tries had scored.

In England, Ireland, Scotland, Wales and later on in France,
The Waratah embroidered on their chest
Became the very symbol of the team that took a chance,
The team that breathed with passion in its breast.

Now when you see a team that plays the game they play in heaven
A team that you would love to call your own,
You're looking at the Waratahs of nineteen twenty-seven;
The finest team of sportsmen we have known.

Peter Fenton.

Fenton provided this short biography in *For The Sake Of The Game*: "Dr. William Beverley James 'Billy' Sheehan, Kings School, Sydney University, aged 24, weight 10 stone 10, was already established as a fine player when the tour began. In 1921, at the age of 18, he played three tests against South Africa and captained New South Wales to New Zealand in 1923. Sheehan's clever stepping was nullified to an extent on the soft British ground, but he still had a fine tour, playing well in the tests against Wales and Scotland, and filling in admirably for Lawton in the games at five-eighth. Billy Sheehan stayed in London after the tour to further his medical studies but came back to Australia and played for New South Wales again in 1930."

Sheehan actually did not travel overseas with the Waratahs because of medical examinations, and did not go to North America with the team, and therefore would have missed some of the bonding experience on the trip to England.

Sheehan's versatility was particularly useful and he played 12 games on the 31–match tour. However, Lawton's genius kept him from appearing in his preferred five-eighth position. In the test against Wales he was in the centre, and Howell, *et al* wrote in *The Wallabies: A Definitive History of Australian Test Rugby* that "Billy Sheehan, next to Tommy Lawton and Johnnie Wallace, was the most dangerous player in the team. He also made the Scottish international in the centre, but after that the Towers-King centre combination won out."

For the rest of his life, Billy Sheehan was glorified as one of the famous Waratahs of 1927–28. He played his last game for New South Wales in 1930.

BILLY SHEEHAN
CAPTAIN: 3 tests (v New Zealand 1923) plus 4 other matches
BORN: 1903
DIED: 1957
SCHOOL: Kings' School, Sydney
CLUB: Sydney University, Randwick
NEW SOUTH WALES REPRESENTATION: 33 matches (1921–27)
AUSTRALIAN REPRESENTATION: 31 matches (18 tests) (1921–27)

TED THORN

The Manly Flanker

Ted Thorn and his younger brother Joe were both forwards and stalwarts of the Manly Club, after their talents came to light at Manly Public School under Harold Austin. Others to develop there were Norm ('Rat') Mingay, the first player to score 100 points in a season in the Sydney competition, and Dudley Beer and Jerry Chambers, who also played for New South Wales.

Joe Thorn was the first to make his mark in representative rugby, bursting on the scene in 1921 and continuing his surge in 1922. He made the highly successful Waratah tour to New Zealand in 1921. Joe played in eight of the 10 games, including the one against New Zealand, surprisingly won by New South Wales 17–0. It should be noted that the 1921 Springboks were in New Zealand at the same time.

Though three years younger than Ted, Joe's star shone early but faded quickly, perhaps through injury, as he retired after playing only 28 games with Manly.

When his brother's career seemed to be declining, flanker Ted Thorn was getting his opportunity. He played three matches against the All Blacks in 1922, New South Wales surprisingly winning two of them.

Ted did not play against the visiting Maori team in 1923, but was selected on the highly unsuccessful 1923 New South Wales tour of New Zealand. He played in every match, showing himself to being a veritable iron man, and scored three tries, but the team won only two of the 10 games. The absence of key players like 'Watty' Friend, 'Johnny' Wallace, 'Wakka' Walker, 'Pup' Raymond, John Pym, Charlie Fox and Larry Wogan was a major factor in the dismal record. The New South Wales team was too young, too light and too inexperienced. The references to Thorn were all favourable: "well supported by Thorn," "Thorn covered a lot of ground," "Thorn and Greatorex the best of a forward pack that struggled against much heavier opposition," and so on. He was one who returned to Australia with his reputation intact.

In 1924 New Zealand arrived, and Ted Thorn played in each of the three New South Wales games. In the final match, on 16 July 1924, he was made captain. He died without knowing he was a test captain. Perhaps he was a trifle lucky, as the captain in the previous games, tough halfback 'Wakka' Walker, had to retire through injury.

Thorn's leadership qualities came to full fruition the following year, 1925, as he was captain in the first two New South Wales matches against the visiting All Blacks. An injury forced his withdrawal in the third match, New South Wales being captained by Charlie Fox.

His sterling captaincy was rewarded on the 1925 New South Wales tour to New Zealand. Again a number of outstanding players were unable to tour, among them Alex Ross, Charlie Fox, Tom Davis, and Otto Nothling. Experienced players Norm Mingay and 'Wakka' Walker had retired. On the other hand, the brilliant and mercurial Tom Lawton was in the team, as were Jack Ford, Charlie Morrissey, Ned Greatorex, Allen Bowers, 'Jock' Blackwood, Wally Meagher, Owen Crossman and Syd King. The manager was test player and all-round sportsman Harald Baker.

The tour was a great success, New South Wales winning nine of their 11 games. Ted Thorn played in the first seven, but received a severe wrist injury and could not play the final three games, which included the test. Tommy Lawton was made captain.

In 1926 the All Blacks toured again, and they played four matches against New South Wales. Ted Thorn captained New South Wales in the first three, before Johnny Wallace, who had returned from the British Isles, took over the captaincy. It must have been a big disappointment for Thorn, who had done everything asked of him, but Wallace was the flavour of the day, having achieved fame as a vital cog in the Scottish three-quarter line while overseas. If it were not for Wallace, Thorn might possibly have been the captain of the 1927–28 Waratahs on their overseas

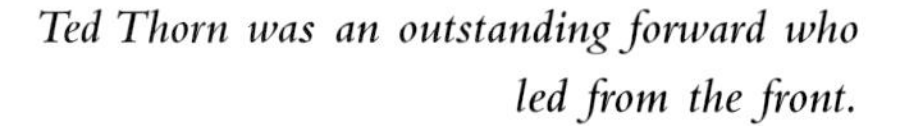

Ted Thorn was an outstanding forward who led from the front.

tour. He was a fine leader of men.

When the 1927–28 team was announced, Johnny Wallace was the captain and Charlie Fox his understudy.

This is that Peter Fenton said about him in his excellent work *For The Sake Of The Game*. "Edward Joseph 'Ted' Thorn, Fort Street Boys' High School [note: we believe it was Manly High School], Manly, aged 30, height 5ft 11in, weight 14st, was a breakaway who had captained New South Wales against New Zealand on six occasions between 1924 and 1926. He was also captain of his club, Manly, for whom he was the regular goal kicker. Though in the veteran class by the time of the tour he played well in 13 games and his experience was invaluable in a very young pack. He was one who matched the British forwards in his ability to keep the ball on the toe and instigate foot rushes.

"On his return Ted Thorn again pulled on the boots to captain Manly, where he also was a member of the selection panel and the administration committee."

Ted Thorn was an outstanding forward who led from the front, always setting the example by his determined and intelligent play. When later the New South Wales matches were accorded test status, he thus became an Australian captain on six occasions. Though he did not play a test on his final tour, he was a vital cog in the Waratah machine.

TED THORN

CAPTAIN: 13 matches (6 tests), 1924 (2), 1925 (1), 1926 (3)
BORN: 26 July 1897
DIED: not known
SCHOOL: Manly High School
CLUB: Manly (78 matches)
NEW SOUTH WALES REPRESENTATION: 44 matches (1921-28)
AUSTRALIAN REPRESENTATION: 41 matches (15 tests) (1921-28)

CHARLIE FOX

Senior Citizen of the Waratahs

CHARLIE FOX, a burly second rower and outstanding lineout exponent, was one of the senior citizens of the 1927–28 Waratah tour of the British Isles, France and North America. He was 29 years of age. Only Ted Thorn, at 30, was older.

His representative career was longer than anyone else on the tour of tours. He had started in 1919, and retired after the 1928 tour.

This is what Peter Fenton wrote about him in *For The Sake Of The Game*. "Charles Leigh Fox, Vice-Captain, Sydney Grammar, Northern Suburbs, aged 29, height 6 feet 1, weight 13 stone 7, suffered a severe leg injury against Oxford University that dramatically curtailed his career. Up to that point he had played 10 of the first 13 games. His long absence was a real blow to the side as he was one of the most experienced players, having represented New South Wales several times since 1919 against the All Blacks, the Maoris and the Springboks. He was a tremendous lineout forward and his injury placed a heavy burden on Finlay and Storey. Charlie Fox recovered in time to play the last four games of the tour, including the French international when he replaced Jack Ford. He retired after the tour."

The Fox representative career started in 1919 with the visit of the AIF team, which did much to revive interest in rugby union in Australia after World War I. On 2 August 1919 he was selected on an Australian XV to play against the AIF, and acquitted himself well. He was 21 years of age at that time.

In 1920 he played in three matches for New South Wales against the All Blacks, and one for the Metropolitan Union. All matches New South Wales played against international teams are now regarded as tests, but Fox died without knowing this. No rugby was being played in Queensland from 1919 to 1929, when the so-called 'Revivalists' brought the game back in the northern state.

Fox had a busy year in 1921, going up against the visiting Springboks once for New South Wales and once for the Metropolitan team, and was also called upon to tour New Zealand. He played seven games on tour, including the 17–0 defeat of the All Blacks in the single test. This tour was the most successful in Australia's history, but it should be noted parenthetically that the Springbok team was touring New Zealand at the same time and the opposition was not of the normal calibre.

In 1922 he went up against the visiting New

Charlie Fox, the vice-captain of the Waratahs of 1927–28.

Zealand Maori in two tests and played once against the full All Black team. He disappeared from the representative scene in 1923, but was back in 1924 (three tests against New Zealand) and 1925. In the latter year he went up against the might of the All Blacks five times; three for New South Wales, once for a New South Wales XV and once for E.J. Thorn's XV. In the third test against New Zealand he was appointed captain, so he lined up in history as one of the nation's one-test captains. In 1926 he again played two tests against New Zealand, and on the basis of his continual solid performances was selected, and as vice-captain, of the touring 1927–28 team.

As noted, Fox was a stalwart on the team, playing in 10 of the first 13 games. It was against Oxford University that the main goals of his tour were smashed, as he had to retire from the field in the first half with what appeared to be a badly sprained ankle. It turned out to be so serious that he was only able to play the last four tour games. One of these games was against France, so at least he played in one international. In all, he played in 13 of the 31 games. It was not the end of his career that he would have wished.

Charlie had been the captain of the Waratahs at the Oxford match, as he had been against Glasgow in Johnny Wallace's absence. Without Fox on the field in the second half, no substitutions in those days, the Waratahs lost their first tour game against Oxford by 3–0.

France lost to the Waratahs 8–11, so this is one example how his formidable presence was missed. The Waratahs thereafter enjoyed the following chorus of "Those Waratah Blues":

The Waratah Blues in gay Paree,
They captured the test, Ah, oui, oui, oui,
With Parlez vous, and oh, such cheers,
They met the girls from Armentiers.
Wherever they went, you heard folk tell
Of our wonderful lads and their famous yell,
Come On, the Blues! Come On, the Blues!
Come On, You Waratah Blues!

One item is still surrounded by mystery on that Waratah tour. The *Western Mail* of

November 21 1927 reported:

'BOWERS GOES HOME. INJURED WARATAH RELEASED TO TAKE NO FURTHER PART IN TOUR.

"A.J.A. Bowers, the Waratahs' wing three-quarter, who has played two games in Wales, will take no further part in the present tour of the colonial side, and has left for his home in Sydney.

"Bowers has been injured seriously in two games, and when he fractured a couple of ribs in a game in England a few weeks ago he asked to be released by the manager (Mr. Gordon Shaw). He left during the weekend and his absence will greatly weaken the side.

"Bowers, who was one of the most popular members of the party, was married only a fortnight before the team left for Australia."

As all rugby players know, "what happens on tour stays on tour." This remains the case with the Bowers situation.

There was no doubt that he was homesick, and that he married shortly before leaving Australia. But he had scored 8 tries in his 10 appearances, and had just played against Ireland. The *Ford Diary*, compiled by his daughter, does not even mention Bowers leaving the team.

What we know is what Peter Fenton wrote in *For The Sake of The Game*: "He was involved in a minor scuffle with vice-captain Charlie Fox, and in an effort to ensure team morale was not affected, asked permission to quit the tour. Gordon Shaw agreed that the big winger should go."

So there was more to the situation than appears. What happened between Charlie Fox and Allan Bowers? Perhaps we shall never know. Both appeared at regular Waratah reunions in Australia.

CHARLIE FOX

CAPTAIN: 7 matches (1 test) (1925 v New Zealand)

BORN: July 2 1898 (Waverley)

DIED: 1984

SCHOOL: Sydney Grammar

CLUB: GPS Old Boys (Sydney 8 matches), Glebe-Balmain (40 matches) North Sydney (40 matches)

NEW SOUTH WALES REPRESENTATION: 35matches (1920-28)

AUSTRALIAN REPRESENTATION: 36 matches (17 tests) (1920-28)

TOM LAWTON, SR.

The Loping Ghost

In the Official Report to the New South Wales RU following the return of the 1927–28 Waratahs after nine months overseas, written by manager Gordon Shaw and captain Johnny Wallace, it was stated:

"We understood... that with regard to the actual play a certain policy was to be followed – firstly, that the winning of matches was not to be our only consideration; secondly, that our type of play should be such that it indicated a desire on our part to make the game attractive to both player and spectator and an exhibition of a contest between friendly sportsmen, and thirdly, that each man was to be played as much as was reasonably possible in order to extend his experience."

'Running rugby' was the credo of the Waratahs, and no one epitomised that philosophy more than the captain Wallace and arguably the Waratahs' top player, Tom Lawton. That Waratah style became central to an 'Australian style' which dominates Australian rugby to the present day.

Tom Lawton was a near-mythical person. He was gifted, a legend in his own time and seemingly did it all.

He is undoubtedly the greatest sportsman ever produced by Brisbane Grammar School. He entered the school, Brisbane's most elite private school, in 1913. He represented BGS in cricket for four years, captaining the school in 1916 and 1917, was adjudged the best fieldsman in 1915 and 1916, and had the best batting average in 1917. His best scores included 176 not out at Armidale School and 137 against Toowong, both in 1917.

He rowed number two in the school crew for three years, and was a fine tennis player. Tom won the All School's open high jump with a leap of 5ft 6in and was second in the 120 yard hurdles. He also gained his swimming colours in 1916 and 1917, won the breaststroke and backstroke races in 1917 and was school champion in that sport and school captain the same year.

However it was at Rugby Union where he really made his mark, playing in the first team for three years and winning recognition as the best back in 1916 and 1917. Playing mainly in the centre, the school magazine said of him, in his last year at school: "His rapidity in taking advantage of any opening offside, his ingenuity in originating passing rushes, his clever 'raking in' of wild passes, and his sure foot, combine to warrant him the position of in-centre in any team. Without in any way detracting from the merits of the other backs, he was undoubtedly superior to them all, and innumerable times he saved a dangerous situation so that in fact the others began to rely so much on his ability that far more than his portion of work was always thrust upon his willing shoulders. A splendid kick with both feet, he could find the line to a nicety."

Brisbane Grammar School has many Wallaby graduates over the years: David Clark (1964), Alex Evans (1962), Tom Baxter (1958), Joe Dixon (1904), Lew (1903–4) and Poley Evans (1899), Duncan Fowles (1920–23), Julian Gardner (1987–88), Charles Graham (1899), Alex Henry (1899), Peter James (1958), Rob (1988) and Tom Lawton Jr. (1893–89), Cameron Lillicrap (1985–91), Dick Marks (1962–67), Greg Martin (1989–90), Bob McCowan (1899), Andy McIntyre (1982–89), Frank (1903–04) and Fred Nicholson (1904), Otto Nothling (1921–24), David Nucifora (1991–93), Charles Parkinson (1907), Con Primmer (1951), Bill Ross (1979–83), "Chilla" Wilson (1957–58) and Keith Winning (1947–51).

Lawton played rugby for his home state in 1919, and later on in 1929, 1930 and 1932. Rugby was resumed in Queensland after a hiatus in 1929.

During the First World War he was a Gunner in France with the 12th Field Artillery Brigade. On his return to Queensland after the war he entered the University of Queensland to do Science, passing first year. Only rugby league was played at the University, so he played for them, the University winning the competition that year. However he did play for Queensland AIF against the touring AIF team in 1919.

Tom Lawton then went to Sydney to pursue a medical course at St. Andrew's College, Sydney, where he was in residence during 1920 and 1921. He played for Sydney University, and got his 'Blue' in 1920.

That same year, 1920, he represented New South Wales in two matches against the All Blacks, which are now considered tests. He played no representative games in 1921 and in 1922 he began his studies at Oxford University as a Rhodes Scholar, residing at New College. He, of all people, represented the scholar-athlete, and with his war-time service included he was the perfect choice. While at Oxford he won three Blues, granted to a player who represents his University in the annual Oxford-Cambridge game.

In 1922–23 he played 60 games for Oxford, Blackheath, New College and the Barbarians. That year was a highly emotional one, as after a challenge he and two other Australians were suspended because they had played rugby league. The underlying reason was that a 'colonial', Lawton, had been selected to captain Oxford. There was much drama involved, but finally the three Aussies played in the 1923 fixture. Tom also won an Athletics Blue in the shot put and represented the University at swimming and water polo.

He returned to Sydney in 1925 and after one game in an invitational XV against the All Blacks he accepted the captaincy of the New South Wales team on their tour of New Zealand. He was an immediate success, playing in nine of the 11 games, all as captain, and being the top scorer. He got 49 points, from three tries and 20 conversions. In *The Visitors* it is stated: "The outstanding personality was Tom Lawton... One of the greatest five-eighths of all time."

His next representative fixtures were on the 1927–28 Waratah tour to the British Isles, France and North America. Known now as 'the Loping Ghost', he played in a remarkably relaxed manner. He was one of, if not *the* star, of the Waratahs, playing in 27 of the 31 games, the five tests (Ireland, Wales, Scotland, England and France) and being the top scorer with 124 points (one try, 48 conversions, seven penalty goals and one dropped goal).

Peter Fenton, in *For The Sake Of The Game*, wrote of the 28–year-old Lawton: "The wonderful five-eighth certainly had no peers at the time of the tour. Though spotted continually by wing forwards and inside backs alike... he played magnificently. His team mate Alex Ross [now deceased] insists to this day that Australia may have produced his equal, but not his superior."

In 1929 rugby re-commenced in Queensland and Lawton was an inspiration. New Zealand visited Australia that year and, with Lawton at the helm, Australia won the series by 3–0. It had never before happened to an All Black team.

In 1930 Great Britain toured. Lawton

captained Australia in the test (won 6–5), and then Queensland and an Australian XV.

In 1932, now 33 years of age, the remarkable Lawton put on his boots once more, captained Australia to a 22–17 victory over New Zealand, captained Queensland and led Australia the second test, which was lost by 3–21.

Thus ended the representative career of one of the true greats of Australian rugby.

The *Daily Express* had this to say of him: "Lawton is a deceptive stand-off half. With his long legs and his long stride, he seems slow to the casual spectator and at times he does not appear to be doing much in what we may call a formal attack – the ball heeled out and passed to Lawton, who runs on a few yards and gives it to some one else.

"That is not all. But watch Lawton closely, and you will see, as likely as not, that in those few yards he draws an unwary opponent, and so times his pass that the attack is likely to prosper. He scores few tries himself; but helps his comrades to many. He is always in the right place. His defence is excellent, his kicking well judged, and as a 'converter' he runs up the goal score within a pitiless accuracy equalled only, in another place, but that of a taximeter".

The loping ghost. A rugby genius, who captained his nation's teams seven times.

His grandsons, Tom Jr and Rob, both became Wallabies. They certainly had the right genes.

TOM LAWTON

CAPTAIN: 10 matches (7 tests) (1925 New Zealand (1), 1929 New Zealand (3), 1930 Great Britain (1), 1932 New Zealand (2))
BORN: January 16, 1899
DIED: 1978
SCHOOL: Brisbane Grammar
CLUBS: University of Qld, Past Grammar, Western Suburbs (Sydney), Sydney University, Oxford University, Valley (Brisbane)
NEW SOUTH WALES REPRESENTATION: 38 matches (1920-28)
QUEENSLAND REPRESENTATION: 13 matches (1919-32)
AUSTRALIAN REPRESENTATION: 44 matches (14 tests) (1920-32)

Tom Lawton greets All Black captain Frank Kirby.

JOHNNY WALLACE

Captain of the 1927–28 Waratahs

JOHNNY WALLACE was one of many Sydney Grammar School products to reach the top level of rugby. Over the years there have been Malcolm Blair, Edwin and Ernest Carr, 'Huck' Finlay, Charlie Fox, Tony Fox, Bill George, Bill Hemingway, Wal Ives, Doug Keller, Bob Loudon, Hyam Marks, Walter Phipps, 'Pup' Raymond, Alex Ross, 'Alby' Stone, Geoff and Keith Storey, Eric Tindall, Alan Walker, 'Wakka' Walker, 'Doss' Wallach, Col Windon, John Bain, Clifford Campbell, Billy Mann and Andy Town.

One of the influences for those in the 1920s at Sydney Grammar was Hyam Marks, Sydney University's first rugby international. One of those he influenced was the young Johnny Wallace, who in 1920 came to Sydney University to study law.

His potential was obvious, and although Wallace had no international experience he was taken to New Zealand with the New South Wales team in 1921. He played in five of the 10 games, including one against New Zealand that is now regarded as a test. He scored four tries in his five games.

Johnny surprisingly never got a 'Blue' at Sydney University, but won a Rhodes Scholarship to Oxford in 1922. Other Sydney University players who preceded him with this great distinction were such as H.V. Porteus and Howard Bullock, while 'Pup' Raymond was awarded the Rhodes Scholarship the next year.

The timing was perfect for Wallace, who won 'Blues' at Oxford in 1922–23–24–25. He also played for Scotland, as did his fellow Oxford rugby backs Ian Smith, Phil Macpherson and George Aitken. He represented Scotland nine times between 1923 and 1926.

On returning to Australia in 1926 he joined the Glebe-Balmain club and played in two games for New South Wales against New Zealand, scoring a fine try in the second encounter.

In 1927–28 he was chosen as captain for the 9–month long tour of the British Isles, France and North America. He had not captained a representative team to this point in his career. It is interesting who might have been chosen if he were not available. The logical candidates were Ted Thorn, Charlie Fox and Tom Lawton.

The choice of Wallace was a master stroke. He was well known in the British Isles through his association with Oxford and Scotland. Peter Fenton, in *For The Sake Of The Game* wrote that Wallace "proved to be a magnificent captain. Despite a strained thigh and a broken wrist which limited his appearances early in the tour, he played 21 matches, including the five internationals and scored 11 tries. His experience in England, as well as his own natural ability, tactical brilliance and influence on the younger players were major reasons for the team's on-field successes. He was a great teacher."

As for his teaching, Cyril Towers, who was barely 21 years of age, always credited Johnny Wallace for his timing of the pass, a feature of his game that later made Cyril famous. Wallace told him firmly: "Give me the ball when I call for it!" When Wallace called "Now!" he got the ball, and Towers slowly but surely started to appreciate the value of the moment when the pass should be given.

The Waratahs were a great success on the field, and despite the injury rate and Bowers asking to go back to Australia, they played 31 games on the tour proper for 24 wins, two draws and five losses. They won three of the five internationals, and in all scored 432 points from 98 tries, 52 conversions, eight penalty goals and two dropped goals. They conceded 207 points which included 43 tries.

Wallace, in a speech on his return, noted: "Every man went into the game wholeheartedly and did his utmost. Australia should be especially proud of the team considering that the Waratahs were picked from nine clubs, while England has 40,000 players to draw from."

One of the songs the Waratahs sang as they

Johnny Wallace, captain of the highly esteemed 1927–28 Waratahs.

were touring seems to typify the tour. It was entitled *The More We Are Together*:

The more we are together, together, together,
The more we are together, the happier we'll be;
For your friends are my friends, and my friends are your friends,
The more we are together, the merrier we'll be.

After they got home the Waratahs had regular meetings, recounting the same good, old stories and the wonderful things that happened to them. 'Jock' Blackwood, Wylie Breckenridge, Wally Meagher and Arnold Tancred became Presidents of the New South Wales Rugby Union, while Blackwood and Breckenridge became delegates to the IRB. Almost all the Waratahs made a significant contribution to the game either through coaching or when acting as selectors.

Johnny Wallace opted out of representative rugby on his return but acted as a selector and coach for both New South Wales and Australia over many years, and went overseas as assistant manager-coach of Wallaby teams. One of his greatest victories occurred in 1937, when New South Wales upset the Springboks 17–6 on a waterlogged Sydney Cricket Ground. Always, until the end of his life, he extolled the Waratah style of play, the running game.

Wallace himself was equally adept anywhere in the three-quarter line, perhaps favouring the wing. He had a good turn of speed with a great outside break and was a magnificent finisher.

Peter Fenton, in summing him up in *For The Sake Of The Game*, wrote: "A man of great intellect, a brilliant orator, and the most popular of men, Wallace did not achieve all that he may have done in his private life. The Rhodes Scholar returned to his home of Macksville (the main road bears the name 'Wallace') to tend to the family business affairs after the death of his father. Later he returned to Sydney to become a non-practising barrister with the crown solicitor's office. When he died, at The Entrance in 1975, his vice-captain Charlie Fox wrote, 'By his death, an era covered by his life-long rugby interest is closed, but he will be remembered by many for his contribution to the remodelling and the rebuilding of the Australian Rugby game."

JOHNNY WALLACE

CAPTAIN: 25 matches (6 tests) (1926 v New Zealand, 1927–28 Ireland, Wales, Scotland, England and France)
BORN: September 5 1900
DIED: 1975
SCHOOL: Sydney Grammar School
CLUB: Sydney University, Oxford University, Scotland, Glebe-Balmain
NEW SOUTH WALES REPRESENTATION: 30 matches (1921–28)
AUSTRALIAN REPRESENTATION: 32 matches (8 tests) (1921–28)

SYD MALCOLM

Newcastle's Finest

When a debate rages over Australia's greatest-ever halfback, the names of Chris McKivat, Syd Malcolm, Cyril Burke, Des Connor, Ken Catchpole, John Hipwell, Nick Farr-Jones and George Gregan are commonly proposed. Three of them came from Newcastle: Malcolm, Burke and Hipwell.

Syd Malcolm started it all. He was idolised by Newcastle residents, and belatedly was inducted into the Newcastle Hall of Fame in 1995. Legend has it that Malcolm coached Burke, who coached Hipwell. Cyril Burke said it was not so, though he would go to Malcolm's brother's home to listen to rugby stories and occasionally Syd was there.

Whatever, Newcastle produced three world beaters. What is intriguing is that in his long career Syd Malcolm never appeared for Newcastle in a major contest. In fact, he had to leave Newcastle in his teens to seek work and finished up working at Ipswich, Queensland, and playing rugby league there. He was a boilermaker by trade.

Syd Malcolm's first representative games were on the 1927–28 tour of the British Isles, France and North America. Surprisingly three half-backs were picked: Wally Meagher and Jack Duncan, who were oddly enough from the same club, Randwick, and the 10st 6lb, 23–year-old Malcolm.

Syd Malcolm: The first of a Newcastle dynasty.

The pecking order had Meagher clearly out in front, with Duncan and Malcolm a fair way behind. Though he showed great promise, Malcolm was untested at the higher level and it appeared to be the end when he dislocated his shoulder in the match against Oxford University. Charlie Fox, the vice-captain, was also seriously injured in this match, and they were both sidelined for many matches.

In fact, Syd Malcolm played in only 11 of the 31 tour-proper games and Meagher was the test halfback against Ireland and Wales. But Malcolm was showing his incredible bag of tricks in the Wednesday games, and he was picked for the final three internationals, against Scotland (lost 8–10), England (lost 11–18) and France (won 11–9).

Syd Malcolm returned to Australia as the number one halfback and when he arrived in Newcastle he was treated like a hero, but surprised everyone by going to Sydney and playing club rugby there.

What were his qualities that shot him to the fore? He had a fast but not overly long pass, he was off and running when he saw an opening, but above all he was hard and courageous. He never backed down when the going got tough.

On his return he was made captain of New South Wales for the 1928 tour of New Zealand. Only three members of the highly successful 1927–28 Waratahs made the tour: Malcolm, Cyril Towers and Geoff Bland. Syd played in seven of the 10 games, of which five were won and five lost. Chester and McMillan wrote in *The Visitors*: "Although the 1928 Waratahs lost as many games as they won, their tour was a successful one in terms of experience gained by the younger players. The tourists also gave a great deal of pleasure to the rugby public of New Zealand with their willingness to open up play. According to one critic, no visiting team had played more delightful rugby than these young Waratahs. Possessing extremely fast backs, the New South Welshmen threw the ball about in dazzling fashion and moved at such pace that they were dangerous even when in their own 25."

Archie Strang and Syd Malcolm toss before the first Bledisloe Cup test in 1931.

The legacy of the 1927–28 Waratahs was going ahead at full speed. The running game became the Australian game.

In 1929 the All Blacks came to Australia, Tommy Lawton taking over as captain from Malcolm and, in a stunning upset, Australia won all three tests: 9–8, 17–9 and 15–13. For the first time since 1914, a full Australian team was fielded as Queensland was playing the union code once more. This was the first that any nation had won a 3–test series against the All Blacks.

In 1930 Great Britain toured Australia, Syd playing four games against them: two for New South Wales (as captain), one for Australia (Lawton being captain) and one for an Australian XV. Australian won 6–5, a real high-point for Australian rugby, as the team now had four test wins in a row.

For the first time since 1913, a fully representative team was sent by Australia to New Zealand in 1931. Syd Malcolm was again the captain. Two Victorians were in the team, Dave Cowper and Owen Bridle, and nine Queenslanders. While there were some outstanding veterans like Malcolm (now 28), Alex Ross (25), Cyril Towers (26), Bill Ritter (27) and Len Palfreyman (26), there were also many young players, including Jack Steggall (21), Harold Herd (26), Harold Tolhurst (20), Phil Clark (19) and Owen Bridle (19)

The team played 10 matches, winning three, drawing one and losing six. Australia beat the Maori (14–3), but lost the single test against New Zealand 13–20. Malcolm played in seven of the 10 games.

In 1932 the All Blacks toured Australia, and Malcolm played for New South Wales (two games, one as captain), and three for Australia, once as captain.

Now 31 years of age, Malcolm made Australia's first-ever tour of South Africa in 1933. He played in 11 of the matches, including two tests, one as captain. He unfortunately injured his shoulder in the fourth game, and did not reappear until the fourteenth match.

Malcolm's swansong was in 1934, against New Zealand. He played in two tests, in an Australian XV match, and one game for New South Wales.

So Syd Malcolm had eight years of representative rugby, playing 45 matches for his country including 18 tests.

During his time at the top, he did it all from the point of view of a happy tourist. He went to the British Isles, France and Canada, he captained two touring sides to New Zealand and went to South Africa. There were no other tours in those days. Not bad for a boy from the other side of the tracks in Newcastle.

The two major tours were the highlight of his rugby career, and he was proud of the 3–match series defeat of New Zealand in 1929 and the defeat of Great Britain a year later. Syd Malcolm always held the respect of his peers. He was courage personified.

SYD MALCOLM

CAPTAIN: 17 matches (6 tests) (1928 New Zealand (2), New Zealand Maori (1), 1931 New Zealand (1), 1932 New Zealand (1), 1933 South Africa (1)

BORN: December 10 1902 (Merewether, New South Wales)

DIED: 1987

SCHOOL: not known

CLUB: Cook's Hill Surf Club, Newcastle, YMCA (6), Glebe-Balmain (12), Manly (41 games)

NEW SOUTH WALES REPRESENTATION: 28 matches (1927-34)

AUSTRALIAN REPRESENTATION: 45 matches (18 tests) (1927-34)

BOB LOUDON

The Forward Who Also Toured As A Back

BOB LOUDON was an unusual character. First, he and sibling Darby are the only brothers to have captained Australia, they both had long careers, and they both only captained Australia once.

Bob Loudon: Versatile enough to be chosen for Australia as both a back and a forward.

Many brothers have represented Australia. The list is long. Harald and 'Snowy' Baker, Andrew and Cameron Blades, Stewart and Jim Boyce, Ernest and Edwin Carr, Pete and 'Son' Burge, Alfred and Tom Colton, Mitchell and Phillip Cox, Gordon and Clarrie Davis, Michael and Edmund Dore, Mark, Glenn and Gary Ella, Poley and Lew Evans, Glen and Len Forbes, Eric and Jack Ford, Vince and Ted Heinrich, Anthony and Daniel Herbert, Bob and Barry Honan, Bryan and James Hughes, Eric and Frank Hutchinson, Paul and Brian Johnson, Tom and Rob Lawton, Darby and Bob Loudon, Graeme and Stuart Macdougall, Doug, Bill and Jack McLean, Paul and Jeff McLean, Jack and Lou Meibusch, Robert and William Marrott, Pat and Bill Murphy, Frank and Fred Nicholson, Ignatius and Jack O'Donnell, Peter and Jim Phipps, Clarrie and Ward Prentice, Tom and Billy Richards, Frank and Norman Row, Tom and Norman Smith, Geoff and Keith Storey, Arnold, Jim and Harry Tancred, Joe and Ted Thorn, John and Dick Thornett, Keith and Col Windon. Naming the brothers who played rugby union for Australia would make for a great quiz question.

The second unusual thing about Bob Loudon is that he toured New Zealand as a back in 1923 and as a forward in 1928. Has any other Wallaby done that? These games, then representing New South Wales, are now regarded as Australian representative games or tests.

In all Bob Loudon made three representative tours, two to New Zealand with New South Wales and one to South Africa in 1933 with a full Australian team. His status in the game would have been much higher if he had gone on the 1927–28 tour. A certainty, he declared himself unavailable and thus missed his appointment with destiny. Almost all the players on that tour became legends on the game. Just think of some of them: Johnny Wallace, Alex Ross, Tom Lawton, Wylie Breckenridge, Cyril Towers, 'Huck' Finlay, Jack and Eric Ford, 'Jock' Blackwood, Geoff Storey, Syd King, Wally Meagher, Syd Malcolm and Ted Thorn. It is a pity that we could not put Bob Loudon on that list.

A superb athlete, this New Zealand-born Australian was 6ft 2in tall and weighed 14st 4lb in 1933. A lifesaver of some distinction, he was stroking Manly Surf Club's boat to win the national championship 1927–28 while the Waratahs were away running around the cold British fields.

Bob Loudon's representative career started the hard way, facing unforgiving and unrelenting New Zealand teams. On the 1923 New South Wales tour of New Zealand he was picked as a three-quarter, the other being Allen ('Sheik') Bowers, Harold Buntine, Dan Erasmus, Billy Sheehan, Norm Smith, 'Bot' Stanley and H.B. Trousdale. Loudon was tall for a winger and at this stage he weighed 13st. He played in eight of the 10 matches, including two tests, and appeared as a centre, fullback and wing. Versatility seemed to be his middle name.

He moved in and out of representative teams, as he only appeared against the All Blacks once between 1925 to 1928, for E.J. Thorn's XV in 1925. He was still playing in the backline, but he was replaced in that game.

By 1928 he was a specialist flanker, and from then on was regarded as one of the best in Australia. He toured New Zealand again in 1928 and proved himself as a real iron man. He, Bill Cerutti and Cyril Towers were the only men to play in every one of the ten games. Loudon played in the four tests on that tour and captained the tourists in the third. Thus he took his place in history. He also captained Australia in two other games, against Hawkes Bay and Southland.

He continued developing in 1929, playing one test against the All Blacks. This was the first year since 1914 that a full Australian team had been put on the field. On the surface it would appear that his representative career was on the wane, as he appeared only twice in 1932, for New South Wales against New Zealand.

However he fooled them all, and in 1933 was selected on the first-ever Australian tour to South Africa. He played a highly creditable 14 matches there, including four tests. He was regarded as one of the successes of the tour.

His representative career ended the following year, 1934, when he appeared twice for New South Wales against New Zealand, and once for Australia, in a test drawn 3–3.

A great athlete, Bob Loudon played 129 first grade club matches for Manly, as well as 32 for two earlier clubs, GPS Old Boys and Northern Suburbs. In all, he played 34 matches for Australia, which included 13 tests.

Whatever else might happen in the future, the Loudon brothers, Darby and Bob, will go down in history as the first pair of brothers to captain their country.

BOB LOUDON

CAPTAIN: 3 matches (1 test) (v New Zealand 1928)

BORN: Leeston, New Zealand March 24, 1903

DIED: October 6 1991

SCHOOL: Christ's College (New Zealand), Sydney Grammar

CLUB: Great Public Schools Old Boys (19), Northern Suburbs (13), Manly (129)

NEW SOUTH WALES REPRESENTATION: 23 matches (1923-34)

AUSTRALIAN REPRESENTATION: 34 matches (13 tests) (1923-34)

JIMMY CLARK

Tackler Supreme

JIMMY CLARK was Queensland born and bred and he was schooled at Gregory Terrace, which over the years has had the habit of turning out Wallabies. His club, University of Queensland, has also produced a great number of Wallabies.

Clark was a week short of his 22nd birthday when he made his first representative appearance, for Queensland against Great Britain in 1930. These were years full of hope in the northern state, as rugby had been resumed in 1929 by the so-called 'Revivalists' after lying dormant since 1914.

In 1931 he was selected as vice-captain of the Australian team to New Zealand. His brother Phil was also on the team, but he only played two matches out of 10, the second and the last, and did not play a test during his career. He was, however, in three University premiership sides and toured Japan with Australian Universities in 1934.

Jim played in seven of the 10 games in 1931, being 22 at the time and weighing 12st, very light for a flanker. The 1931 side was captained by the evergreen Syd Malcolm.

Jimmy Clark: Danie Craven said he was the hardest tackler he had known.

Clark played in two tests on the 1931 tour, one against New Zealand and one against New Zealand Maori. The latter match, against New Zealand Maori, is now regarded as a test in Australia. New Zealand does not award test caps for such matches and quite controversially Australia has. Players at the time had no idea they were in a test match. As a matter of fact such matches were played mid-week, and the 'Wednesday boys' or 'dirt trackers' comprised the Australian team. It is for this reason the touring captain, Syd Malcolm, did not play. He was resting himself for the 'real' test against New Zealand three days later, so Clark could be deemed lucky to be forever hailed as a test captain. This was his only test captaincy.

Clark did, however, lead the team in one of the mid-week games, against Waikato-King Country. He thus joined a growing list of Australians who captained non-test teams. They receive no recognition, and this does not seem to be quite fair. Clark captained Australia twice (only one was a test). The Maori match was won by Australia 14–3, and the Waikato-King Country game 30–10, so he has a 100 percent win rate as Australian captain.

In 1932 New Zealand toured Australia, and Jimmy Clark played in two tests and the Queensland match.

Perhaps the highlight of his career was being in the first Australian team to South Africa in 1933. The team was led by brilliant fullback Alex Ross, and consisted of 29 players. The Queenslanders were Billy Warlow, Doug McLean, Jack Steggall, Gordon Bennett, 'Bernie' Doneley, Graham Cooke, John Ritter, 'Bimbo' White, Clark, Max White and Eddie Bonis.

Clark played in nine of the games, which included the first test. An injury prevented him from playing for over a month and limited his other test and playing opportunities.

Clark will forever be honoured as captaining his country in Rugby Union. Quite fast and agile, South African guru Danie Craven used to say that the hardest tackler he had known in his career was Jimmy Clark.

JIMMY CLARK

CAPTAIN: 2 matches (1 test) (v New Zealand Maori 1931)
BORN: September 9 1908 (Bundaberg)
DIED: 1978
SCHOOL: Gregory Terrace (Brisbane)
CLUB: University of Queensland
QUEENSLAND REPRESENTATION: 15 matches (1930–34)
AUSTRALIAN REPRESENTATION: 18 matches (5 tests) (1931-33)

DAVE COWPER

Elegance Personified

DAVID COWPER was a Newington College graduate, and many other Wallabies have been given their formative rugby coaching there. Among them are Eric Bardsley (1928), Scott Bowen (1993–96), Jim Brown (1956–58), Harry Bryant (1925), Alan Cameron (1951–58), Jack Carroll (1958–59), Nick Farr-Jones (1984–93), Aub Hodgson (1933–38), Peter Jorgensen (1992), Peter Johnston (1976), Bruce Judd (1925–31), Phil Kearns (1989–99), Reg Lane (1921), Dinny Love (1932), Graeme Macdougall (1961), Stuart MacDougall (1971–76), George Mackay (1926), John Manning (1904), Bill McLaughlin (1936), Charles Morrissey (1925–26), Tom Perrin (1931), Roy Prosser (1967–72), Bill Tasker (1913–14), Lisle Taylor (1923–24) and John Williams (1963). So the sport of Rugby Union owes much to this private school.

In 1929 Cowper moved to Melbourne, and with Gordon Sturtridge (a Brisbane Boys' College lad), Owen Bridle (UK born and bred), Evan Jessep (New Zealand) and 'Weary' Dunlop (Victorian born), changed the face of Australian rugby, all these players finding their way into test teams.

Dave Cowper was a tall, distinguished, curly-haired elegant gentleman who looked the picture of tranquillity both on and off the field. He was ever graceful in his movement, statuesque even, though it is normally not said of males. A high-stepping runner, he was blessed with unusual speed, so much so that he placed third in the national trials in the 100m which were held to select the athletes for the 1932 Olympics at Los Angeles. There was little money in those days in amateur sport, and he did not make it because Australia only sent a small team.

He was a fine cricketer, but he was well surpassed by two of his three sons, Bob and David. Bob Cowper played 27 cricket tests, while brother David was in the Victorian XI of 1965–66. Bob and the other brother, Trevor, played rugby for both Victoria and Australian Universities.

After moving south, Dave's first representative appearance was against Great Britain in 1930. Victoria lost 36–41 but Cowper, in a sensational display, scored three tries.

As a consequence of this performance, he found himself on the Syd Malcolm-captained tour of New Zealand. During his career he fluctuated between centre and wing. He was an indispensable part of the touring party, playing in nine of their 10 games, three as a

Dave Cowper: On and off the field he was elegance personified.

winger and the remainder as a centre. Alex Ross was the top scorer with 35 points, while next in line were Cyril Towers and Dave Cowper, with six tries each. His impact was noted by Chester and McMillan in *The Visitors*: "the flying wing three-quarter," "Cowper did some fine defensive work," "Cowper, whose pace was too much for the opposition," "Cowper... showed amazing speed as he flew for the corner to touch down," "Cowper finished off as passing bout with a brilliant try under the bar" and "Cowper... outstripped the defence."

In 1932 New Zealand toured Australia and Cowper played against them in two tests.

Australia made its first-ever tour of South Africa 1933, with Alex Ross as captain and Syd Malcolm the vice-captain. The dashing three-quarter was elevated to the captaincy in the absence of these two through injury and performed magnificently with the added responsibility. He played in 17 of the 23 games, and was the team's top scorer with 34 points, from four tries, nine conversions and a dropped goal. In all he captained Australia in three tests (out of five) as well as three mid-week games, against Rhodesia twice and Orange Free State. Ian Diehm, summing up the 1933 tour in *Giants in Green and Gold*, wrote: "Without a doubt, the star of the backline was Jockey Kelaher, who proved a world-class winger. Jack Steggall was not far behind and would have made a greater impact had he a settled position. Of the others, Doug McLean made great strides and Dave Cowper was often impressive. The best was not seen from Ross and Malcolm because of illness and injury and the team was poorer for this." Though born in New South Wales, Cowper was the first Victorian to captain Australia.

After the tour the 25–year-old came back to Sydney for a few years, playing for New South Wales against New Zealand in 1934. In 1935 he appeared for Victoria and New South Wales against New Zealand Maori and Queensland respectively.

Dave Cowper became an Australian selector and assistant manager (coach) with the 1957–58, Bob Davidson-captained side, that went to the British Isles, France and North America. The tourists had a poor record, and many of the players criticised the antiquated coaching methods of Cowper. As many people have found throughout the years, their coaching improved with better players. Cowper unfortunately found himself with weak personnel. He had some brilliant players, to be sure, but also some very ordinary ones.

The author was privy to Cowper's coaching methods, and they followed those acceptable in the time period. Ever the gentleman, he never criticised the players, even when he had every right to.

Dave Cowper personified the true amateur, playing always to the rules with a strict code of ethics.

He had speed to burn, a great outside swerve, was sound in defence, and was a born leader of men. He will ever be known as the first Victorian to captain his country in Rugby Union.

DAVE COWPER

CAPTAIN: 6 matches (3 tests) (v South Africa 1933)
BORN: December 28 1908 (Mosman)
DIED: 1981
SCHOOL: Newington College
CLUB: Northern Suburbs (Sydney), Melbourne, New South Wales
AUSTRALIAN REPRESENTATION: 29 matches (9 tests) (1931–33)

ALEX ROSS

The Rock of Gibraltar

Sydney Grammar School has been an excellent breeding ground for Rugby Union players, and Alex Ross was arguably the best. Others to have represented Australia from there are: Malcolm Blair (1928–31), Edwin (1921) and Ernest Carr (1913–14), 'Huck' Finlay (1926–30), Charlie Fox (1920–28), Tony Fox (1958), Bill George (1923–28), Bill Hemingway (1928–32), Wal Ives (1926–29), Doug Keller (1947–48), Bob Loudon (1921–22), Hyram Marks (1899), 'Fob' O'Brien (1937–38), Jim Phipps (1953–56), 'Pup' Raymond 1920–1923), Alby Stone (1937–38), Geoff (1926–30) and Norm Storey (1936), Eric Tindall (1973), Alan Walker (1947–50), Arthur Walker (1912–24), 'Doss' Wallach (1913–14), Col Windon (1946–52), John Bain 1953), Cliff Campbell (1933), 'Billy' Mann (1927–28) and Andy Town (1962).

Peter Fenton, in *For The Sake Of The Game* has this to say of Alexander William Ross: "A wonderfully gifted all round player, Ross had the essential anticipation for full back play as well as superb handling and kicking skills. His courage and technique in stopping the foot rushes of the British forwards became a feature of his play. He rarely missed a tackle and many attackers preferred to kick past him rather than try to beat him."

Alex Ross made his first appearance on the international circuit in 1925 against the All Blacks on 13 June. From 1919 to 1929 Queensland stopped rugby union in the state, and hence it was later (1986) adjudged that when New South Wales teams played against international teams these could be considered tests. The players at the time had no idea that this would be the case.

Four days later Ross was in a New South Wales second team against New Zealand, and to the surprise and everyone the locals won by 18–16. Though only 19 years of age at the time and weighing about 10st, the rugby aficionados knew they were witnessing a genius of the playing fields. Some of the players on that Second XV who would make their mark in the game were Norm Smith, Charlie Morrissey, Owen Crossman, Bill George, Harold Snell, Ted Thorn, Arthur Erby and Ken Tarleton. The great Wylie Breckenridge came on as a replacement.

In a busy year the young Sydney University medical student played two more games against New Zealand with New South Wales (now tests), and another for A New South Wales XV. He played 13 tests with New South Wales from 1925 to 1930 and received five 'Blues' from the University, 1925, 1926, 1927, 1928 and 1929.

Alex Ross: A towering punt and rock-like defence.

He was later voted into Sydney University's greatest team and named as one of the University's 10 greatest players.

In 1926 he played in three more tests against New Zealand, the Waratahs winning the first 26–20 and losing the following two narrowly, by 6–11 and 0–14.

His performances were good enough to make him a virtually automatic selection of the much sought-after 9–month long 1927–28 tour of the British Isles, France and North America. Though a New South Wales team, the Waratahs were the best available players in Australia. This team are all considered legends of Australian rugby, and the tour legendary.

The Waratahs were captained by Johnny Wallace, with Charlie Fox the vice-captain. Alex was 21 and weighed 10st 6lb. Small in stature, at 5ft 8in in height, he had a solid build and very strong legs. Compact might be a word to describe him.

Alex Ross was one of the sensations of that tour. He played in 29 of the 34 games, more than any other player. Tom Lawton was second in line with 27 matches to his credit. Ross also starred in the five tests, against Ireland (won 5–3), Wales (won 18–5), Scotland (lost 8–10), England (lost 11–18) and France (won 11–8). Sydney University was well represented on the tour: besides Alex there was 'Billy' Mann, 'Billy'Sheehan, 'Huck' Finlay, Geoff Storey, and two ex-Uni players, the captain Johnny Wallace and the immortal Tommy Lawton.

Peter Fenton, in *For The Sake Of The Game*, penned a poem called: *The Waratahs*:

The Waratahs who packed their bags in nineteen twenty-seven

And sailed away to play the running game,

Spent six weeks on the high seas as they made their

way to Devon
With neither thought of riches nor of fame.
But they were meant for greatness, and it was somehow pre-ordained,
They thrilled the crowds at every rugby ground,
They played the game with passion and the glory they attained
Is tribute to the legends that abound.

For here were people playing for the magic of the sport
The simple thrill of running with the ball,
No thought of breaking records, no immortal claims were sought,
The game was all that mattered to them all.

And twice a week they gave their all and never cried 'enough'
In rain and sleet, in weather foul and fair,
And always with a smile that said: we know you boys are tough
Come match us as we give the ball some air.

Their names will live forever when the greatest deeds are done
Like Lawton, Wallace, Ross and big Jack Ford,
And Breckenridge, the iron man, who spoiled the half-backs' fun,
And Towers who so many tries had scored.

In England, Ireland, Scotland, Wales, and later on in France,
The Waratah embroidered on their chest
Became the very symbol of the team that took a chance,
The team that breathed with passion in its breast.

Now when you see a team that plays the game they played in heaven
A team that you would love to call your own,
You're looking at the Waratahs of nineteen twenty-seven;
The finest team of sportsmen we have known.

The year 1929 was a big one for rugby in Australia, as Queensland had re-entered the fray and a national team could finally be fielded. The most recent one had been chosen in 1914. So Alex Ross became a part of the history of the game as he was selected in the first Australian team following the revival, against New Zealand. Others in the match were Eric Ford, Cyril Towers, Syd King, Cam Gordon, Tommy Lawton (capt.), Syd Macolm, Jack Ford, Len Palfreyman, Wylie Breckenridge, Harry Hamalainen, 'Huck' Finlay, Bill Cerutti, Eddie Bonis and Eddie Thompson. Some 38,111 spectators were present at the match and were delighted when Australia was victorious by 9–8. This series saw the first clean sweep by Australia over New Zealand with 3–0 series scoreline, but Ross was injured and could not play in the final two tests.

In 1930 Ross took a year off to finalise his medical studies, but he was needed on the field and was chosen by the selectors after watching him play for St Andrews in an intra-varsity match. He answered the call, being in a winning international against Britain (6–5) and in a victorious state team (28–3).

He went to New Zealand with Australia in 1931, and though he was not the captain he played in every one of the 10 matches and top-scored with 35 points. Chester and McMillan, summarizing the tour in *The Visitors*, wrote: "[Ross] showed that his reputation as one of the world's finest fullbacks was well warranted," "Ross gave a brilliant exhibition at fullback," "Ross... was the outstanding Australian back, giving one of the soundest exhibitions of fullback play seen on Athletic Park for some time," "Ross again proved a regular sheet-anchor," "Ross left no doubt as to

Alex Ross: He was nicknamed 'Chatterbox' because he spoke so little and 'The Rock of Gibraltar' for his solid defence.

his ability" and "All [New Zealand] players interviewed by the authors considered Ross, Towers, Steggall, Malcolm, Cerutti and Bonis to be among the best opponents they ever encountered." Famous Maori and All Black fullback George Nepia always contended that Ross was the best player he had ever come up against.

In 1931 Alex Ross linked with the Eastern Suburbs Club. Historian and noted sportswriter Eddie Kann, in *Easts Rugby Story*, had this to say: "Taciturn Alexander William Ross, regarded by most old-timers as without peer among Australian full-backs, led Eastern Suburbs to their fourth premiership victory in 1931.

"So impressive was Dr Alex Ross at full-back that he was dubbed 'The Rock of Gibraltar'. His close associates also had another nickname for this silent, modest, smiling young player... 'Chatterbox'." He was so-named because he spoke so little.

New Zealand toured Australia in 1932, and Alex Ross played once for New South Wales and twice for Australia. All games were lost.

In 1933 he went to South Africa with Australia's first-ever team to visit the Republic. Now 27 years of age and weighing 11st 10lb, Ross was at the height of his considerable powers and was honoured with the captaincy. Struck down with appendicitis early on in the tour, he was unable to play from 28 June to 16 August. Thus he only played in 11 of the matches, leading the side every time, and could only play in the last test of five. This was his first national captaincy. Australia, elated by his return, won the final test by 15–4. The loss of the captain was a severe blow to the team, as he was the anchor, the stabiliser.

Alex Ross' swansong was in 1934. After playing for New South Wales in a narrow 16–18 loss to the All Blacks, Ross captained Australia to a resounding 25–11 victory at the Sydney Cricket Ground. Ross himself kicked two conversions and three penalty goals in the match. Tries were scored by Cyril Towers (2), Doug McLean and Owen Bridle.

The second test team was also captained by Alex Ross, and Australia eked out a 3–3 draw, Bob Loudon scoring a try. It was a great time to retire, as Australia had won the Bledisloe Cup for the first time. Who would have thought that it would be 45 years before Australia before the Wallabies would again beat New Zealand in Australia?

The author interviewed Alex shortly before he died. He was 90 years of age. I had found his home in the North Shore, and noted that it was the surgery of Dr A.W. Ross. A kindly, small gentleman, obviously Dr Ross, opened the door. I asked: "Does your son keep the surgery going?"

He laughed and replied: "No, it is my surgery. I still see patients."

He took me inside, answered all my questions and showed me his scrap-books. It was a wonderful few hours. He had been a bit of a 'Chatterbox', belying what team-mates generally thought of him. He was still keen of eye and mind, and he had a firm handshake. It was not hard to imagine him in the last line of defence, bringing down to earth another opponent. He had been an inspiration to the teams he played with. They felt safe with Dr Alex Ross behind them.

Jack Pollard said of him in *Australian Rugby*: "One of rugby's greatest fullbacks. He was a masterly tactician, not particularly fast, but gifted with great anticipation and a guileful grasp of positional play, a marvellous exponent of the punt kick, and a safe tackler and catcher of the ball in all conditions. His duels with the great New Zealand Maori fullback George Nepia provided some of the great highlights of Australia's rugby past."

ALEX ROSS

CAPTAIN: 13 matches (3 tests) (1 South Africa 1933, 2 New Zealand 1934),
BORN: November 24 1905
DIED: August 30 1996
SCHOOL: Sydney Grammar
CLUB: Sydney University (66), Eastern Suburbs (22), Manly (18)
NEW SOUTH WALES REPRESENTATION: 33 matches (1925-34)
AUSTRALIAN REPRESENTATION: 65 matches (20 tests) (1925–1934)

RON WALDEN

Rugby Player, Boxer & Policeman

RON WALDEN was one of those hard-rock types that you did not fool around with. A country boy originally, his family gravitated to Manly. As well as the rugby game that fascinated him he was a noted amateur heavyweight boxer. In real life he was a detective, and received a great deal of notoriety in leading the famous Thorne kidnapping case.

He had three years at the top, 1934, 1935 and 1936. At representative level he shone as a front-rower, but could perform equally well in the second row. At 5ft 11in and 14st 6lb, he was an ideal build for the front row. Not overly fast, he revelled in tight forward play, and was known to always give of his best. Durable, he played 127 matches for Manly.

Manly has a proclivity for developing outstanding athletes. At the 1924 Olympic Games in Paris, Australia received three gold medals. All the winners were from Manly: 'Boy' Charlton (1500m freestyle), Dick Eve (plain high diving) and Nick Winter (hop, step and jump). As for Wallabies at Manly, as well as Ron Walden there have been James Black, Geoff Bland, Spencer Brown, Bill Calcroft, Ernest Carr, Roy Chambers, Brian, Mitchell and Phillip Cox, Clarrie Davis, Gordon Davis, Wal Dawson, Lenny Diett, Peter Dunn, Charlie Eastes, Keith Ellis, Peter FitzSimons, Nathan Grey, Rob Heming, J. Hill, Aub Hodgson, John Kelaher, Stephen Knight, Bob Loudon, Don Lowth, Tony Miller, Norman Mingay, Rex Mossop, 'Larry' Newman, 'Willy' Ofahengaue, John O'Gorman, John Pashley, Barry Roberts, Norm Smith, Tom Smith, Don Telford, 'Joe' Thorn, Ted Thorn, Alan Walker and Geoff Wyld. There is something about that beach-side community that seems to assist the growth of such talented athletes.

Ron Walden had his first big-time experience in 1934, going up against the All Blacks for New South Wales (lost 13–16) and then he made a name for himself in the second test for Australia. This 3–3 draw followed the upset 25–11 victory in the first test and, as there were only two test matches in that series, it meant that Australia had recorded its first victory over New Zealand in the Bledisloe Cup.

There was a trifle of luck involved in his selection, as the famous 'Weary' Dunlop cried off with influenza.

Howell, *et al* wrote in *The Wallabies: A Definitive History of Australian Test Rugby*: "When play closed, the teams gathered and sang Auld

Lang Syne and exchanged sweaters ... Sir Henry Braddon said that the visitors had maintained the highest traditions of the rugby game, and losing the Cup was nothing so long as the game was played in the proper spirit."

In 1935 the Maori team came to Australia, and Ron Walden appeared three times against them, winning once and losing twice.

The year 1936 was the pinnacle of Walden's career, as he was made vice-captain of the Australian tour of New Zealand. The team was captained by Queensland's 'Dooney' Hayes, a centre. There were some giants in the Wallaby team such as Bill Cerutti, Aub Hodgson, Eddie Bonis, Doug McLean, Ron Rankin, Owen Bridle, 'Shirts' Richards and 'Jockey' Keleher. There were also three Victorians: winger 'Ru' Dorr, five-eighth Bill Hammon and flanker Owen Bridle.

Ron Walden turned out to be the iron man of the tour, as he played in all 10 games, the only one to perform the feat. A rib injury early on side-lined the captain, 'Dooney' Hayes, and Walden took on the added burden of the captaincy. As a consequence, he was captain in seven of the 10 games, which included three tests; two against New Zealand and one against the Maori. Walden was in the right place at the right time, and thus became an Australian test captain.

Chester and McMillan, in *The Visitors*, remarked about Walden's play: "Walden and Hutchinson worked hard in the tight", "Walden... played an excellent game," "Walden played a solid game and led his team effectively", "Walden and Bridle were the best of the Australian forwards" and "Walden worked like a Trojan in the tight."

Ron Walden: As tough as they come in the 'engine room.'

Now 27 years of age, Walden never appeared again in a representative game other than for New South Wales.

In 1949 he went to New Zealand as manager of the Australian team, with Bill Cerutti as assistant manager. Howell, *et al* have this to say of them in *Bledisloe Magic*: "The management was a perfect combination, men amongst men, as they say. The Manager was Ron Walden, a rugged forward of rare leadership qualities who captained Australia in three of the four tests he played. His first was against the All Blacks in 1934. He was a policeman by profession, who rose through the ranks to occupy senior positions. He was a no-nonsense type.

"His Assistant Manager was the one-and-only 'Wild Bill' Cerutti. Winston McCarthy in *Listen...! It's a Goal!* had this to say of Cerutti: "He was a wonderful person, a ball of energy, had a tremendous sense of humour and was always 'one of the boys'. No matter what kind of society he was in Bill was soon on a Christian name basis with everyone."

This management team was much beloved by the 1949 tourists, captained by Trevor Allan. By winning both tests of the tour – and 11 of 12 games – the 1949 Wallabies became the first Australian team to win the rubber in New Zealand. It was due in no small measure to the management team of Ron Walden and Bill Cerutti.

A story is told in Sir Nicholas Shehadie's autobiography *A Life Worth Living*. Col Windon, a team-mate on the 1949 tour, had a good win at the races in Sydney, and invited Nick to a nightclub. As he described it: "At about 11 p.m. there was a huge bang when the bar doors were suddenly thrown open by two huge, plainclothes policeman. 'Nobody move!' they shouted. Apparently it was illegal to sell liquor on the premises. Col and I got the shock of our lives when we saw that the cops were in fact Ron Walden, who had managed our New Zealand tour some weeks earlier, and his partner, Frank ('Bumper') Farrell, a former great rugby League player. When they spotted us among the nervous patrons, Ron called again, 'Nobody move!' Then he came over to us and whispered, 'You two, buzz off!' and we did. Ron wasn't only a good cop, he was a good bloke."

RON WALDEN

CAPTAIN: 7 matches (3 tests) (2 v New Zealand 1936, 1 v Maori 1936)
BORN: August 27, 1907
DIED: 1985
SCHOOL: Dubbo High School
CLUB: 127 matches (Manly)
NEW SOUTH WALES REPRESENTATION: 24 matches (1933–1937)
AUSTRALIAN REPRESENTATION: 11 matches (4 tests) (1934–36)

CYRIL TOWERS

Football Genius & First Voice of Rugby

AUSTRALIA HAS POSSESSED many fine centres over the years. Just conjure with these names, even if time has dimmed the memories of some: Percy Colquhoun, Bob McCowan, Stan Wickham, Frank Row, Lonnie Spragg, Frank Bede Smith, Larry Wogan, 'Bot' Stanley, Syd King, Cyril Towers, Gordon Sturtridge, 'Dooney' Hayes, Max Howell, Trevor Allan, John Solomon, Herb Barker, Rod Phelps, Beres Ellwood, Dick Marks, John Brass, Phil Smith, Stephen Knight, Barry Honan, Geoff Shaw, David L'Estrange, Bill McKid, Andrew Slack, Michael O'Connor, Michael Hawker, Gary Ella, Brett Papworth, Lloyd Walker, Tim Horan, Jason Little, Daniel Herbert, Pat Howard and Nathan Grey, to mention but a few.

Arguably the best in this list was Cyril Towers, Melbourne-born, Queensland-raised and eventually a Randwick icon. The running game's greatest advocates in those early years were Waverley College's Arthur Hennessey, Randwick coach Wally Meagher and Waratah and Randwick centre Cyril Towers. 'Attack' was their credo, setting up the wings their main goal, and kicking for touch became a 'no-no'.

Towers was a legend while he was still playing and was a rare student of the game. The two most knowledgeable rugby people the author has known in his lifetime are Cyril Towers and 'Mick' Cremin, and Cremin was a student of Cyril's and carried on the same fundamental philosophy. It is interesting that both had their detractors, Towers being inexplicably omitted from the 1933 tour of South Africa because he was too 'strong' a person to have in the team, and Cremin was reduced to playing in mid-week games in 1947–48 because of personality clashes with the establishment. As the saying goes, they had forgotten more than most people knew.

The author came under the influence of Towers, and Cremin for that matter, when he was an emerging talent at the Randwick club. They had a common trait, that is they did not suffer fools gladly. Some of Towers' sayings are a reflection of the man. He would say "anyone that takes him for a fool is no mug", when discussing a selector he would observe that "he's a little like the Chinese: if you can't be wise be mysterious", and of certain coaches and managers he would remark, "if he got a bright idea on rugby it would die from solitary confinement."

In the case of Towers and Cremin knowledge was power, but it also provoked fear from lesser lights.

Towers was often disdained because he never did anything in halves. When Cyril decided to give you or anybody else opinions on your

Cyril Towers: A master tactician and student of the game.

game or tactics you got it all, an hour-long diatribe where you contributed little to the conversation. The advice opened up countless new worlds for the neophyte player, but only those who listened and practised what Towers preached would benefit from what was to him the gospel, the running game.

He was a mere 19 years of age when he served notice of his rare ability, going up against the All Blacks at the Sydney Agricultural Ground in 1926. New South Wales won the match 26–20, with the young tyro playing against two of the greatest ever to don the All Black jersey, Mark Nicholls and Bert Cooke. Mind you, it was a highly talented New South Wales backline, with Wally Meagher, Billy Sheehan, Owen Crossman, Towers, Syd King, Allen Bowers and Alex Ross, and there were in the few in the forwards who would leave their mark on the game, including Charlie Fox, Jack Ford, 'Huck' Finlay and 'Jock' Blackwood.

Though he missed out on the next two New South Wales games, Cyril was brought back for the final one against New Zealand. Although the match was lost by 21–28, Towers scored a try and kicked three penalty goals. The following day was his 20th birthday. These two matches are now regarded as tests.

Howell, *et al* said of him in *They Came To Conquer*: "Possessed of every skill, he had intuition that marks only the finest players and never stopped adding parts to his game. Superbly aware of tactics, he could control matches as a conductor controls an orchestra..."

On the basis of these performances he was selected to the magical 9–month 1927–28 tour to the British Isles, France and Canada. He turned 21 on the ship going over.

On this tour Cyril Towers played in 25 matches, exceeded only by Wylie Breckenridge (26), Tom Lawton (27) and Alex Ross (29). He was the equal top try scorer, with the mighty Jack Ford (15), and was the equal second highest point scorer with Ford (45 points). Tom Lawton easily took the prize with 124 points.

As for his contribution to the tour, Peter Fenton wrote, in *For The Sake Of The Game*: "Towers made the most of this magnificent tour. Though he did not play all the test matches, by tour's end it was obvious the strongest back line had Towers at outside centre. He was a most effective tackler, and had a wonderful swerve which often allowed him to beat his man on the outside. His 15 tour tries were testimony to his attacking skills, and his ability to set up his wingers improved under Wallace's guidance."

As for the last statement, the captain, Johnny Wallace, felt that Towers needed improvement on when he should give the ball to the winger. So Wallace would call "Now!" and the young Towers would immediately provide him with the ball. It must have been one of the few times in his football life he took orders from anyone. In 1928, 22 years of age and a solid 12st 4lb, Towers went on the tour to New Zealand, captained by Syd Malcolm. Only he, Malcolm and Geoff Bland had been on the 1927–28 Waratah tour. The tour was not overly successful, the team winning only five of their 10 games, but Cyril Towers – and Bob Loudon – played in every game, three of which are now tests. He was also top scorer with 29 points, which included eight tries. Chester and McMillan wrote, in *The Visitors*: "... he was hailed by many critics as the best centre in world rugby and was certainly one of the great Australian players of all time."

One of the highlights of Towers' career was in 1929, when for the first time since 1914 a full Australian team took the field and Australia won the three games, 9–8, 17–9 and 15–13. Cyril played in two of the three tests. A whitewash was a new experience for the All Blacks and most of the team, apart from George Nepia, Herb Lilburne, Charlie Oliver, 'Beau' Cottrell, Rube McWilliams, Athol Mahoney, Bert Palmer, Cliff Porter and Dick Steere never won national selection again.

In 1930 the British team captained by Doug Prentice arrived, and Towers played against them in four matches. In the single test Australia won a nail-biting contest by 6–5.

There was another tour to New Zealand in 1931, by the first fully representative side sent since 1913. Syd Malcolm was again the captain. It was even more of a representative tour this year as two Victorians were included, winger-centre Dave Cowper and flanker Owen Bridle. The team only won three of its 10 games, but Towers again displayed his sturdiness by playing in nine matches. With Dave Cowper, he was top try scorer with nine. During the tour, for the first time, Towers captained Australia in a mid-week game against Seddon Shield Districts.

In 1932 Towers only went up against the All Blacks once, for New South Wales, and injury prevented him playing again that season.

In 1933 it was assumed that Towers would be on the tour of South Africa, and the rugby world was stunned when his name was not on the list. Pollard, in *Australian Rugby*, summed up the situation: "Towers' omission from Australia's first tour of South Africa in 1933 caused wide-spread controversy and he made no secret that he was hurt by it. The manager of that team, Dr. Wally Mathews, said Towers' forthrightness was so disruptive it would upset team morale and, forced to choose between Mathews and Towers, Towers was omitted." It was probably the most ridiculous omission in Australia's long rugby history.

The irony is that Towers' best days were still to come. He played in two tests against the All Blacks in 1934, and then finished his representative career playing against the Springboks. He was captain in the two tests. After being dropped in 1933 as a disruptive influence, he was Australia's captain in 1937.

Pollard in *Australian Rugby* had this to say of his final game: "Old timers single out from Towers' many triumphs his display against the 1937 Springboks, hailed as the finest side in the world at the time, in the first test at Sydney. The Springboks worked the touch line monotonously to produce a record 119 lineouts, but Australia held them to a four points margin, South Africa winning 9–5, with Towers scoring all Australia's points from a try and a goal."

In fact Cyril Towers played in the final trial in 1939 to pick the team to go to the British Isles. He captained The Rest against Australia and The Rest slaughtered Australia by 48–3. Cyril was the best player on the field, scoring two tries himself and setting up his wingers for five more. But when the team was announced, he was not in it. The manager was the same Dr. Wally Mathews who refused to have him on his team to South Africa. Towers retired the next year at 34 years of age, saying: "I'm tired of the Union's petty meddling and stupid administration. They've killed my enthusiasm for football." Little wonder.

His was a wonderful career. He played 233 games for his beloved Randwick and 57 matches for his country, of which 19 are now recognised as tests, and he captained Australia twice.

His career was rejuvenated when he was asked to do rugby broadcasts for the ABC, and he became known as "the voice of Rugby".

A strong personality, he was a brilliant centre, perhaps the greatest Australia had seen since 'Dally' Messenger.

CYRIL TOWERS

CAPTAIN: 3 matches (2 tests) (v South Africa 1937)
BORN: July 30 1906 (Mansfield, Victoria)
DIED: 1985
SCHOOL: Roma High School, Waverley College, Randwick Boys' High School
CLUB: Randwick (233 first grade)
NEW SOUTH WALES REPRESENTATION: 82 matches (1926–38)
AUSTRALIAN REPRESENTATION: 57 matches (19 tests) (1926–37)

VAY WILSON

A Career Snuffed Out

VAY WILSON is one of the least known of the reasonably modern Australian captains, and this is so for three reasons. First, he only played five games for Australia. Second, he was captain of the 1939 Wallabies to the British Isles when war broke out and no games were played. Third, he was a Queenslander.

Only a handful of Queenslanders had preceded Vay Wilson to the highest honour in rugby union, the captaincy of Australia in a test. They were Bob McCowan (1899), Frank Nicholson (1904), Allen Oxlade (1907), Jimmy Flynn (1914), Tom Lawton (1929,30,32) and Jimmy Clark (1931).

Vay Wilson first came to public attention

Vay Wilson on the ship to England in 1939. His team did not play a match due to the outbreak of war.

when he made the Australian Universities team in 1934. His home club was the University of Queensland. He was equally proficient in the front row and second row.

He made the Queensland team in 1935, and had his first taste of international experience when he went up against the touring Maori team that year. Some of the Queensland team on his debut were winger Doug McLean, centre 'Dooney' Hayes, five-eighth Wally Lewis, halfback Gordon Bennett, and forwards Bernie Doneley, Vince Birmingham, Eddie Bonis and John Ritter. Eddie Bonis, the 'prince of hookers', won a vast majority of the scrums and Queensland ran out surprise winners by 39–22. This was Queensland's second victory over any touring team from New Zealand, the first coming against the 1913 Maori team.

In the second match, the Maori team won a rugged match 15–13, Queensland being hampered by an injury to fullback Fitz Vincent.

Vay Wilson did not go to New Zealand with the Australian team in 1936, and no touring teams played in Australia that year. In 1937 the mighty Springboks came to Australia, and Wilson found himself in the Australian team to play them at the Sydney Cricket Ground. Cyril Towers was Australia's captain in this match. The only other Queenslanders were Eddie Bonis and Vince Birmingham.

The match was played in atrocious conditions, buckets of water being placed on the sidelines to allow players to wipe mud from their eyes. The captain of South Africa was 'Flip' Nel, and the five-eighth was rugby immortal Danie Craven. The result was a hard-fought, 9–5 win to the Springboks, who had surprisingly lost 6–17 to New South Wales in similar conditions a week earlier.

South Africa then stormed through Newcastle (58–8), an Australian XV, of which Wilson was a member (36–3), Toowoomba (60–0) and then Queensland (39–4). Wilson played for Queensland in the latter game, and was again picked for Australia in their final game. Australia was again competitive, losing 17–26. This match was one in which Towers had to leave the field and flanker Keith Windon went out to centre, sparking a marvellous comeback which fell short of victory. As for Wilson, Ian Diehm had this to say in *Red! Red! Red!*: "Vay Wilson, who always played with his sleeves rolled up and revelled in the hard-slogging forward exchanges, was the only Queenslander to hold his spot for the second test but he was knocked out in the brutal start to the match. The manner in which Wilson came back into the game and his dignified bearing led the selectors to name him captain of the Australian team the following season against the All Blacks."

In 1938 New Zealand toured, led by 'Brushy' Mitchell. In the first test Vay Wilson found himself as captain although he had only played two tests for his country. Wilson went into the front row, his preferred position. It was a singular honour, as there were great players including Ron Rankin, 'Dooney' Hayes, Eddie Bonis and Vic Richards in the team who could have captained Australia.

Australia lost against the All Blacks 9–24, but Wilson captained Queensland against them (a 9–30 loss). In the Brisbane test, with Wilson as captain again and very impressive throughout, Australia made a fine showing to lose 14–20. He retained his captaincy in the final match which was also lost, 6–14. During this period Wilson showed himself to be a fine leader of men who was never overawed by the occasion.

Jack Pollard, in *Australian Rugby*, described him as: "A studious, contemplative second row or prop forward ... was popular, companionable and a keen student of rugby tactics and an automatic choice for the Queensland team from 1935 to 1939. He was in the University side which won the 1938 Brisbane grade premiership."

When the trials for the 1939 British Isles team were held, Cyril Towers made a brilliant comeback, but he and other veterans like Dave Cowper and Bill Cerutti were ignored and the selectors stuck with Wilson as captain. Though he did sterling work getting his team fit on the ship going to England, the team was destined never to play a match as war broke out. He was at the peak of his rugby career, only to have it snuffed out. We shall never know the heights he may have climbed as Australian captain.

Few people know the names of the unlucky tourists of 1939. The backs were Mick Clifford, Ron Rankin, Max Carpenter, Basil Porter, Vaux Nicholson, 'Jockey' Kelaher, Len Smith, 'Blow' Ide, Des Carrick, Vic Richards, 'Wally' Lewis, Paul Collins, Eric Gibbons (vice-capt), Cec Ramalli; forwards Vay Wilson (capt), 'Steak' Malone, Boyd Oxlade, Aub Hodgson, Bill McLean, 'Bill' Monti, 'Straub' Turnbull, Stan Bisset, Keith Ramsay, Brian Oxenham, 'Cracker' McDonald and Keith Windon. The manager was Dr. W.F. Mathews and the secretary was Jeff Noseda.

Vay Wilson came back to Australia with the team, but left soon to go to England. He had finished his MA at the University of Queensland, and had received a Carnegie Fellowship to study in England. A studious and quiet man, he frequently attended games and functions when the 1947–48 Wallabies toured. What thoughts must have flashed through his head as he witnessed the reception they received?

He joined the British Navy in the war and was awarded the DSC for his action in the English Channel in a P.T. boat.

VAY WILSON

CAPTAIN: 3 matches (3 tests) (v New Zealand 1938). Captained to British Isles 1939, did not play
BORN: 18 January 1912 (Gympie, Queensland)
DIED: 1962
SCHOOL: Gympie High School
CLUB: University of Queensland
QUEENSLAND REPRESENTATION: 1935–39
AUSTRALIAN REPRESENTATION: 5 matches (5 tests) (1937–38)

BILL McLEAN

A Commando With No Luck

BILL McLEAN was a hard-rock, pure and simple. In the war he was a Captain in the AIF Commandos, and was dropped by parachute behind enemy lines. As team-mate Max Howell observed: "If only the Japanese had known, they would have thrown down their arms and run for their lives."

Bill McLean's rugby life was certainly not blessed. Though he had no representative experience other than inter-state, the selectors realised his potential and selected him for the 1939 tour of the British Isles. The other Queenslanders on the team were Vaux Nicholson, 'Blow' Ide, 'Wally' Lewis, captain Vay Wilson, 'Bill' Monti, and 'Cracker' McDonald. War broke out after the team arrived in England, and no games were played.

After the war, a super-fit, lean McLean was selected in an Australia versus The Rest match. The two candidates for the captaincy were the veteran Keith Windon, captaining Australia, and Bill McLean, in charge of The Rest. The Rest won the match, and thus Bill became the captain. In the match, with The Rest on their goal-line, Bill punted the ball, which went into touch over 100 yards away. It was the longest punt ever seen, in either code.

Bill was injured in this game, and he went on the 1946 tour to New Zealand, the first post-war overseas tour by any country, unable to play the first six games.

The author was 19 years of age, on his first tour, and will ever remember the speech of the captain before he ran on the field. It went something like this, though one has to imagine this wild-eyed captain looking at each and every one of his team, his sleeves rolled up showing biceps like volleyballs: "Listen to me. You're playing for Australia today. Your country, do you understand? Our aim is to kick the shit out of them and no one takes a backward step. Nobody! You're playing for your country! If you do, you'll cop this from me!" A fist that would not have disgraced Mike Tyson was shown to all.

At the time I weighed 9st 13lb and a good wind would blow me over. I was not certain if I could live up to the captain's tactics.

Certainly, Bill McLean never took a backward step. Never once in his life. The vision of McLean remains, this strong and svelte athlete never sparing himself. A flanker, he was always harassing the opposition.

Bill had some old-timers on the team, like

One of the authors, Max Howell (left) and Bill McLean who is showing his father Doug's caps.

Keith Windon, Graham Cooke, Jimmy Stone, 'Chappie' Schulte and Phil Hardcastle, but also a number of youngsters, such as Trevor Allan, Terry MacBride, Cyril Burke, Max Howell and Arthur Buchan. The team responded to his leadership, and most were thereby earmarked for the 'tour of tours', the 1947–48 gambit to the British Isles, France and North America. It would be nine months long and include a circumnavigation of the globe.

In 1947 Freddie Allen's All Blacks arrived to test the mettle of the candidates for the big tour, and Bill captained Queensland twice against them, and played in both tests. Phil Hardcastle was the captain of the first test, and Bill was captain of the second. The die was cast. One or the other would captain the Wallabies overseas.

The two candidates, McLean and Hardcastle, were extremely different personalities. Bill was direct, up-front, confrontational at times and an Aussie to his boot-strings. What you saw was what you got. He never expected anyone to do any more than he would do himself. He led, he never followed. Phil Hardcastle was more urbane, a medical doctor who stuttered uncontrollably, a person who liked to sweat it out with the troops but never really led the charge and a really loveable bloke who got on well with everyone.

In the final trial, Phil led Australia and Bill The Rest. McLean seemed to relish the underdog role and, sure enough, The Rest won hands down against Australia, so another Queenslander was captain of Australia.

So he was off to the British Isles for the tour of tours, and there were no war clouds to interrupt the melody. Bill plotted and planned on the trip over, honing in on the fitness of his charges. He was to act as coach as well as captain, with a little assistance from the manager, ex-Waratah Arnold Tancred.

After a delightful stay at Penzance to get their land-legs and fine-tune their tactics, the Wallabies started their tour, with the captain leading his charges in the first six games, against Cornwall and Devon (won 17–7), Midland Counties (won 22–14), Gloucestershire and Somerset (won 30–8), Arbitillery and Cross Keys (won 6–3) and Cardiff, in a terrible brawl (lost 3–11) before coming to the spiritual home of rugby, Twickenham, against Combined Services (won 19–8).

Disaster struck at Twickenham. Coming out of a ruck, sleeves rolled up and the ball tucked under his arm, McLean was hit by three tacklers from different angles. There were 62,000 at the game, and spectators interviewed afterwards, said the loud snap could be heard at the top of the stadium. Australia's captain was down, and in agony. It turned out he had a spiral fracture of the tibia and fibula.

The author was one of the first to him, and said that we would get him off the field.

"I ain't going!" he said emphatically.

"What do you mean? You can't even stand up."

"I'm the captain of Australia. I'm staying!"

"But what good can you do?"

"If someone runs by I'll get him."

Reason prevailed, however, and he was carried off the field. As he did he turned to his vice-captain, the youthful Trevor Allan, and said: "It's all yours now, Tubby."

Bill McLean had played his last representative game, though he made an abortive attempt to return with Queensland in 1952, at 34 years of age.

It was obvious that Bill McLean was not Australia's luckiest captain. He was on the 1939 tour to the British Isles that did not play a game, he missed the first six games through injury on the 1946 tour of New Zealand and was pole-axed in the sixth game of the 1947–48 tour. The number six was never to be his favourite.

The 1947–48 Wallabies had arguably the best record of any Australian touring team to the British Isles in its long history. What sort of a record might it have been if the captain had remained at the helm and if the best player, Charlie Eastes, had appeared again on tour after a broken wrist at Newport, is open to conjecture.

Sir Nicholas Shehadie picked McLean on the best team among those he played with. He said, in *A Life Worth Living*: "McLean brought his former commando skills onto the rugby field. A tough, hard-hitting forward who led by example, he was speedy around the field and a huge punt kicker of the ball."

Jack Pollard, in *Australian Rugby*, wrote: "A brave resourceful forward of rare technical skill who captained Australia in four of his five tests. He remains [now deceased] one of the most respected men in Australian rugby, yet his career was studded with cruel luck, and his talents enjoyed only a brief airing at the international level."

As well as his rugby, Bill McLean was goal-keeper in the 1938 Queensland Water Polo Team, was on a Surf Boat Crew the same year that won the Queensland Championships, and in 1946 was captain of the Burleigh Heads Surf Life Saving Club.

McLean coached Queensland in 1951 and 1952, and Australia 1951–52, thus putting back into the game something of a measure of what he got out of it.

BILL McLEAN

CAPTAIN: 13 matches (4 tests) v New Zealand (2), New Zealand Maori (1) 1946, New Zealand (1) 1947)

BORN: 28 February 1918 (Ipswich)

DIED: 9 December 1996

SCHOOL: Brisbane State High School

CLUB: GPS Old Boys (captain 1938–1951)

QUEENSLAND REPRESENTATION: 1939–52

AUSTRALIAN REPRESENTATION: 15 matches (5 tests) (1946–47)

PHIL HARDCASTLE

The Stuttering Giant

PHIL HARDCASTLE was your typical gentle giant, a real pussycat off the field, a real pest on it. In the lineout in particular he was always tempting fate, as he was one of the world's greatest in holding an opponent's jersey, or using his elbows, or stopping a player from jumping by pushing down on his shoulder. Most of the time he got away with it, but there were occasions when frustrations reached boiling point.

Phil's problems were exacerbated because he had a terrible stutter, and after being warned to desist he could not get his reply out soon enough to prevent the mayhem that would follow.

Phil Hardcastle: Words may have failed him but he gave his all every time.

In one memorable clash, Australia versus The Rest in 1947, Hardcastle was captaining Australia and was up to his usual shenanigans. Not blessed with great jumping ability himself, he had figured out his own ways to equalise matters. He should have known better than to irritate Graham Cooke from Queensland, maybe the hardest man to ever play for Australia. Cookie was not very well educated, so he relied on simplistic notions like 'an eye for an eye and a tooth for a tooth' and 'God metes out punishment to those who sin' and he had the perfect solution to any problems, a straight right that was lethal.

It was an important match, every player endeavouring to impress as the team to tour for nine months to the British Isles, France and North America was to be selected that night. Cooke's fantastic abilities were being thwarted by Phil's antics, so he curtly said to Phil, out of the corner of his mouth: "Phil, do that once more and I'll belt you one."

Phil was holding Graham's shoulder again at the next lineout, but was trying to say: "Graham, what's wrong?" But all he got to was "G-g-g-g-Graham, W-w-w..." when 'Cookie' whirled around and threw his thunderbolt right. Phil ducked, and the punch kayoed an innocent Eric Tweedale, who was carried off the field. Phil thereafter came to the conclusion that discretion really was the better part of valour. He left 'Cookie' alone and The Rest won a magnificent game. Phil had been captain of Australia and Bill McLean was captain of The Rest, so McLean was appointed the touring captain.

One time, playing against the great New Zealand 'Iron Man', Johnny Simpson, Phil was being subjected to a fair hammering from the same Simpson.

Hardcastle protested: "F-f-f-fair d-d-d-dinkum, J-J-Johnny, it w-w-w- wasn't m-m-me!"

"You'll do," said Johnny, and hit him with a terrific right cross.

Winston McCarthy in *Rugby In My Time* tells another Hardcastle story that happened on the New Zealand tour of Australia 1947. Holding in the lineouts was anathema to 'Iron Man' Simpson and Phil was at it once again. "And old John [Simpson] said: 'Look,' he used to mark Phil Hardcastle – 'I'm going to tell Phil' – and of course Phil stuttered and had to listen, he couldn't tell you anything in the heat of the moment – 'I'm going to tell Phil that if he hangs on to my jersey when I go up I'll have to clock him – he can't go upsetting our team.' So they all decide that if these things happen they'll warn him, and if they happen again they'll have to clock him.

"Well, they go into the first lineout, and Simpson goes to jump in the air, and sure enough old Phil's got him anchored. So Johnny turned around and I can almost see the look on his face now from the sideline – you could hear it all over the paddock. 'Hardcastle, if you do it again I'll clock you.' Old Phil didn't have time to say anything, and they go into the next lineout and it happens again. So then Johnny gave the signal to Wally Argus on the wing to toss it in to Phil. Now every time Phil took the ball in the lineout above his head he used to bring it straight down, with his arms straight between his legs, and he'd stand up and they'd come in behind and take the ball from there. Well, he goes up and down he comes. Down go his arms and the next moment you've got a perfect scrum. It was just like a billiards table, and the only thing sticking up into the centre of it was Hardcastle, his arms pinned to his sides right down and just his torso showing and Simpson said: 'Now!' and Johnny was a tremendously built man with big hands and everything, and he drew back his fist and let fly. Now just at this moment Charlie Willocks, one of our locks, decided that he'd better put his head up to find out what was going on and he found out. He got between Johnny and Phil Hardcastle, and Johnny hit him fair in the eye. It split Charlie's eye - seven stitches - and he didn't play again the rest of the tour. Johnny was always a bit wild about that, because he didn't get another chance at Phil Hardcastle for the rest of the tour and Phil was a bit worried about that one."

As can be readily seen, Hardcastle could be a real pest on the field.

The one story that always comes up when Phil is discussed occurred on the 1947–48 tour. As is generally known, touring players really abhor the interminable after-dinner speeches following games. Bill McLean takes up the story: "I told Dr Phil 'Wallaby' Hardcastle before the Swansea match it would be his turn to respond. He had a great game and in the dressing room afterwards I reminded him. This caused a lot of consternation to some members and to others sadistic laughter as he had a speech impediment in the form of a stutter. I asked Dr. Doug Keller what he thought of the idea, he just said 'great'. So the dinner went on and Hardcastle and his three doctor team-mates proceeded to make sure the beer stewards did not miss them on the way past their area on any occasion. The moment we were all waiting for came when Arnold Tancred called upon the esteemed Dr Philip Hardcastle to reply. A deathly silence fell over the team members in apprehension and anticipation.

"Dr Phil stood up with a wave of his hand from left to right said 'Gee-gee-gee-gee-Gentlemen, w-w-w-words f-f-f fail me!' and sat down. He was given a Churchillian acclamation." All Wallabies of this time period universally agreed that it was the greatest after-dinner speech they ever heard.

Phil, who was born in Buenos Aires, played pre-war in Sydney so he was one of the few to continue when war ended. While doing his medical studies at Sydney University he received 'Blues' in 1937, 1939 and 1941 and made the New South Wales team in 1938.

In 1946 he was still playing well and made the Wallaby tour to New Zealand, captained by Bill McLean. He showed himself to be an indispensable member of the pack. Not fast afoot, he was a real tight forward, and revelled in the softer grounds and tougher rucking in New Zealand. He proved his durability, playing in 10 matches, including the two tests against New Zealand and the one against New Zealand Maori.

His status increased after the New Zealand tour and he was the captain who led New South Wales to one of the Blues' greatest wins, 12–9 over Freddie Allen's 1947 All Blacks. His most memorable moment, however, was when he was asked to captain his country in that series. It was obvious to everybody that either Bill McLean or Hardcastle would captain the 1947–48 Wallabies overseas. Bill captained Queensland that year and Australia in one test, whereas Phil captained New South Wales and Australia in one test.

When the final trial was announced, Hardcastle captained Australia and McLean The Rest. It was The Rest that won out, and Bill McLean, the unlucky British tourist of 1939, was appointed captain.

Phil Hardcastle never once displayed any chagrin over the decision, and became one of the most popular of the tourists. He did not play in a single test, 'Joe' Kraefft and the remarkable veteran Graham Cooke being preferred. He was the perfect 'dirt tracker', never objecting to his mainly mid-week role and never playing a bad game. Because of his leadership and example, he was selected for the final UK match against the Barbarians. He played 22 matches on tour.

A high percentage of the 1947–48 Wallabies finished their representative career after the tour of tours, but Phil played against New Zealand Maori for New South Wales in 1949 and in the third test. In 1950 played for his state against the British Isles.

A prince of a man, the stuttering second rower was universally beloved. There was no malice in him, no jealousy. He was forever proud to play for his country and he was so very close to being the captain of the famous 1947–48 Wallabies.

Sadly, he was the first of the 1947–48 team to die, at 43 years of age. His team-mates openly wept when they received the news.

PHIL HARDCASTLE

CAPTAIN: 1 match (1 test) (v New Zealand 1947)

BORN: December 23, 1919

DIED: 1962

SCHOOL: Scots College

CLUB: Eastern Suburbs (17), Sydney University (71)

NEW SOUTH WALES REPRESENTATION: 9 matches (1938–50)

AUSTRALIAN REPRESENTATION: 34 matches (5 tests) (1946–49)

TREVOR ALLAN

The 'Boy Centre' and Captain

TIMING IS IMPORTANT in life, and that was certainly the case with Trevor Allan, the 'boy centre' who captained Australia at 21 years of age. He graduated from North Sydney Technical High School in 1945, and found himself almost immediately playing first grade for Gordon Rugby Club and centre for New South Wales. There were no tours or tourists that year, so he had time to settle in with his club and show all and sundry the enormous talent at his disposal.

He was knocked out in one of the first games, and thereafter wore a scrum helmet. Both Terry MacBride and Max Howell wore enormous aluminium noseguards, so when these three ran out together in representative games they looked like something out of *Star Wars*.

His nick-name became 'Tubby', emerging out of calls of 'Fatty' when he was young. 'Tubby' he certainly was not; rather he was a finely tuned athlete who could canter with the best in cricket and athletics as well. Stamina he had in plenty, as he had an ice-run while he was playing and running up and down stairs was a great way to keep fit. These were the pre-refrigerator days, when households would buy 25lb blocks of ice for their ice-chests.

Trevor's father 'Slab' was a big influence on Trevor, and wherever he went in his early years his father would be trotting along beside him. A war hero, he coached Gordon to its early successes. 'Tubby' worshipped his father, and one of the great and emotional days of his life was when he visited the battlefields overseas where his father had fought.

Australia has had some superlative centres over the years such as Dave Cowper, Gordon Sturtridge, Cyril Towers, Dick Marks, John Brass, Andrew Slack, Jason Little, Michael O'Connor and Michael Hawker, but the experts have rated Allan as arguably the best of all.

His first move towards international rugby was in 1946, when Australia went to New Zealand. It was the first international tour post-World War II. Australia was captained by ex-commando Bill McLean and other veterans were Keith Windon, Bernie Schulte, Jimmy Stone, Graham Cooke and Phil Hardcastle. Then there were a bunch of newcomers, including Trevor, Charlie Eastes, Max Howell, Cyril Burke and Terry MacBride.

The world's best centre at the time was the famous JB (Johnny) Smith, and Trevor did not back down in marking him. Smith was an outstanding offensive player, but Trevor was a hard-rock defender and even when he made a mistake he recovered quickly. One facet of his play throughout his life was his utter determination; he never gave up and entered

Col Windon (left) and Trevor Allan hold the Bledisloe Cup in 1949

every game with a positive outlook.

After the tour the rugby aficionados realised that the young Allan was a star in the making, and this was reinforced during the trials in 1947 and the battles against the All Blacks who came to Australia. Up for grabs for those who could make it was probably the world's greatest-ever sporting tour, nine months in the British Isles, France, Canada and the United States.

When the team was announced, no one was more surprised than 'Tubby' to find out he was named as vice-captain. The team captain was the rugged Queenslander Bill McLean and it was obvious that Trevor was being groomed as Australia's captain of the future.

In the sixth game of the tour, against London Counties at the 'home' of rugby, Twickenham, McLean suffered a tour-ending injury, sustaining an horrendous spiral fracture of the tibia and fibula. As the captain was carried off the field he waved and said to Trevor: "It's all yours, now, Tubby."

All this occurred a few days after his 21st birthday, and so he became the youngest-ever Wallaby touring captain. The team never questioned the new captain's selection; rather they all simply rallied behind him. It was a tremendous responsibility for such an inexperienced player but he took it all in his stride, as if this was his destiny.

The 1947–48 Wallabies are arguably the most successful in Australia's rugby history and set a record that can be equalled but never beaten. They did not have their line crossed in any of the 'home' internationals. Yet they lost one, to Wales, on two penalty kicks. Australia had three kicks at goal from reasonably close distances and missed them all. England, Ireland and Scotland were beaten.

Probably the highlight for Trevor was against England, when D.W. Swarbrick rounded two Australian players and seemed certain to score. Trevor Allan hit him with a sensational tackle to prevent the try.

When Allan returned to Australia he was automatically named captain of the Wallabies against the 1949 New Zealand Maori team and took Australia to New Zealand the same year. They won 11 of 12 games and became the first Wallaby team to come home with the Bledisloe Cup. New Zealanders sneer somewhat as 30 of their best players were in South Africa at the time, but the fact is Maoris could not travel because of apartheid, and there were some great players left home because of that, including

Alan Blake, Ben Couch, Vince Bevan, Johnny Smith and Ron Bryers.

Trevor Allan was selected as one of the five best players of the year by *The Rugby Almanack of New Zealand*. They wrote: "Captain of the 1949 touring side Allan on his second trip to this country confirmed the good opinions entertained concerning him three years earlier. An extremely speedy and elusive centre, 'Tubby' Allan puts every ounce of energy into his football, one minute in a terrific and startling burst through the opposition, the next saving brilliantly on defence. Never stinting himself Allan does the work of two men, his cover defence and his backing-up being outstanding. A deadly tackler, Allan is always in the thick of the fray, and is ever ready to open up an attack with one of his devastating straight dashes up field; often he has caught the defence on the wrong foot by a sudden change of direction, and flashed through to either score a try or make one possible."

Trevor's decision to turn professional with Leigh in 1950 shocked the world of rugby union, and he was at the time expelled from the game. This was later rescinded, and a few years after he became the 'voice of rugby' on the ABC, taking over from the esteemed Cyril Towers.

In all, Trevor played 17 matches for New South Wales during his career and 52 matches for Australia, 14 of which were tests. He captained Australia in 40 of his 52 matches. A great athlete and a fine human being, Trevor Allan is certainly a legend of the game.

TREVOR ALLAN

CAPTAIN: 40 matches (10 tests) (1947–48, 5 Scotland, Ireland, Wales, England, France, 1949 New Zealand Maori 3, 1949 New Zealand 2)

BORN: 26 September 1926 (Bathurst)

SCHOOL: North Sydney Tech

CLUB: Gordon

NEW SOUTH WALES REPRESENTATION: 17 (1946–50)

AUSTRALIAN REPRESENTATION: 52 matches (14 tests) (1946–49)

NEV COTTRELL

The First Hooker To Captain Australia

NEV COTTRELL was the first Queensland hooker to captain Australia. Mind you, his mentor Eddie Bonis perhaps should have, and he passed on many of the tricks of the trade to young 'Notchy', as he was called. Bonis was called the 'prince of hookers' and represented Queensland from 1929, when the game was revived in the north, to 1939, before making a comeback in 1945. Bonis made 21 test appearances.

Bonis's reputation was built on determination, perseverance and sportsmanship, and the same could be said about Cottrell. 'Notchy's' name is rarely mentioned these days, but he was a world class player, described by Bert Bickley in *Maroon* as "a fine hooker and a bustling battler." He played 23 matches for Australia, including 14 tests, and captained Australia twice, against the British Isles in 1950.

Jack Pollard, in *Australian Rugby*, was more extravagant in his praise. He wrote: "One of the best hookers to play for Australia. He was a key player in the Australian team which, in 1949, defeated New Zealand for the first time in a series in New Zealand. Apart from his skilful scrummaging, he was a splendid worker in tight play, and a dogged tackler."

Ian Diehm in *Red! Red! Red!* noted that in the Queensland-New South Wales games he outhooked Don Furness, considered the fastest striker of his day, and that he "not only outhooked all opponents but proved a bustling, harassing forward around the lineout. 'I used to come around the front of the lineout and pounce on New South Wales halfback Cyril Burke, who'd always be saying, 'Watch Cottrell'."

Ian Diehm quotes Cottrell on his games with New South Wales: "There was a friendly rivalry. You got to know the blokes from playing them over the years. Nick Shehadie was a great bloke. You could stand on his toes in a lineout and he wouldn't do much about it. Once when we were having trouble in the scrums, I was lying down and trying to rake the ball back from the New South Wales second row, when Nick said, 'Don't do that, Notch. Don't come through the scrum.' I kept doing it until eight sets of boots raked over me in a ruck."

While a student at St Laurence School he showed little athletic ability, but he and Neil Betts started a West End rugby side in 'B' grade competitions. It was Eddie Bonis who 'discovered' Cottrell and inveigled him over to the YMCA team. There it was he came under the teaching of the master.

'Notchy's' entry into the big time was when,

as a 20–year-old, he played for Queensland against the All Blacks in 1947. It was a rude awakening as he realised that it was necessary to go up a gear in such competitions. Has Catley, an enormous All Black hooker, looked after Cottrell on his debut. Fortunately the genial and rugged Bob McMaster was in the front row to help him. The All Blacks were captained by Fred Hobbs that day, and they had a few rugged ones like Nev Thornton, Johnny Simpson and Charlie Willocks in the pack. When it came to selecting the 1947–48 team to the British Isles, 'Notchy' was considered too young, and Ken Kearney and Wal Dawson were selected as the hookers. Don Furness was a surprise omission.

In 1949 the New Zealand Maori came over and Nev was now the number one hooker. He played three tests against them and one match for Queensland.

His first tour was to New Zealand with the 1949 Wallabies captained by 'Tubby' Allan. Though Australians whisper it with a soft breath, the fact is that thirty of New Zealand's finest were playing in South Africa at the same time, though Maori players were not allowed to go because of South Africa's apartheid policies. The Wallabies won 11 of 12 matches, both tests, and brought the Bledisloe Cup home from New Zealand for the first time. 'Notchy' played in both tests and seven of the matches. He was praised because of his displays as a general purpose forward. He made the specialist striker a thing of the past.

Trevor Allan turned professional in 1950, and 'Notchy' was honoured to accept the captaincy in two tests against the British Isles. He would captain Queensland in the future, but not his country.

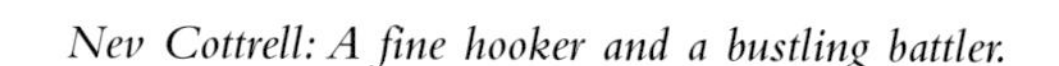
Nev Cottrell: A fine hooker and a bustling battler.

In 1951 New Zealand toured again under Peter Johnstone and they had great players like Ron Jarden, Laurie Haig, 'Ponty' Reid, Graham Mexted, whose son Murray would become a legendary All Black, Tiny White and Bill McCaw. 'Notchy' appeared in two tests, for Queensland and for an Australian XV. He was now well established as Australia's top hooker.

In 1952 he played for Queensland and Australia against Fiji, and then toured New Zealand for the second time, again playing both tests and four other games.

In 1953 a severely injured knee ended his test career, although he made a few comebacks.

Only Eddie Bonis had more tests as a hooker than Nev Cottrell when he retired, and opened the gate for so many fine hookers that were to wear the Queensland and Wallaby jersey in the future, such as Paul Mooney, Tom Lawton Jr. and Bill Ross.

Jack Pollard said of him: "Before each game, he excluded everything but the approaching challenges from his mind. He talked of nothing else, pacing his hotel room hitting his hands together, grunting in a most aggressive manner. He maintained it at meals and kept muttering to himself and when the whistle went he played like a runaway train. It was frightening to even sleep with him during this pre-match period, but after the game he relaxed and joined in socialising with gusto. Conrad Primmer who played with him, regarded Cottrell as the best forward pound for pound in either the Australian or New Zealand pack." High praise indeed!

NEV COTTRELL
CAPTAIN: 2 matches (2 tests) (v British Isles 1950)
BORN: 16 March 1927
SCHOOL: St Laurence
CLUB: YMCA/Souths
QUEENSLAND REPRESENTATION: 1947–55
AUSTRALIAN REPRESENTATION: 23 matches (14 tests) (1949–52)

KEITH WINNING

The 'Baby' of 1947–48 Becomes the Captain in 1951

'ARCH' WINNING, as he was called, was certainly one of the luckiest players to captain Australia.

He burst upon the scene in 1947, a 19–year-old playing breakaway for Queensland. He was squat and solid and looked and acted older than his years. His entry into top-class rugby came in an important year, as following the New Zealand tour of Australia that year a 30–man team was to be picked for the 'tour of tours', a 9–month long tour of the British Isles, France, Canada and the United States.

The youngster did not figure into too many pre-tour selection predictions. Australia has always been blessed with outstanding flankers, and Bill McLean, Col Windon and the giant Roger Cornforth seemed to be dead certainties, with Jimmy Stenmark, John Fuller and Winning fighting out the remaining position. The team announcement provided an enigma that still has the aficionados shaking their heads in astonishment. One of the apparent certainties, Cornforth, was dropped and players and spectators alike wondered why. Fuller, Stenmark and Winning took up the slots, although Stenmark could back up number eight Arthur Buchan. The breakaways, then, were the captain McLean, Windon, Fuller and the 19–year-old Winning.

Roger Cornforth played with distinction twice for New South Wales against the All Blacks and scored a try in the first test, the only one for Australia. Winning played twice for Queensland, Stenmark captained a New South Wales XV, while Fuller never appeared once

Keith Winning: Fast and mobile, his career was fraught with injuries.

against the All Blacks. This analysis is not meant to disparage any individual, but to point out the mysteries that occasionally accompany selections.

The cold hard facts are that Stenmark played 22 matches on tour and this despite a period with an injured shoulder, Winning played in only eight matches because of a lingering groin injury, and Fuller played 11 games, three of those in Canada and the United States, and he was not injured. There were 41 games on the tour. The captain, breakaway Bill McLean, could not play after the sixth game, and front rower Doug Keller picked up the slack by playing breakaway.

In 1951 Arch Winning appeared again, as captain of Australia against New Zealand. He backed up again a week later captaining an Australian XV in a match in which his jaw was broken. Thus he ended his representative career. He had played in nine matches for Australia, one of which was a test, and he was captain in his lone test.

All this may seem unduly harsh on 'Arch' Winning. After all, it was not his fault that the selectors opted for he and Fuller, and it certainly was no fault of his that he incurred a genuine groin injury in the British isles which severely restricted his training and playing.

Ian Diehm in *Red! Red! Red!* refers to Arch Winning as "a squat, powerful former BGS star" and Jack Pollard wrote: "A nuggety, strongly built back row forward with outstanding leadership qualities."

The author travelled with Arch Winning on the 1947–48 tour, and the above analysis may sound overly critical and clinical. 'Arch' Winning the man should be presented as well. The Wallabies of 1947–48 felt genuinely sorry for Winning, and the players themselves knew that a groin injury is one of the worst sporting injuries. It is virtually impossible to tape, deep heat in those days was not overly penetrative, and when you tried to push off you tore the muscle again.

'Arch' Winning was the 'baby' of the 1947–48 Wallabies with respect to age, and yet was one of the most popular members of the touring party. He was always supportive of the team, had a great sense of humour and in difficult circumstances gained everyone's admiration. All the players who played with him and against him said he was a rare talent, fast on his feet and a punishing tackler.

He died tragically in 2004 at a Wallaby reunion lunch. Though everyone was shocked, the general feeling was it was a good way to go, surrounded by his best friends.

And though he only played one test for Australia, he captained Australia in that test. Only 72 Wallabies have captained Australia, and 'Arch' Winning's name will ever be there as one of them.

KEITH ('ARCH') WINNING

CAPTAIN: 1 match (1 test) (v New Zealand 1951)

BORN: 2 February 1928 (Maleny, Queensland)

DIED: 2004

SCHOOL: Brisbane Grammar

CLUB: University of Queensland, GPS, Randwick

QUEENSLAND REPRESENTATION: 1945–53

AUSTRALIAN REPRESENTATION: 9 matches (1 test) (1947-51)

COL WINDON

He Ran Like The Wind

COL WINDON was one of the great players of the twentieth century. He was never bested in his seven-year career at the top. They called him 'Breeze', because he ran like the wind, and in his entry into first grade in Sydney for Randwick, as a winger, he was equal-top try-scorer in the competition that year.

In the Second World War he was a 'runner', a time-honoured military role thousands of years old. His role was to run messages from the front line to a command post, for example, and no Japanese bullet ever touched him as he weaved his way expertly across a battlefield. He was a wizard on attack when he transferred these abilities to the rugby field. He swerved, used a great 'don't argue' as a fend was called in those days, and could smell the line like no other flanker in Australian rugby's long history. He was Australia's leading try-scorer for over thirty years, an incredible feat, until winger Brendan Moon surpassed his record.

Col always deferred to his brother Keith, a rare student of the game, who was both a pre-war and post-war international. A football genius, like Col, Keith's best years were lost to the Second World War. He was an absolute star in 1937 against the Springboks in their tour of Australia. Cyril Towers had to go off the field during the second test and Keith went out in the centre, where he masterminded one of the great comebacks in Wallaby history. Australia lost, but Keith became a legend through his efforts.

Keith was selected on the 1939 Wallaby tour to the British Isles, but war broke out and the team did not play an official game and he went into the Air Force. A fitness fanatic, like Col, Keith was a premier breakaway with Randwick in 1945 and 1946. In 1946, Australia made its first post-war tour to New Zealand and the candidates for captaincy were Keith Windon, Ron Rankin, Phil Hardcastle and Queensland's Bill McLean. In the final trial, Keith captained Australia and McLean led The Rest. McLean's team prevailed and the captaincy went his way. Still, Keith and his brother Col both were selected, but what was thought to be an injury was diagnosed as gout, and Keith hardly played. His career ended, sadly, on that 1946 tour.

Col, however, blossomed, and at the end of the tour he and Charlie Eastes were selected as two of the five players of the year by the prestigious *New Zealand Rugby Almanack*. Col always said his best coach was his brother Keith, who schooled him in the finer points of flanker play. One of his dictums was to always look up while packing down in the scrum, to analyse the position of the opposition backs. Another was to always run to the lineout, and rest then.

The *New Zealand Rugby Almanack* said of Col: "Whether in the tight scrummaging or in the open play, Windon was equally at home, whilst he was adept at linking up with his backs in attack. Probably the feature of Windon's play that impressed most was his determination, which attribute enables him to score tries that others were unable to accomplish. He was the outstanding forward on either side in the first test, and at Wellington, particularly. His try at New Plymouth was the result of a swerving run after he had accepted a pass from his backs, whilst both tries at Wellington were outstanding efforts, the reward of tireless following up, determination, and the ability to seize opportunities."

On that tour to New Zealand, Col played nine of the 12 games, including both tests. Against the powerful Wellington team, he scored two brilliant tries.

In 1947 the All Blacks toured Australia, and it was heralded as the final trial for those who were vying for the 'tour of tours', the 9–month 1947–48 Wallaby tour of the British Isles, France, Canada and the United States. He played for New South Wales twice against the All Blacks, including the famous 12–9 victory at the SCG, engineered by Randwick's 'Mick' Cremin. His one test appearance was in the first match. He was left out of the second match, as were many others, to test other players and the All Blacks won both matches handily.

There was no doubt that Col was Australia's leading flanker, and he was one of the first selected for the 1947–48 tour. He played 27 games on tour, exceeded only by winger Arthur Tonkin (28), centre Trevor Allan (32) and winger Terry MacBride (29). The kickers

Col Windon: Perhaps the greatest attacking flanker in Australian rugby history.

always lead the way in tour scoring, but Windon did his part by scoring eight tries.

Col captained Australia against Leicester, a non-test match, and also against Aberdeen. He showed himself to be an iron man, playing 11 games in a row at one stage. Against Leicester, Australia was rattled as the local player Watkin kicked two dropped goals and three penalties. Col said: "I couldn't let him get away with that," and scored three magnificent tries.

When Australia played Llanelly the match resembled an all-in brawl, with manager Arnold Tancred endeavouring to climb over the fence to stop the game, unheard-of in international rugby. Bob McMaster shoved him back, saying: "They started it, we'll finish it!" The giant veteran Graham Cooke flattened three opponents with magnificent straight rights, and the referee blew his whistle and pointed to the stands.

Cookie started to walk off and bumped into Windon. "What are you doing, Cookie?"

"I've been sent off, that's what!"

"It's not you, Cookie, it's me."

For the first time in his life Col was sent off the field of play, and then for a very innocuous offence.

Probably his most glorious moments on the 1947–48 tour were in the English test. Experienced reporter Phil Tressider said: "I saw him single-handedly destroy England at Twickenham."

Col Windon scored two tries in that match and one of them was heralded as among the finest ever seen at 'Headquarters'. A reporter described it: "Windon, seizing upon a knock-on by [five-eighth] Kemp, tore through their defence like a red-hot rocket. He had 50 yards to go, and three men after him, but this prince of breakaway forwards had the speed and stamina to get there. Tonkin kicked a goal, and although there was still plenty of fight in the English pack, the game was now lost and won."

It is interesting that Col, following his brother's advice, looked over the opposition and heard Kemp tell his halfback: "I don't want it!" The halfback ignored him and sent out the pass, which Kemp dropped and Windon seized upon. He thought: "If you don't want it, I do!"

Col Windon scored eight tries on tour, exceeded only by wingers Terry MacBride (10) Charlie Eastes (10) and centre Trevor Allan (10). He played in all five tests, despite having a bout of malaria prior to the Scottish test.

When Col got back to Australia, he played in three tests against the touring Maori team in 1949, and appeared for New South Wales once against them.

There were so many highlights to his superlative career, but one most certainly was to accompany captain Trevor Allan, himself as vice-captain, to New Zealand in 1949 for his second tour there. He played in 10 of the 12 matches, and scored eight tries. In a remarkable performance, Col scored a try in the three Maori tests, and one in each of the New Zealand tests, meaning he had scored in five consecutive internationals. All this paled with the defeat of the All Blacks in the two tests, and Australia brought back the Bledisloe Cup from New Zealand for the first time in its history. He was also captain in a mid-week game, against Manawatu-Horowhenua.

Incidentally, Col got engaged during 1951, and to show how times have changed, invited all the All Blacks to his house to celebrate. They all arrived, and every scrap of food in his house was ravenously demolished. It was necessary to keep going out for more beer, and during the evening all sang "Life is just a bowl of cherries," followed by:

The bubbles on the beer
Keep haunting me,
Every time I have a drink
I'm happy as can be.
The bubbles on the beer
When on a spree,
Why don't you come
And have a drink with me.

That next year, 1952, the exciting Fijians came, with the freakish Josefa Levula on the wing. That and other Fijian tours were a God-send for the Australian Rugby Union, as its finances were restored since the Fijians captured public imagination. Col played in both tests and in the New South Wales game.

In 1952 Col made his third trip to New Zealand, again showing his stamina in playing in nine of the 10 games, including both tests. He scored in the first test, and in all scored five tries on tour.

When 1953 came around, despite being 32 years of age, he decided to try to make the team to South Africa. Just before he left, however, he tore his hamstring training at Coogee, but was passed fit by the authorities. He missed the first seven games, then he rallied to play in six matches, but his leg gave out and he was unable to play in any of the last ten games.

It was a sad end to an illustrious career, but he had done it all. He captained his country twice in tests, played 70 matches for Australia and was captain four times in mid-week matches. He was selected in the *Sporting Life* All Australian team, in 1947, 1948, 1949, 1951 and 1952, and was elected to the Randwick City Council Sporting Hall of Fame. He later coached Randwick from 1954 to 1957, and was a co-owner of outstanding horses 'Heat of the Moment' and 'Dolceeza'.

His team-mate Sir Nicholas Shehadie, in his autobiography *A Life Worth Living*, picked the greatest players he had ever played with, and one was Col: "As back-row forwards go, he was the very best. A try-scoring machine, a superb attacker with the speed of a three-quarter, the man they nick-named 'Breeze' was simply peerless in supporting play."

COLIN WINDON
CAPTAIN: 6 matches (2 tests) (v New Zealand 1951)
BORN: 8 November 1921
DIED: 2004
SCHOOL: Sydney Grammar School/Randwick Boys' High School
CLUB: (98 matches) Randwick
NEW SOUTH WALES REPRESENTATION: 26 matches (1946–53)
AUSTRALIAN REPRESENTATION: 70 matches (20 tests) (1946–53)

JOHN SOLOMON

Versatility and Leadership

JOHN SOLOMON was one of those players who really did it all. He gained Sydney University 'Blues' in 1948, 1949, 1950 and 1951; he captained and later coached Sydney University, as he was to captain and coach Australia. Moreover, he captained Australia on two tours to New Zealand and one to South Africa. The only other major tour in those days was to the British Isles, and they went roughly every ten years. He unfortunately was too young in 1947–48 and too old in 1957–58.

Sir Nicholas Shehadie, in his autobiography *A Life Worth Living*, picked the best players he had played with. One was John Solomon: "Quick enough to play centre or wing, equipped with a skilful swerve and sharp acceleration when a gap appeared. Much admired for his astute captaincy."

Jack Pollard, in *Australian Rugby*, wrote: "One of the most intelligent utility backs Australian rugby has known, a resilient, scheming winger, inside centre or fly half who captained Australia in eight of his 14 tests. His teams helped revive Australia after a series of disappointments. He later became a successful coach."

An icon at Sydney University, John Solomon reflected on back-line play in the 1950s in Tom Hickie's *A Sense of Union*: "There was very little coaching of the backs in those days. We just used to play standard backline outside overlap play. It went on for years in international football which you never see played today [1993] and I never quite understood why. It was all designed to send the winger away. You couldn't make a break inside. If one of the centres made a break you always worked out to the winger and he scored tries and if not, you worked to try to get an overlap for your winger and throw him outside his man. Nowadays they are so engrossed with getting across the advantage line and cutting back inside and having maul after maul after maul. We used to be able to make breaks from set play. We loved the loose play but we could in fact made a break from set play."

These remarks are very pertinent from a player who captained and coached his country, and certainly got to the core of the difference in philosophy from the past to the present.

The glory of Solomon was touched on by Jack Pollard. It was his great versatility. He was a mere 19–year-old when he played his first test at the Sydney Cricket Ground in 1949, as a winger. Then he went to New Zealand with the 1949 Bledisloe Cup-winning Wallabies, led by Trevor Allan, and played three different positions in his first five matches: five-eighth, fullback and centre. He played in seven of 12

John Solomon: Fast and gifted, he was at home anywhere in the backline.

matches, and made the team for the final test, won by Australia to the tune of 16–9, and he scored his first test try. It was the first time an Australian team had won the Bledisloe Cup in New Zealand. At the time of the tour, Solomon was 5ft 9½ in and 11st 10lb, so he had a compact build.

Having established himself as a valuable utility back, he played twice for New South Wales against the visiting British Isles team in 1950, and in both tests. His appearances for Australia were at five-eighth to the halfback wizard, Cyril Burke. Trevor Allan and Nev Emery had turned professional, and hence there

John Solomon and All Black captain Kevin Skinner with the Bledisloe Cup in 1952.

were openings for a player as gifted as Solomon. In the first test, Howell *et al* note in *They Came To Conquer*: "Solomon, at five-eighth, played soundly, and his handling was faultless."

The Lions were unbeaten on their tour until the final match, when a gritty New South Wales team won 17–12, Solomon finding himself in the centre. The Lions had some brilliant players on the field that day, including fullback Lewis Jones, winger Ken Jones, centre Bleddyn Williams, and hooker and captain Karl Mullen. The young Solomon more than held his own.

New Zealand toured in 1951, and Solomon played in two tests and for New South Wales, as a centre. This was a period when the captaincy of Australia became a problem with the departure of Trevor Allan to rugby league. 'Arch' Winning was tried, then Col Windon, but neither met the demands of the Australian selectors.

It was no surprise when John Solomon emerged as Australian captain in 1952 when Fiji appeared on the scene. In the first test, Howell *et al* wrote: "Six minutes from the end captain John Solomon clinched the game for Australia when he dived over near the corner after a strong run. The final score was Australia 15, Fiji 9." He made an outstanding debut as captain, playing at inside centre. The Fijians came back to win the final test 17–15, but the Australian public gloried in the exciting play of the Fijians and the ARU filled its previously empty coffers.

The very next day Australia went to New Zealand for a 10–match tour. The captain was the 22–year-old John Solomon, and the manager ex-Waratah hooker 'Jock' Blackwood. Despite his age, this was John Solomon's second tour. Seven of the team had already toured New Zealand, Jack Baxter, Nick Shehadie, Keith Cross, Col Windon, Cyril Burke, Nev Cottrell, and of course Solomon.

Solomon's tourists played attractive, attacking rugby, and won eight of 10 matches, an outstanding record in New Zealand. Australia won the first test by 14–9, but lost the second 8–15. Chester and McMillan in *The Visitors* wrote of the second test: "Stapleton was the best of the Australian backs, with O'Neill showing up in the second spell. The rest of the visiting rearguard all had their moments, especially Solomon. Windon, Cameron, Baxter and Cottrell stood out in the Wallaby pack."

John Solomon played in nine of the 10 matches, and scored three tries. He also captained Australia in his seven non-test appearances.

In 1953 Solomon was again appointed captain, on Australia's second excursion to South Africa. This was universally known as a particularly arduous tour, with hard grounds and variable altitudes.

The management team appeared to be perfect, with Wylie Breckenridge and Johnny Wallace, two ex-Waratahs, at the helm. Breckenridge, in his autobiography *Breck*, observed that Wallace was ill on tour and was in no shape to fulfil his duties, which meant a lot more responsibility lay on the shoulders of Solomon. There were some handy players on the tour: Nick Shehadie, Dave Brockhoff, Johnny Bosler, Jack Blomley, Cyril Burke, Herbie Barker and Col Windon among them.

John Solomon took ill and missed the first three games, and Col Windon became a virtual passenger, so it was tough going. Solomon played in 14 of 27 games, which included three of the four tests. The first test was lost 3–25 in front of 70,000 spectators. The Springboks played in white sweaters with a Springbok badge on the left breast.

The highlight of the tour was the second test, won by Australia 18–14. The score was 14–8 when Solomon left the field with an injured knee, which forced Brian Johnson out to the wing. Showing plenty of courage, Solomon returned, there was inter-passing between himself and Jimmy Phipps, and 'Spanner' Brown was sent through an opening. When confronted he sent a long pass out to Johnson, who scored, and Eddie Stapleton kicked a mighty conversion from the side-line to make the score 14–13.

With time running out the ball went loose, Cyril Burke got to it first and sent a long pass to Brown. He passed it on the Phipps, then to Solomon, who despite his injury surged on before giving the ball to Stapleton. Stapleton drew the cover defence and threw the ball to the Queensland winger Garth Jones, who got over the try-line after covering half the length of the pitch and ran round to place the ball between the posts. The conversion heralded a sensational victory, and the Springboks, in a surprising gesture, chaired Solomon off the field.

The fairy-tale ended with this victory, as the Springboks rallied to win the third test, and it surprised most followers of the Wallabies when the captain was dropped for the final test. The team badly needed a kicker, and Herb Barker took his place. It was widely held as an error of judgment, and so it proved, South Africa winning 22–9.

John Solomon took a year out to attend to his medical studies, but returned triumphantly to captain Australia to New Zealand in 1955. Again, the Wallabies had an excellent management team with Wylie Breckenridge as manager and the wily and popular Bill Cerutti as assistant manager/coach. Although he was still only 25 years of age, this was Solomon's touring swan-song. Despite having a very experienced team, it was criticised because it only had one fullback, Dick Tooth, and one five-eighth, John Solomon. This was a huge gamble because of the arduous nature of all New Zealand tours, and this one had 13 matches, including three tests.

Solomon only played six of the 13 games, his tour ending against South Canterbury-North Otago-Mid Canterbury when, after 20 minutes, he was thrown heavily and had to leave the field with a dislocated shoulder. His loss was devastating for the Wallabies, who despite this won 10 of their 13 games.

That was the end of John Solomon's representative career, though he coached both his University and Australia. One might ask what his best position was, as he seemed to play wing, fullback, centre and five-eighth with class. It was probably inside centre, as he was an intelligent player who could read a game, and following the backline strategies of his day he was extremely adept at setting up his wings.

John Solomon captained his country in eight of his 14 tests and in 23 tour games. A leader of men, he made an outstanding contribution to Australian rugby.

JOHN SOLOMON

CAPTAIN: 31 matches (8 tests) (2 Fiji 1952, 2 New Zealand 1952, 3 South Africa 1953, 1 New Zealand 1955)
BORN: 15 October 1929
SCHOOL: Scots
CLUB: Sydney University
NEW SOUTH WALES REPRESENTATION: 19 matches (1949–55)
AUSTRALIAN REPRESENTATION: 43 matches (14 tests) (1949–55)

SIR NICHOLAS SHEHADIE, OBE, AC

The Wallaby Who Did It All

SIR NICHOLAS SHEHADIE is one of two Australian Wallabies knighted, the other one being Victorian 'Weary' Dunlop. Neither knighthood was bestowed for rugby; Shehadie's was for his contribution to local politics, though in his case it could have been for rugby.

Shehadie, more familiarly known as 'Sir Nick' or plain Nick or 'Black Nick', did it all for rugby. He at one time held the record of most tests for Australia (30), played 175 first grade games for Randwick, captained Australia, was made an honorary member of the Barbarians Club, became chairman of the NSWRU and ARU, managed the Wallabies in 1981–82 and was Joint Chairman of the inaugural World Cup in 1987.

When his other achievements are included one realises the enormous contribution he has made to Australia, as well as sport. He was chairman of TAFE, Chairman of SBS, Chairman of the Trustees of the Sydney Cricket and Sports Ground Trust, Lord Mayor of the City of Sydney, received the OBE and AC, had the Nick Shehadie Stand named after him at Aussie Stadium, received an honorary doctorate degree from the University of Western Sydney and in 2004 was husband of the Governor of New South Wales.

All this is not bad for a boy from Redfern, who went to Cleveland Street and Crown Street Public School and had to enter into the work-force at the early age of fourteen. His father, a Lebanese minister in the Orthodox Christian Church, made little money, and Nick worked because there was inadequate money to support the family.

A 12lb monster at birth, Nick soon found a love of sport intrinsic in his make-up, and joined the Coogee Surf Club and then the Randwick Rugby Club. Many of the surfers were avid rugby players, Keith and Col Windon among them.

Shehadie likes to recount that he began as an inside centre in the fourth grade at Randwick, though few of his friends believe him, but he was pulled out of a game one day because a person was injured in reserve grade, and gained instant promotion. Another injury brought him into the first grade, still 15 years of age. By 1942 he was a regular first grader, but when Keith Windon returned from the Air Force he was relegated once more. In 1943, when he gravitated to the second row, he went back to the firsts. Still sixteen years of age, he was selected to play for New South Wales against Combined Services.

'Sir Nick' was unlucky to miss the 1946 Australian tour to New Zealand, but he resolved to train harder as he felt he was in with a chance to make the 1947–48 tour to the British Isles, France, Canada and the United States.

The New Zealand team came to Australia in 1947, as a final test for those aspiring to the long tour. The manager was Norman McKenzie, considered the brains behind New Zealand rugby, and as the team was staying at the Coogee Bay Hotel, the All Blacks wandered down to the ground to watch Randwick play Gordon. Later McKenzie informed the Australian selectors that he had seen a real international prospect, one Nick Shehadie. On the basis of this he was thrown even more into the selection mix. He played for a New South Wales XV against the All Blacks, and then was selected in the final test for Australia. This was his first of 30 tests, and despite concealing a gashed hand he made a favourable impression.

Two days later the team to go on the tour of tours was announced, and the 20–year-old Shehadie was included as the utility forward. He was the fourth youngest, behind Arch Winning, Max Howell and Terry MacBride.

The Wallabies bonded on the *Orion* to England, and the team soon found out that young Shehadie was a person of rare good humour and somewhat of a prankster. He roomed with 'Wallaby Bob' McMaster, and they formed a great comedy team that kept the players laughing the nine months they were away.

It was a marvellous experience for the boy from Redfern. As he wrote in his autobiography *A Life Worth Living*: "For a young man like me,

'Sir Nick' appreciated life and all the chances it offered a boy from Redfern.

seeing the world for the first time, each day was an adventure. I didn't have a care in the world." The team met the Duke of Gloucester at St James Palace, and King George VI and the Queen, as well as Princesses Margaret and Elizabeth, at Buckingham Palace. It was heady stuff.

Nick played a highly creditable 24 matches on tour, playing both second and front row, despite dislocating his shoulder at Cardiff. His form improved the longer the tour went and he made the final two internationals against England and France. He also made the Wallaby team to play the Barbarians, the first time this fixture, now a regular one, had occurred.

This was merely the start of the run for Nicholas Shehadie. He played five games against New Zealand Maori in 1949, including three tests, and then toured New Zealand the same year with Trevor Allan's team. Nick played in 10 of the 12 tour matches, including the two tests, which Australia won. For the first time in history, a team came back from New Zealand with the Bledisloe Cup.

The British Lions arrived in 1950, with Nick going up against them five times, for New South Wales twice, the Metropolitan Union and two tests. Then New Zealand followed in 1951, Nick adding three more tests to his growing score, and two more against Fiji in 1952.

In 1952 Shehadie went on his second tour of New Zealand, and played seven of the 10 games, including one test.

Another of his life's ambitions was fulfilled when Nick Shehadie was chosen as vice-captain in the Wallaby tour of South Africa under John Solomon. At one stage it was thought that Shehadie could not tour because of his Lebanese association, but manager Wylie Breckenridge rightly stated: "No Shehadie, no Wallabies."

John Solomon was taken ill prior to the first game, and Nick took over as captain. He played 20 matches, leading the side in nine matches including one test. Solomon was overlooked for the final test because Herbie Barker was a fine kicker, so Nicholas Shehadie led the Wallabies out.

One of Shehadie's most treasured moments, over and above his first captaincy, was the Wallaby victory over South Africa 18–14 in the second test. As he wrote in *A Life Worth Living*: "Danie Craven, together with so many other diehard South African supporters, took the defeat hard, but it was pure champagne for us. We lost the series, but that defeat by the Wallabies of the 'Boks and the sight of Garth Jones in his breathtaking match-winning scamper down the wing will live on. It was a truly famous victory."

Though many other highlights would occur in his life, the year 1954 was sheer magic for him. The exciting Fijians arrived, and Shehadie played in five matches against them, all as captain: for South Harbour, New South Wales (2), and Australia (2).

Nicholas Shehadie made his third tour to New Zealand in 1955, under John Solomon, and played in 12 of the 13 matches including all three tests. Australia won one test of three.

In 1956 South Africa came to Australia and Nick played for New South Wales and in both tests against them. New Zealand toured in 1957, and Nick played single matches against them for New South Wales, Australia and the Australian Barbarians.

Later in 1957 Nicholas Shehadie made history, as he became the first Wallaby to repeat as a tourist to the British Isles, France, Canada and the United States. Although he was the only 1947–48 Wallaby to repeat, Cyril Burke was unlucky not to be included and therefore match the feat. The real mystery was associated with the non-selection of Australia's captain Dick Tooth and the premier back-rower Keith Cross on that tour. Bob Davidson was appointed captain.

It was a disastrous tour, as the team lacked depth and was always up against it. As Shehadie wrote in *A Life Worth Living*: "The 1957–58 tour (I did, in fact, become the first player to tour ten years apart) was a huge disappointment for me, having experienced the thrill and success of playing with the 1947–48 Wallabies. This time we weren't winning our share of matches and there wasn't the same feeling of commitment."

Shehadie, however, did more than his part, playing in 24 matches, which included tests against England and France. He had played 30 tests, more than any Wallaby who had preceded him and in total he had played 114 matches for Australia, the first ever to reach a century. He was also the first tourist to be asked to play for the Barbarians in the final match against his own team, being made an honorary 'Baa-Baa', a signal honour in rugby circles.

After the tour Nicholas Shehadie went on to bigger things, as cited earlier. When he played for his country he always played with pride and deep commitment. He was a tough but scrupulous forward who loved it in the tight, but could also handle himself in the open. What was remarkable was that he never lost his basic innocence, his ingenuousness, his openness.

Despite all the kudos that have come his way, Nick Shehadie remains unchanged, a nice man, certainly a man of the people, a person of high principles and ethics.

SIR NICHOLAS SHEHADIE, OBE, AC

CAPTAIN: 11 matches (3 tests) (1953 v South Africa, 1954 v Fiji)
BORN: 15 November 1926
SCHOOL: Cleveland Street Public School/Crown Street Public School
CLUB: Randwick (175 matches)
NEW SOUTH WALES REPRESENTATION: 37 matches (1946–57)
AUSTRALIAN REPRESENTATION: 114 matches (30 tests) (1947–58)

ALAN CAMERON

The Forgotten Hero

ALAN CAMERON is one of the forgotten heroes of Australian rugby. When the top 100 Wallabies were selected, he was not among them. Of course one can argue interminably about such selections, and much depends on the individuals who selected this mythical 100. Only one of the selectors saw him play and that was when Cameron was beginning his career. The other six selectors would not have had a clue.

Let us look at Alan Cameron and what he accomplished. He played 26 matches for his state, New South Wales and played an incredible, for those days, 72 matches for Australia, which included 20 tests. He toured New Zealand twice, in 1952 and 1955, South Africa in 1953 and the British Isles, France, Canada and the United States in 1957–58. His representative career spanned the years 1951 to 1958. He played against visiting All Black teams in 1951 and 1957, Fiji in 1952 and 1954 and South Africa in 1956.

On tour, he played nine out of 10 games for the 1952 Wallabies to New Zealand and 12 of 13 in 1955, backed up in 20 matches in South Africa in 1953 and even at the tail end of his career played in 22 matches in the 1957–58 tour.

The measure of the man is in his captaincy. It is a great honour to captain one's country, and in Cameron's day virtually any of the tour matches was near test match intensity. Alan

Alan Cameron: Worked like a Trojan in the engine room.

Cameron captained Australia in four test matches, two against New Zealand in 1955 and two against South Africa in 1956. Yet in non-test matches he was selected to captain Australia against King Country in 1952 at just 22 years of age. His leadership qualities were recognised early in his career. He was not overly ostentatious in his play, he was a hard, grafting individual who often went unnoticed, but did the job where it counted, in the tight. He was a second rower and occasional number eight.

In 1953, still a relative youngster, he captained Australia twice in South Africa in non-test matches, and in 1955 in New Zealand he was Australia's captain in seven matches, which included two tests. On his final tour in 1957–58, he captained his country seven times. This is a quite remarkable record. He was selected because they knew he led from the front and would give his all for his country. He did not get his distinctive cauliflower ears standing outside of the rucks.

One of the greatest authorities in the game was ex-Waratah flanker Wylie Breckenridge, who managed the 1953 tour to South Africa and the 1955 Australian team to New Zealand. His experience was of the 20s, 30s and 50s, and he maintained after the 1953 tour that Alan Cameron and Tony Miller were the most outstanding second row combination that Australia had ever produced. The case rests for Cameron being selected in the nation's top 100 rugby players.

There are a few other factors to be considered. The rugby community in Australia have, surprisingly until recent years, been a non-literary lot. The only books written by Australians up to the 1960s were Herbert Moran's *Viewless Winds*, and only one chapter was on rugby, and John Thornett's book which was really an instructional manual. The point is that players like Cameron, and so many others in his time period and before, never had books written about them extolling their feats. In New Zealand, on the other hand, there has been a continuous literature on their game. Perhaps it is all because rugby is New Zealand is *the* game of the nation, whereas in Australia rugby has been fighting for recognition against Australian Rules and rugby league. Australian rugby people are now learning of their rugby past and giants of the game like Alan Cameron.

A Newington College graduate, his ability was recognised at the school level by making the GPS Combined Team in both 1946 and 1947. The following year he joined the rather unfashionable St George club. Randwick and Sydney University dominated the international selections. After only five matches for his club he was chosen in the New South Wales team to tour Queensland. He eventually played 26 matches for his state and captained the Blues.

In 1951 he entered the big time, being selected for New South Wales and Australia in three tests, at 20 years of age. Some of the All Blacks that worked him over were captain Peter Johnstone, 'Tiny' White, Bill McCaw, Bob Duff and Kevin Sinner. There were some outstanding Australians at this time in the forwards, like Keith Cross, Nick Shehadie, Col Windon, Nev Cottrell and Dave Brockhoff.

In 1952 Cameron played four matches against the visiting Fijian team, whose exciting play, epitomised by mighty long-striding winger Josefa Levula, was embraced by Australian spectators. Howell *et al* have called it 'Champagne Rugby' in *They Came To Conquer*.

There was no doubt that he would tour New Zealand in 1952 with John Solomon. Chester and McMillan in their monumental work *The Visitors*, noted that "Cameron.... was in fine form," "Cameron and Shehadie did splendid work in the lineouts," "Cameron gave a superb exhibition in the lineouts and was one of the best Wallaby forwards in general play", "Shehadie, Cameron and Baxter were splendid in the tight", "Cameron and Shehadie again worked hard in the tight", "Miller, Shehadie and Cameron standing out for their work in the lineouts" and so on. Despite his age he showed himself to be somewhat of an iron man, playing in nine of the 10 games. The highlight for him was the Australian 14–9 defeat of the All Blacks in the first test.

He was firmly entrenched as a Wallaby and was a certainty for the South African tour. As stated, he played in 20 matches including all four tests and was the captain in two mid-week games. Led by John Solomon, it was a reasonably successful tour, which livened up when Australia won the second test 18–14. Outstanding South African journalist A.C. Parker, in *The Springboks (1891–1970)* said of them: "The 1953 Wallabies turned out to be a team very much like their 1933 predecessors. In pursuing their policy of keeping the ball in play they took risks and made numerous costly errors. Yet they scored more points (450) than any other touring side up to then, though they played more games (27). In reverse, they also conceded more points (416) than any touring side." He also concluded: "Cameron, 23 at the time, established himself on the 1953 tour as a lock of true international calibre."

Cameron played against Fiji again in 1954 and then went to New Zealand in 1955 with Solomon's team as vice-captain. He again showed his iron man tendencies by playing in 12 of the 13 matches, captaining the team in two tests and five other matches, through an unfortunate shoulder injury suffered by John Solomon. Again, Chester and McMillan observed in *The Visitors*: "Cameron was the outstanding Australian forward, being very effective in the lineouts and in forward rushes", "Cameron played his usual solid game in the visiting pack and did his best to rally support," "Their forwards were out-rucked but held their own in the lineouts, mainly through Cameron's superb display".

In 1956, in Australia, Cameron captained Australia in the two tests and in 1957 played a test against New Zealand. Then came the 'tour of tours' to the British Isles, France, Canada and the United States. It marked the end of his representative career and the results were very disappointing.

Cameron was no longer supreme in his position, but his 22 matches on tour show that he more than did his part to set an example for the team. He only played in one test but he was captain in seven mid-week matches, a superb contribution.

Alan Cameron is one of the unsung legends of his time period. He was Australia's lineout supremo, and he held his head high against the best players in the world. As captain, he led Australia with great pride and distinction.

ALAN CAMERON

CAPTAIN: 18 matches (4 tests) (2 v New Zealand 1955) (2 v South Africa 1956)
BORN: 18 November 1929
SCHOOL: Newington
CLUB: St George
NEW SOUTH WALES REPRESENTATION: 26 matches (1948–57)
AUSTRALIAN REPRESENTATION: 72 matches (20 tests) (1951–58)

DICK TOOTH

Missing Tooth Left a Big Gap

ALMOST EVERYONE knows one thing about Dick Tooth; he was not selected for the 1957–58 tour of the British Isles, France, Canada and the United States. Two other superb athletes also unexpectedly missed out, dynamic flanker Keith Cross and the mercurial halfback Cyril Burke. Tooth's case was even more ridiculous, as he had been the Australian captain in the two previous tests. The whole thing was mystifying, similar to the non-selection of Cyril Towers in the Wallaby team to South Africa in 1933.

Tooth was born in Bombala, New South Wales, and his family moved to Newcastle when he was seven years of age. He attended Newcastle Boys' High School, where he played rugby league; he was introduced to the union code when he enrolled to study science at Sydney University in 1948. While in residence at St Andrew's College he played inter-collegiate

rugby and played in fourth grade for the University.

He switched to medicine in 1949 and from that moment on his ability came to the fore, moving up rapidly to second grade. The team was coached by the astute Harold Masters, who was a 1922 All Black. He had moved to Australia in 1938 and coached both Sydney Grammar School and Sydney University. He had been a national selector in New Zealand, and was on the New South Wales and Australian panel in 1946 and 1947.

Tooth had the good fortune to be selected from second grade to the Australian Universities team to play New Zealand Universities, and played in the three 'tests' as an inside centre. Keith Walsh, who later coached the University, was the halfback and the five-eighth was Nev Emery, who went overseas with the 1947–48 Wallabies. Tooth gravitated to the First XV in 1950, but was unimpressed with the coaching at the University until Wallaby 'Joe' Kraefft took over in 1951. 'Joe' stressed the basics and moving the ball.

Dick Tooth: One of Australia's most versatile backs, his non-selection on the 1957-58 tour was a sensation at the time.

Tooth, in Hickie's *A Sense Of Union*, noted: "I remember after the Grand Final... saying to Joe 'What a great year it is. You've done a great job in coaching us to win.' He looked at me and said 'You know all you need to do to get a University team to win is to be a psychiatrist not a coach.' And I remembered those words very well when I started coaching... He was absolutely right!'

In 1950 Dick Tooth had played in the centre with Jack Blomley against the British Isles, but was overrun by the Lions' centres Bleddyn Williams and Jackie Matthews, and five-eighth Jackie Kyle. They were considered the best in the world at that time.

His first real break-through came against the visiting All Blacks in 1951. He played for New South Wales and for Australia in all three tests as a five-eighth, marking the very experienced All Black Laurie Haig. Although the series was lost 3–0 Tooth, a thoughtful man and a rugby scholar, learned two things, as he stated in *A Sense Of Union*:

1. "As a five-eighth one very basic lesson I leant was that you never kick the ball when you won a quick ruck. I remember that being brought home to me after one of the tests we played and I did just that and one of the All Blacks said: 'That's a fundamental mistake. You never kick from a quick ruck. A quick ruck is your best opportunity you're ever going to have of scoring.'
2. "Laurie Haig passed the ball out every time all through the first half and until halfway through the second half. And then

on one occasion he went to pass it, Brockhoff, I, and everybody else assumed he would. He just pulled it back and walked through and put it under the posts... There's another lesson – you only make the break when the break is there. You don't make them, you take them."

There were many things he learned from the All Blacks, above all their overall grounding in the basics.

He took somewhat of a sabbatical after 1951 for study purposes, but was back at full throttle in 1954 with the arrival of the Fijians. He played five times against them, for South Harbour, New South Wales in two matches and Australia in both tests. A centre in his first outing, he was a fullback in the remaining four.

Dick Tooth's only overseas tour was to New Zealand in 1955 under captain John Solomon. He played 12 of the 13 games, eight as the fullback, and after Solomon was seriously injured he finished the tour with four games at five-eighth, Rod Phelps going to fullback. He was 25 years of age at the time, 5ft 11in and 13st 7lb, so he was quite powerful. Chester and McMillan, in *The Visitors*, wrote: "Tooth proved a competent fullback", "Tooth was very sound", "Tooth's exhibition could hardly be faulted," "Tooth provides a fine link and an accurate punter" and "Burke, Tooth and Phipps all had splendid games for the visitors."

In 1957 New Zealand came to Australia and Dick Tooth played against them for New South Wales and in the two tests. It was in these tests that he was appointed captain. Despite solid performances, the 27–man Wallaby team of 1957–58 did not include the current captain. It did not make sense and despite the passage of time still defies explanation. That the 1957–58 Wallabies had a disastrous tour makes the decision even more ludicrous.

What Dick Tooth brought to the table was unusual versatility. He proved in the international arena that he could play fullback, inside centre and five-eighth equally well, which would have made him an invaluable member of a touring party on a long tour, and he was considered as one of the greatest tacklers of his day.

While others ranted and raved about the unfairness of the situation, Dick Tooth took it all in his stride, never complained openly, and instead was in the United Kingdom while the Wallabies were there, doing medical studies.

Jack Pollard wrote, in *Australian Rugby*: "Dick Tooth concentrated on enjoying his rugby after his absurd omission from the Wallabies. He captained Rosslyn Park, played for Middlesex and, when he went to work in a Belfast hospital for a year, displaced his idol Jackie Kyle from the North of Ireland Wolfhounds, the Irish equivalent of the Barbarians. There is no bitterness from a tour on which he should have been captain, an action which had nothing to do with football form but stemmed from a clash of personalities."

DICK TOOTH

CAPTAIN: 2 matches (2 tests) (v New Zealand 1957)
BORN: 21 September 1929 (Bombala, New South Wales)
SCHOOL: Newcastle Boys' High School
CLUB: Sydney University, Randwick, Rosslyn Park (Eng.), Middlesex and North of Ireland
NEW SOUTH WALES REPRESENTATION: 14 matches (1950–57)
AUSTRALIAN REPRESENTATION: 19 matches (10 tests) (1951–57)

BOB DAVIDSON

Dick Tooth Out, 'Davo' In

BOB DAVIDSON was a Newcastle product, as was the previous Australian captain, Dick Tooth. Other captains to come from Newcastle were Syd Malcolm, Tooth and John Hipwell, and there was another who should have been, Cyril Burke.

'Davo', as he was called, was a graduate of Newcastle Technical High School, and captained the school as well as the rugby team. He played five-eighth in those days. His objective was to become a teacher, which was the main career objective of many bright kids from the working class. The mothers would say: "My son is a teacher, you know." For the girls, it was nursing or teaching.

Bob dutifully attended Sydney Teachers' College with the one pound a week government stipend that was handed out in those days. He soon gravitated to the Sydney Teachers' College rugby team, which won the mid-week competition two years in a row, in 1945 and 1946. Now he was a speedy and gutsy breakaway, and lined up with the author, Max Howell, who played for Australia from 1946 to 1948. They were life-long friends. Competition was pretty rugged to get into the team, many first graders not making it.

Cyril Towers used to still turn out for the Bank, and the Police had notables in Rugby League international 'Bumper' Farrell and Olympic wrestler Jim Armstrong. Bob's wife-to-be, Fay Engell, who was also at the college, would bring the oranges and even run the line occasionally.

Among Bob's team-mates was one of the greatest athletes Australia has ever produced, decathlete Peter Mullins. He happened to be Australian high jump champion, so he was inveigled into his first-ever game of rugby. Marking him was the infamous 'Bumper' Farrell and Bob was supposedly protecting Mullins. When the ball was thrown into the lineout Mullins jumped and took the ball cleanly, about two feet higher than 'Bumper'. Everyone gasped as Mullins went up. At the second lineout Mullins started to jump when he was hit with a lightning right and was knocked right out of the lineout. Mullins said nothing, and at the following lineout received another right. There was deathly silence as Mullins picked himself up, went chest to chest with his adversary and said: "You do that once more and I'm liable to get angry!" Everyone on both teams collapsed laughing, and he was thereafter left alone.

Bob did play for Eastern Suburbs during his College days, a third grade breakaway, but played no sport in 1947 as he was studying for his Science Diploma and he had married.

He joined Gordon in 1947 and was graded in third grade as a lock. Fortune favours the brave, and when first grader 'Bomber' Miles broke his

Bob Davidson was an engaging personality and a true leader of men.

wrist Bob was promoted to the firsts and performed well in his six games. Now recognised as a valuable utility forward, he slipped in and out of first grade. He became a regular in the front row in the team that won the premiership in 1949.

His ascent into the 'big time' was rapid, so when the exciting Fijian team arrived in 1952 Bob was on the State side which drew with them, and then was selected for Australia in the two tests. From that time on he was a regular in the national team.

'Davo's' first tour was in 1952 to New Zealand under captain John Solomon, and he played prop in seven of the 10 tour games. The top front row was 'Tarakan Jack' Baxter, 'Notchy' Cottrell and Davidson. The All Black captain in the two tests was the mighty Kevin Skinner, who played 63 matches for New Zealand, including 20 internationals. He was also the New Zealand heavyweight boxing champion.

Much has been made of 'Davo's' weight during his playing career, and the then 24–year-old weighed in at 13st 7lb, exactly the same weight as his partner 'Tarakan Jack'. He would add a stone in future years. Though perhaps a trifle light, he handled himself with the best in the world and was more mobile than the normal front rower. After all, the scrum is only part of a forward's assignment. He played in both tests.

In 1953 he toured South Africa with John Solomon's team, and played in 15 games. Little did he know he would work in South Africa when his playing days were over. The tour was something of a personal disappointment, as he only played in the first test. Colin Forbes and Nick Shehadie won out against the enormous pack fielded by the 'Boks, with 'Jaap' Becker and Chris Koch in the front row.

The year 1957 was an important one in Bob's career as the All Blacks were touring, as a final test before selecting the 1957–58 tour of the British Isles, France, Canada and the United States, the dream of every Australian player. Bob played for New South Wales and then both tests under the captaincy of Dick Tooth. Davidson captained the Australian Barbarians against the All Blacks. When the touring team was announced Tooth was dropped and Bob Davidson was the captain. It was the biggest boil-over since Cyril Towers was overlooked on the 1933 tour to South Africa.

The reasons for Tooth being dropped have never been adequately explained, a hint of personality differences entering into the general conjecture. Why was Davidson selected? Others who might have been chosen were Nick Shehadie, making his second tour, Alan Cameron or Tony Miller. What has to be remembered is that Davidson was chosen, for whatever reason. Some of the obvious reasons were he was a born leader of men, he was immensely popular, he met people well, he was highly intelligent and spoke well in public. He was an experienced captain, having led Gordon to premierships in 1952 and 1956. For such a long tour, a leader with a public persona was needed. 'Davo' had an engaging personality. Why Tooth was dropped is a mystery, why 'Davo' became captain is not.

The 1957–58 tour was, comparatively speaking, disastrous. Some 41 matches were played, the Wallabies winning 22, drawing three and losing 16. All five tests were lost.

It is possible to attribute blame, and too often the captain is singled out. There are 15 men on the field. The problem with the 1957–58 team (the author coached a local team against them in Canada) was that they lacked depth. Some 13 to 15 players could be mustered who were of international standard, but many of the others were club players who lacked the commitment necessary at the next level.

Davidson did everything in his power to right the wrongs. He played in 32 of the 41 games, more than anyone else. As for the tests, Wales won 3–9, Ireland 6–9, England 6–9, Scotland 8–12 and France 0–19. With luck Australia could have won any one of the games except the French test. It must have been agonising for the players and the captain.

When 'Davo' came back to Australia he captained the winning test team against the New Zealand Maori and the losing New South Wales game. His run was over.

Bob Davidson played 16 matches for New South Wales and 61 for Australia, of which 13 were tests. He captained Australia in six tests and led Australia out on the field in 27 other matches.

Phil Wilkins in *The Highlanders* takes up the story: "Whatever the disappointments of his test captaincy, Bob Davidson assured himself of Rugby immortality with his inspiring captaincy on the field when he led Gordon to three premierships in 1952, 1956 and 1958. But even the most astute leader can be absent-minded. Early in one game at Chatswood Oval, there was a delay as Gordon's captain fumbled with his mouth. 'I've got my tatts in!' he exclaimed. 'Davo' handed his top plate to a team-mate who transported it to the ball boy on the sideline and then, and only then, the game resumed. He succeeded Trevor Allan as club coach in the Melbourne Olympic Games year of 1956 and remained in the position until 1961. Bob succeeded the inexhaustible Tommy Harrison as club president in 1964 and after deciding to end his association with the teaching profession, he graduated to become Chief Executive with the Castrol oil company in South Africa. He was later to become Castrol's Managing Director in Canada."

Bob Davidson returned to Australia and died in Brisbane in 1992. He was staying in the author's home until a few hours before he died.

BOB DAVIDSON

CAPTAIN: 33 matches (6 tests) (England, Ireland, Scotland, Wales, France 1957–58, New Zealand Maori 1958)

BORN: 18 October 1926 (Newcastle, New South Wales)

DIED: 1992

SCHOOL: Newcastle Technical High School

CLUB: Eastern Suburbs/Gordon

NEW SOUTH WALES REPRESENTATION: 16 matches (1952–58)

AUSTRALIAN REPRESENTATION 61 matches (13 tests) (1952–58)

DES CONNOR

A Wallaby and an All Black

DES CONNOR did what no other Australian had ever done. He played 40 matches for Australia (12 tests) and 15 matches for the All Blacks (12 tests). This was a superb achievement, especially when it is realised that he captained Australia in two tests and New Zealand in one midweek match against Queensland. A remarkable player, leading New Zealand journalist Terry McLean [later Sir Terry] said Connor had "a long clumping breakaway from the scrum, a long and fast pass, long and prodigiously powerful punt, a reverse pass which no opponent could possibly foresee, a character so fine that players were attracted to him and inspired by him."

A Queenslander, he graduated from Ashgrove Marist Brothers College and went to Brothers Rugby Club, and was immediately drafted into the Queensland team as an 18–year-old. That same year, 1954, he played for both Brisbane and Queensland against the visiting Fijians, and his promise was immediately recognised. Though he was the premier Queensland halfback, there were some outstanding ones in the southern states such as Johnny Bosler, Brian Cox and Cyril Burke.

He captained Queensland against South Africa on their 1956 visit, although he was only 20 years of age. Queensland had many a fine player in 1956, like Ashley Girle, Garth Jones, John O'Neill, Kev Ryan and Neil Betts, so his selection as captain was a considerable honour.

Des Connor was one of the great players of his generation, and the first to be an All Black after becoming a Wallaby.

One of the most important matches of his career was in 1957 when he represented Queensland against the visiting All Blacks, because the competition was fierce and the 1957–58 team to visit the British Isles, France, Canada and the United States was soon to be announced. He was selected, and was overjoyed to be seeing the world. The other halfback was Don Logan. The omission of Australian captain Dick Tooth, flanker Keith Cross and 1947–48 tourist Cyril Burke surprised the pundits. Connor seized his opportunity and played 27 games, including the five tests. It was a difficult tour, overall the worst performance by a Wallaby team to date, but people like Des Connor, Arthur Summons, Jim Lenehan, Alan Morton, Terry Curley and Rod Phelps were among those whose reputation was enhanced.

The 1957–58 Wallabies were short on luck, losing their 'home' internationals 6–9 (Ireland), 6–9 (England), 8–12 (Scotland) and 3–9 (Wales). With any luck they could have won any or all of these vital games. As Jack Pollard wrote in *Australian Rugby*, "when Connor or Summons made a break there was seldom anyone backing up to continue the move."

Highly respected Queensland writer Frank O'Callaghan wrote that Connor "was astounding opponents and spectators with a pass which thudded into his flyhalf, running beyond the reach of marauding flankers. Connor had added to his repertoire a reverse pass which he flipped beneath him.

"Connor, always willing to learn, copied the reverse pass of the Cambridge University half-back of the day, Andy Mulligan, the Irish international, and Philip Horrocks-Taylor, the England fly-half.

"Mulligan had borrowed it from his predecessor at Cambridge, Olwyn Brace, who could be called the pioneer of the new skill. But if Brace was the pioneer, Connor made it an art form."

The year 1958 was also pivotal for Des Connor, as he played against the touring New Zealand Maori team for the Australian Barbarians and then in two tests, when he captained his country for the only time in his career. The second test was drawn (3–3) and the third was lost 6–13. He was still only 23 at the time.

The third test loss was unfortunate for him, as when the 1958 team to tour New Zealand was announced the captain was 'Chilla' Wilson, who later became one of the most respected of all Australian managers.

Connor played in nine of the 13 tour games, including the three tests. The prestigious *Rugby Almanack of New Zealand* selected three of the tourists among their five players of the year: Alan Morton, Arthur Summons and Des Connor.

Chester and McMillan observed, in the voluminous *The Visitors*, that Connor was the star of the Australian backs with his long passing and powerful punts.

Howell, *et al* in the two-volume tome *They Came To Conquer*, observed: "If there was a better halfback in the world than Connor during this time, his name does not spring to mind and the Queenslander was expert at operating with any ball and under pressure."

The end of his playing career in Australia was 1959, when he played in one match for Queensland and two tests for Australia against the visiting British team.

A teacher, he was offered an enticing appointment in Auckland, and decided to move there.

Chester and McMillan briefly tell what happened next in *The Encyclopedia of New Zealand Rugby*: "Moved to Auckland 1960 and was one of the key players during that unions' long tenure of the Ranfurly Shield. Selected for the All Blacks against France in the three tests 1961 then toured Australia 1962 and played both tests, appearing in three more internationals against his native country when the Wallabies returned the All Blacks' visit later in the season. Connor was the All Black half-back in the two tests against the 1963 England team but was a surprise omission from the British tour at the end of the season. He ended his international career with two tests against Australia 1964."

Lindsay Knight in *The Shield* wrote: "Some, indeed, rate him with his superb passing, clever and accurate kicking and tactical nous as the premier player of the entire era."

On his return to Australia, with the All Black experience behind him, he coached Brothers to a premiership victory, and then coached both Queensland and Australia.

His first Australian coaching assignment was against New Zealand, and who should be the All Black coach but Auckland's Fred Allen, his mentor. Realizing that Australia was outgunned, he put on his thinking cap, looked up the rules, had discussions with referees, and introduced the first short lineout in the southern hemisphere. Relations between the two coaches soured overnight, the All Blacks labelling the innovation a disgrace which could ruin the game. Now common-place, the innovation was not good enough for Australia to win, but it brought the Wallabies close, with 11–27 and 18–19 losses.

A thoughtful man, a rare tactician and theoretician of the game, he continued coaching a number of years, against France, Scotland and South Africa at home, and to overseas tours to Ireland and Wales, plus South Africa. He was also an Australian selector in 1970 and 1971.

Des Connor must surely be one of the greatest players to ever run out on the field for Australia. It is somewhat sad that he tends to be hailed more in New Zealand than Australia. As Lindsay Knight put it in *The Shield*: "From 1960–63 Connor played in nearly all of Auckland's Shield matches, and in most estimations was considered the one player who was pretty well indispensable."

As a dual Wallaby-All Black Des Connor occupies a unique place in Australia's rugby history. A great competitor, he was a player with the highest of ethics. He formed one of the great halfback-five-eighth combinations with Arthur Summons, who moved on to further fame in Rugby League. A considerable stylist, Connor had a perfect pass and introduced the reverse pass in the southern hemisphere, as he was later to do with the short lineout.

DES CONNOR

CAPTAIN: 2 matches (2 tests) (v New Zealand Maori 1958)
BORN: 9 August 1953
SCHOOL: Ashgrove (Brisbane) (Marist Brothers College)
CLUB: Brothers (Brisbane), Marist (Auckland), North Island (New Zealand)
QUEENSLAND REPRESNTATION: 1954–59
AUSTRALIAN REPRESENTATION: 40 matches (12 tests) (1958–59)

CHARLES ('CHILLA') WILSON

From Captain to the Manager's Manager

THERE ARE PROBLEMS endeavouring to balance any university course and an international rugby career, but it is just that much more difficult when a medical degree is being pursued. Some of the captains who were faced with this dilemma and overcame any of the concerns are 'Paddy' Moran, Billy Sheehan, Darby Loudon, Alex Ross, Phil Hardcastle, John Solomon, Dick Tooth, Mark Loane and Charles ('Chilla') Wilson.

A graduate of Brisbane Grammar, which was a great Queensland rugby nursery, 'Chilla' signed up with the University of Queensland when he left school, and he still contributes to that institution to the present day. His brother, Fergus, was also an important influence at the University, coaching various teams.

'Chilla's' first appearance against a touring team was in 1952 for Queensland, but it was four years later before he made his second major appearance, against the visiting South African team in 1956 for his state. Selection for the national team still eluded him. In that match giant winger Garth Jones was seriously injured and it signalled the end of his career. 'Chilla' Wilson found himself on the wing in his stead and acquitted himself well.

In 1957, 'Chilla' came to the forefront, getting his first cap for Australia, against the touring All Blacks. It turned out to be unfortunate for him, though he captained Queensland later on. As for his test, Ian Diehm, in *Red! Red! Red!*, quoted 'Chilla': "Ponty Reid's side in 1957 used to stand right up in line with the scrum. Max Elliott, the prop, whinged to McLaughlin (the coach), 'Chilla Wilson's not pushing', but it was second rower Cameron who wasn't pushing." The net result was that Wilson was dropped for the second test and missed out on the 1957–58 tour. He was not included in the final trial, though he was Queensland's captain. Only Ken Donald, Des Connor and Kev Ryan from north of the border made the side. Des said of Wilson that he was "a fearless breakaway who got to the ball first and put his body on the line. He was also an enormous copy-book tackler."

'Chilla's' luck turned around in 1958 when the Queensland team, trained for a week by 1947–48 five-eighth Eddie Broad, beat New South Wales 10–6 for only the second victory over the Blues in Sydney since the war. This performance vaulted him into the captaincy of the 1958 Wallabies to New Zealand. The other

'Chilla' Wilson: The likable flanker, who would become arguably the most popular manager in Australia's rugby history.

Queenslanders selected were Tom Baxter, Des Connor, Col Forbes, Kev Ryan, Harry Roberts and 'Buster' McLean.

The 1958 team was the youngest-ever to tour New Zealand, and only three had visited that country previously: Eddie Stapleton, John Thornett and Rod Phelps. The manager was Charlie Blunt and the assistant manager was 1936 Wallaby 'Bill' McLaughlin. An interesting feature of this team was the inclusion of two Victorians, 'Danny' Kay and J.R. Cocks, and one South Australian, Malcolm Van Gelder. The general opinion was that the team was one of the weakest ever sent to New Zealand, but critics did not count on the tenacity of the captain and the determination of the team generally.

Australia had a mediocre record, winning six of 13 games and drawing one. 'Chilla' Wilson did more than his share, captaining Australia in 11 of the 13 games and, to the surprise of all the pundits, this gallant team won the second test by 6–3.

The undoubted stars of the tour were fullback Terry Curley, halfback Des Connor, winger Alan Morton, utility back but mainly centre Rod Phelps, five-eighth Arthur Summons, and Wilson. 'Chilla' displayed magnificent leadership throughout the tour, and clearly pointed out what an asset he would have been on the 1957–58 tour. Summons, Connor and Morton were honoured by being selected as three of the five players of 1958 by the Rugby Alamack of New Zealand. Jim Lenehan and Eddie Stapleton were injured on the tour and this did not aid the tourists.

Chester and McMillan, in *The Visitors*, wrote that "Wilson shone in the Australian pack, where he received good support from Ryan, Ellis and Carroll."

'Chilla' did come back in 1959, captaining Queensland against the Lions, but this was his last game against a touring team although the selectors were criticised for his omission from the tests that year.

Wilson played 12 matches for Australia, four of which were tests. He captained his country every time except for his first test in 1956.

'Chilla' left Australia for five years of post-graduate medical studies in Scotland and England, and concentrated on enjoying his rugby. He allied himself with the Edinburgh Wanderers, but was selected for the London Counties team which played against the All Blacks in 1963 and 1964.

On his return to Brisbane, he became captain-coach at Wests and started to manage teams, starting with Queensland and then ending up with the Wallabies. He managed the Australian tour to New Zealand in 1982, to Italy and France in 1983, and the 'Grand Slam' tour of 1984. Chilla was really the manager's manager.

The style of Charles Wilson is summed up in the delightful book by Mark Ella and Terry Smith, *Path To Victory*.

First of all Smith has his say: 'It's always fun to be around Chilla Wilson, bon vivant, ex-Australian captain, Brisbane gynaecologist, chain-smoker and surely one of the greatest of Australian team managers. Unorthodox in his methods perhaps, but somehow the job always seemed to get done. The essential Chilla surfaced when observers spoke in awe of Australia's pushover try against Wales. 'Farr-Jones had to run really fast to keep up with the scrum', he said. It was always open house in Chilla's room, and the players loved him. His role was that of a benevolent big brother. While Alan Jones couldn't help but be high profile, Dr Wilson preferred to stay low key, although he made some hilarious speeches."

Alan Jones added to this in *Path To Victory*: "The aim of management is to create an environment to do well, but too often management imposes itself to find a place in the sun. Chilla has never done that, and that is his greatest virtue. He probably isn't the Harvard model of a manager and the books may not always balance, but that was one of many endearing features of him."

The concluding remarks come from Mark Ella: "I couldn't think of a better manager. I played for Australia for six years. Thank God I had Chilla Wilson for three of them. With Jonesy up there dominating everything, Chilla was the perfect foil. He was quiet, unobtrusive and didn't make a lot of noise. In fact, you wouldn't know Chilla was the manager until the time came for somebody to get up and say the right thing.

"The biggest thing Chilla had in his favour was that everybody loved him. We gave him a hard time, but nobody wanted to be the one that let him down... He was the perfect players' manager."

Chilla Wilson made an enormous contribution to Australian rugby, as player, captain and manager. He is universally beloved.

CHARLES WILSON

CAPTAIN: 11 matches (3 tests) (v New Zealand 1958)

BORN: 4 May 1931

SCHOOL: Brisbane Grammar

CLUB: University of Queensland, Edinburgh Wanderers, London Counties, Western Districts

QUEENSLAND REPRESENTATION: 1952–59

AUSTRALIAN REPRESENTATION: 12 matches (4 tests) (1957–58)

PETER FENWICKE

The Boy From Walcha

PETER FENWICKE was the 'boy from Walcha', the first purely country player to captain the Wallabies. His is a wonderful story, which is brilliantly told in Graham Coker's book *Memories From Scrum and Ruck: A History of the Walcha Rugby Union Club.* His achievements remind one what rugby union is all about.

Walcha is in the New England area and was one of the first areas occupied by Europeans after John Oxley travelled through the region. Rugby has been played continuously there since 1894. Walcha's first test player, Bill Laycock, only had his 1925 match against New Zealand recognised as a test in 1986. Reflecting on that game, he said: "By jeez, I livened them up. I was causing a bit of concern when I was paid the greatest compliment I've ever had. No less than the All Black captain said, 'Stop that mad bastard.'"

Peter Fenwicke: A country hero.

Somewhat of a character, he even wrote his own epitaph:

"Here, let us bury him here,
Under the bar-room floor
Where the sweet stale stench of beer
Will haunt him for evermore."

One had to be a rugby tragic to play for Walcha. As Coker put it: "Travelling long distances is nothing new to the players of the Walcha Club. The Walcha Shire is one of the biggest in area in New South Wales and many players travel over 40 miles (65 km) into town just to get to training. With the closest competition match in Central North being at Tamworth, some 60 miles (100km) distant, and the furthest competition matches at Moree and Coonabarabran, well over 200 miles away, a return trip for some can mean 500 miles for the weekend. To put that in perspective, Walcha could play in the Hunter Valley competition and travel to Newcastle for their furthest match."

Peter Fenwicke was the club's second Wallaby. He was truly gifted. After a stint at Walcha Public School he attended The King's School at Parramatta 1945–50. Coker tells the story of this part of his life: "Academically, he was selected in the exclusive club for the 12 most intellectual boys in the final year of school. He was also a school monitor and a cadet lieutenant, the highest rank in school cadets. He also excelled at sport. During 1949 and 1950 Fenwicke represented the school in senior tennis, shooting, cricket and rugby union. He was captain of the shooting team in both years and won two shooting awards for being the best marksman in the school. He also won the Honour Cup in cricket in 1950, was vice-captain of the First XV in 1950 when he won the Brabazon Honour Cup for senior rugby and the goalkicking cup and captained the GPS Second XV to a 13–9 victory over Hawkesbury Agricultural College.

"On arrival home from school in 1951 the 17–year-old Fenwicke was made captain of the Walcha club, a position he held until his retirement in 1963. He made an immediate impact. At 6ft 2in and 13st 7lbs – his playing weight never went much above 14st – he had grown into an ideal build for a backrower. After a handful of games he was selected in the New England side to play at Country Week and was reserve for New England when they met the All Blacks that year. He also set a trend at Walcha that wasn't to change for another seven seasons; he was the highest pointscorer for the season and won the C.R. Fenwicke [his father] Memorial best and fairest trophy. Although he scored his share of tries, Fenwicke was a very accurate goalkicker..."

Peter's first foray into the 'big time' was in 1954, when he captained New England in Tamworth against the visiting Fijians. There were 7000 on hand for the match.

It was in 1956 that he first came to the attention of the Sydney press as, following an effort in a New South Wales Country side against the visiting Springboks, experienced rugby reporter Phil Tressider rated Fenwicke as a potential test player. The Country side was defeated by 8–15.

His timing was right, as in 1957 the All Blacks toured and he played three matches against them, for New South Wales, Australia and New England, who he captained. But his big break was being selected for the test match, where he played number eight behind two of Australia's finest second rowers, Alan Cameron and 'Slaggy' Miller. Dick Tooth, the captain, was inexplicably dropped when the 30–man side under Bob Davidson was announced but Peter Fenwicke made it. It was big stuff for Walcha.

As Graham Coker described it: "Such was the esteem in which Fenwicke was held in the Walcha community and, because of his achievements, he was given a civic farewell before departing for Sydney to join the Australian team for the 1957–58 tour. News of his selection reached town several days before Walcha played Inverell in the Group 5 rugby league grand final played at the Showground. Fenwicke was invited to the grand final by the Walcha Rugby League and introduced to the 2000 strong crowd who stood as one and cheered, clapped and tooted motor horns. He was then accorded the honour of commencing the match with a token kick-off.

"A public farewell was organised by the Walcha Shire Council... The Walcha Rugby Union Club then organised a formal farewell in the Parish Hall where representatives of all sporting bodies in the community and from the New England Rugby Union attended."

He played in 19 matches on tour, including the tests against Wales and England, but he was injured in the following game against North-West Counties and could only play three of the remaining games. The 'boy from Walcha' had impressed, however, being compared in ability to the great Arthur Buchan of the 1947–48 tour.

On his return in 1958 he played in two New

South Wales wins over Queensland and by 1959 was captain of the Blues. They had five straight wins under his leadership. In his year of years he captained New South Wales, New South Wales Country and Australia against the touring Lions side. The British team was loaded with talented players, including Bev Risman, Dickie Jeeps, Peter Jackson, Tony O'Reilly, Ron Dawson and Noel Murphy. Australia also fielded some outstanding players in Jim Lenehan, Alan Morton, Arthur Summons, Des Connor, John Thornett, Tony Miller and Peter Johnson.

The New South Wales match was a major victory for the 'Blues', as they unexpectedly toppled the Brits by 18–14. Peter Johnson, in *A Rugby Memoir*, discussed a crucial point in the game: "With our skipper, or 'Phenol' as he was known, leading with voice and deed, we lifted the tempo." It was sufficient for the historic victory.

In the tests, the Lions were simply too strong. In the second test, as Johnson described it: "During the half time break our skipper, Peter Fenwicke, tried everything from vilification to persuasion in his efforts to lift us. The more the poor fellow tried the stronger the smell of defeat became. It seemed to me words only won battles in history books." The loss marked the end of both Fenwicke's test captaincy and his career.

He wound his representative career down with a game for New South Wales Country against the All Blacks in 1960, and captained Northern New South Wales and the Australian Barbarians against Fiji in 1961.

Peter Fenwicke made an enormous contribution to country, state and national rugby, and was and remained an institution in Walcha.

Coker endeavoured to sum up his life and career:

"Fenwicke was a lock forward in the classic mode. Those who played alongside him marvelled at his positional sense and cover defence. He could just as easily lead the way through the thick of the forward action or, as in the 1961 grand final, play a deft hand at five-eighth. He could encourage, cajole and be heeded and he was a high percentage goalkicker.

"Having devoted 13 seasons to the code Fenwicke's retirement allowed him to devote to his young family, develop his 'Branga North' property, produce some of the best fat lambs of the district, and assist the P.A. and H. Association into making the annual Walcha Show one of the best in the north. He became involved with the Junior Rugby Union Association for a number of years and was 'putting back' into Country Rugby Union some of the vast experience when his days were shortened by cancer. A most personable man with that rare gift of leadership that sets some apart, he has been sorely missed in Walcha, both on and off the field."

Australia's first real country captain died at a mere 54 years of age.

PETER FENWICKE

CAPTAIN: 2 matches (2 tests) (v British Isles 1959)

BORN: 14 November 1932 (Walcha, New South Wales)

DIED: 1987

SCHOOL: Walcha Public School, The King's School, Parramatta

CLUB: Walcha, New South Wales Country

NEW SOUTH WALES REPRESENTATION: 9 matches (1957–59)

AUSTRALIAN REPRESENTATION: 21 matches (6 tests) (1957–59)

KEN CATCHPOLE

A True Genius On The Paddock

THERE HAVE BEEN many great players in Australian rugby, and the names keep rolling off the lips: Alex Ross, Charlie Eastes, Trevor Allan, John Hipwell, Mark Loane, Tony Shaw, Syd Malcolm, Johnny Wallace among the very best. Then there are some that have that little extra, that has the pundit shaking his head, like Michael O'Connor, Cyril Towers, Colin Windon, Eddie Stapleton, Arthur Summons and Dick Thornett.

Every now and then a true genius trips the world stage. They provide that occasional magic which does not come from hard work alone. They do things we have never seen before. Some of those that fit this category are David Campese (on attack, we will neglect defence), Mark Ella, Brendan Moon, John Eales and most certainly Ken Catchpole. It was as if they were not controlled by their own thought processes. They were truly gifted, possessed of a certain magic that transcends other mere mortals. It can never be constant, of course, but the moments, the flashes, are there to see and one feels fortunate to have witnessed those magic moments.

Ken Catchpole had the fastest pass in rugby.

Ken Catchpole was schooled at Scots, but he was from the working class and made it to that school by sheer academic ability. He started off at Randwick Primary School and was fortunate that his parents enrolled him at Coogee Preparatory School where he came under the influence of the principal, a somewhat eccentric but demanding individual by name Bill Nimmo. It was at Coogee Preparatory School

Ken Catchpole: Arguably the finest halfback Australia has produced.

that his abilities were developed, as Nimmo was an advocate of *mens sano in corpore sano*, a sound mind in a sound body. He learned to study, to express himself not only in the classroom but on the playing fields and he found himself having a go at five or six sports. He loved swimming, and tennis and his father even took him to boxing lessons from ex-Australian champion Mick Lacey. At Coogee Preparatory School he earned an academic scholarship to Scots College.

Scots College has been a nursery for rugby players over the years, and some of the Wallabies who learned their skills there are Tom Bowman, the twins Stewart and Jim Boyce, Dave Brockhoff, Murray Buntine, Bill

Calcraft, David Carter, Phil Crowe, Max Elliott, Tim Gavin, Phil Hardcastle, Jim Hindmarsh, Terry MacBride, Bill McKid, Rupert Rosenblum, John Solomon and Warwick Waugh.

Wallaby Barrie Ffrench was at the school to put some finishing touches to the then 9st, 5ft 5in Ken Catchpole. He started off at inside centre, but his potential as a halfback was soon realised and he had three years in the firsts, making the GPS thirds the first year and the GPS firsts in his two remaining years.

When he left Scots he entered Sydney University to study science, but decided to play for Randwick. It took little convincing from coaches of such renown as Wally Meagher and Cyril Towers that the running game was where it was at.

His first year at Randwick was as an 18–year-old in the Under-21s, but the word spread via the Randwick rugby mafia that there was something extra special cavorting with the Under-21s.

His rise in 1959 was meteoric. After just a few first grade games he was selected for the New South Wales team against the British Lions. Some of the best in the world were up against him that day; the halfback-five-eighth combination was Dickie Jeeps and Bev Risman, but 'Catchie' and the great Arthur Summons, who later became a dual international, more than held their own. In one of the major upsets of the 50's New South Wales triumphed by 18–14 and the 19–year-old 'Catchie' scored a try to mark his debut. Now all of Sydney knew that this lad was something special.

Peter Johnson has recorded one moment in the match in *A Rugby Memoir*: "It wasn't long before the scoring began and with it the crowd erupted. From a ruck Kenny Catchpole took off on a twisting run which covered fifty metres before he was confronted by fullback Terry Davies at which point Ken stopped dead. Backing up in some depth, I thought: 'God's trousers, what's the young twit up to?' as no doubt did Terry. The young twit's answer was to locate a surprised Alan Morton, who was just passing by, with a pinpoint pass."

Des Connor was the Australian halfback at that time, and he was one of Australia's greatest-ever, but he left Australia in 1960 for a teaching job in Auckland. He became an All Black and had a distinguished career there. What it meant, however, was that the field was now open for the brilliant youngster.

In 1960 New Zealand came to Australia, but no tests were played. However Catchpole captained New South Wales while still 20 years of age.

France arrived in 1961 for two matches, one against Queensland and the other against Australia, and Catchpole not only participated in his first test but also captained Australia. The Wallabies lost by 8–15, in atrocious conditions, his five-eighth Harry Roberts having a tough day at the office. The other players in Catchpole's first test were Jim Lenehan, Michael Cleary, Rod Phelps, Beres Ellwood, Ted Magrath, Rob Heming, John O'Gorman, the Thornett brothers Dick and John, Ted Heinrich, Tony Miller, Peter Johnson and Jon White.

He next played against Fiji in one match for New South Wales (won 17–13) and three tests, two won by Australia and one drawn. He was not only New South Wales captain but also Australian captain that year. The Wallabies made a short, 6–game tour to South Africa to complete the year. 'Catchie' was not only captain but also found himself in a coaching role as well. It was too much to expect of 'Catchie' in the cauldron that is South African rugby and the team won three games and drew one, but lost both tests 3–28 and 11–23. As Peter Johnson put it in *A Rugby Memoir*: "The selection of Catchpole as captain was widely accepted but many, including me, thought saddling him with the coaching was too much to ask." It was some time before Catchpole captained Australia again.

In 1962 the All Blacks toured for two tests, Peter Johnson being called to the captaincy. Later the same year Australia was off to New Zealand for a 13–match tour, John Thornett being the new Wallaby captain. 'Catchie' played in only six matches, as a knock against Horowhenua was enough to keep him from selection in the first test and an injury at Wanganui took him out of the third. For the first time in his career Catchpole was seriously challenged, Wagga Wagga's Ken McMullen playing 'blinders' every time he stepped onto the field. Despite the challenge, 'Catchie' was still brilliant. As Chester and McMillan put it in *The Visitors*: "Catchpole demonstrated his class with his beautiful passing and intelligent breaks", "Lenehan and Catchpole were the best Australian backs", etc.

In 1963 he was off to South Africa again, this time for a 24–match tour. Catchpole played in 12 matches, including three of the four tests, and captained Australia in three midweekers. Ken McMullen was also on tour, but 'Catchie' was the preferred scrum half. His non-appearance in the first test was noted by Peter Johnson: "The [first] test training session increased my optimism but this was shattered when Ken Catchpole, who had missed training, appeared sporting a cast on his right hand. It was a tragedy which instantly lowered team morale. Brave faces were quickly put on with pronouncements on the extraordinary gifts of Ken McMullen lacing every conversation. 'Nipper' was of the very first rank but Catchpole was on a different plane to him and the rest of us for that matter."

Leading South African journalist A.C. Parker, in *The Springboks* had this to say of 'Catchie' on the tour: "Catchpole, with his razor-sharp reflexes and cat-like quickness in everything he did, had a superlative tour and was undoubtedly the world's finest scrum-half at this stage."

In 1964 Catchpole was back in New Zealand with the Wallabies, and he played in five of the eight matches. It was his second tour there, and at last Australia seemed to have found its captain, as John Thornett was at the helm once more. The New Zealanders were still ecstatic in praise of the now 25–year-old Ken Catchpole. The other halfback was Laurie ('One Lung') Lawrence, who later coached some of Australia's finest swimmers. 'Catchie's' partner at the time was Phil Hawthorne, and they were as good a combination as ever seen. Chester and McMillan wrote, in *The Visitors*: "Catchpole confirmed his status as a world-class halfback", "Catchpole revealed superb qualities behind the Australian scrum and was clearly superior to Laidlaw," "Catchpole was a lively halfback who combined well with Hawthorne", and "Catchpole gave a masterly exhibition for the Wallabies."

In 1965 he played two tests against South Africa at home and in 1966 there were also two against the visiting Lions team.

One of his fondest wishes came to fruition in 1966–67 as he toured the British Isles, France and Canada with the Wallabies. Due to a skin complaint contracted by Thornett much more responsibility came to Catchpole, who took it in his stride. He took over the captaincy against Wales (won 14–11), Scotland (lost 5–11), England (won 23–11) and Ireland (lost 8–15). Thornett had recovered sufficiently and resumed the captaincy against France.

As well as his test captaincy, Catchpole led Australia in seven additional matches. At the dinner following the English test the President of the Rugby Football Union, Duggie Harrison, stated to all and sundry: "I have become very fond of our Australian friends and have had hours of enjoyment out of the magnificent type of football they play. I have also had the pleasure of watching the greatest halfback of all time!"

When 'Catchie' returned to Australia, the selectors realised his leadership qualities once more. He played three times against the touring Irish, for New South Wales, Australia and Sydney, and captained each of those teams. He also captained Australia in the 75th Jubilee Test, played to mark the anniversary of the New Zealand RFU.

His last year in representative football was in 1968, and what happened was both horrendous and freakish. The All Blacks were touring in 1968 under the mighty Brian Lochore, and Catchpole captained Sydney, New South Wales and Australia against them.

The story is told in Howell, *et al*'s *They Came To Conquer*: "Australians were enraged by an incident that put their great halfback Ken Catchpole off the field and, as it turned out, out of test rugby forever. He was dragged from a ruck by Colin Meads and suffered muscle and ligament damage to his leg as a result of the rough handling. What Meads did not realise as he grabbed Catchpole's leg to pull him out of the All Black ruck – and as far as the home fans were concerned, did not care about – was that the other leg was trapped under a pile of bodies and would not move. There was terrible certainty about the resulting damage and the great Wallaby's career was finished."

'Catchie' was 28 years of age when the accident occurred. The rugby community was enraged, then saddened. A genius had appeared on the rugby fields of the world, and was now gone.

The memories of Ken Catchpole in action never left the memories of those who were privileged to see him.

KEN CATCHPOLE

CAPTAIN: 18 matches (13 tests) (3 v Fiji 1961, 1 France 1961, 2 South Africa 1961, 1966 Wales, Scotland, England, Ireland, 1 Ireland 1967, 1 New Zealand 1967, 1 New Zealand 1968)

BORN: 21 June 1939

SCHOOL: Scots College

CLUB: Randwick

NEW SOUTH WALES REPRESENTATION: 26 matches (1959–68)

AUSTRALIAN REPRESENTATION: 64 matches (27 tests) (1961–68)

PETER JOHNSON

Striker and All-round Hooker Extraordinaire

PETER JOHNSON was an Eastern Suburbs lad, who first of all went to Waverley Public School, and showed enough academic potentiality that he gained entrance to Sydney Boys' High School. It was the flag-ship of the state education system, and was the only school to compete in both the Combined High Schools and the Great Public Schools in sporting competitions. The school also had an outstanding rugby man on the teaching staff, ex-Rugby League international Frank ('Paddy') O'Rourke, who had even done a stint in the professional code in the north of England.

Sydney Boys' High School turned out quite a few internationals besides Peter Johnson over the years. There was John Bosler, John Brass, Roy Cawsey, Roy Cooney, 'Mick' Cremin, 'Charlie' Crittle, Keith Cross, Wal Dawson, Keith Gordon, Russ Kelly, Syd King, Tom Pauling, Alan Skinner, Phil Smith, Gordon Stone, Ken Tarleton, John Thornett, Chris Whitaker and Stan Wickham.

Johnson made the GPS Second Combined Team in his last year of high school, and first went to play at Eastern Suburbs, being graded in their fourths. He next went to Randwick, to be confronted by the fact that the first grade hooker, Jim Brown, was also the Wallaby hooker. As he was studying Economics at Sydney University, he played for them for a time, until he was cajoled back to Randwick by rugby legend Col Windon. He remained there the rest of his career.

When Jim Brown was away Johnson occasionally stepped into first grade, and was unexpectedly selected out of second grade to participate in the trials for the 1957–58 Wallabies tour. It did not turn out like the Phil Kearns story many years later, but the fact is he went agonisingly close to selection on the long tour. Instead Brown and 'Twinkletoes' Ron Meadows got the nod. Brown retired in 1958, thus providing Johnson with the opportunity he had been dreaming about.

Now 21 years of age, Peter Johnson started to get a look-in at the representative level, and came up twice against the visiting Maori team, playing against them for South Harbour and the Australian Barbarians. As a result of these performances he was selected on the 1958 tour to New Zealand. So he had gone up the ladder of rugby success very rapidly indeed.

That New Zealand experience was invaluable for a number of reasons. First, he proved that he could handle himself at the very top level. Second, he revealed himself as an affable tourist, a humourist and wit, and such people form an invaluable service in bonding a team.

Peter Johnson: Australian test record holder, he was a marvellous striker at the ball.

Peter played in only five of the 13 matches, and no tests, as Meadows had established himself at this time as the test hooker. Johnson, however, had him in his sights, as he demonstrated a remarkably quick strike, and with Randwick had developed his all-round ability. The captain of the Wallabies was Charles ('Chilla') Wilson from Queensland, who later managed many Australian teams overseas. The most outstanding players were Des Connor, Alan Morton and Arthur Summons, who were named as the five players of the year by the *Rugby Almanack of New Zealand*.

Johnson reflected on himself at the end of 1958 in *A Rugby Memoir*. "For what remained of 1958 I managed to alert every living creature within ten kilometres of Bronte Beach to my Wallaby status. By new year however it was all wearing a little thin, even with me. Like the hippopotamus, to which I was to show more than a trifling resemblance, I could only wallow for so long." He doubled his fitness and hooking training to make his mark.

The British Lions were on tour in 1959, and Peter Johnson played against them three times, for New South Wales and then in his first two tests. Few would have predicted at that stage that he would get 42 caps and play in 92 matches for his country. The captain of the Lions was the hooker, Ron Dawson.

In the New South Wales match in 1959, rugby followers were ecstatic when the 'Blues' beat the Lions by 18–14. As he put it, "Our dressing room was inundated with all those supporters you never see when you lose, so I thought, damn it, it must be true, we had beaten the Lions!" New South Wales was captained by 'the Walcha boy', Peter Fenwicke, and Manly's Keith Ellis and Peter Dunn were his front rowers. They were also his props for the first test at the Brisbane Exhibition Ground. Johnson was not disgraced in the 6–17 loss, and held his place for the second test, which again was lost.

The only visitors in 1960 were the All Blacks on their way to South Africa and no tests were played. However he was in the New South Wales team which lost to them 0–27. The All Black front row was a mighty one, with the captain Wilson Whineray, Ron Hemi and Mark Irwin, while he had as props two of Australia's greatest-ever, Tony Miller and Jon White, the latter a strong country player from Yeoval.

The year 1961 was a big one, as Peter Johnson played a test against France and three against Fiji. But that was not all, as there was a short 6–match tour to South Africa. Peter played four of the six matches and both tests.

In 1962 the All Blacks toured, and the New South Wales game was surprisingly won by the home side 12–11. Jim Lenehan, who captained New South Wales, withdrew from the first test and Johnson was appointed as captain. Australia was outgunned by 6–20, and when Lenehan had recovered he captained Australia in the second match. The strong All Black team won again, by 14–5.

Later in 1962 the Wallabies, captained by John Thornett, returned that visit. Johnson played in eight of the 13 games and all three tests. The first was drawn 9–9, the second lost 0–3 and the third 8–16. The gap was narrowing between the two countries. Phil Tressider wrote of Johnson at the end of the tour: "As a combination of hooker and forward he's Australia's best since Ken Kearney. He is a lightning quick striker who has prospered despite playing in some indifferent packs over the years."

In 1963 Australia defeated England in a single test before Peter was off to his second sojourn to South Africa, only this time for a 24–match tour. Johnson, at the height of his playing career, 25 years of age at the start of the tour, played in 16 matches and all four tests. Phil Tressider wrote: "Peter Johnson showed once again that he is the outstanding hooker in international Union today. He won set scrums solidly against the best hookers South Africa could put on the field and his all round forward play was so sound that he could have held down a test position simply as a prop forward." By winning of two of the four tests, the 1963 Wallabies achieved the greatest performance by a touring team since the 1947–48 side's run through Britain.

Another tour to New Zealand followed in 1964. This was his third tour, and he played six of eight matches and all three tests. The last won in sensational style by 20–5.

South Africa came in 1965 and the British Isles in 1966, and he racked up another four tests. Then, in 1966, he was selected for the 36–match tour of the British Isles, France and Canada. Johnson played in 21 matches and all five tests. Wales and England were defeated, but the Wallabies came up short against Scotland, Ireland and France. It was not an overly successful tour.

When he returned to Australia he made himself available against Ireland, recording one more test, and then embarked on a remarkable visit to New Zealand with the 1967 Wallabies for the New Zealand 75th Anniversary test, won by New Zealand 9–29.

In 1968, in one of the highlights of his career, he captained the Wallabies to Ireland and Scotland for a short tour and played in all five matches, including losing tests against Ireland and Scotland. The same year New Zealand toured Australia, and he played for Sydney, New South Wales and two tests against them. He was captain for the second test. He also captained Australia against the visiting French that year, won 11–10 by the Wallabies.

In 1969 Fiji visited Australia, Scotland toured in 1970 and South Africa in 1971. After that heavy workload Johnson played in six of 10 matches in a short tour of France and North America. In the game against the Combined French team, for the first time in his career, he was replaced in a match through injury. He played in the first test, but had to be replaced in the second test. At 34 years of age, it marked the end of a most remarkable career.

In all, the great Peter Johnson, striker and all-round hooker extraordinaire, captained his country in five tests and three other matches. He surpassed the amazing Tony Miller with most tests played by an Australian, 42, and in all played 92 matches for his country from 1958–71.

Australian captain Bob Davidson averred he was "the fastest striking hooker I have ever seen." He was a perennial choice as a member of the Australian team of the year, and won many accolades by his performances. What does not show in such a short biography is what the man was really like, what made him tick.

What is certain is that he was highly motivated. He had a high aspiration level, and when he achieved his goals he had amazing drive to keep going. Few people can keep their motivation level as high as Peter Johnson. He was also a wonderful asset to a team, as he had a highly developed sense of humour and wit, and such individuals are worth their weight in gold on tours.

When the Randwick team of the century was announced, Peter Johnson was chosen as Randwick's hooker. Phil Kearns and Jim Brown were also candidates. What is neglected herein is that he played 215 first grade matches for his club, often finishing a test match or a tour and backing up the next day for his club.

Peter Johnson wore the green and gold jersey with pride on eight overseas tours. He never played a bad game, and was a credit to his country.

PETER JOHNSON

CAPTAIN: 8 matches (5 tests) (1 v New Zealand 1962, 1 v New Zealand 1968, 1 v France 1968, 1 v Ireland 1968, 1 v Scotland 1968)

BORN: 27 July 1937

SCHOOL: Sydney Boys' High School

CLUB: Eastern Suburbs, Sydney University/ Randwick (215 first grade, 239 all grades Randwick)

NEW SOUTH WALES REPRESENTATION: 34 matches (1959–71)

AUSTRALIAN REPRESENTATION: 92 matches (42 tests) (1959–71)

JIM LENEHAN

The Country Boy From Riverview

Jim Lenehan was a country boy from the Wagga Wagga region, who now runs 'Beggan Beggan', near Cootamundra. Like many other graziers' sons he was sent to a private school in Sydney, in his case Riverview. There are some other Wallabies who graduated from that school: Ian Comrie-Thompson (1926-28), John Coolican (1982-83), Bryan (1913) and Jim Hughes (1907), John Manning (1904), 'Tug' Morrissey (1925-26), 'Iggy' and Jack O'Donnell (1899) and Bob Westfield (1928-29).

The greatest of them all was 'big Jim' Lenehan. His representative career ran from 1957 to 1967, and in all he played 81 matches in the green and gold, including 24 tests. He only captained Australia in one test, but he was the only one from his old school to be accorded such an honour. He went on five tours: to New Zealand 1958 and 1962, to the British Isles, France, Canada and North America 1957-58 and 1966-67 and to South Africa in 1961.

While at Riverview he was a hurdler of some note, and his potential at rugby was recognised by Australian coach Alan Roper, who was coaching at the school. Though he had no representative experience he found himself on the bench for the 1957-58 trials, and while he did not play he was one of the selected tourists, at 19 years of age. This was the tour where the current Australian captain, Dick Tooth, flanker Keith Cross and halfback Cyril Burke were passed over.

The glory of Lenehan and his usefulness on tour was that he was equally good at fullback, centre and even on the wing. At 14st and 6ft 2in he was enormous for an Australian back of that period and he could kick a football a prodigious distance.

So the country boy found himself on one of sport's dream tours, some eight months long and travelling first-class all the way. Despite his age he played in 32 of the 41 matches, and four of the five tests; injury prevented him from playing against Ireland. He was the leading points scorer on tour, with 114 points from 13 tries (in which he also led the team), one

Jim Lenehan: Equally good at fullback, centre and wing.

dropped goal, 18 penalty goals and nine conversions. Though he started out as a fullback he moved into centre because of injuries, with Terry Curley being the number one last line of defence.

Jim Lenehan, with his weight, was a punishing tackler and when he hit an opponent they were often injured or concussed. The British crowds, unused to seeing such kamikaze behaviour, often booed the youngster. This occurred in Wales, at Swansea, and the so-called 'home of rugby', Twickenham, in the England test which Australia narrowly lost.

The Times had this to say: "It was rough justice that the Australians should have lost in injury time. Rugby football is no namby-pamby game, but there is a point where ruggedness must stop. Booing at a Rugby match is fortunately an ugly rarity, and hitherto almost unthinkable at Twickenham, but there were several instances where the crowd's indignation was justified. Johnson was knocked cold by an act of irresponsibility [by Lenehan] so unexpected that the referee did not see it, and there were other instances of totally unnecessary petulance. But, it was perhaps an even bigger pity that parts of the crowd should be unable to distinguish between such performances and robust give and take."

Lenehan was accused of the occasional suspiciously late and extra tigerish defence, but the preceding 1947-48 team had similar accusations levelled at them. They claimed, in their defence, they were doing nothing different to what was done in Australia.

The 1957-58 Wallabies had a very poor record in comparison with the 1908-09, 1927-28 and 1947-48 tourists. They lost all five tests, although four were close, and overall lost 16 and drew three out of 41 matches. Despite their lack of success, players such as Jim Lenehan, Des Connor, Alan Morton, Rod Phelps, and Terry Curley and Arthur Summons enhanced their reputations.

In 1958, on the return of the Wallabies, Jim Lenehan played once for New South Wales and three times for Australia against the visiting New Zealand Maori team and then embarked on his second tour, to New Zealand. He only played in two of the 13 games, being injured at Southland. Chester and McMillan, in *The Visitors* noted that "Lenehan played well until he aggravated a leg injury. He remained on the field because of the no-replacement rule but was obviously in pain and did not play again on tour."

The British Lions came in 1959, and Lenehan played both tests against them. He also fronted up for New South Wales and New South Wales Country.

He did not reappear on the national scene in 1960, but went to New Zealand for the second time with New South Wales Country. The following year he was selected for the short 6-match tour to South Africa and played in five of the six matches, including the two unsuccessful tests. Peter Johnson wrote in *A Rugby Memoir*: "Like most others I rated Dick Thornett and Rod Phelps our best performers, but Jon White, John Thornett, Jim Lenehan and Mike Cleary also deserved consideration were a combined team to have been selected."

On return Lenehan was at fullback in the single test against France in atrocious conditions, lost by 8-15. He made the *Australian Almanac*'s 1961 Australian team.

1962 was a year that would live long in Jim Lenehan's memory, as it opened with New South Wales beating the All Blacks, and then, for the first and only time, he captained his country, although to a 5-14 loss. He would have been captain in the first test as well but had to withdraw at the last moment with an injury.

The thing that set him apart from other mere mortals was that he could punt a ball almost the length of the field, something like Bill McLean in the 1940s, and he showed this ability in the test. Though his team did not win he was not eclipsed by Don Clarke, the phenomenal All Black fullback who also had a thundering boot.

The captaincy, however, went to John Thornett on the tour to New Zealand in 1962, with Lenehan as vice-captain. His old school coach, Alan Roper, was the Australian coach. Lenehan played in nine of the 13 games including the three tests, one of which was drawn 9-9. Lenehan also captained the mid-week team against Horowhenua.

Chester and McMillan, in *The Visitors*, reported: "Lenehan also impressed with a useful all-round display," "Lenehan dropkicked a goal 48 yards", "Lenehan fielded, kicked and tackled well, but the main feature of his game was his evasive running", "Lenehan then dropkicked a penalty goal from centre-field near halfway", "Lenehan played superbly and was the best of the Australian backs", "Lenehan was a polished and reliable fullback who looked the best of the visiting backs", "Lenehan and Catchpole were the best Australian backs" and "although not fully recovered from a leg injury, Lenehan played very soundly and his two dropkicks were fine efforts."

In 1963 Lenehan was picked to tour South Africa, and even flew with the team to Perth, only to be sent back because of a severe knee injury.

It appeared as if his career might be over but he reappeared in 1965, playing in both tests against the visiting Springboks, and for New South Wales. The Springboks were unexpectedly defeated in the three matches. Jack Pollard wrote in *Australian Rugby*: "His tackling in both matches was devastating, frequently making spectators wince as he barrelled his men." These were fantastic wins for Australian rugby. He was again named in the Australian team of the year by the *Australian Almanac.*

In a rugby rarity in those days, Jim Lenehan was picked to tour the British Isles, France and Canada in 1966-67. Only Nick Shehadie had previously repeated in the classic tours, doing so in 1947-48 and 1957-58. In those long-off days such visits were roughly ten years apart. So Lenehan, despite his punishing tackling, demonstrated to one and all his rugby longevity.

Jim Lenehan played in 23 of the 36 matches, including all five tests. He was also second top scorer to Phil Hawthorne, with 74 points.

On his return his representative career ended with games for New South Wales and then Australia against the visiting Irish. He was 29 years of age.

Jim Lenehan was an outstanding athlete, equally good in attack and defence, with a massive boot. He only captained Australia once, but much of that was due to leaders such as Ken Catchpole and John Thornett being available at the time. His career spanned 11 years and during that time he appeared in 81 matches for his country, 24 of them tests. The All Blacks had the mighty D.B. Clarke, Australia had the mighty Jim Lenehan.

JIM LENEHAN

CAPTAIN: 2 matches (1 test) (1 v New Zealand 1962)
BORN: 29 April 1938
SCHOOL: Riverview
CLUB: Wagga Wagga
NEW SOUTH WALES REPRESENTATION: 21 matches (1958-67)
AUSTRALIAN REPRESENTATION: 81 matches (24 tests) (1957-67)

JOHN THORNETT

The Captain of Captains

JOHN THORNETT is recognised by all and sundry as one of Australia's greatest leaders in rugby union. He captained Australia in a remarkable 63 matches, 16 of which were tests.

When test captaincies before him are evaluated, the only ones close to him were 'Wakka' Walker (11 tests), Ken Catchpole (13), Trevor Allan (10) and John Solomon (8). After he retired, Greg Davis captained Australia the same number of tests, and only Andrew Slack (19) and Nick Farr-Jones (36) exceeded him in the amateur era. Since that time John Eales (55) and George Gregan have exceeded his tests in the professional era. But one must keep in mind that John Thornett captained Australia in 47 additional games.

A graduate of Sydney Boys' High School, he was the eldest of three brothers. Dick Thornett went to Randwick High School, and Ken went to Paddington Junior Technical High School. What an athletic trio they were, spending their winters on the playing fields of Sydney and their summers in the surf and swimming pools.

Both Ken and Dick Thornett eventually went to rugby league. Dick was a superlative rugby union test player before switching to the professional code, and had represented Australia in water polo at the Olympics. All the boys were outstanding swimmers and water polo players, playing for the Bronte Water Polo Club.

Australian rugby players have been slow to take up the pen. Herbert Moran, the 1908 captain, was the most literate, penning three published works. One of them, *Viewless Winds*, has a very enlightening chapter on rugby. It took almost 30 years before there was another attempt, *This World of Rugby* by John Thornett.

Although Thornett's book was mainly an instructional one, there are snippets in it about what made Thornett tick. For example, he wrote:

"Above all, Rugby is an amateur game played by men who should always stand for the highest standards of sportsmanship. By amateur I do not only mean that Rugby players are not paid for playing the game. There is far more in being an amateur than the money factor. The amateur spirit to me is a state of mind about how you approach a match in the fields..."

What made John Thornett such a good captain? The whole question of captaincy is an interesting one. There are the table thumpers, the lead from the front captains, the mad dog captains, the laid back captains, the theoretical captains, the quiet captains, the noisy captains and so on. The fact is each can be successful, there is no magic to it all.

John Thornett was the quiet achiever type. His players followed him because they knew he had the experience, and that he was a man of sterling character and high ethics. He was rarely the most brilliant player on the team, but rather the essential cog in the machine. Men followed him into battle because he was solid, dependable, unwavering, a man of undoubted modesty and tangible principles. This is what he offered to a team, and in his case it worked. They all knew he was a fine human being.

Bill McLaughlin wrote in *This World of Rugby*: "He is quiet by nature, but a very staunch character with the vision to see beyond Sydney football grounds and take in the overall international picture in Rugby. I doubt if he has ever failed to do anything asked of him if he thought it would help Rugby – and these demands have been considerable."

Thornett started off as a breakaway, and played 17 tests in that position, but as the years went on and perhaps his speed diminished he was often placed in the second row, and finally gravitated to the front row. It was in the latter position that he gained particular acclaim, and the front row of Jon White, Peter Johnson and Thornett was heralded throughout the rugby world. No one bested them when they got together.

He was a mere 20-year-old when he was thrust into the international cauldron, touring New Zealand with the 1955 Wallabies. He had previously served notice of his potential when touring New Zealand with Australian Universities in 1954 and played in 10 of the 13 matches with the Wallabies, including the three tests on the John Solomon–captained tour. The highlight of the tour from Australia's viewpoint

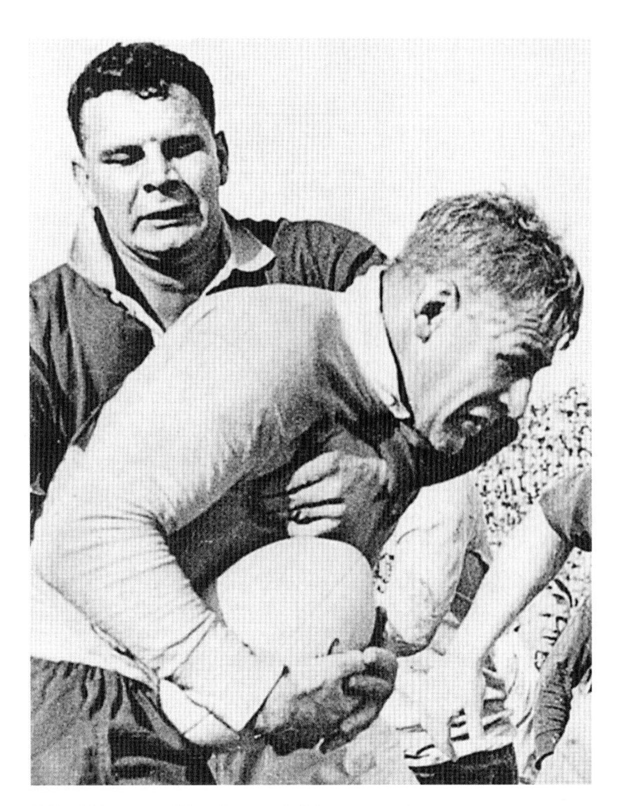

John Thornett: He always led by example.

was the 8-3 victory in the final test. Chester and McMillan wrote in *The Visitors*: "The loose trio of Keith Cross, Hughes and Thornett were in devastating form."

South Africa came to Australia in 1956, and he played against the Boks for New South Wales and in both tests. Then, in 1957-58, he was off to the British Isles, France and North America with captain Bob Davidson. The tour as a whole was a big disappointment as all tests were lost, although four were by narrow scores, but injury limited Thornett's appearances. He ultimately played in 18 matches and four tests, an injury keeping him off the field against England.

The New Zealand Maori team was next on tap at home in 1958, and after that he embarked on his second tour to New Zealand with captain 'Chilla' Wilson. Thornett missed the first test but played the remaining two. As he wrote: "Of all the matches I have played, one of the most memorable was the second test against New Zealand at Christchurch in 1958. We had left Australia described by one sportswriter as the worst team Australia had ever sent in any code. We had lost the first test by a big score... We slogged it out with New Zealand's forwards all through the first half and midway through the second half it was 3-3 and it suddenly dawned on us all that we had a real chance to win. This realisation, together with the fact that we were such strongly criticised underdogs, inspired us. Then Alan Morton scored his brilliant try and we were in front. From then on the forwards literally threw themselves into the rucks, really playing superbly. We came off winners against all the forecasts of the experts and I can still remember the gleeful figures jumping up and down for joy on the top deck of the stand – the Australian reserves who had not played."

In 1959 the Lions came, and Thornett played in two tests. 1960 was quiet but 1961 was a big year, as Fiji visited (Thornett played two tests), France arrived for one test and the Wallabies undertook a short 6-game tour of South Africa with a young Ken Catchpole in the near-impossible situation of being captain-coach. Both tests were lost. There were two lingering highlights of the tour, apart from the magnificent scenery and generosity of the hosts. The first was that Thornett had his initial run-on as captain of an Australian team. It was not a test match, but it was a great honour to lead the Wallabies out on the field against South-West Africa, and the team eked out a draw.

The other highlight was memorable in other ways: "For different reasons, the test against South Africa at Ellis Park, Johannesburg, on the short tour in 1961 will linger long in my memory. We went into this match a little cockier than we should have after a couple of good wins against provincial sides and we were absolutely overwhelmed. I have never had such a feeling of helplessness on a football field as when wave after wave of Springbok players poured through our defences. It was my first test as a front-rower and I remember that we were pushed back so fast in some scrums that even when we won the ball Catchpole had to dive to escape being trampled on by our own scrum which seemed to be almost running back."

From 1963 to 1967 Thornett was clearly in charge and was recognised as Australia's leader, captaining the Wallabies more times than any player to that point in Australia's rugby history.

First he captained the 1962 Wallabies to New Zealand, playing in 11 of the 13 matches including the three tests. Australia was on the move, as the first test was drawn 9-9, the second agonisingly lost 0-3, and the final one lost 8-16. Australia's standards had dramatically risen, no doubt after the lessons learned from the back-breaking scrummaging of the Springboks the previous year.

His brother Dick was on that 1962 tour, and he was a brilliant player who strengthened the Australian pack. Chester and McMillan, in *The Visitors*, said: "John Thornett and White were the best of the forwards," "Dick Thornett was the best of the tight forwards," "The best of the Australian forwards was Thornett," "The Thornett brothers and White were outstanding in the Australian pack," "The Thornett brothers, Chapman and Heming constantly made their presence felt in the forward encounters," "The Thornett brothers stood out among the visitors' forwards," etc.

In 1963 Thornett captained Australia to an 18-9 victory over England. As he wrote: "Rain had fallen for 10 hours before the match and three inches fell between 2 p.m. and 5 p.m. on the afternoon of the match...Despite the conditions the Australian team in the first 20 minutes probably functioned better than it has ever done in my experience. Everything we tried succeeded and we led 18-0 in as many minutes."

South Africa beckoned next, this time for a full 24-match tour. Thornett played in and captained the side in 16 of the 24 games, and Australian rugby reached heights it never had previously scaled. Australia lost the first test 3-14, won the second 9-5, incredibly won the third 11-9 before losing the last 6-22. The series was squared. It was one of the real success stories of Australian rugby.

In 1964 Thornett was off to New Zealand again, playing in and captaining Australia in all eight matches. The first test was lost 9-14, the second lost 3-18 and then Australian romped home 20-5 in the third. As Chester and McMillan wrote in *The Visitors*: "All of the visiting forwards rose to the occasion magnificently, and the result must have been an exciting reward for John Thornett, the Wallaby skipper."

The seemingly impossible occurred in 1965, as the visiting Springboks lost all three games in which captain Thornett played, for New South Wales and two test matches.

The culmination of Thornett's career was being selected as captain of the 1966/67 tour to the British Isles, France and Canada. Earlier that season there were three matches against the visiting Lions. Thornett's final tour was not the way that he would have liked to go out, as he caught impetigo (a contagious skin disease) from an opponent in England. It made it hard to train, and his form deteriorated. It must have been a tough decision on his part as he was a selector, but he did not play the internationals against Wales, Scotland, England and Ireland. He had recovered sufficiently to play against the Barbarians and the last test against France. Now 32 years of age, he hung up his boots.

John Thornett had performed unbelievably for the cause of rugby in Australia. He had played 114 matches for his country, 37 of them tests. He was captain of his country in 16 tests and 47 other matches. A proud man, a born leader, he had been one of those instrumental in bringing an international reputation once more to Australian rugby. Modest, intelligent, hard-working, he was arguably the greatest captain Australia has ever had.

JOHN THORNETT

CAPTAIN: 63 matches (16 tests) (3 New Zealand 1962, 1 Eng. 1963, 4 South Africa 1963, 3 New Zealand 1964, 2 South Africa 1965, 2 British Isles 1966, 1 France 1967)
BORN: 30 March 1935
SCHOOL: Sydney Boys High School
CLUB: Sydney University/Northern Suburbs (approx. 170 games)
NEW SOUTH WALES REPRESENTATION: 21 matches (1955-66)
AUSTRALIAN REPRESENTATION: 114 matches (37 tests) (1955-67)

GREG DAVIS

His Body On the Line

Greg Davis was born in New Zealand, and became a wool classer by trade. He played in the Thames Valley, Auckland and Bay of Plenty, and was in the New Zealand trials in 1961. He came to Australia in 1963 and immediately joined the Drummoyne Club.

The rugby game in Australia owes much to New Zealand, as constant tours of the All Blacks and Maori teams, and invitations to Australia to tour, did much to save the game when it was a low level. There have been a host of New Zealand-born players as well as Davis who represented Australia over the years, such as James Carson (1899), Jim Clarken (1905, 10, 12), Arthur Corfe (1899), John Cornes (1972), Walter Davis (1899), John Hammon (1936, 37), Ross Cullen (1966-67), Keith Gudsell (1951), Bill Hardcastle (1899,1903), Mark Harding (1983), Wilf Hemingway (1931, 32), Ernest Hills (1950), Rod Kelleher (1969), Bob Loudon (1929, 32-32), Barry McDonald (1969, 70), Doug Osborne (1975), Charlie Redwood (1903, 04), Sid Riley (1903), 'Jum' Sampson (1899), Owen Stephens (1968), Bob Thompson (1971, 72), Pat Walsh (1904), Peter Ward (1899), Willie Watson (1912-14), Bill Webb (1899), Bob Westfield (1929) and Larry Wogan (1912-14). This was certainly an influx of talent over the years.

Of these, Willie Watson, Bob Loudon and Greg Davis captained Australia. Watson led Australia three times, Loudon once and Davis sixteen times. Though Watson had a considerable influence through his work with the AIF team reviving the game in Australia, it had to be concluded that of all the New Zealanders to come to Australian shores Greg Davis made the greatest contribution.

As well as his test captaincy, Davis captained Australia in 31 other matches, mainly but not solely midweekers. He captained Australia on the 1967 and 1972 tours to New Zealand, the 1969 South African tour, the 1968 tour to Ireland and Scotland and the 1971 tour to France and North America. In all Greg Davis played a remarkable 102 matches for the Wallabies, which included 39 tests. He was the supreme flanker. Whereas Col Windon was all style, Davis was all effort.

What kind of a leader was Greg Davis? Never overly voluble, he led from the front in the 'into the Valley of Death' mode, with a complete disregard of his own body. He never asked anyone to subject himself to the same complete commitment as he did, but it rubbed off on the other players. Greg Davis was a kamikaze type player and he found his playing soul-mate in the equally hyped-up Jules Guerassimoff. Together, when they were both on song, they absolutely terrorised and horrified the best inside backs of the world.

Whatever degrees of pain tolerance there are,

Coach Bob Templeton (left) makes a point to his captain, Greg Davis.

Greg Davis set new boundaries. One story tells it all. He broke his nose in a match, and when he returned to the dressing room simply belted it back in place with a bottle, to the horror of his team.

His entry into top-class rugby was immediate. He arrived in Australia in 1963 and forced his way into the test team that year that beat England 18-9. From that moment on selection in Australia's top teams was virtually automatic. He offered a 'never give up' approach that rallied the troops.

That year he was selected to tour South Africa in a team captained by John Thornett. There were some all-time greats in that 1963 team, including Jon White, Dick Marks, Phil Hawthorne, Ken Catchpole, Peter Johnson, Rob Heming, Thornett and Guerassimoff. Davis played 14 of the 24 matches, including the four tests.

That series against the Springboks is among the finest any Australian team has ever played. No one would have predicted that Australia would lead 2-1 going into the final test, when the South Africans equalised the count.

Respected journalist A.C. Parker wrote, in

The Springboks: 1891-1970: "The defence was excellent, and here the part played by the loose forwards, Greg Davis and Jules Guerassimoff, cannot be over-emphasized. Davis, with his tearaway speed and devastating tackling proved a scourge to fly-halves and, in particular to Oxlee. Guerassimoff, reputed to have been the last man chosen for the tour, started off poorly but developed into an outstandingly forceful flank forward, tighter than Davis and a perfect foil to him."

The next international venture was the John Thornett-captained tour of New Zealand in 1964. It must have been a rare feeling for Davis to tour his homeland and play against the All Blacks. He played in seven of the eight matches, including the three tests. Although the first two tests were lost, the Wallabies shocked the rugby world by trouncing New Zealand 20-5 in the final test. Davis and Guerassimoff simply took up where they left it in South Africa.

Chester and McMillan, in *The Visitors*, commented: "Guerassimoff and Davis stood out for their speed and intelligence in the loose," "Davis was fast in the loose," "Davis and Guerassimoff overshadowed the All Black loose forwards and were two of the best players on the field."

Back in Australia, the Wallabies beat South Africa in two tests in 1965 but lost two to the British Isles the following year.

Then Davis was selected for the 1966-67 tour of the British Isles, France and Canada, once more captained by John Thornett. Davis played in 20 of the 36 matches and all five tests. This was the infamous Ross Cullen ear-biting tour, and in retrospect this incident affected the tour as there was dissension in the team over the manner in which it was handled.

The Wallabies beat Wales and England, but lost to Scotland, Ireland and France. It signalled the passing of the guard for such sterling performers as Thornett, Rob Heming, 'Charlie' Crittle, Jim Miller, Guerassimoff, Peter Ryan, Alan Cardy, Paul Gibbs, John Francis, Russ Tulloch, Tony Moore, Dick Taylor and Dick Webb.

On his return to Australia in 1967, Davis was honoured to be one of the Wallabies in New Zealand for the 75th Jubilee Test, to which all living All Blacks were invited, and they came to the dinner afterwards. He met many of his childhood heroes that day.

New Zealand came to Australia in 1968, as did France, and Davis went on the short tour of Ireland and Scotland. Only one test was won that year, a narrow 11-10 victory over France.

In 1969 Greg Davis became part of history, being called upon to captain his adopted country. On 21 June 1969 he led Australia in a narrow 16-19 loss against Wales.

That year he took the Wallabies to South Africa, where he played in 21 of the 26 matches, a considerable feat of endurance. It was not a repeat of the charmed 1963 tour, as the Wallabies went down in all four tests. With so many retirements, the game in Australia was in a re-building phase. Greg Davis, whose bald and distinctive head kept bobbing up everywhere on the veldt, was the sole survivor of that 1963 team to tour.

The coach was Wallaby and All Black Des Connor, a great thinker and student of the game. He was innovative, having introduced the short lineout to the horror of Fred Allen and the All Blacks, but during his tenure he simply did not have the personnel to put his ideas into practice.

Although the record of the 1969 team was not a good one the team scored 465 points, beating the record set by the 1953 Wallabies. A selection error became obvious, as the Australian youth policy was overdone, and there were two Wallabies still playing in Australia, 'Charlie' Crittle and Jules Guerassimoff, who might have turned the table on the tour.

The bald-headed warrior remained the servant of the game, and did everything humanly possible to restore Australia's rugby prestige. In 1970 he was captain against Scotland in a major win (23-3), while he went up against South Africa in three tests and the British Isles (for New South Wales) in 1971. He then captained a Wallaby team to France and North America, winning one and losing one against France.

His representative career wound down in 1972. In two home tests against France, one was lost and one drawn. Then he took the team to New Zealand that year, and though he personally held up and played 11 of 13 games, Australia lost the three tests by wide margins. Chester and McMillan summed it up in *The Visitors*: "So the Wallabies completed their tour with the dismal record of just five wins in their 13 matches. They had been totally outclassed in the test series, conceding 97 points to 26 in the 0-3 loss."

That result was a considerable disappointment to Davis but it was also a low point in Australian rugby. There were few geniuses on the paddock and the Australian game as a whole had virtually no depth.

Greg could hold his head high. He never faltered, never compromised. His determination at the end of his career differed little from the start, but he was 33 years of age in 1972 and there are limits to human endurance. He had captained the Wallabies in 16 tests and led Australia out on the field in another 31 matches, a fantastic achievement. He was a leader of men, who believed that a leader should lead. That was the nature of the man, a single-minded flanker who gave no quarter and asked for none.

The Greg Davis story had a sad ending. He went back to the land of his birth, where it was discovered that he had a tumour on the brain. He died in Rotorua in 1979.

Jack Pollard concludes the tragic story in *Australian Rugby*: "When former team-mates in Australia heard of his illness, they formed a committee headed by Charlie Blunt, John Freedman and the Drummoyne club president, Eric Paton, to raise money to pay his medical bills. Drummoyne Club played a Barbarian XV which included French star Jean Pierre Rives, as part of the Davis benefit. Small Rugby clubs from the far corners of Australia contributed to the fund, which raised more than $60,000. The trustees of the fund paid for Davis's house before he died in 1979, invested the balance for his widow, two sons and daughter, and have since paid their school and medical fees."

GREG DAVIS

CAPTAIN: 47 matches (16 tests) (1 Wales 1969, 4 South Africa 1969, 1 Scotland 1970, 3 South Africa 1971, 2 France 1971, 2 France 1972, 3 New Zealand 1972)
BORN: 27 July 1939 (Matamata, New Zealand)
DIED: 24 July 1979 (Rotorua, New Zealand)
SCHOOL: Sacred Heart College (Auckland)
CLUB: Katikati (Thames Valley), Otahuhu (Auckland), Tauranga HSOB (Bay of Plenty), Drummoyne (Sydney)
NEW SOUTH WALES REPRESENTATION: 27 matches (1963-72)
AUSTRALIAN REPRESENTATION: 102 matches (39 tests) (1963-72)

PETER SULLIVAN

He Would 'Bust His Guts' in Every Game

Peter Sullivan was the third player from the Gordon club to captain Australia, after Trevor Allan and Bob Davidson. The club has always been a proud one. As the Club song goes:

A Gordon for me, A Gordon for me,
If you're no a Gordon you're no use to me,
The Eastwoods are braw, the Randwicks on a'
But the cocky wee Gordon's the pride of them all.

Some of Gordon's other Wallabies are 'Fob' O'Brien, Des Carrick, Brian Piper, Arthur Tonkin, Bevan Wilson, Brian Johnson, Jimmy Phipps, Peter Phipps, Neil Latimer, Arthur Summons, Eddie Purkiss, Ken Yanz, Don Logan, Dave Shepherd, Rod Batterham, Bruce Taafe, Dave Burnet, Laurie Monaghan, John Ryan and Steve Cutler.

Sullivan was the first and only Wallaby to have come out of Chatswood Boys' High School.

Peter Sullivan's early years are told in *The Highlanders*, by Phil Wilkins: "His early Rugby was with the Forest Club in Forestville on Sydney's North Shore after which he played Rugby in Wollongong. He had an extraordinary rise to prominence, one which he was to regret. In his initial season of first grade Rugby in 1966 he won a position in the Illawarra representative side for the New South Wales Country carnival and overnight found himself in the New South Wales team to play Queensland after just six senior games. He was barely out of school, just eighteen years of age. Upon his return to club football, Sullivan found himself a marked man. Injuries followed and his form deteriorated, and his confidence with it. In 1969, Sullivan came back to Sydney, joining Gordon because of the presence there of his old coach from the Forest, Bevan Wilson. Even then he found the rise in standard difficult, spending time in reserve grade. The summer of 1969-70 saw a fitter, harder, more enthusiastic breakaway appear for the 1970 season and after a four-year absence, he regained his State position in the back row."

His first match against a touring team was against Scotland in 1970, and the Blues were victorious by 28-14. Peter was impressive in his comeback, and was selected in the Sydney team to play the Scots. He had served notice.

Things really went his way in 1971. South Africa came to Australia that year, and Sullivan played against them for Sydney, New South Wales and three tests for Australia after appearing for the Blues against the visiting Lions earlier in the year. He was selected for his first tour, a

Peter Sullivan was never afraid to mix it with the opposition.

short, 10-game trip to France and North America. Greg Davis was the captain, and the team included some excellent players in 'Hollywood' McGill, 'Bunter' Shaw, John Hipwell, Stuart Gregory and Roy Prosser. Sullivan was doubtless relieved after the first test against France at Stade Toulouse, as it was his first test win in four matches. This period was certainly not a high-point of Australian rugby. Still, he and Davis were Australia's top flankers, and he personally was playing well. As Gordon coach Fred Testone described him: "The trouble is he only knows one way to play - and that's to bust his guts in every game." Davis, of course, was of the same ilk.

Jack Pollard, in *Australian Rugby* is somewhat critical: "Sullivan was a big, strapping forward who worked tirelessly in the rucks, but he seldom used his height to advantage in line-outs, and lacked vigour in tackles." The latter statement seems unfair.

He reached the peak of his rugby union career

in 1972, playing three times against the visiting French team, for New South Wales and then in both tests.

The first test, which was drawn 14-14 in front of a crowd of 31,694, was notable in the unsavoury incidents that occurred. Referee Warwick Cooney enraged the crowd by allowing two doubtful tries by the visitors, tough Australian prop David Dunworth was stretchered off the field after a free-for-all and Russell Fairfax, who was targeted mercilessly by the French, was concussed but refused to leave the field. Jim Webster wrote, in the *Sun-Herald*: "The match as a whole ... was marred by strong ill-feeling between the teams. The Australians were particularly incensed at the treatment meted out by the Frenchman to Fairfax. Early in the second half he was twice flattened, the first time in a late tackle and again when he jumped high to retrieve a ball, and ended by being carried off on a stretcher. When he returned to the field after treatment he was again late-tackled."

There were unprecedented scenes at the finish as touch judges Roger Vanderfield and Jim Reilly were jostled by the French players.

The final test, narrowly lost 15-16, was considered by the Ballymore spectators as one of the most vicious seen in years. As Howell *et al* put it in *They Came To Conquer*: "There was an early flare-up among the forwards and Australian flanker Peter Sullivan was left sprawled on the ground."

Jim Webster, in *The Sydney Morning Herald*, wrote: "Rugby was the real loser today, as it was the most spiteful of nearly 30 tests that I have covered. The man, and not the ball, was the target."

Later that year Peter Sullivan toured New Zealand with the Wallabies, captained by the now 33-year-old Greg Davis, who had been a magnificent Australian captain but was nearing the end of the trail. There were 13 games and Australia won five, drew one and lost seven. The tour was a complete disaster, and occasioned Davis's retirement.

Sullivan played in six of the 13 games and two of the three tests. He was injured in the first test and had to be replaced, as he was against North Otago. One personal bright light was that he was called in to captain Australia in two non-test matches.

Chester and McMillan wrote in *The Visitors*: "The best of the forwards were prop Roy Prosser and flanker Peter Sullivan, whose appearances were curtailed owing to injury."

On the way home, due to Davis's injury and subsequent retirement, Peter Sullivan was brought in to captain Australia against Fiji. In his test captaincy debut, Australia won narrowly by 21-19. One source of concern during the match was Fiji's 17-stone winger Vuniani Varo. As Ian Gleeson wrote in *The Australian*: "Varos' speed and weight caused the Australians considerable concern... Australian captain Peter Sullivan is carrying a slightly injured right shoulder he received when he tackled Varo. After the match Sullivan described the experience as 'trying to tackle a mobile rock.'"

What was for certain was that Australia had to have a hard examination of its game, and new players had to be brought in. Twenty-five players then came from Tonga in a historic 10-match tour, and Sullivan was captain in his four games against them, for Sydney, New South Wales, and both tests. Some new players put into the mix were Trevor Stegman, Owen Stephens, Ron Graham and Mark Loane.

The first test was won comfortably by 30-12, and Frank O'Callaghan wrote in *The Courier Mail*: "Outstanding Australians were flankers

Peter Sullivan and Dick Cocks, and wingers Stephens and Cole."

The result of the second test was a sensational boil-over, Tonga winning by 16-11, and even to this day many consider it to be the lowest-ever point of Australian rugby.

The year 1973 finished with a short tour of Wales and England, with Sullivan retaining the captaincy. He played in six of the nine matches, but Australia continued its poor form and lost to Wales 0-24 and England 3-20. Sullivan, who carried a knee injury, did not take the field against England.

Sullivan led Australia manfully in four tests and nine other games. His role is often underrated, and what must be kept in mind is that he played 28 matches for his country, 13 of which were tests. A captain's role can be exaggerated when a team is not of sufficient calibre, and this appears to be the situation in his time period. He was a vigorous, aggressive player who played to the maximum when wearing the green and gold.

In 1974 Peter Sullivan shocked the rugby world by turning professional, the first captain to do so in over 20 years since Trevor Allan went to rugby league. Many players had turned professional from the Union code, but many considered it was not the right thing for the Australian captain to take the plunge. He signed a five-year contract with St George, but his career was cut short by a serious knee injury.

PETER SULLIVAN

CAPTAIN: 11 matches (4 tests) (1 Fiji 1972, 2 Tonga 1973, 1 Wales 1973)
BORN: 19 March 1948
SCHOOL: Chatswood High School
CLUB: Gordon
NEW SOUTH WALES REPRESENTATION: 18 matches (1966-73)
AUSTRALIAN REPRESENTATION: 28 matches (13 tests) (1971-73)

JOHN HIPWELL

Cover Defender Supreme

THERE HAS TO BE something about the air in the Newcastle region, as every ten years or so it seems to develop world-class halfbacks. Syd Malcolm was the first, and he captained Australia and played in 18 tests from 1927 to 1934. Then came that will-o'-the-wisp Cyril Burke, who surprisingly never captained Australia but played in 26 tests from 1946 to 1958. Next in line was John Hipwell, tutored by the same Burke, and he played 36 tests between 1968 to 1982.

John Hipwell: Another master halfback from Newcastle.

'Hippie' burst on the scene in 1966, and though a mere 18 years of age he went to the British Isles, France and Canada with the 1966-67 Wallabies. Captained by John Thornett, it was somewhat of a dramatic tour, as Thornett contracted impetigo, a virus, missed a considerable number of games and did not appear in any of the tests. The captaincy load on the field was taken over by Ken Catchpole, and Hipwell, as the number two halfback, played when he could, sat back, listened and learned. His potential was obvious, and his squat, heavily muscled lower body was perfect for his position. The tour was not successful, but 'Hippie' played in 10 matches and only one of these was lost.

In 1968 New Zealand and France toured Australia, and misfortune to another opened the door for 'Hippie'. He had captained New South Wales Country against New Zealand though a mere 20 years of age and in the first test he came on as a replacement for captain Ken Catchpole. In a terrible incident, Colin Meads was endeavouring to pull Catchpole out of a ruck. 'Catchie' was trapped, Meads twisted his leg and this caused severe muscular and ligament damage. Catchpole never played top rugby again. In an odd occurrence in rugby history both captains had to be replaced, as the New Zealand captain Brian Lochore was also injured.

This was the test during which Australian coach Des Connor introduced the short lineout to southern hemisphere rugby, and the All Blacks were aghast. The All Black manager did not mince words: "I deplored the manner in which Australians played the game today. This has been a setback for Australian rugby." This, however, was the 20-year-old John Hipwell's first test, and he was picked in the second test as well, narrowly lost by Australia 18-19. Australia's only try was scored by Hipwell after a sortie on the blind side. One great one, Catchpole, was gone; another great, Hipwell, had emerged. He held his place for the single test against France, which Australia won 11-10.

Still in 1968, 'Hippie' was selected on the Australian 5-match tour of Ireland and Scotland under new captain Peter Johnson. Hipwell played in four of the five matches and both tests. Australia went down 3-10 to Ireland and 3-9 to Scotland. Though it was a disappointing tour, Hipwell had shown his class.

In 1969 there was a single test against Wales (lost 16-19), before a 26-match tour of South Africa. During this arduous tour, 'Hippie' played in 14 matches, including the four tests. A.C. Parker wrote, in *The Springboks*: "They had an outstanding scrum-half in John Hipwell, a strong player with a long pass. All four tests were lost." Ian Diehm, in *Giants of Green and Gold*, entitled his chapter on this tour 'Lambs to the Slaughter.' He concluded: "Throughout the tour, the Wallabies struggled against bigger, more physical packs and could never play to their strengths. For want of a few big, experienced forwards, the tour was lost!"

Scotland toured in 1970 and South Africa in 1971, with Australia thrashing Scotland but losing heavily to the Springboks. Hipwell was an automatic selection but missed the last test against South Africa as he had to undergo an operation for a thigh calcification.

One quality not mentioned to this point is that John Hipwell had no deficiencies in his game, and he was arguably the greatest and most effective cover defender yet seen. He was a second number eight, or fullback, and when he hit them it was with a punishing tackle.

'Hippie's' next tour was to France and North America in 1971, and Australia won and lost a test in France, always a difficult country to tour. Again, there had been changes aplenty in the Australian team, through the defection to Rugby League in previous years of people like Michael Cleary, Phil Hawthorne, John Brass, Phil Smith, John Ballesty and Dave Grimmond. Every time a great layer of talent was unearthed in rugby union players would invariably leave for financial reasons. The last test in France marked the farewell, but not for financial reasons, of Peter Johnson, who had played 42 tests, one more than Tony Miller.

France came to Australia in 1972 and these games were blood-baths which left a sour taste in the mouths of Australian supporters. Blatant punches and kicks were the order of the day. Robert Messenger wrote in *The Australian* after the first test: "One might almost be able to forgive the French for their lack of knowledge of Marquis of Queensbury rules if it were not for the aiming at the groin by one particular forward who has displayed his complete disregard for the welfare of Australian opponents in both the Sydney match and the test." 'Hippie' had to be replaced in the second test, and subsequently failed the fitness test and could not go to New Zealand on the 1972 tour. John Cornes and Gary Grey took over as half-backs on that tour.

In 1973 he went up against the surprising Tongan team, and though he played in the winning first test he must have felt happy to be ruled out of the second encounter, through injury, as Australia was defeated in one of the great boil-overs in all rugby history.

'Hippie' was the same year selected for the short 9-game, tour of England, Wales and Italy, with Peter Sullivan as captain. With Sullivan injured, John Hipwell led Australia out against England for his first test captaincy.

For the next two years, 1974 and 1975,

John Hipwell's passing was superb but his cover defence was simply the best ever seen from a Wallaby halfback.

Hipwell was the undisputed Australian captain. New Zealand toured in 1974 and 'Hippie' captained New South Wales Country, New South Wales and Australia in all three matches. Space does not allow for an exposition of his contribution to New South Wales Country rugby, but the fact is that he, coach Daryl Haberecht, and players like Stuart Macdougall, Peter Horton, Lars Hedberg, Brian Mansfield, Peter Prince, John Lambie, Chris Onus, Tony Gelling, Bill McKid, Geoff Shaw, John Weatherstone and Geoff Shaw raised the status of country rugby to unheard-of levels.

In 1975 Japan arrived and 'Hippie' captained Australia against them, as he did against England, for New South Wales, New South

Wales Country and Australia. He was then an automatic selection to captain Australia on their 26-match tour of the British Isles and the USA.

It was not the tour that Hipwell hoped for. The team, managed by Ross Turnbull and coached by Dave Brockhoff, won 19 of their 26 games, losing six and drawing one. They won only one of the four tests in the British Isles, against Ireland, and won an unofficial test against the United States on the way home. Hipwell was captain in two of the tests, against Scotland and Wales, but he had been injured in the North-Eastern Counties game. Though he battled on his injury worsened and he had to be replaced against Wales. He had serious damage to the cruciate ligaments in the leg. However, he captained Australia in nine mid-week and two test matches.

It appeared as if this was the end of the mercurial Hipwell, but he bounced back in 1978, joining Tony Shaw's tour to New Zealand. Though he played in only five of the 13 matches, he was selected for each of the tests and regarded as one of the many highlights of his tour the 30-16 demolition of New Zealand in the third. All this occurred when his friend, and Australian coach Daryl Haberecht, had a heart attack and the team had to train themselves. Haberecht was an innovator, who brought the 'up the jumper move' and the 'flying wedge' into country rugby.

The ARU originally felt that John had enough representative football and he was not originally selected for the 1978 tour, the two halves being Peter Carson and Rod Hauser. Australia asked for a replacement because of an injury to Roger Gould, and instead of sending a fullback a third halfback, John Hipwell, was sent. New Zealand writer Bob Howitt called it an "Aussie con trick." Whatever, Hippie became a key player.

Once more it looked like John Hipwell was finished, as he was not available for tours of Argentina and Fiji.

In 1981 the miracle worker was back. France was in Australia in 1981, and Hippie represented New South Wales, and then was in two winning tests against them. He made himself available once more to tour and was on Tony Shaw's 1981-82 tour of the British Isles. There were some brilliant players on that tour, such as Roger Gould, the three Ellas, Andrew Slack, Paul McLean, Mark Loane, Tony Shaw, Michael O'Connor, Greg Cornelsen and Tony D'Arcy.

For 'Hippie' it was a sad tour, as he had to leave the field with a torn hamstring against Wales. To his credit, the gutsy halfback made it back for the international against England. This would be his 36th and last test; he led the Wallabies in nine of them. In all, he played 81 matches for Australia, a mighty performance.

Howell, *et al* wrote about him in *Wallaby Greats*: "His was a career of great honour and devotion. The players who toiled with him in the sweat-box swear by him, as well they should. He always played an honest, courageous game, but he also had remarkable strength, as would readily be attested to by players he grounded in cover defence."

JOHN HIPWELL

CAPTAIN: 18 matches (9 tests) (1 England 1973, 3 New Zealand 1974, 1 Japan 1975, 2 England 1975, 1 Scotland 1975, 1 Wales 1975)

BORN: 24 January 1948

SCHOOL: Wallsend High School (New South Wales)

CLUB: Waratahs (Newcastle), New South Wales Country, Armidale, New England

NEW SOUTH WALES REPRESENTATION: 27 matches (1968-81)

AUSTRALIAN REPRESENTATION: 81 matches (36 tests) (1968-82)

GEOFF SHAW

The Master of Second Phase Play

Geoff Shaw was a talented centre who could match it with the world's best. He was squat and solid, could read a game well and was a punishing tackler.

In many ways, however, he was thwarted by a tactic that swept the rugby-playing world but was perfected by the All Blacks. It was to use the inside centre as something of a battering ram straight down the middle of the field to force a tackle and a ruck, at which time the attacking team could use the second phase ball to attack on either side. It was not a ploy for the faint-hearted, but Geoff had the will and the strength to do it and he subjugated some of his own attacking skills to these changing demands.

Geoff was a country boy from New South Wales who played 22 matches for his home state before coming north to Queensland, where he became a fixture in his highly creditable 47 games for the Reds.

Stan Pilecki, in Howell, *et al*'s *Stan the Man: the Many Lives of Stan Pilecki*, when picking his best-ever touring team, said of him: "Invaluable. After all, we would need someone to steady the game if the forwards were not going well."

For much of the time, he provided a team with stability, as he was remarkably cool in tight situations. People liked to play with him because he would never let anyone down, he was dependable and rock-like.

Ian Diehm, in *Red! Red! Red!* wrote of his arrival and influence in the northern state: "Pound for pound, the man dubbed 'Lizard' was one of the toughest tacklers in the game." He was also versatile, at various times in his career playing centre, five-eighth or even wing.

His first representative game of note was as a 19-year-old for New South Wales Country against New Zealand. Brian [now Sir Brian] Lochore led the All Blacks that day, and Shaw found himself up against Grahame Thorne and Bill Currey. The Country team was led by John Hipwell, and had a few that would make their mark in the game including Rod Batterham, Richard How, Dick Cocks, Tony Gelling, Hugh Rose, Bruce Bailey and Ross Turnbull. The Country lads fought bravely without much ball, going down to a formidable All Black team by 3-29.

His rare skills were soon recognised as he made the test team against Wales as a 20-year-old in 1969 in the only match they played. Wales was loaded, with legends of the game like J.P.R. Williams, Barry John, John Dawes, Gerald Davies, Gareth Edwards,

Geoff Shaw was steady, reliable, dependable and a fine example.

Mervyn Davies and Brian Price. Des Connor was the Australian coach, and Greg Davis the Australian captain in Shaw's first international. Australia led 11-0, but went down in a disappointing loss by 16-19.

That same year Geoff Shaw was off to South Africa with the Wallabies, again captained by the bald-headed tyro, Greg Davis. Former great Australian winger Charlie Eastes was the manager, and Des Connor the coach.

The Wallaby team was weakened by retirements and defections to rugby league, and two able tourists were left out, 'Charlie' Crittle and Jules Guerassimoff. As one of the new boys Geoff Shaw more than held up his end, playing in 16 of the 26 games, which included one test, though he was replaced in that match. The experience was invaluable for the youngster, but Diehm in his book *Giants in Green and Gold* entitles the chapter on this tour as "Lambs to the Slaughter." South Africa was much too strong. Diem noted, after the Orange Free State game that: "Geoff Shaw, the 20-year-old baby of the team, made a big impression..."

In 1970 Scotland arrived in Australia, and Geoff Shaw went up against them three times, for New South Wales (won 28-14), New South Wales Country (lost 15-18) and Australia (won

23-3) in the sole test. Geoff was in the centres with Stephen Knight. Each winger, John Cole and Rod Batterham, scored two tries, which attests to the ability of the centres. Phil Tressider, the Sydney rugby journalist, acclaimed it as "Australia's greatest victory in 71 years of test football," which was slightly over the top.

Shaw had a heavy year in 1971. First of all the British Isles arrived for two matches against the state teams, New South Wales going down narrowly by 12-14. Then South Africa toured and Shaw played against them five times, for New South Wales (lost 3-25), as captain for New South Wales Country (lost 3-19), and in the three tests, all lost. All games were subjected to violent anti-apartheid demonstrations, which made concentration difficult. Smoke bombs were thrown, and *The Argus* reporter noted: "It was the most incredible sight and deafening sound I have known on a sporting field. It was like a garish nightmare..." The tour left a bitter taste, and was most certainly the most controversial tour to occur in the history of rugby in Australia.

Then Australia was off to France and North America for a 10-match tour. Poor or at least strange food and accommodation, interminable speeches in French and match after match against French Selection teams chosen to unsettle the Aussies did not make for an overly enjoyable tour, but the two tests were shared, Australia winning the first and France the second. It was a relief to play in the United States and Canada where they could throw the ball around once more with rare abandon. Geoff played in six of the ten tour matches, including both tests.

Geoff Shaw married in 1972, and took his wife with him to South Africa, then the British Isles and Europe. Everywhere he went he took his rugby strip with him and played wherever and whenever he could. He made the Eastern Province Currie Cup team and the Junior Springboks; in London he fronted up for London Scottish, and even picked up games in France and Italy.

When he returned to Australia in 1973 he was fortunate to miss out on the Tonga debacle, but was selected for the 1973 9-match tour of England, Wales and Italy. He had lost little over his year's sabbatical and played in eight of the nine matches, including both tests.

In 1974 New Zealand came to Australia, and he went up against them five times, for New South Wales Country, New South Wales and the three tests, one of which was drawn and the other two narrowly lost.

Japan arrived in 1975, and he played for New South Wales Country against them and then in both tests. The first test was captained by John Hipwell, but he was unable to play the second test and thus the lad from Kiama was appointed Australia's captain. Howell, *et al* wrote in *They Came To Conquer*: "Geoff Shaw scored two tries, and the Japanese seemed to be intimidated by his bulk."

In 1975-76 Geoff was selected for the tour of the British Isles and the USA, with John Hipwell as captain. Once again 'Hippie' was injured, and Shaw took up the slack. He captained the Wallabies in six mid-week matches, as well as the England, Ireland and USA tests. In the Irish test, won by Australia 20-10, Peter West wrote in *The Times*: "The hefty G. Shaw varied his game shrewdly in the centre and always worried the Irish defence." Overall the tour was disappointing, injuries certainly affecting the team. The Wallabies played 26 games, winning 19, drawing one and losing six.

When Fiji arrived in 1976, Geoff captained New South Wales once and Australia three times, all matches won by the locals. This leadership success led to his selection as touring captain to France and Italy the same year. The French format was much the same as on his previous visit, the Wallabies facing rabid French Selections to soften them up. This appeared to have been successful, as the French won both tests.

'Bunter', which was Shaw's other nick-name after the roly-poly schoolboy character Billy Bunter, had always been a close friend and admirer of Bob Templeton, who lost his Australian coaching position after the French tour. Shaw moved north to Queensland, and eventually played 47 matches with them, including tours to New Zealand in 1977, Japan, British Columbia and the United States in 1978, and the United Kingdom, France and Italy in 1980.

This was really a wind-down period, and Shaw's career closed with matches for Queensland against Wales in 1978, his final test against New Zealand in 1979, games in 1979 for Queensland against New Zealand Maori and Ireland, and in 1980 for the Reds against New Zealand. He had certainly enjoyed a wonderful career.

Geoff Shaw had played 68 matches for Australia, which included 27 tests. He captained Australia in nine tests as well as 10 other matches and he saw the world as few rugby players had done before.

Bret Harris wrote of him in *Marauding Maroons*: "Shaw was a fine tactician and totally reliable under pressure. A big, burly centre, he was punishing in both attack and defence. He was also a skilled ball-handler and played the game with unusual finesse for a man of his bulk. Shaw provided the Queensland backline with authority and relieved the pressure which had been mounting on Paul McLean's young shoulders. All of the Maroons drew confidence from Shaw's presence on the field."

Team-mate Peter Horton said of him: "Geoff always loved a debate and would often hold court, cigarette in hand, on topics from football to politics. He also had his own brand of wit which at times was acidic, at times subtle – he coined Tempo's real nickname of 'Elmer Fudd'! And of course their friendship/partnership is legend. Tempo loved the banter of 'Bunter', it seemed to invigorate him! Geoff Shaw is a total rugby man, someone who has been able to make his passion his career, though he always kept things in perspective with his family coming first."

A deep, intelligent, passionate, committed, sentimental man, he has put back much into the game, working first for the QRU in various coaching and leadership roles, and now for the ARU. He is a fine man, as he was a fine captain.

GEOFF SHAW

CAPTAIN: 19 matches (9 tests) (1 Japan 1975, 1 England 1976, 1 Ireland 1976, 1 USA 1976, 3 Fiji 1976, 2 France 1976)

BORN: 27 December 1948 (Kiama, New South Wales)

SCHOOL: Edmund Rice College

CLUB: Illawarra, New South Wales, Port Elizabeth (SA), Univ. of Queensland

NEW SOUTH WALES AND QUEENSLAND REPRESENTATION: New South Wales 22 matches (1969-76), Qld 47 matches (1977–80)

AUSTRALIAN REPRESENTATION: 68 matches (27 tests) (1969-79)

TONY SHAW

A Hard Man At The Helm

TONY SHAW was the hard man's hard man. The only other Australian captain to compare with him is Greg Davis. They both went in where angels fear to tread. One of his nick-names was 'Crazy Eyes', which came from his water polo days, in which sport he was good enough to play for his state. In rugby his own players would notice this steely gaze of his when in mortal combat. He was uncompromising, of the 'take no prisoners' school.

His early rugby experiences were at Gregory Terrace, an institution which has turned out quite a few Wallabies over the years: Bill Campbell, Phil Clark, Len Forbes, Geoff Gourlay, Frank Leville, Phil Carmichael, Bill Canniffe, Mark Chisholm, Jim Clark, Michael and Bruce Cooke, David Croft, Mick and Edgie Dore, David Dunworth, Jack Fihelly, Pete Flanagan, Jimmy Flynn, Colin Forbes, Damien Frawley, Chris Handy, John Howard, Sam Kreutzer, Michael Lynagh, Mark McBain, Bob McMaster, Brendon Nasser, Vay Oxenham, Tony Parker, Peter Reilly, Harry Roberts, Nick Stiles and Clem Windsor.

When they were team-mates for the 'Reds', Stan Pilecki always enjoyed tongue-in-cheek banter about Tony Shaw. These are some of his masterpieces in *Stan The Man: The Many Lives of Stan Pilecki*: "In the early years in the Queensland team I was so mild-mannered that Tempo [Bob Templeton, Queensland coach] used to assign Shawry to king-hit me in the first ruck just to get me going. Well, it worked and pretty soon I developed into the meanest s-o-b ever to pull on a maroon jersey.

"Only trouble was that Tempo forgot to cancel his instructions to Shawry... 122 games for Queensland and 122 king-hits! Geez, is it any wonder I have a go at him about his [bald] head. Look what he did to mine."

"There's nothing I wouldn't do for Tony Shaw and I know there's nothing he wouldn't do for me. To prove it, we do absolutely nothing for each other."

"Shawry's no extremist, mind you, although he told me once he believed in the death penalty. How else are you going to stop hookers losing tight heads, he wants to know?"

"Shawry was the only rugby player in Queensland on a retainer from Norbert Byrne and Col Waldron, the QRU's two resident optometrists, and you've got to gouge a lot of eyes to attract the attention of those two discerning talent scouts."

Tony Shaw was a tough man, who could easily have graced a Springbok or All Black pack.

AUSTRALIA
RUGBY 1979

"He also doubles in finger-breaking, but this is something of an acquired taste, for the connoisseur only..."

"A real role reversal is the switch Shawry makes every time he walks off a football field and reverts to a nice bloke again."

"When I put out my newspaper column I had to rely on a ghostwriter [Wayne Smith] who took on more liberties than Tony Shaw used to when the referee was on the far side of a ruck."

"Where the All Blacks are concerned, what you see is what you get – as opposed to Shawry, when what you don't see is what you get!"

"In a recent game Australia showed as much imagination as Tony Shaw choosing his hairstyle." [In his later years Tony went as bald as the proverbial billiard ball, becoming locally famous for an egg commercial.]

"The selectors did as much for consistency as Tony Shaw has done for Brisbane barbers. There is no way he would ever win the Queensland Barbers' Association most valuable customer award."

All this was in great fun. The real Tony Shaw was better summed up by Bret Harris in The *Marauding Maroons*: "Tony is the rare blend of toughness and technical brilliance which separates a good player from a great player. He was probably the most completely equipped forward in Australian rugby in the past decade. A hard-driving forward in the best All Black tradition, Shaw was an outstanding rucker and mauler. His forte was protecting his team's possession but he could spoil the opposition's ball with equal effectiveness. In the short line-out Shaw was second to none as he outwitted taller and more spring-heeled opponents. Shaw was a cunning lineout technician and the majority of Queensland's and Australia's variations can be attributed to him. Shaw was not as naturally talented as Loane or McLean, but he shared their fanaticism for physical fitness."

Chris Handy spoke of Shaw in Diehm's *Red! Red! Red!*: "Shaw wouldn't fight anyone but frightened everybody in the international world. He couldn't run and score tries. He'd always look for someone else, even at training. He wasn't the athlete that Loane and Cornelsen were, but he wouldn't give in and tried to match it with them at training. His mauling was better than anyone's and he came into his own because mauling became the game. He epitomised what the Queensland struggle was all about.

"He never left it for a moment to retaliate. 'Otherwise', he'd say, 'you were always in the other guy's pocket.' There was an incredible bond between Shaw and McLean. If someone bumped McLean, Shaw would be there in an instant to deal with him.

"'Switch on' was Shaw's catchcry to get the concentration going. As a leader Mark Loane was Conan the Barbarian. His tactics were simple. 'Follow me', he'd say. If we were in trouble, he'd gather us around and say, 'I'll pick the ball up from the back of the scrum and drive it forward. You follow me. Right?" Shaw was different. I would do anything for Shaw – not that I wouldn't for Loaney – it was just different. There was a contract between us. Shaw could ask anything of me. By the way, when he finished school, he had all that long, curly hair and was doing male modelling for Myer and David Jones."

Paul McLean added his sentiments in *Red! Red Red!*: "Shaw was physically and mentally hard – all that and a bit more. He was not too compassionate on the field but he was very helpful to new players and always made people feel welcome in the team. He was a terrific ambassador on tour. Some guys aren't great mixing with the black blazer brigade but Shaw was and took pressure off people. There were things he did that the public didn't see. He was very supportive of teams in which he played. Technically, he was a great player with enormous strength and stamina."

What was for certain was that the triumvirate in the back row, Tony Shaw, Mark Loane and Greg Cornelsen, was never bettered in Australian rugby history.

It did not take the young Tony Shaw long to get into the swing of top-level rugby. At 20 years of age, he showed up well for Queensland against Tonga in 1973, and forced his way into a 9-match tour of England, Wales and Italy that same year. He was chosen as a second rower. Shaw played in five of the nine games, including the tests against Wales and England, both of which were lost. Though so young, he was already a test player.

In 1974 Shaw was in the Queensland team against the visiting All Blacks, and his career seemed to have stalled as he was not picked for any of the three tests. He realised at this time that number eight was long-gone, as the legendary Mark Loane 'owned' the position, and so he decided to concentrate on the flanker position or second row, where Roger Davis and John Lambie were favoured.

It was just a momentary stutter in his career, and when Japan and England visited in 1975, he once more secured his place at the top. The 'go-forward' style with physical confrontation put zip into the Australian pack.

After the English tour, Tony was off to tour the British Isles and France in 1975-76, with John Hipwell as captain. Shaw played in 19 of the 26 matches, including the five tests, against Scotland, Wales, England, Ireland and the USA. It was not an overly successful tour, as only the final two tests were won. An injury to Hipwell did not aid the team, and Geoff Shaw had to pick up the pieces as playing captain. Tony was the only backrower to play in all the tests.

On his return to Australia he played three tests against Fiji, as well as one match for Queensland, and all were won. The resurgence of Queensland rugby was complete by this point, the 'Blues' being defeated 42-4 in 1976, to the complete and ecstatic joy of Queensland fans. The same year was a tour to France, which was unsuccessful and proved to cause the demise of national coach Bob Templeton. Tony played in eight of the 10 games, but the 15-18 and 3-34 test losses were humiliating. It appeared as if many players' careers were in jeopardy as well. It was not to be the case for Tony Shaw.

In 1978 innovative coach Daryl Haberecht took over as Australia's coach, and he began discussions with Tony Shaw and Paul McLean. He felt that these two were pivotal in his plans, and selected Shaw as his captain. Tony was not even captain of Brothers at the time, and Mark Loane was the obvious choice in many minds. But it was Shaw and the qualities he brought to the game that Haberecht wanted.

It was an interesting situation, for when Wales came the captain of Queensland was Mark Loane, but Tony was appointed as test captain. This Loane-Shaw rivalry continued over the next few years at both the state and national levels, and though no enmity existed between the two they were absolutely contrasting personalities and their philosophies or ethics of the game certainly did not match. They were different types of leaders, and it was entirely debatable as to which style was superior.

Australia won the two Welsh tests, by 18-8 and 19-17. After the first test coach Haberecht said: "It is a great credit to Wales that they could apply such pressure. It is even more credit to the Australians that they withstood it." He went on, however: "I was appalled by the deliberate kicking from some of the players, and I cannot recall any Australian player who indulged in this nasty exercise."

The stage was set for an horrendous second test, and so it proved, with Graham Price sustaining a badly broken jaw, attributed to Australian prop Steve Finnane. It remains one of the most controversial incidents in Australian rugby history. The Welsh manager presented his view somewhat forcibly: "One of my players is in a hospital bed tonight with a double fracture of the jaw. If we are rugby people and condone thuggery then I don't want any part of it." The Australian pack on that day of infamy, as some called it, was: Greg Cornelsen, Mark Loane, Tony Shaw (capt.), Garrick Fay, David Hillhouse, Stan Pilecki, Peter Horton and Steve Finnane.

Tony Shaw was retained as captain on the 1978 tour of New Zealand, and he played 11 of the 13 matches, including the three tests. The first two were lost 12-13 and 6-22, and then Daryl Haberecht had a heart attack and was hospitalised. The team rallied in his absence, and in a remarkable display overran New Zealand by 30-16, Greg Cornelsen scoring a record four tries. As veteran reporter Bob Howitt wrote: "Stewards order swabs at racetracks for the sort of form reversal that saw the Wallabies go from 6-22 down in Christchurch to 30-16 up in Auckland.

"But blood samples weren't needed to establish the cause of this dramatic turnaround. It could be described in one word.... motivation."

Tony Shaw's speech when the game was slipping away was held to be vital. As Adrian McGregor reported it: "Captain Shaw knew... he gathered the team together, his face angry, and told them (major expletives deleted) that they'd bloody well lose unless they got committed again.

"We haven't come this far to throw it away, have we?" he asked. "Look around you. Look at each of us. Look at your mates. You'd do anything for them, wouldn't you? Well, do it now. Give me your guts." The rest is history, and 'Crazy Eyes' had rallied the troops.

Dave Brockhoff took over the coaching in 1979, and there was a single test against New Zealand for the Bledisloe Cup. The Australian captain was now Mark Loane, and Australia beat the All Blacks 12-6. Quite staggeringly, this was Australia's first home success over New Zealand in 45 years, and one of the greatest rugby scenes ever followed with the Aussies running round the stadium brandishing the Bledisloe Cup. As Howell *et al* put it in *They Came To Conquer*: "Australia's win, and the subsequent lap of the SCG with the Bledisloe Cup, put more fire into these contests than had been present for many years. This match, more than any other, is responsible for lifting the trophy to the important position in world rugby that it now enjoys and also did a great deal to drive the Wallabies towards the top handful of test-playing nations."

There were games for Queensland against New Zealand Maori and Ireland in 1979, but the only two tests, against Ireland, were both lost under Shaw's captaincy.

Mark Loane was back into the captaincy later that year for the 7-match Argentina tour, but Shaw played in six of the seven matches and did lead Australia in one mid-week game.

Loane went off to South Africa in 1980, and Tony Shaw was the undisputed captain once more. In a remarkable home series against the All Blacks, Australia won two of the three tests.

As Howell, *et al* put it in *They Came To Conquer*: "Australia retained the Bledisloe Cup with this emphatic win and thoroughly deserved it." This win remains one of the highlights of Tony Shaw's long rugby career.

Shaw's captaincy was retained on a tour of Fiji in 1980 and home games with France in 1981, when Australia won all the tests.

Next he captained the 1981-82 Wallabies to the British Isles. He was the first Queenslander since Bill McLean in 1947-48 to captain Australia in the U.K. Tony Shaw married Bill McLean's daughter so the genes are certainly right for their children.

Sir Nicholas Shehadie was the manager and Bob Templeton the coach on this tour, and it was disappointing considering the strength of the team, as only 16 of 23 games were won. Tony played in the Ireland, Wales and Scotland tests, but in the latter match disaster struck. He was questioning the referee while the Scottish captain, Bill Cuthbertson, kept niggling him. Shaw turned and hit Cuthbertson with a right, knocking him down in front of the referee, 60,000 at the game and millions watching on TV.

Thus Shaw was dropped for the English match and Loane took over as captain. The incident had happened in a split second, and unfortunately, and perhaps unfairly as Cuthbertson aggravated the situation, it was the end of his test captaincy.

In 1982 he played against Scotland, of all teams, for Queensland and then two tests, and against Argentina in 1983.

There was a token appearance in 1984 for Queensland 'B' against the All Blacks, but he himself rang down his own curtain on his representative career. He was 31 years of age.

Tony Shaw had a remarkable career, and it should be not be stained by a single rush of blood. He captained his country in 15 tests, and captained Australia in 14 other matches, a rare feat. He played 84 matches for his country in all, 36 of them tests.

Tony Shaw should be remembered for what he was, a tremendous competitor who never took a step back. It was Shaw and a few like-minded types who brought not only Queensland but Australia to the forefront of rugby countries throughout the world. Tony Shaw was without doubt one of the greatest captains Australia has ever had.

TONY SHAW

CAPTAIN: 29 matches (15 tests) (2 Wales 1978, 3 New Zealand 1978, 2 Ireland 1979, 3 New Zealand 1980, 2 France 1981, 1 Ireland 1981, 1 Wales 1981, 1 Scotland 1981)
BORN: 23 March 19153
SCHOOL: Gregory Terrace
CLUB: Brothers
QUEENSLAND REPRESENTATION: 112 matches (1973–83)
AUSTRALIAN REPRESENTATION: 84 matches (36 tests) (1973-82)

MARK LOANE

The Thinking Man's Number Eight

Mark Loane is universally held to be among the premier number eights in Australian rugby history. Choosing the best is a matter of conjecture, but the pundits will never cease debating and analysing. Picking teams of the greatest this and that will, however, never cease despite the impossibility of making comparisons over time.

Which other names, if any, might be thrown up for debate? Well, Arthur Buchan of 1947-48 fame would be one, then there were Syd Middleton, Nev Greatorex, Charlie Fox, Jack Ford, Wylie Breckenridge, Bob Loudon, Aub Hodgson, Keith Cross and Dick Thornett. Many of these players were intermittently picked as flankers as well.

What is for certain is that Mark Loane, and players like him, occasioned a revolution in Queensland rugby. They were men of steel and resolve. As well as Mark there was the mighty Tony Shaw, who had a rough edge to his play that is rarely seen in Australian rugby. He and Loane, in particular, would have been automatic selections in any team in the world when they were in their prime and when one includes the brilliant Paul McLean and hard rocks like David Dunworth, Bill Ross and Stan Pilecki, any opponent knew there would be trouble.

Mark Loane was a country boy, born in Ipswich, Queensland. His father was a judge who moved around the north of Queensland on judicial matters, and because of this Mark went to Gympie Christian Brothers before being sent to Nudgee Christian Brothers as a boarder. It did not take him long to fit into the rugby ethos of the school.

Throughout the years Nudgee had been one of the great nurseries of rugby talent, with players like Mick Freney, Duncan Hall, Ross Hanley, Bernie Doneley, Shane Sullivan, Sean Hardman, Pat Harvey, John Fogarty, Voy Oxenham and John O'Neill emanating from there.

It was thought that he would proceed to another nursery of rugby, Brothers, but instead gravitated to the University of Queensland Rugby Club because he was studying there. It also had more than its share of internationals and a couple of old Wallabies, Jules Guerassimoff and a former Wallaby captain 'Chilla' Wilson, were still coaching the Uni lads. Wilson's brother, Fergus, was also involved. 'Chilla' later emerged as a much-beloved Australian manager. Stan Pilecki said of him in *Stan the Man: The Many Lives of Stan Pilecki*: "The ultimate in the laid-back manager. Great in taking off pressure put on the players...

Mark Loane ran like a train without a station.

Didn't manage anything. The type of manager you wanted when you didn't need a manager." Mark was drawn to him: "He was a mystic, like most of those playing rugby at the University." Queensland and Australian coach Bob Templeton, who had a particular affiliation with the University, attended most of their games.

It did not take 'Tempo' long to realise that the young Loane was a prodigious talent and in 1973, at 18 years of age, he was selected to play for Australia against the first Tongan team touring. Australia had picked 18-year-old backs before, but such young forwards are rare as generally they are still physically immature. This was not the case with Loane, who was well-built, solid and fast. And he thought then, as he still does, that the number eight position was the best position on the field. Somewhat of a mystic himself, he outlined that it was the geometric centre of play, the number eight having an unparalleled view of both sides of the field.

Tonga was handled easily in the first test (30-12), as expected by the general public who had no notion of Tongan rugby, but those same pundits were horrified when the Wallabies stumbled in the second test, losing a hard-fought game 11-16. The loss was heralded as the worst in Australian rugby history, and Evan Whitton inferred that Loane would never be capped again. How wrong he was! Only some years later did the world come to realise the high standard of Tongan rugby. Their players, raw-boned and disruptive, proved that they could tackle any team out of its rhythm.

Before the match Loane was told that he had to remain in the scrum until it had broken up, and twice the Tongans exploited him. As he said, on reflection, it was the last time he took notice of anyone on how to play his position.

His period in the dog house did not last long, as his obvious talent and single-minded commitment rose to the surface. He got in one match against the All Blacks in 1974, Australia losing narrowly in a nail-biter by 6-11. The mighty Loane, heralded as playing like a train with no station, was well and truly back.

In 1975 he played a single test against Japan (37-7) and three games against a touring England team. Both tests were won, by 16-9 and 30-21, although the Reds went down to them.

On the basis of these performances Mark was picked on the 1975-76 tour of the British Isles and North America, captained by halfback John Hipwell. It was no longer a 9-month, 41-game tour like the 1947-48 Wallabies embarked on, but it was still most attractive. Mark was injured after playing four consecutive matches, and from 12 November until 27 December he was unable to play, thus missing the Scottish and Welsh internationals.

When he did recover he played in eight straight games, which included the English international (lost 6-23) and the Irish (won 20-10).

Stan Pilecki in *Stan The Man: The Many Lives of Stan Pilecki*, was asked by the authors to select his all-time touring team. 'Loaney' was one of them. As he said: 'Let's face it, we need a captain. Besides, someone should be in charge of our Culture Club, and he is the only one who could have got me to Hadrian's Wall and Stonehenge."

A Culture Club was regularly formed on touring teams and they would organise tours to places of cultural interest, like the British Museum and the National Gallery. There were few takers, but Loane would persist. Somewhat of a perfectionist, he had certain obsessive qualities and had a black book in which he would tick off what he had seen and done. Pilecki reflected that once Mark was visiting a church and there were 133 steps to the turret, which he counted as he walked up, and ticked it off in his little black book with a wry smile.

Fiji came to Australia in 1976, and Mark played in the three tests and led Queensland in one match. All matches were won convincingly.

The same year there was a short tour of France and Italy, which was not for the faint-hearted. The Wallabies kept coming up against French Selection after French Selection, each loaded with hatchet men bent on mayhem. Geoff Shaw was Australia's captain, and both tests were lost, 15-18 and 6-24. They even had trouble against an Italian XV, winning narrowly 16-15. The performances placed Bob Templeton's tenure as coach in jeopardy. Strange food, poor accommodation, and interminable speeches in French did not make for an enjoyable tour.

Wales visited Australia in 1978, Mark captaining Queensland to a close loss and then Australia won two spiteful tests, during which Steve Finnane became part of Australian rugby folklore. As Howell, *et al* put it in *Stan The Man: The Many Lives of Stan Pilecki*. "Then there was Steve ('Sort 'Em Out') Finnane. The first word he ever learned as a child was 'aggression.' He was a barrister who always advocated equal rights, particularly espousing the credo 'an eye for an eye and a tooth for a tooth'. He had another name, 'the Gunfighter', and in good western tradition always added a notch to his belt when he knocked an opponent out.

"Pilecki, Horton, Finnane! They were involved in a shoot-out, like that at the legendary western site the O.K. Corral, only this was on the hallowed Sydney Cricket Ground.

"The test started with the ever-loquacious Price [Welsh prop] directing his verbal harangue at the Wallaby front row. He said to 'the Gunfighter'! 'It's going to be a long day for you, Finnane.'

"'Sort 'Em Out' replied calmly: 'Not for you, mate!'"

"In the first five minutes [of the second test] Price had to leave the field holding a badly broken jaw..."

All this was a bit much for Loane. Tough, rugged and ever willing to put his body on the line, he never transgressed the mythical ethos of the game. He was always scrupulously fair.

In 1978 Loane was picked to tour New Zealand. Though he was normally the Queensland captain, coach Daryl Haberecht figured that Tony Shaw was the one he wanted to lead the Wallabies. The Loane-Shaw rivalry was not of their making, but they were the two most dominant forwards in the game at this time, and there was also Paul McLean on hand from the northern state with leadership qualities.

What is for certain is that Loane and Shaw were poles apart in philosophy and mode of thought. Mark was single-minded in his approach to the game, while Shaw was a 'blood and thunder' type who revelled in the physicality of it all. In later life they have become much closer, but in those days one led Brothers, the other University and never did the twain meet other than on a rugby field.

The 1978 tour to New Zealand did not turn out well for Mark, as he only played against Hawkes Bay and Manawatu because of injury. As he later said: "There was nothing worse travelling from town to town and listening to the variant advice of local physiotherapists and succumbing to their treatment." A tourist carrying an injury, particularly a serious one, is not a happy camper, and he lamented: "How many cold meat pies and sausage rolls can one eat at after-game functions?"

One of the ambitions of his life was realised in 1979 as he was selected as Wallaby captain, in a one-off test against New Zealand which Australia won by 12-6. The standard of Australian rugby had now reached the point where any Wallaby-All Black match was fiercely contested. New Zealand Maori came that same year, and Mark captained Queensland to an exciting 18-18 draw.

Also, in 1979, a surprising and spirited Irish team toured and although he captained Queensland, Loane was not captain in the two tests, both won by Ireland.

It was a topsy-turvy time for him, as he was selected to captain Australia on a 7-match tour to Argentina. Mark played in six of the seven matches, including the two tests, one won and one lost.

Stan Pilecki had called Mark "the kiss of death" by this time. When a player was injured Mark was called on to provide a medical prognostication, at which time 'Loaney's' imagination would run wild: "It looks like a medial tear," or "It could be fractured ribs, on the other hand it might be an injury to the spleen." Invariably the player went off, with Mark ever the prophet of doom.

Following this tour Mark went off to South Africa, ostensibly to gain medical experience and play a little rugby, both of which he did. But Mark Loane was and is an inquisitive man, a Renaissance type and he wanted to live in this wonderful country and see apartheid at first hand. Over the years he has climbed mountains in Nepal, visited Easter Island, travelled by ship to the Antarctic and visited ancient Indian sites in Arizona with the author. He no longer has the little black book to tick off what he has seen, but the world's wonders are his oyster. He hears a different drummer, as they say, and is interested in the arts and archaeology. He is a one-man Culture Club.

While in South Africa he played in the Currie Cup and was selected as a Junior Springbok, two unusual feats. On his return to Australia in 1981 he immediately went into the test team against France and captained Queensland against Italy.

1981-82 included another tour to the British Isles, with Tony Shaw as captain. This was probably the peak of Loane's rugby career, as the 18-year-old who started against Tonga was now a rampaging 27-year-old. In a remarkable feat, he played 17 of the 23 matches, including all tests. In the game against Scotland Tony Shaw punched his opposing captain during a disagreement in front of the referee, but those close to the incident claim Cuthbertson should have received an Academy Award for his performance that day.

After that event, Shaw was dropped from the captaincy and Mark took over against England. He also captained Australia in four non-test matches.

His career ended in 1982 against the visiting Scottish team. He captained Queensland against them, and then led Australia in the two tests. The first was lost 7-12, the second was a runaway 33-9 drubbing by the Wallabies.

Mark Loane, now an opthamologist, has put his rugby years in perspective as he searches out other goals and other interests. He is no ordinary rugby man. He is a man of the world, a deep thinker who understands the transient nature of sport and the never-ending glory of all those other things the world has to offer.

One of his lesser known qualities is compassion. Though there is a generation gap between the author and Mark Loane, the author was confronted by a terrible situation, as he found himself in Sydney with his wife unexpectedly dying of cancer. Mark found out about it and flew to Sydney to be at her side. His visit bucked her up and revived her spirits, albeit temporarily. One has to understand that moments are treasured in such heart-rending tragedies. As he put it so well: "It's at moments of crisis that true friends come together." So add compassion to those qualities that make the great one tick.

MARK LOANE

CAPTAIN: 13 matches (6 tests) (1 New Zealand 1979, 2 Argentina 1979, 1 England 1982, 2 Scotland 1982)

BORN: 11 July 1954 (Ipswich)

SCHOOL: Gympie Christian Bros/Nudgee Christian Brothers

CLUB: University of Queensland

QUEENSLAND REPRESENTATION: 1973–82

AUSTRALIAN REPRESENTATION: 61 matches (28 tests) (1973-82)

PAUL McLEAN

'The Boot'

Bret Harris, in *Marauding Maroons*, wrote: "Paul McLean was a rugby thoroughbred. Spanning three generations his famous family produced seven international rugby players. This unique record is unmatched by any code of football anywhere in the world. The McLean dynasty began in 1904 when Doug McLean played tests against the British Lions. Three of his sons, Doug Jr, Jack and Bill played for Australia. Bill was the captain of the 1947-48 tour of Britain. A fourth son, Bob, did not play representative football, but he fathered Jeff and Paul, who did. Bill's son, Pete, was the seventh member of the family to wear the Gold jersey.

"McLean inherited an innate rugby intelligence from his footballing forebears. He was the pivotal figure around which all of Queensland's strategies revolved. Dextrous of both hand and foot McLean's skills were universal. He could quite easily fit into an Australian Socceroo team and his mammoth punt-kicks would delight any Australian Rules supporter. Of all the Maroons McLean was the most naturally gifted. His powers were subtle and precise... McLean is unflappable under pressure. His icy-cool exterior is legendary and he rarely makes a mistake. He possesses a ruthless eye for opposition weaknesses and is able to read a game better than any of his contemporaries."

Malcolm McGregor wrote an excellent biography of McLean, and in it he stated: "There is a certain irony in the fact that someone of Paul McLean's self-effacing nature should have been one of Australia's most controversial figures."

And such he was, and the controversy had a specific line of demarcation - the line dividing the state of Queensland from that of New South Wales.

For all those north of the border, McLean was a rugby genius, born and bred to right the embarrassments of Queensland's rugby over the years. The hopes and prayers of Queenslanders were passed onto him. David Dunworth, tough Wallaby prop, immortalised him when he defined Queensland's Holy Trinity. God the Father was Mark Loane, the Son was Tony Shaw and the Holy Spirit was Paul McLean.

How apt his designation was, for McLean had this certain ghost-like quality, sifting his way effortlessly through opponents when he felt like it and stitching the side-line and splitting the goal-posts as if some hidden hand was directing him. His coolness was legendary. While everyone else's heart would be fluttering, McLean's pulse rate would be normal.

There were no two ways about it, he was a footballing genius, among those who flit across the world's stage every now and then.

Paul McLean supplied what Australian rugby had missed over the years – a reliable kicker.

But there was controversy, not of his making other than his continued brilliant play. It just so happened there was another genius strutting his stuff, Mark Ella, and he had captivated and entranced the New South Wales supporters of the code just as McLean had done in the north. It was a pity, really, as both were gifted, almost freakish, and they unfortunately came to the fore at approximately the same time. Ella was a genius. McLean was a genius. And vociferous support came on state lines.

The controversy was not particularly of their making, other than through their feats on the field, and both were quiet, restrained and unostentatious. Not so the supporters.

There were differences between them to be sure. McLean was more of a tactician, controlling time and space. Ella's game was attack, and he could drift between players like few before or since. One's position on the controversy, if one endeavoured to be fair, was really a philosophical clash on styles. But McLean had one extra thing to offer to the debate, and that was that he was a world-class kicker, which Australia had prayed for over the years, but Wallaby teams had too often lacked. The All Blacks would confront the Wallabies over the years, and the Aussies continually paled as their penalties and conversions missed and the All Blacks maintained a high percentage of success. Paul McLean was the first pure kicker to ever appear in an Australian team.

So the selectors had a real dilemma, as they wanted Paul, and they wanted Mark. McLean it was who was considered more adaptable, so he often found himself at fullback or even centre. McLean was a superb athlete. While at Nudgee he received the James Baxter Memorial Prize as the most outstanding cricketer, student and footballer in the school.

Paul McLean came to national notice in 1974 as a 20-year-old. After a handful of interstate games, he went straight into the Australian test team against the All Blacks. In his first match, at the Sydney Cricket Ground, he played five-eighth to John Hipwell, who captained Australia that day. Paul's brother Jeff was on the wing. It was a tough first test, as the weather was atrocious, but he held up well despite the conditions, New Zealand winning 11-6.

He went up against the All Blacks for Queensland, kicking two penalty goals, and then was selected for the remaining two tests. He again kicked two penalty goals, and a conversion, in the second test, a 16-16 draw. Howell, *et al* wrote in *They Came To Conquer*: "Hipwell and McLean both played well for Australia, controlling play in the final stages." The final test was won by New Zealand 16-6, McLean scoring all of Australia's points. Paul McLean had proven himself against the toughest competition in the world at that time.

Japan was next to visit, and McLean played one match for his State and two internationals, all won. In the first test in Sydney, Paul was placed at fullback, and he scored two tries, a penalty goal and five conversions. He made six of eight kicks to establish a new Australian test record of 21 points in a 37-7 victory.

In the Queensland game, he scored a try, nine conversions, a dropped goal and a penalty goal, for 28 points. An international star had been born. In the final test, playing five-eighth, he kicked six conversions and two penalty goals, 18 points in all. He had scored 39 points in the two tests.

In 1975-6 he was selected to tour to the British Isles and the USA, and played in 18 of the 26 matches, mainly as fullback. It was a disappointing tour, as the only two tests won were against Ireland and the USA.

Malcolm McGregor, in his biography, wrote: "For Paul McLean the tour marked his emergence as a player of world class. In eighteen matches he scored 154 points, the greatest ever contribution by a Wallaby tourist. His general play was consistently excellent and on some occasions, inspirational. The realisation that he was the only reliable good kicker, and the only available fullback, placed him under intense pressure, but he handled it with a coolness and aplomb that endeared him to team mates and spectators alike. His eighteen appearances in twenty-four games afforded him almost no rest, especially as two of the games he missed were the final two. But he proved that he was both resilient and unflappable. The more demanded of him, the more he produced. The tour was the crucible in which Paul McLean's talents took positive shape. The earmarks of his game were impeccable handling, perfectly judged kicking, and an accurate football intellect."

Fiji toured in 1976, and he played for Queensland once and Australia three times against the visitors, all matches being won.

That same year there was a tour of France and Italy and although McLean more than did his part in playing in all ten matches, only four were won and both tests were lost. Coach Bob Templeton was replaced after the tour.

In 1978 the Welsh came, and this has been developed elsewhere. The two tests were won, with Paul at five-eighth, but the general thuggery was criticised and Graham Price's broken jaw dominated the pages.

He made his first New Zealand tour in 1978 under captain Tony Shaw, but an injury prevented him from playing in more than five matches. He had to be replaced during the second test after being unable to play in the first.

Games for Queensland and Australia against New Zealand, New Zealand Maori and Ireland followed in 1979, after which he toured Argentina with Mark Loane's team. The experience was a great one, but the Argentinians proved a handful and the tests were split.

In 1980 Paul McLean captained the Australian team to Fiji, leading the side in one mid-week game against Nadi and the single test, won 22-9.

This gave McLean a 100 percent record as test captain, as surprisingly this was the only time he led his country. Though quiet and unassuming he led by his brilliant example, and it does not seem right that he only captained Australia once in a test. Paul McLean was a born leader, but Tony Shaw and Mark Loane were occupying the captaincy position. He has to be deemed unlucky. Mark Ella, in contrast, captained Australia ten times.

France and Italy visited in 1981, and then McLean went back to the British Isles in 1981-82. At the time of departure it was generally held that this was the best Australian team, under Tony Shaw, to ever leave Australian shores. Paul McLean played in 15 of the 23 games and at five-eighth against Ireland and Wales, inside centre against Scotland and full-back against England. He was easily the top scorer with 118 points, but for once the magic from his boot deserted him in the tests.

The end of Paul's international career could not have been more dramatic if it were scripted. New coach Bob Dwyer, in 1982, dropped two of Queensland's favourite sons, Roger Gould and McLean, for the first test against Scotland. It was the first time a Queensland crowd ever booed an Australian team, and it is little wonder that the visitors won by 12-7.

The public clamour was such that Gould and McLean were reinstated for the second test against Scotland at the Sydney Cricket Ground. In one of his finest-ever displays, McLean kicked five penalty goals and three conversions, equalling his own Australian record of 21 points, and Gould scored two tries, which was an Australian record for a fullback. Paul's retirement was announced before the game, so it was a perfect finish.

With characteristic modesty, he said, after the game: "Having lost three of the internationals in Britain and then again last week, it was very satisfying. I can't say any more than that."

Paul McLean was a true genius, and a leader of men. He played 70 matches for Australia, 30 of them tests. After he retired, his leadership qualities have been clearly evident, as he has reached the highest administrative levels of the game both in Queensland and Australia.

That the McLean Stand at Ballymore is named after his family is evidence of how Queenslanders feel about the contribution of his family to the game. Their names live on through this honour.

PAUL McLEAN
CAPTAIN: 4 matches (1 test) (1980 Fiji)
BORN: 12 October 1953
SCHOOL: St Edmunds CBC, Ipswich/Nudgee
CLUB: Brothers Club
QUEENSLAND REPRESENTATION: 1973–82
AUSTRALIAN REPRESENTATION: 70 matches (30 tests) (1974-82)

MARK ELLA

A Genius Trips The World's Stage

Mark Ella: An instinctive genius.

MARK ELLA occasionally did things on the playing field that smacked of pure genius. It had to do with seeing an opening, knowing where to be, instinctively recognising where others were, gliding between players, finding another gear, and so on. When he played with his brothers Gary and Glen, it is as if they had some inner knowledge. They made it all look so easy, and we are left to wonder what might have been if they had consistently been placed together in a test team, as they had been at Randwick.

His former coach Bob Dwyer said of him, in *The Winning Way*: "Mark Ella, as we know, was in a class of his own. Mark was very correct in his play and very confident. He was also extremely coachable...

"Mark Ella was, like Glen, a beautifully balanced runner, and he had a superb change of pace. He was also blessed with a superb running style. When he accelerated, he had a way of sinking his hips in a manner reminiscent of one of those prestige cars, which lower their suspension as they are about to take off. He also had a way of extending his legs out in front of him when he ran which, strangely enough, used to remind me of an emu. When he accelerated, he did not lean forwards and push off, as many runners do, but rather reached forwards with his legs in long, smooth strides...

"One of Mark's greatest strengths as a player – and this was true of his brothers, too – was an intense power of concentration. It sometimes seemed to me that the Ellas had eyes like laser beams. If there was a loose ball, they would fasten their eyes on it, not allowing anything to distract them, and pounce on it like birds of prey...

"Mark played with a natural flair..."

David Campese, in his autobiography *On A Wing And A Prayer*, picked his All Australian team: "I wouldn't have to think too long and hard about my choice for the first five-eighth position. Mark Ella is, in my opinion, the best rugby player I have ever known or seen. Why? Just the way he played, the manner in which he could release others and turn up in the unlikeliest of positions or places simply because of his telepathic reading of a game. Nothing worried Mark, and his skills were unbelievable. Even years after his apparent retirement from top-class rugby, his skills remained of a high quality. He was always a great thinker of the game but opponents could never legislate for Ella, because he would suddenly do something no other player in the world would ever think of achieving."

All too often people generalise and define rugby as a middle or upper class sport. The Ellas alone negate that statement. Their grandfather, one Alfred Ella, was a white man who worked in a Sydney woolshed, married a part-aboriginal woman and they went to Yarra Bay to live in an aboriginal settlement.

Gordon and May Ella, the boys' parents, were itinerant workers who moved around the east coast until settling at La Perouse. They had a family of five girls and seven boys. Frank Keating elaborated on the story in Gordon Bray's *The Spirit of Rugby*: "May and Gordon Ella brought up their 12 children in a shanty hut, which a nailed-up plywood partition turned into a two-roomed job. They daily slept on shared mattresses on the floor; no privacy, no sewerage; there was one cold tap; a bath was a communal trough in the yard, a shower was when it rained, for the roof was a sieve.

"Yet it was, the boys will tell you, a home with a lot of love and laughter. May was the feared matriarch; Gordon... was the romantic who loved to catch mullet off the cliffs when he had time away from the factory where he worked."

One of their emotional releases was sport, and La Perouse had a junior rugby and cricket team. Mark and Glen were twins, while Gary was born twelve months later, so a lot of their physical outlets were practised together. When they attended Matraville Boys' High School, they came to the attention of Geoff Mould, who coached them at the school and later with the record-breaking 1977 Australian Schoolboys Team. Many of the moves that they performed at Matraville found their way to Randwick, as coach Bob Dwyer inveigled them there, and then to New South Wales and the Wallabies.

Each of the Ellas was tailor-made for rugby league, particularly from the socio-economic viewpoint, but despite dazzling offers they never seriously considered leaving the rugby code.

It was not long before they were ensconced in the Randwick firsts, and from that point on they were worshipped by Randwick supporters. They provided a new dimension to the running game.

Mark made an immediate impact on New

South Wales rugby when a few days short of his 20th birthday he was put up against the visiting Irish team, which has ever been renowned for the quality of its fly halves. He found himself up against the brilliant Tony Ward, but as usual took it all in his stride. Paul McLean from Queensland was the Australian five-eighth at that time.

The next match saw Sydney play Ireland. Once more Mark went up against Tony Ward, and to everyone's surprise Sydney broke the Irish 6-game winning streak, recording a 16-12 victory. There were some outstanding Australian players in the Sydney lineup including Laurie Monaghan, Phil Crowe, Mick Martin, Tony Melrose, captain Peter Carson and Mick Mathers.

After the Irish tour Mark was on his first overseas tour, to Argentina under Mark Loane, and he was one of the 'dirt trackers', filling in on the mid-week games. He missed out in the two tests, Tony Melrose being preferred.

The following year, 1980, Mark came into his own. He played for Sydney, New South Wales and in all three tests for Australia against the All Blacks. Dave Loveridge was the All Black captain and Tony Shaw led the Wallabies.

Sydney was no longer an easy beat as they had brilliant, committed players and fierce pride. The All Black match was drawn 13-13, and then New South Wales took the All Blacks to the limit before succumbing by a 4-12 score. On 21 May 1980, still 20 years of age, Mark Ella played his first of 25 tests. His opposite number was the experienced and clever Wayne Smith but Australia ran out winners by 13-9, with Ella kicking a dropped goal.

The second test at Brisbane was lost 9-12, and the third was a 26-10 Wallaby victory. This was the infamous 'food poisoning' match, with All Black suspicions suggesting the wave of sickness that swept through their team might have been deliberately caused. A general euphoria surrounded the victory as Australia had retained the Bledisloe Cup, won the previous year.

Australia went to Fiji with a team captained by Paul McLean, and Mark played in two of the three matches, but not the test. Michael Hawker was selected as five-eighth.

In 1981 France came to Australia, and Paul McLean was picked for the Ballymore test. In Sydney, the five-eighth was Mark Ella. It was at this time that rugby supporters were savagely divided, by state boundaries, as to which player should be in the test team. McLean had the added advantage that he was the main kicker, but he also could play at fullback which allowed both of them to get onto the paddock.

The young Ella was seeing the world in a hurry, as after the French visit he was off to the British Isles for a 23-match tour under captain Tony Shaw. Mark played in 14 of the 23 matches, including two tests, but McLean got the nod in the first tests against Ireland (won 16-12) and Wales (lost 13-18). The weather was so hopeless that the Barbarians match was cancelled.

In 1982 Scotland came to Australia and then Mark Ella was selected to captain Australia on its New Zealand tour. The Australians arrived as holders of the Bledisloe Cup. This was the tour when ten of Australia's top players ruled themselves out of the trip. All but one were Queenslanders, and though the cited reason was that there was too much rugby and too much travelling, most observers believe that the real cause of the defection was that Bob Dwyer had taken over as coach from the popular Queenslander, Bob Templeton. The three Ellas were selected. Many new players, including Andy McIntyre, Steve Cutler and David Campese, took their opportunity. The players who opted out were Paul McLean, Brendan Moon, Mark Loane, Tony Shaw, Peter

McLean, Tony D'Arcy, Bill Ross, Stan Pilecki and Michael O'Connor, all Queenslanders, and Gary Pearse from New South Wales.

Mark played in nine of the 14 matches but New Zealand won two of the three tests, which was expected following the defections. Chester and McMillan, in *The Visitors*, wrote: "Ella was the big influence in the backs [in the first game], and much of the credit for the win must go to his contribution of 11 points." "In Mark Ella and 19-year-old Campese the Wallabies had two outstanding players who exhibited a confidence that approached arrogance," "The Ella brothers all had impressive games," "Ella was a classic general," "The three Ella brothers were all great performers, particularly Mark."

Mark Ella had impressed with his leadership and demeanour as captain of Australia, and retained the position during visits in 1983 of the USA, Argentina and New Zealand teams. Following these visits, Mark was honoured by captaining his second tour overseas, an 11-match visit to Italy and France. The French section of the tour was rugged, playing French Selection after French Selection who seemed to be intent on working over the Wallabies. One test was drawn and the other lost.

In 1984, with Alan Jones at the helm, Andrew Slack took over the captaincy. Jones had resolved that whichever team won the interstate clashes would provide Australia's captain.

New Zealand toured in 1984 and then there was a short tour to Fiji. Then came the 1984 excursion to the British Isles. Mark played in 10 of the 18 games, and all tests. This was the greatest tour in Australian rugby history and is now called the 'Grand Slam Tour.' The Wallabies won all four tests, the first time an Australian team had accomplished the feat. And even more remarkably Mark Ella scored a try in each of the tests, a Wallaby first.

Afterwards, a mere 25 years of age, Mark Ella announced his retirement. He seemed to be reaching a new pinnacle in the sport. He did make a comeback with Randwick later on, but he stepped aside with humility and style. There was world-wide disappointment, as they knew of the Ella genius and hoped it would never end.

Mark Ella played 61 matches for his country, which included 25 tests. He was captain in 10 of these tests and he also led Australia out in 10 other matches.

The jacket of *Path To Victory* endeavoured to sum up his career. "Mark Ella is as indigenous to Australia as kangaroos, koala bears, Paul Hogan and a Foster's tinny. The first Aborigine to captain Australia in any sport, he won twenty-five test rugby caps, leading his country on Wallaby tours of New Zealand and France. He was Young Australian of the Year in 1983 and was made a Member of the Order of Australia a year later. Gloriously instinctive, Ella wound up his career by making history with a try in each of the four tests on the Wallaby tour of the British Isles. Quitting when only twenty-five, he became a lucid TV commentator with the ABC. Ella and wife Kim live just up the hill from Coogee Oval – the scene of so many of his triumphs with brothers Glen and Gary for Randwick."

MARK ELLA

CAPTAIN: 20 matches (10 tests) (3 New Zealand 1982, 1 USA 1983, 2 Argentina 1983, 1 New Zealand 1983, 1 Italy 1983, 2 France 1983)

BORN: June 5 1959

SCHOOL: Matraville High School

CLUB: Randwick

NEW SOUTH WALES REPRESENTATION: 26 matches (1979-84)

AUSTRALIAN REPRESENTATION: 61 matches (25 tests) (1980-84)

ANDREW SLACK

The Grand Slam Captain

Whatever else in life Andrew Slack will do, he will forever be known as Australia's first 'Grand Slam' captain. This feat might be equalled, but it will never be surpassed.

Andrew Slack is an interesting case study of a captain. He is quiet, thoughtful, introspective and intelligent. At the same time he can pull out his guitar and bring everyone together with a few songs. He was not of the 'Into the valley of death' mode, but he led by example. When there was a kick through he would never give up the chase, and players notice that. He led by force of character.

In *Path To Victory*, Terry Smith wrote of him: "On the rugby field, Andrew Slack, former Queensland University student of literature, ex-schoolmaster, once a fledgling journalist and now stockbroker [back to TV journalism now], is a quiet achiever. An organiser in midfield with a sharp, cool brain. Master of the half-break. A man not lacking in the social graces. A man who realises that life doesn't exactly revolve around a sporting encounter.

"And without being pushy, Slack proved a remarkably popular captain of the Grand Slam Wallabies. Whether leading the players in song as he played his guitar or providing a steadying influence on and off the field, this engaging chap unquestionably was in charge. Slack had style, he had sincerity, he set the example.

"Slack is a survivor, too. A slim, trim veteran of nine Wallaby tours and more than 120 matches for Queensland, he lost his test spot on several occasions but always managed to bounce back. Since making his test debut against Wales in 1978, Slack's centre partners have been Martin Knight, Billy McKid, Michael Hawker, Michael O'Connor, Geoff Shaw, Paul McLean, Michael Lynagh and Brett Papworth. On all his tours he wore a maroon beanie knitted by his mother Julia, who was worried he might catch cold in New Zealand in 1978.

"With no worlds left to conquer, Slack quit rugby after the 1984 tour of the British Isles, but regained the captaincy when he made a comeback two years later. Captain Slack was back to lead a World XV in Cardiff and bring the Bledisloe Cup home from New Zealand. On his return, he deservedly was given the Order of Australia for his services to rugby."

Mark Ella added his comments in *Path To Victory*: "Slacky probably was the only person who could have handled the captaincy in the British Isles. He was fantastic. Every team needs a cornerstone, and Slacky was it. We all had lots of respect for him. He's been around for a long while, but he's not really that old.

"With players like Gould, Campese, Moon, Lynagh, Farr-Jones and myself, we had a backline full of exciting individuals. I'm not saying

Andrew Slack led by the force of his character.

Slacky lacked initiative and flair, but his role was to settle the play down. Be the link man. Not be happy-go-lucky or adventurous. Slack did it to perfection and always seemed to be there when he was wanted.

"Although he's a quiet person, Slacky is a great communicator. Because he had the respect of the team, he could come up and say, 'I don't think you're doing this right', or, 'Why don't you try this?' Slacky didn't have to get up and rant and rave. He preferred to listen to people and do things in a quiet sort of way. Because of his experience, he could analyse things and understand how people are feeling."

Andrew made his state debut at 19 years of age in 1975 against Combined Services as a five-eighth, a position which he specialised in originally. However the retirement of Wallaby centre David L'Estrange left a big gap at outside centre. The selectors experimented with Andrew Slack and he did not let them down. From that moment on he proved he could be an outside centre, though many thought his best position might be at inside centre because of his safe hands and clever ball-distribution skills.

In 1976 the Australian centres were Geoff Shaw, then in New South Wales but later to come to Queensland, and Greg Shambrook, and 'Slackie' teamed up with Shambrook against an exciting Fijian team. The experiment was successful, Queensland downing Fiji by 28-16.

By 1978 the qualities that Slack brought to the game were evident, and he appeared for Queensland against the visiting Welsh team. Geoff Shaw, now north of the border, was in the centres with 'Slacky', and though the Reds lost by 24-31 both men proved more than capable of holding the Welsh centres Ray Gravell and Steve Fenwick.

When the test team was announced there were two newcomers in the Australian line-up, Andrew Slack and Martin Knight. The previous match between the two countries was at Cardiff during the 1975-76 tour, and Australia had been trounced by 3-28. There was plenty of drama surrounding the 1978 tests. In an extremely physical first match, which Australia won 18-8, coach Daryl Haberecht exclaimed: "I was appalled by the deliberate kicking from some of the players, and I cannot recall any Australian player who indulged in this nasty exercise."

Slack's performance was such that he and Knight were retained for the second test, won by Australia to the tune of 19-17. This test was infamous for the Graham Price-Steve Finnane clash, which resulted in a badly broken jaw for the Welshman. These tests, both brutal encounters, were a tough introduction for Slack, but he showed that he kept his cool, fed his wings, and had a minimum of mistakes.

On the basis of his form Slack was selected on his first Wallaby tour the same year, to New Zealand, with Tony Shaw as captain. He played in two of the three tests. The three-quarters on that tour were Paddy Batch, Martin Knight, Bill McKid, Brendan Moon, Slack and Steve Streeter. He played in the two losing tests, and was replaced by five-eighth Ken Wright in the third, which was won by Australia 30-16 after Daryl Haberecht suffered a heart attack.

In 1979, with Slack partnering Geoff Shaw, Australia beat New Zealand in a one-off test 12-6, thus presenting Australia with the Bledisloe cup. As Howell, *et al* put it in *They Came To Conquer*: "Australia's win, and the subsequent lap of the SCG with the Bledisloe Cup, put more fire into these contests than had been present for many years. This match, more than any other, is responsible for lifting the trophy to the important position in world rugby that it now enjoys and also did a great deal to drive the

Wallabies towards the top handful of test-playing nations."

The same year there were games for the Reds against New Zealand Maori and Ireland, Andrew being injured in the Irish match. In the two Irish tests Bill McKid and Tony Melrose filled the centre berths. There were many good centres plying their trade in those years.

Later that season 'Slacky' was off to Argentina with Mark Loane's Wallabies, where he played in six of the seven matches. The first test was surprisingly lost by 13-24, but the Wallabies came back to turn the tables in the final encounter by 17-12. The centres in both tests were Andrew Slack and the brilliant Michael O'Connor.

There was a short tour to Fiji in 1980 with captain Paul McLean, a first for Australia, and 'Slacky' played in the three games there, including one test. O'Connor was again in the centre with him. Slack had many partners over the years, and he fitted in with all of them, subjugating at times his own game to play to the strengths of the other person.

'Slacky' liked the travelling life-style he now found himself in, so he departed Australia in the summer of 1980-81 to visit his roots in Ireland, and while there he played for the Wanderers Club. It is little wonder that he was so popular in Ireland whenever he visited there on tour.

After matches for Queensland against France and Italy in 1981, he was away from Australian shores again, to the British Isles with the 1981-82 Wallabies. Tony Shaw was the captain, and Sir Nicholas Shehadie and Bob Templeton manager and coach, respectively. Slack more than proved his worth by playing in 17 of the 23 matches, which included all four tests. 'Slacky' had Michael O'Connor with him in the first test against Ireland (won 16-12), Michael Hawker in the second against Wales (lost 13-18), Paul McLean in the third against Scotland (lost 15-24), and Hawker again in the England test (lost 11-15). He showed himself as 'Mr Consistency'. The tour was a fabulous experience, soured somewhat by the poor test record.

On his return to Australia, he played for Queensland and Australia in 1982 against the visiting Scottish side, and then was off to New Zealand with Mark Ella's Wallabies for a 14-match tour. The up-and-down nature of test rugby was driven home to him on this tour. Hawker and Gary Ella paired in the centres for the first two tests, but once more he rebounded to partner Hawker in the final test.

One feature of this tour, however, was that his leadership qualities came to fruition, as he captained Australia in three mid-week, non-test matches.

In 1983 Slack played tests against the USA, Argentina and New Zealand before embarking on an 11-match tour of Italy and France under Mark Ella. His only test was against Italy, though he played in eight of the 11 matches. Gary Ella and Michael Hawker occupied the centre slots against France.

It looked as if his test career might be on the wane, but in 1984 mercurial coach Alan Jones decided that whichever captain was on the winning side in the New South Wales-Queensland clashes would be his Australian captain. It was Andrew Slack, then captain of the Reds.

When New Zealand came, in 1984, 'Slacky' was elevated to the test captaincy. The tests were all close, Australia on top in one and New Zealand in two. Michael Hawker was his partner.

Slack led the Wallabies on a short three-match tour to Fiji, and in an ominous sign for Hawker, though he did not tour, Michael Lynagh was tried at inside centre. Coach Alan

Jones had a real dilemma with two outstanding five-eighths, Mark Ella and Michael Lynagh. He did not want to drop Ella because of his attacking skills, and he had to have Lynagh in the team because of his kicking skills. A consummate player, Lynagh fitted into inside centre easily.

Then the Wallabies were off to the British Isles for the fabled 1984 tour, with Andrew Slack as captain. Books have been written on this tour, now known as the 'Grand Slam tour'. In a first-ever performance by an Australian team, every one of the tests was won. It was a high point in Australia's rugby history, and the captaincy of Slack, the brilliance of Ella, the coaching of Jones and the balance within the team were lauded throughout the world. It was now a matter for the history books. Australia had won the Grand Slam.

On his return to Australia, 'Slacky' retired temporarily. But the love of the pig-skin proved to be too great, and after all he was just 30 years of age. His friend Stan Pilecki, tongue-in-cheek, had this to say: "I had a little inside information about why Slacky was so keen to get back into the action. You see, he was having trouble settling into his new job as a journalist. Now I'm not saying he couldn't recognise a good story when he saw one, but I reckon if he'd been covering the Last Supper, the best quote he would have come up with would have been: 'Pass the wine!'"

He later returned to the test captaincy and in 1986, after matches against France and Argentina at home, he captained a team to New Zealand which returned with the Bledisloe Cup.

His final sortie was in the 1987 World Cup. A disastrous semi-final loss to France ended Australia's aspirations. Ignominy followed when Wales beat Australia by 22-21, Australia's hopes disappearing with the send-off of David Codey.

This was to be Andrew Slack's final test. He had been an outstanding example for all Australian rugby players. He played in 133 games for his state and an incredible 87 matches for his country, 39 of them tests. He was captain in 19 tests, and led Australia out in an additional 15 matches. Slack is the most capped Queenslander of all time.

Bret Harris said of him, in *Marauding Maroons*: "Always mindful to pack his guitar on tour, Slack was a great source of entertainment to his teammates. A deeper thinker than most rugby players, Slack was the Maroons' resident poet and philosopher. He delighted in seeking out subterranean cafes in foreign cities and playing to unknown audiences through smoky hazes and dim lights. If a Welshman could sing and play rugby as well as Slack, a statue of him would be standing in Cardiff Square."

Andrew Slack was Queensland Sports Star of the Year in 1985 and in 1986 was made a member of the Order of Australia.

ANDREW SLACK

CAPTAIN: 34 matches (19 tests) (3 v New Zealand 1984, 1 Fiji 1984, 1 England 1984, 1 Ireland 1984, 1 Wales 1984, 1 Scotland 1985, 1 Italy 1986, 1 France 1986, 3 New Zealand 1986, 1 South Korea 1987, 1 England 1987, 1 USA 1987, 1 Ireland 1987, 1 France 1987, 1 Wales 1987)

BORN: 24 September 1955

SCHOOL: Villanova College

CLUB: Souths

QUEENSLAND REPRESENTATION: 133 matches (1975–87)

AUSTRALIAN REPRESENTATION: 87 matches (39 tests) (1978-87)

STEVE WILLIAMS

The Uncontested Captain of 1985

Andrew Slack will always be heralded as the captain of the Wallabies on their sensational 1984 Grand Slam tour of the British Isles. A good question for a quiz show would be: Who was the vice-captain? It was towering second row forward Steve Williams.

Steve, or 'Swill' as he was nick-named, was forever the hard man of the various packs in which he played. All teams need such an individual in the trenches when it counts. When the giants Steve Cutler and Bill Campbell were introduced to world rugby the opposition needed to negate their obvious height advantage, and they therefore had to be protected by their own team. This was one of 'Swill's' roles, but it did not end there. He was not simply a hatchet man, he was an excellent jumper in his own right, and surprisingly fast in the open.

Born in the country, a grazier's son, he was sent to 'Joeys', where the second great religion was rugby. What Wallabies had been produced there over the years: Des Bannon (1946), Mark Bell (1996), Jack Blomley (1949-50), Mathew Burke (1993-2004), Chris Carberry (1973-82), 'Bill' Cody (1913), Declan Curran (1980-83), Tony Daly (1989-95), Ted Fahey (1912-14), Eric (1927-29) and Jack Ford (1925-30), Bill Gunther (1957), Ted (1961-63) and Vince Heinrich (1954), 'Jake' Howard (1970-73), Paul Johnson (1946), Darren Junee (1989-94), Tim Keleher (1992-93), Ted Larkin (1903), John Malone (1936-37), Bruce Malouf (1982), 'Bill' Monti (1938), John O'Gorman (1961-67), Brian Piper (1946-49), Ernie Reid (1925), Barry Roberts (1956), Peter Ryan (1963-66), Bill White (1928-32), Steve Williams (1980-85), Harry Woods (1925-28) and Bill Young (2000-04).

Terry Smith wrote about 'Swill' in *Path To Victory*: "Born in Narromine, New South Wales as a grazier's son, Steve Williams learnt his rugby at the greatest of rugby nurseries, St Joseph's College at Hunter's Hill, Sydney. Not only was he Australia's captain when he quit after the 1985 season, but he was his country's most capped second-rower with twenty-eight tests. A deep thinker, he played a dominant role running through the game plan with his colleagues just before the Wallabies took the field.

"Williams went into Australia's pack in 1980 and stayed there to make five Wallaby tours. Twice his jaw was broken by unscrupulous rivals, but he bounced back to figure in some of Australia's most dramatic test victories. Never has he played a more dominating game than in Australia's 16-9 win over Ireland in 1984. His scrummaging, lineout jumping and work-rate were simply phenomenal. At times he got out to the loose ball like a breakaway. For such a big man, Williams' co-ordination and ball sense were uncommonly good.

"The towering stockbroker they call Swill can be playful as a puppy when relaxing off-duty or making an after-match speech. Nobody queried his right to take over from Andrew Slack as Australia's captain in five tests after being vice-captain in the British Isles. With a quiet authority, Steve Williams commanded respect because he never shirked the issue."

Mark Ella provided his own slant: "When Alan Jones made Steve the senior forward, it was the best thing that could have happened. He took the responsibility and really drove the forwards. I must say Steve's lineout ability surprised me. Some of his jumping was sensational, particularly in the Irish test. It enabled us to take pressure off Steve Cutler by being able to throw to 2, 4 or 6. To Williams up front, Cuts in the middle or Steve Tuynman at the back. Our lineout was complete.

"Apart from his work in the lineouts, Swill wasn't there just as a motivational-type forward. He was the big scrummager in the pack, a powerhouse in the second row. That undoubtedly was his best point. I think his all-round game improved 100 per cent in 1984. As vice-captain, Steve Williams had a very big role to play and he handled it beautifully."

Steve had all the requisites for success, but in life a little luck and the right timing can come together to make for success. In Steve's case, it was the fact that he was at Manly, when a dynamic and talented Alan Jones became the coach. When Jones took over coaching of the Australian team, he had Williams clearly in his

Steve Williams: A no-nonsense, multi-skilled contributor to fine Wallaby teams.

sights, as he was aware of his value in making a pack cohesive.

In May 1980 Steve Williams went to Fiji for a 3-match tour and played in every match. His first test came against Fiji, Australia winning easily by 22-9.

It was also in 1980 that he first got his breakthrough at home, being picked for New South Wales to go up against the All Blacks. Mick Mathers was the state captain, and they had as their opponents probably the best in the world at the time, Andy Haden and John Fleming. New South Wales went down in a tight match by 4-12. Williams' performance secured a place in the first test, at the Sydney Cricket Ground, the captain of the Wallabies being Tony Shaw. Williams had a great test and easily held his place for the second encounter at Ballymore.

That second test was a nightmare for Williams, for when he unloaded a punch on Mark ('Cowboy') Shaw he got one in return, which broke his jaw and he had to leave the field. Up to this point he had been very successful in the lineout, gaining several opposition throws.

Sometimes an accident like a broken jaw can end a career, the individual becoming 'gun shy', but Williams took it all in his stride and fronted up in 1981 in four matches against the visiting French, for Sydney (won 16-14), New South Wales (lost 12-21), and two tests (won 17-15 and 24-14).

This earned him a tour with Tony Shaw's team to the British Isles in 1981-82, but Shaw went into the second row with his Queensland partner Peter McLean, so Williams acted the role of a 'mid-weeker', always performing to his highest. When the captain was dropped for punching the Scottish captain Bill Cuthbertson, Williams came into the test team against England at near the end of the tour.

Still in 1982, Williams found himself in a Mark Ella-captained squad to New Zealand, and he played in eight of the 14 matches, including the three tests, one of which was won. Duncan Hall was his main partner until he was injured, then Peter Clement took over. In the background, however, and very significant, was a young giant named Steve Cutler who was gaining invaluable experience. The coach at the time was Bob Dwyer.

1983 was a busy year, as he played for Australia against the USA, Argentina twice and New Zealand, and then went on tour with Mark Ella's Wallabies to Italy and France. On the latter tour, he played in the three tests, against Italy (won 29-7), and France (drawn 15-15 and lost 6-15).

The year 1984 was perhaps the most significant in Australia's long rugby history. There were three matches to toughen the team up and give them the final test before the team led by Andrew Slack was off to the British Isles. What is not generally known is that Williams captained Australia in the first match of that tour, against London Division, won by 22-3. Though not a test, he led the team out with great pride. He captained the team on another mid-week occasion.

The Grand Slam was won by this 1984 team, the first time ever for an Australian team. Steve Williams led the pack in the four tests, and his role was pivotal, though mainly unsung. He ran the engine room, gave the pack a hard edge, protected Steve Cutler, and won lineout ball.

The Grand Slam was won in the final test against Scotland on a chilly day. Although Australia only led 12-9 at the half it was a romp at the end, by 37-12. Over the tour Australia had scored 12 tries to one, Mark Ella scored in each of the tests, and Michael Lynagh's 21 points against Scotland equalled Paul McLean's record against an IRB country. The victory included Australia's highest-ever test score and greatest winning margin over an IRB country. It was heady stuff, and that evening Steve Tuynman, Andy McIntyre and Nick Farr-Jones, dressed in kilts, sang 'Auld Lang Syne' with the dinner guests.

Terry Smith wrote, in *Path To Victory* that "... the next morning, as the hungover Aussies stood in their overcoats outside the North British waiting for a bus to take them through the Scottish countryside to Gleneagles and St Andrews, Steve Williams, Bill Calcraft and Steve Tuynman suddenly plucked three big brooms from nowhere and started sweeping the footpath. Whistling as they worked, they swept the gutter, the street, and when a bus or car stopped, they swept the windows. It broke everybody up. A clean sweep, indeed."

While many key figures in the Grand Slam squad retired or took a sabbatical in 1985, Steve Williams kept going and it provided that little extra to cap a distinguished career. He captained New South Wales and Australia to victories over Canada and Fiji, before finishing his career with a close, 9-10 loss to New Zealand in a one-off test.

The big man then bowed out, at the top, as the captain of his country. He had played 56 matches for his country, 28 of them tests, and was on six Australian tours: twice to the British Isles, once to Fiji, twice to New Zealand and once to Italy and France. Not bad for a grazier's son from Narromine.

Steve Williams gave marvellous efforts for a country he loved. A big and hard man, he was not a captain of the screaming variety, or 'into the valley of death' mode. Generally a quiet person, he led by the example he set.

STEVE WILLIAMS

CAPTAIN: 7 matches (5 tests) (2 v Canada 1985, 2 Fiji 1985, 1 New Zealand 1985)
BORN: 29 July 1958 (Narromine, New South Wales)
SCHOOL: St Joseph's, Hunter's Hill
CLUB: Manly/Drummoyne
NEW SOUTH WALES REPRESENTATION: 21 matches (1980–85)
AUSTRALIAN REPRESENTATION: 56 matches (28 tests) (1980-85)

SIMON POIDEVIN

Mr Consistency and Mr Fitness

Simon Poidevin was a country boy, born and bred at 'Braemar', a 360-hectare property not far from Goulburn. His parents raised fat lambs and some cattle. A few other Wallabies of reasonably recent vintage hail from there as well, including Jim Roxburgh, John Klem, Barry McDonald, Jim Hindmarsh and Alan Cardy. That country upbringing never left Simon Poidevin. Among the sophistication, a certain naivety remains in his own basic value system, his pride in playing for his country and his desire for perfection in anything he undertakes.

There were a few athletic genes in the family that might have helped him somewhat. His mother and brothers were excellent runners, and mother, while at Sydney University, plunged into the cricket and basketball teams while his father, who was as strong as a horse, indulged in a little boxing.

His mother's father was Les Hannon, a three-quarter who was on the verge of travelling with the 1908 Wallabies but broke his leg prior to departure. On his father's side, his cousin was Dr Leslie Oswald Poidevin. He was the first Australian to score a hundred centuries at all levels of cricket, and was one of those who founded inter-club cricket in Sydney. The Poidevin-Gray shield remains as testimony to his efforts. He also played Davis Cup tennis in the early days.

So the genes were right, but no one could ever have foretold that young Poidevin would have one quality in spades, unbelievable determination. All his peers have commented on his motivation, how he pushed himself relentlessly. When the others had finished training, 'Poido' would be still out there doing one-arm push-ups. He was an example to all rugby players with his innate desire to improve and excel.

One of the coaches who worked with him for many a year, the mercurial Alan Jones, said: "But then we've got Poidevin, a rugby freak..... There is no saying what Poidevin is capable of. Some have been as good, none better."

Rugby writer Greg Growden said: "Without Poidevin, Australia most probably would not have won the World Cup, as the Wallabies relied enormously on his rat cunning, enthusiasm, and ability to inspire others. Poidevin proved yet again he is as good as any rugby player Australia has yet produced."

Perhaps the only flanker who can be spoken of in the same breath is Col Windon. They were different types. Windon was never as fit as Poidevin – but who was? – but he was uncanny with the ball in hand. All one can say is what a double they would have been if they had played together.

Nick Pitt, in *The Sunday Times*, wrote: "His task is to tackle, to rip, to put his head in the mangle without question, and having done it, to rush to another part of the field and do it again. But Poidevin's importance to Australia is also symbolic. He is the exorcist, the exploder of the All Black myth."

Poidevin shot into the rugby limelight in 1980. Spectators realised that there was something special with this redhead who kept cropping up all over the field, making tackles, rucking, forging ahead. In that breakthrough year he played two games in Fiji, one a test, and six times against the All Blacks, for Sydney (drew 13-13), New South Wales (lost 4-12), three tests (won 13-9, lost 9-12 and won 26-10) and a match for Australian Universities. What a start to a representative career.

The Fijian tour was his first as a Wallaby. He played against Nadi and then was selected for his first test. Little did he realise at the time that there would be many more tours to come and another 58 tests. As he put it in his autobiography *For Love Not Money*: "We went down to Pacific Harbour, the lovely resort just along the Coral Coast from Suva, to train and have a game of golf, and it was there that the test team was announced. Number six was Simon Poidevin. I've made many, many test teams since, in varying and surprising circumstances, but nothing will ever replace the elation at hearing my name read out the first time."

The Fijian adventure was a walk in the park compared to the All Black games that followed. Despite the rugged encounters, Steve Williams having his jaw broken, Australia had won the series, the first in a home series in almost half a century. The Bledisloe Cup was Australia's. As Poidevin put it: "My first season of international rugby was a dream start to my career. After succumbing for generations to All Black-forward power, it looked like we had at last found a dominant pack of our own to complement the marvellous backs that Australia seems to produce year in and year out."

In 1981 France came to Australia, and Poidevin went up against them four times, including two winning tests. Australian rugby was on a high and much was expected of the Tony Shaw-captained team to the British Isles

Supreme fitness was one of the secrets of Simon Poidevin's success.

1981-82. Hailed as the greatest team to leave Australian shores, the side had a disappointing tour as only one of four internationals, the first against Ireland, was won.

There were many reasons offered after the event. Paul McLean's kicking was not up to his usual standard in the tests, the scrum lacked size and power, Tony Shaw showed his pique in Scotland by dropping Bill Cuthbertson and John Hipwell getting injured was a blow. The cancellation of the final match against the Barbarians because of the snow was symptomatic of their luck and Douglas Lord, the journalist, did little to assist matters as he wrote venomously of a Queensland-New South Wales rift in the team.

Disappointed, Simon Poidevin decided to change clubs from the University of New South Wales to Randwick, a move which he never regretted.

In 1982 Scotland played in Australia and then Simon was off to his third Wallaby tour, to New Zealand. He played in nine of the 14 games, including the three tests, New Zealand regaining the Bledisloe Cup with a 2-1 series win. This was the tour for which ten Wallabies declared themselves unavailable, Bob Dwyer believing to this day it was because of his selection as coach instead of the popular Bob Templeton. The defection opened the way for many young hopefuls, including David Campese and Andy McIntyre, to get their chance.

In 1983 Simon played against the USA, Argentina and New Zealand, and toured with Mark Ella's team to Italy and France for an 11-match tour. The latter was a sad tour because of poor accommodation, poor refereeing and dirty play. Mark McBain finished up with a fractured skull with cerebral fluid dripping down his throat. As only Australians can, the team nick-named him 'the Leak'. Then Steve Tuynman finished the last test with a broken nose and his ear hanging off. It was all a bit too much.

If 1983 was disappointing, 1984 was one of the highlights of Simon's career, as after a short tour to Fiji he was a vital part of Andrew Slack's Grand Slam team, the first from Australia to beat the four 'home' countries, and then the Barbarians.

Poidevin summed up the occasion in *For Love Not Money*: "It was easily the best Rugby team I'd ever been associated with. Four years beforehand when we won the Bledisloe Cup we had some fantastic backs, but for a complete team from front to back this outfit was almost faultless. There was nothing they couldn't do. We could play open attacking rugby, as shown by the number of tries we scored, or else percentage stuff when we needed to. And our defence throughout the tour was almost impregnable. It was the complete side. We also had Jonesy: the ultimate coach, an absolute workhorse, extremely smart, able to get his message across and with an extraordinary ability to read players' moods and know precisely when to increase or ease the workload."

In *Path To Victory*, Terry Smith evaluated 'Poido': "Simon is the personification of the Exocet missile. He is so proud to play for Australia that I get the feeling one day he will run through the dressing room without feeling the splinters. That's how much it means to this man of almost suicidal commitment.

"With a heart in the Phar Lap category and fitness that is fathomless, Poidevin is arguably the world's No. 1 breakaway now he has improved his skills with the ball. Like Jean-Pierre Rives, who captained France, he isn't frightened to spill his blood for the cause...

"When the red-haired Randwick player returned from the Grand Slam of the British Isles, league's supercoach Jack Gibson said bluntly: 'Simon Poidevin is the best prospect to come along in rugby since Ray Price. With his intensity, he's no risk.'

"Poidevin beats most of the backs in the sprints at training, and has scored test tries against the All Blacks and England as a result of tailing breaks by super-quick David Campese. He has legs that can run for ever, and prides himself on being in front of the pack in the laps at training. While the others seek a cooling drink after the tackling and mauling drills, Poidevin stays on the field doing push-ups.

"I see Poidevin as standing for the thousands of Diggers who went in at Gallipoli, or fought and swore in the trenches and stood by their mates to the end."

In 1985 Canada came to Australia, followed by Fiji, and at the end of the year Australia played a losing test against New Zealand. In the following year Poidevin reached another of his goals. After helping to dispose of Italy and France, Simon Poidevin captained Australia in two winning matches against Argentina. As he put it in *For Love Not Money* "... words can't describe how happy I was when I was made Australian captain for the opening test. I was absolutely overjoyed. It's a responsibility that deep down I'd always wanted; I felt that I'd served my apprenticeship for it and my time had come. .... to lead Australia in any test match had always been my big dream, so there was no prouder person in the world than me on July 6, 1986 when I led the boys onto Ballymore."

Andrew Slack, however, came back to captain Australia on a 14-match tour to New Zealand, and 'Poido' stepped aside. Another great moment in Australia's rugby history came when the Aussies won the Bledisloe Cup once more.

The World Cup was next on the list, and it was a great disappointment to be so narrowly beaten by France, and then lose the play-off for third place to Wales at Rotorua. As 'Poido' put it: "When the final whistle went, I ran off the ground. I wanted to get away from that cauldron of hatred and smell of defeat. It was one of my biggest Rugby disappointments."

Still in 1987, Simon achieved another of his goals as he captained the Wallaby team to Argentina and Paraguay. As he wrote: "That tour suddenly brought a breath of fresh air into my Rugby. The apartheid issue had surfaced, and for a time it appeared as if Australia would mount a rebel tour." Though this did not occur, the issue left a bad taste in everyone's mouth. However, after a 19-19 draw against Argentina, an injury to his hand ruled him out of the final test, which the Pumas won.

On May, 1988, Poidevin announced his retirement from international rugby, but it was no sooner proclaimed in June than he captained New South Wales against England, before playing for Randwick, New South Wales and Australia in three tests against the All Blacks. It was the shortest retirement on record.

He hung on in 1989, playing a single test against New Zealand. In 1990 he proved it was not all over by playing tests against England (1) and New Zealand (2). Thus he made the 1991 World Cup squad. This was the pinnacle of his career and a wonderful way to end it, as Australia won the World Cup.

The ticker-tape parade accorded the Wallabies "was an incredible experience. We just couldn't believe the wholehearted support and happiness. George Street was chock-a-block with thousands of people... office-workers, pensioners wanting to kiss your cheek, young kids wanting to shake your hand and a smattering of migrants whose backgrounds were obviously far removed from the game of Rugby. But they all simply wanted to help celebrate the greatest team achievement ever by Australia in a truly international sport and be part of Rugby's finest hour in this country."

Thus his international career ended, although a little-known fact is that he did make one more international appearance for Australia. The Australian team of 1992 was in the British Isles, and he happened to be there as a visitor. Because of the number of injuries, they asked him to turn out against the Welsh students, which he did. He had played for New South Wales and Sydney in 1992 against New Zealand so he was fit and ready.

Simon Poidevin did it all. He captained his country in four tests and five other games. His career covered a remarkable 96 matches for Australia, 59 of them tests. He was a member of teams that won the Bledisloe Cup and the World Cup, and not mentioned herein are the grand final wins for Randwick and the 58 matches for New South Wales. And there was the 1984 Grand Slam.

All this was accomplished by a country boy with a dream and aspirations beyond the normal human being. Good-looking and well mannered, modest and polite, he was a fantastic representative of Australia. He had all the requisites to captain Australia more often, but he happened to get sandwiched between great captains and got limited opportunities. By his efforts he became one of the truly greats of Australian Rugby.

Mark Ella had this to say about him in *Path To Victory*: "Simon is such a perfectionist, it's almost a disease. Not only is he the best rugby player in Australia, he's the most determined. He wants to win. He wants to go forward. He hates missing tackles or doing anything wrong. He hates losing. Simon Poidevin just wants to be the perfect rugby player.

"You need guys like that to drive you and the team. Watch Simon's performance and physical aggression and you are inspired by it. Because he wants to play the game to the limit, for the whole eighty minutes, he works harder than anyone I've seen at being super-fit. He actually enjoys the physical work and exertion of training. Because he's worked overtime at it, I don't have too many doubts about Simon's hands now. If he had a weakness, it was his handling.

"Poidevin is so determined to do well in anything he tries I won't be surprised in anything he achieves. He could become a millionaire stockbroker or finish up in Parliament. Simon has done well in triathlons and once came second in a big road run with Eastern Suburbs League Club. He wasn't happy with that, though. He wanted to win."

SIMON POIDEVIN

CAPTAIN: 9 matches (4 tests) (2 v Argentina 1986, 1 Japan 1987, 1 Argentina 1987)

BORN: 31 October 1958

SCHOOL: St Patrick's, Goulburn

CLUB: University of New South Wales/Randwick

NEW SOUTH WALES REPRESENTATION: 58 matches (1979-92)

AUSTRALIAN REPRESENTATION: 96 matches (59 tests) (1980-92)

DAVID CODEY

A Country Boy Who Captained Australia

A bloodstained David Codey (right) and Simon Poidevin toss one down after a hard encounter against the French.

Born in Orange, New South Wales, Codey weighed 101.6kg, carried no superfluous fat and stood 193cm in height, which would weigh heavily in his favour in certain critical decisions. Above all he was a tough, unrelenting player who gave his all whenever he put on the green and gold. He added muscle to the pack whenever he was in it.

He came to the notice of New South Wales selectors while playing for Orange City and burst upon the representative scene in 1983 with the visit of a strong Argentinian team. His entry could not be called dramatic, as he played in three matches against them, for New South Wales, New South Wales Country and Australia, and every one was lost.

In the New South Wales game the 'Blues' went down by 7-19, with the fabulous flyhalf Hugo Porta doing all the damage, scoring a try, kicking a conversion, two penalty goals and a dropped goal. His opposite number, Mark Ella, was overshadowed on the day. *The Sun Herald* criticised the Blues: "They were ragged in defence, slow to the breakdown and unable to find any of the sparkle needed to lift themselves above the mediocre."

However 'Codes' had another opportunity to impress with New South Wales Country, and although the country lads were defeated by 3-46 he found himself in the first test at Ballymore, partnering Simon Poidevin. The Pumas surprised everyone with a comfortable 18-3 win.

The flankers for the second test were Simon Poidevin and Chris Roche, the latter a highly talented player who was lightning-fast to a breakdown.

In 1984 Codey did not make the state or Australian team against Fiji or New Zealand and only appeared, as the captain, for New South Wales Country against Fiji, leading his team to a 43-0 victory.

It would have to be said that with his limited big-match experience he was lucky to make Andrew Slack's team to the British Isles in 1984, but it turned out to be an excellent selection.

On that tour he played in eight of the 18 games, and so impressed against South and South West Division and then Swansea that he was selected for the first test against England. It was a considerable blow to for the 177cm Chris Roche, who shone every time he took the field, but Alan Jones decided that he was not tall enough for the strategies envisioned in the lineout. Codey was given the nod in a considerable gamble and proved most effective. Australia won the lineouts 21-8 and the Wallabies won the match 19-3, the first leg of the Grand Slam.

David Hands wrote in *The Times*: "Let us instead praise the positive virtues of these Australians. Their scrummage and their lineout were the best they have been so far on tour."

Chris Roche got his chance in the next test against Ireland, which Australia won by 16-9, and he was brilliant, but when it came to planning the strategy against Wales David Codey found himself back in and Roche out. The score was 28-9 to the Wallabies, who were now only a game away from Australia's first-ever Grand Slam.

John Billot wrote in the Western Mail: "Steve Cutler played perhaps his greatest lineout game with Steve Williams, in the front, and David Codey at the back also making their presence felt." Though Roche had done nothing wrong, Codey was selected in the final test against Scotland, and the Wallabies demolished their opponents by 37-12 and completed the Grand Slam.

So it had been some year for the boy from Orange.

Terry Smith wrote in *Path To Victory*: "At one stage David Codey seemed doomed to be one of those unfortunates who are dumped forever after a single test match. Luckily for the Grand Slam Wallabies, he got a second chance when given the fourth breakaway spot ahead of Peter Lucas, whose omission drew a storm of criticism. Codey proved an inspired choice, playing with combative, spikey abrasiveness in the tests against England, Wales and Scotland.

"Codey's lone test before the tour was against Argentina at Ballymore in 1983. A year later he lost his spot in the New South Wales team, precipitating a switch from Orange to Brisbane and an immediate call up to Queensland's team against New South Wales. Codey doesn't tackle people as much as break them for scrap. The big fellow scored a Murray Mexted-type try with a powerful run against Swansea to clinch his test spot against England, and his height gave the Wallabies a fourth jumper.

"Before the test against Scotland, staunch

team man Codey popped out a couple of vertebrae when he bent to tie his bootlaces at training. But he shrugged off the injury and turned in a mighty game... Andrew Slack said: 'Codey's attitude is French. He's arrogant in the field like them. In fact, he's as arrogant a player as I've ever seen."

Mark Ella added his impressions: "Codes isn't one of those people who does one good thing and then sits back and basks in his own glory. When he pulls on the Australian jumper, this guy wants to make an impact on the game for the full eighty minutes. He is a terrific trier and team man.

"Codey went away a bit of an underdog, but when Jonesy gave him a chance, he grabbed Chris Roche's test spot with a storming game against Swansea. He had really big games against England, Wales and Scotland. David is big, fast, and his height at the back of the lineout gave us a genuine fourth jumper. Some of his hits in defence were just awesome. Apart from that, Codes has good ball skills and always is eager to support. He loves being part of the game."

Now residing in Brisbane, he played tests against Canada and New Zealand in 1985, and in 1986 played for Brisbane against Italy, and for Australia against France and Argentina. In 1987 he played for Queensland against Fiji and was selected by Alan Jones in the World Cup squad. Codey played against the USA and Japan, and was one of those in the disappointing, tragic defeat by France.

In the French game Codey played superbly after coming on as a replacement for an injured Bill Campbell and scored a sensational try to enable the Wallabies to regain the lead by 24-21. Winger Camberabero kicked his second penalty to level the scores at 24-24. With full time up on the clock, fullback Serge Blanco scored in the corner, allowing France to end Australia's World Cup chances by winning 30-24.

Totally dispirited, the Wallabies found themselves in a play-off in far away Rotorua for third place. Howell *et al* tell what happened in *The Wallabies: A Definitive History of Australian Test Rugby*: "The Wallabies' recent Bledisloe Cup success meant the large New Zealand crowd of 30,000 became Welsh supporters for the day. In this difficult atmosphere the sides made a lively and niggly start. David Codey was in trouble almost immediately, being warned by referee Fred Howard for elbowing an opponent. After only four minutes Codey was sent off for stomping in a ruck, and became the first Australian to be sent off in a test."

Playing against 14 men, Wales won 22-21.

David Codey was appointed captain of Australia in the next test, against New Zealand at Concord Oval. It was his first and only captaincy and Australia lost the Bledisloe Cup game 16-30. Now 30 years of age, David Codey gave the game away. He was proud to have captained Australia, if only once. He played one bad game in the green and gold - Rotorua does not qualify as a happy memory - and one wonders what he might have achieved if he had gone to a major rugby centre early in his career.

DAVID CODEY

CAPTAIN: 1 match (1 test) (v New Zealand 1987)

BORN: 7 July 1957

SCHOOL: Shore/Balgowlah High School

CLUB: Orange City/Souths (Q)

NEW SOUTH WALES AND QUEENSLAND REPRESENTATION:
6 matches (New South Wales 1983-84) (Qld 1985-87)

AUSTRALIAN REPRESENTATION:
18 matches (13 tests) (1983-87)

MICHAEL LYNAGH

A Kicker With Brains

For years Wallaby teams had gone onto fields without an internationally recognised kicker, and had suffered accordingly. Yet over the years New Zealand and South Africa always had a kicker who made an opponent pay for its glitches. Australian rugby was always under the delusion that their brilliant backs would score enough tries to make up the points difference. It rarely worked out that way.

Then came Paul McLean and Wallaby teams were at last on even terms. Next there was Michael Lynagh, the heir apparent, who was virtually a point-scoring machine. But he was more than a 'pure' kicker, he was a phenomenal ball player with the moves of a magician when he wanted to use his full bag of tricks. He could sidestep, swerve, use change of pace, 'read' a game and control a match, and he could lift the morale of a team as he kept kicking points between the uprights. Even with his kicking he was versatile, being equally good at place kicks, dropped goals, kicking for the line and putting up a garryowen. He was safe on defence, his hands were impeccable and he had guts. There is no doubt about it, Michael Lynagh was one of the greatest players to wear the green and gold, a multi-talented athlete of rare dimensions.

The real Michael Lynagh is hard to grapple with. Somewhat reticent - shy is not the right word - he is a thoughtful individual who is his own man. He was never one for the grandiose gesture or statement and was somewhat conservative in matters from politics to racial issues. Above all, he was never a follower. He may have not been a conventional leader but, after perusing these short biographies describing Australian captains, who is the conventional Wallaby skipper? In most instances he let his boot and play do the talking.

As Ian Diehm put it in *Red! Red! Red!*: "For more than a decade, the man affectionately known as Noddy played at a skill level few could dream about. Everyone who knew Michael Lynagh agreed with Bob Dwyer that 'Noddy is the epitome of good sportsmanship and gentlemanly behaviour and at the same time he was a fantastic player!'"

By the time he retired at 31 years of age after 14 years at the top, Diehm noted that "he set points scoring records of Bradmanesque proportions, among them the world record for individual test match points, most conversions and most penalty goals in tests, as well as most

Michael Lynagh was both a fine kicker and a phenomenal rugby player.

Schweppes

tests (47) as a halfback combination with Nick Farr-Jones. In 72 tests, he amassed 911 points, comprising 17 tries, 140 conversions, 177 penalty goals and 9 dropped goals, while for Queensland he scored 1166 points with 24 tries, 193 conversions, 205 penalty goals and 23 dropped goals in exactly 100 games."

He was a schoolboy wonder at Gregory Terrace in both cricket and rugby, but in 1978 his father Ian set off for Oregon State University to do a doctorate degree in psychology. Michael played a little American football and his father still feels that this stint gave Michael a harder, more competitive edge.

When back in Australia, his studies led him to Human Movement Studies at the University of Queensland, and he immediately signed up with the University team. He went straight into the first grade and was immediately placed in the state training squad. The author was Head of Human Movement Studies at the time, and I went to see his first game at St. Lucia. As a former international centre I felt I might be able to give a few tips to the youngster. Incidentally, it was against Souths and his future biographer, Australian captain Andrew Slack, marked him in that game. What impressed me was how cool and measured he was, and how his handling was immaculate. It was some debut as he left Slack on the ground a few times, and he was an excellent defender.

After the game I went up to congratulate him, and he asked me if I could give him any advice. It wasn't easy, but I suggested that he might work a bit more on a side-step. He nodded, and the next game threw about a hundred side-steps at his hapless opponent. He asked if there was anything else, and I shook my head.

It was tough for Queensland fans to accept anybody in the fly-half position other than Paul McLean, but it was soon a case of "The King is dead! Long live the King!" Lynagh took over without missing a stride, and in 1983 his impact was complete. He played for Queensland against the USA, and kicked two penalties in the 14-10 victory. He would kick 203 more penalty goals for Queensland in ensuing years.

A 28-34 loss to Argentina by Queensland followed and then he found himself on his first Wallaby tour, with Mark Ella as captain, to Italy and France. Ella was the number one five-eighth and 'Noddy' performed in a supportive role, gaining invaluable experience in his three matches, but unfortunately broke his collar-bone at Agen and did not play again. Over the years the Ella-Lynagh debate divided supporters in the same way as the Ella-McLean rivalry had. What became increasingly obvious was that Ella had to be in for the magic he could perform, but Lynagh had to be in for the points that he could produce. In 1984 Australian coach Alan Jones came up with the answer, putting Lynagh at inside centre. It was a calculated gamble, but it worked, mainly due to the athleticism and professionalism, in an amateur game, of Michael Lynagh.

History was made on that tour, the 'Grand Slam tour' as it is called, as for the first time Australia won the four 'home' internationals. Before the tour Mark Ella had informed 'Noddy' that he would retire after 1984, and he followed through on that statement although only 25 years of age. This made Lynagh even more excited over the tour. In the final match, against Scotland, Lynagh equalled the Australian points-scoring record, making eight kicks out of a possible nine to post 21 points.

Terry Smith summed him up in *Path To Glory*: "By the time he turned twenty-three, this Brisbane sport psychologist's son known to his peers as Noddy incredibly had posted exactly 200 points in only fifteen tests, including

23-point hauls against France, Argentina and Canada and 21 points against Scotland. That puts him into the Hugo Porta-Naas Botha bracket. It's safe to predict that one day Lynagh will be Australia's captain. In spite of his individual deeds, he is respected by his fellow Wallabies as a genuine team man.

"Lynagh's play can be a marvellous blend of athleticism and skill, courage and concentration... Lynagh is one of those wonderfully gifted individuals with the ability to excel in any ball sport.

"Lynagh was a schoolboy prodigy who was whisked almost straight from the 1981-82 Australian Schoolboys team into Queensland's State side as the successor to Paul McLean. Apart from inheriting McLean's No. 10 jumper, he had the great man's humility, superlative kicking game and knack of always having plenty of time in which to do things. It would seem to be just a matter of time before Lynagh surpassed McLean's record of 263 points in thirty-one tests. 'I see Noddy as the best footballer we have ever produced,' says Queensland coach Bob Templeton, never a man to go over the top. 'He has unique, God-given talents.'...

"With Mark Ella guaranteed the five-eighth spot, the chance to play inside-centre was a lifesaver for Lynagh in the British Isles in 1984. Freed from a tactical straightjacket, Lynagh scored a try against England, made a break that led to Ella's winning try against Ireland and got another try against Wales. He topped the tour scoring with 98 points, including 42 in the tests."

Ella added: "Noddy is a very, very gifted footballer. He can kick the ball with both feet. He can step, which I couldn't do, and he can kick goals. He's a complete team man who's right out of the Paul McLean mould. A future Australian captain."

With Ella out of the picture prematurely, the gate had opened for Lynagh to be Australia's dominant fly half. However, 1985 was a quiet season with only three tests played, two big wins over Canada and a narrow loss to New Zealand.

The year 1986 was a big one for Noddy, as he was now linked with Nick Farr-Jones and their pairing was to be legendary. He went on a month-long tour of the British Isles and Europe, then played the Hong Kong Sevens, and went to England to play for a World XV before the Australian season had even started.

Tests against Italy, France and Argentina followed, and then a 14-match tour to New Zealand under Andrew Slack. It was tough being a student, and even tougher being a University student. But winning the Bledisloe Cup on this tour somehow made it all bearable.

The first World Cup was contested in 1987 and Michael played against England, the USA, Japan and Ireland before Australia was unexpectedly downed by France 24-30 in the semi-final. Motivation was at an all-time low in the play-off game in Rotorua, feelings exacerbated by the sending-off of David Codey. The Wallabies felt humiliated as they lost to Wales 21-22.

Following the World Cup 'Noddy' departed on a 9-match tour of Argentina and Paraguay, with Simon Poidevin as captain.

Every year was full-on now. In 1988 there were matches against England and New Zealand, and a 15-match tour of England, Scotland and Italy. In 1989 opponents were Fiji, the British Isles, Western Samoa, New Zealand and a 10-match tour of Canada and France. Rugby league offers came through at this time, and though they were considered they were in turn rejected in Lynagh's careful and analytical way.

Visits from France and the USA and a 12-match tour to New Zealand with captain Nick Farr-Jones highlighted 1990. New Zealand won the series 2-1.

It was another World Cup year in 1991, and in turn Australia beat Argentina, Western Samoa, Wales, Ireland, New Zealand and England. Just like George Gregan's famous tackle and Mark Ella's four tries in the Grand Slam Tour, Michael Lynagh's decisions in the Irish test which turned defeat into victory will ever be remembered. This occurred after Farr-Jones had to leave the field through injury, and the situation was almost hopeless after Ireland had scored a late try to take the lead. Greg Growden tells the story in *The Wallabies' World Cup!*: "It was Lynagh's cool head that saved Australia today. In the frenzy which greeted Hamilton's try, the acting captain gathered the Wallabies into a tight huddle behind the goal-posts and told them to remain calm and focussed – victory was still within reach.

"Sure enough, some clever kicking from the Queenslander saw Australia move threateningly to within range of the Irish line, and then it was Lynagh himself who fittingly scored the winning try, having master-minded the back-line move which split an Irish defence perhaps prematurely celebrating." A lot of experience plus consummate skills saved the day for Australia. Nick Farr-Jones was too ill to speak at the World Cup dinner, and Michael, though at first appalled, performed that evening with the class others expected of him.

It was then time for a change of pace for Michael. He had been at the top for seven years and needed a different view of life. So he 'pulled a Campese' and signed a contract to play for the Benetton Club in Treviso, Italy. It was a wonderful experience for him, as he learned Italian, experienced 'spaghetti rugby' and met his future wife.

Though there were occasional complications as the ARU had to deal with their overseas Wallabies, 1992 had a full calendar. One part of his rugby life had been incomplete due to the exclusion of the Springboks from world rugby because of apartheid, but that was rectified when he toured South Africa with the Wallabies.

After that, with the departure of Nick Farr-Jones from the scene, Lynagh at last became Australia's captain. But for the consistently brilliant captaincy of Andrew Slack and Nick Farr-Jones, the honour would surely have been his well before this. He was captain between late 1992 and the 1995 World Cup.

His first excursion into this new zone of responsibility was when he captained a Wallaby team to Ireland, Wales and England, with Bob Dwyer as coach. He was nervous about this new direction, and seriously wondered if he had the personality to lead a team. As is his custom, he thought about it a lot, and discussed it with others. Andrew Slack explained what happed in *Noddy*: "Although he had the (c) beside his name, Lynagh still maintained his old role of the less outspoken voice of authority, when the assured Kearns took over some of Farr-Jones' duties. 'Noddy know himself pretty well', agrees Kearns. 'From day one he said to me that he wasn't type of person to carry on too much in the dressing room. He told me he wanted me to help him get the boys in the right frame of mind.' A bit of strong motivation was necessary from time to time. Lynagh realised that, and he understood it would be more effective coming from Kearns. It was sensible delegation. 'I made a real effort to be more accessible and a little more talkative,' recalls Lynagh, 'but at the same time, I wanted other people to play their roles as well.'"

Thus, a new type of captain emerged who delegated responsibility, something that had no parallel up to this point in Australia's history. The question has to be, was it successful?

His first appearance as a captain against Ireland on the 13-match tour was not the experience than he would have wanted. He dislocated his shoulder badly and returned to Brisbane for an operation. In an Australian first, he returned to accompany the team on the Welsh leg of the tour. The team stopped calling him 'Noddy' and instead nick-named him 'Neale Fraser', after the Davis Cup non-playing captain.

After that tour, he captained Australia against Tonga in 1993 and then took the Wallabies to North America and France on an 11-match tour. Then in 1994 he captained the Wallabies against Ireland, Italy and Western Samoa.

At 31 years of age, he called it quits after captaining Australia against Argentina and taking the team to the World Cup in South Africa in 1995. So was he successful with this new style, and his reticent personality? By any comparison with the past he was highly successful. It opens the question for debate on the personality characteristics of a captain. Perhaps the quality of the person is more important than anything else. Leadership takes many forms.

What is for certain is that Lynagh showed his genius on the rugby grounds of the world from 1983 to 1995. He played 108 matches for Australia, 72 of them tests. 'Noddy' also played exactly 100 games for Queensland. Calculating, conservative and thoughtful, Michael Lynagh was expert in all disciplines of his sport, and left a mark that might possibly never be equalled.

MICHAEL LYNAGH

CAPTAIN: 21 matches (15 tests) (1 v Argentina 1987, 1 1991 Wales, 1 Ireland 1992, 1 Tonga 1993, 1 Canada 1993, 2 France 1993, 2 Ireland 1994, 1 Italy 1994, 2 Argentina 1995, 1 South Africa 1995, 1 Canada 1995, 1 England 1995)
BORN: 25 October 1963 (Brisbane)
SCHOOL: Gregory Terrace
CLUB: Univ. of Queensland
QUEENSLAND REPRESENTATION: 100 matches: (1982–94)
AUSTRALIAN REPRESENTATION: 108 matches (72 tests) (1984-95)

NICK FARR-JONES

A Born Leader at the Helm

Australia has had some fantastic captains in its glorious rugby history, such as Tommy Lawton, Johnny Wallace, Trevor Allan, John Thornett, John Hipwell, Geoff Shaw, Mark Loane, Tony Shaw, Andrew Slack, John Eales and George Gregan, but arguably the greatest has been Nick Farr-Jones. He was electric on the field, switching play from right to left like no other half-back in history, urging his forwards on, marshalling the backs, surging forward when the occasion demanded it, and cover-defending ferociously and with a natural fervour that simply cannot be taught.

It is always difficult to compare captains or half-backs, as there have been periodic changes in the game, the most significant being that Australia in recent years has developed packs equal to any in the world. In the dim and distant past, Australian halfbacks worked off twenty to thirty percent possession from scrums and lineouts, and a different kind of half-back was required, one with unbelievable guts and the skills of a magician.

Farr-Jones could not sidestep with the audacity of a Cyril Burke, and lacked perhaps the elegance of Des Connor, the inspired running of Ken Catchpole or the marvellous cover defence of John Hipwell, but his all-round attributes were perfect for the modern game. Farr-Jones was an incomparable artist who covered the canvas with broad and confident strokes, not restricting his finished product to a particular school of artistry. Like Picasso and other greats, there was a variation in his work over time. What he was at the conclusion of his career was not what he was at the start.

The authorised biography of Nick Farr-Jones, by his friend, fellow Wallaby tourist Peter FitzSimons, paints to our mind a picture of the youngster as he was growing up as undisciplined, over-competitive, with an explosive temper. Nick's father's philosophy of life that he imparted to his sons is told in his biography: "life is about winning. I wanted them to know that that's what counts – to be competitive, to get better, to succeed." In fairness to Nick he always gave the impression that he played the game to the ultimate maximum and could generally put any loss into the correct perspective.

There is no doubt that the family genes were right, mother and father being University Blues and grandfather being a gifted athlete, and certainly there was massive encouragement to find sporting outlets for an obviously physically talented and hyper-active youngster. Soccer, swimming and surfing, athletics, golf and cricket, even skiing, were all an essential part of Nick's early life. He was fortunate to be born in a

Nick Farr-Jones was an incomparable artist who covered the rugby canvas with broad confident strokes.

sports-mad family.

Interestingly enough, Newington's most famous rugby player never made the First XV at this school, with Murray McGavin being the coach's choice. Another future Wallaby captain, Phil Kearns, also missed out on selection for Newington's First XV a few years later. Perhaps it was a blessing in disguise, as Nick concentrated on his studies sufficiently to gain entrance to study law at Sydney University.

While at the University Nick made the University Colts team, and in his second year boarded at St Andrew's College. Sport provided him with an outlet for his considerable energy, and when the Colts coach, Lindsay McCaughan, took over Sydney University's First Grade team, Nick found himself as the first team's scrum half.

Rugby politics and a disappointing start to the season by the firsts saw his coach displaced, first by Rupert Rosenblum and Johnny Rouen, and then by the one and only Dave Brockhoff. His own demise at halfback was only temporary, and was completely rejuvenated by 'Brock', a legend in coaching circles through his blood-and-guts approach and a conversation continually littered with extraordinary similes and metaphors. Chris Handy wrote of the infamous 'Brock' in *Well I'll Be Ruggered*: "I found him to be different to say the least. His style could be described as bombastic buffoonery. He knew what he wanted, but he couldn't explain it in simple terms. It was disguised by flowery phraseology that had you smirking or giggling when all was meant to be deadly serious. You tended to laugh at Brock rather than laugh with him."

In 1984 Alan Jones, a virtual neophyte in coaching ranks, took over as national coach from Bob Dwyer. At the time Sydney University was relegated to the Sydney competition's Second Division. On the surface it appeared as if the career of Nick Farr-Jones was on a slide, but the selectors at Sydney figured the youngster had the makings of a test player, and selected him on a Sydney tour to Europe. As is often said, the rest is history.

Simon Poidevin was the Sydney captain on that fateful tour, and though he also recognised the latent talent of the University scrum half, he took it upon himself to talk to Nick about his undisciplined play, and off-the-field behaviour. And always watching, in the background, was new coach Alan Jones, who had his own particular game plan in mind. Farr-Jones met most of the criteria. In a fairy-tale year, a Second Division player was selected on the Wallaby tour to Fiji as the number two scrum half to the diminutive Phillip Cox. Though he did not force his way into the single test, he almost did, and created a most favourable impression.

Farr-Jones, like the other Wallabies, was enormously impressed with their coach, and Jones, indulging in what is now referred to as 'Jones-speak', continually exhorted all players to greater physical and mental challenges for the good of Australian Rugby. It was as if they were all caught up in a surging wave propelling them forward, this highly articulate man continually urging them to keep going. Chris Handy, in *Well I'll Be Ruggered*, wrote that what Alan Jones "brought into our rugby was a professionalism that it really needed... He sought from their players an ultimate commitment."

Farr-Jones was a reserve for the first All Black test that year, which Australia won 16-9. A sensation occurred when eight test players withdrew from Sydney's upcoming encounter with the All Blacks. The press, and Sydney coach Peter Fenton, were staggered at the Jones-led decision, but it was fortuitous as it gave Farr-Jones the opportunity to play for Sydney against the All Blacks as he was only a reserve, and he showed he could mix it with the very best in the game. Nick was solidifying his own future by his on-field magic. Despite his evident claims, Nick was not selected for the remaining two tests of a series Australia narrowly lost 2-1.

In 1984 Farr-Jones was selected for the Wallaby tour to the UK, now known simply as the famous Grand Slam tour. Nick was 22 years of age and was reaching his physical maturity. What was becoming obvious was that having him at halfback was tantamount to having a third breakaway on the field because of his size and strength. Farr-Jones had an early opportunity to impress on tour as the incumbent test halfback Phillip Cox had an injured shoulder and Nick seized upon his unexpected good fortune in the first match against London Division, scoring a try and demonstrating his effectiveness with a fine, robust, all-round game.

Farr-Jones was never, in his career, averse to a little nocturnal activity, and after a night on the town in the UK he was summarily summoned to coach Alan Jones' room and was subjected to a 20-minute tirade. The story is told in *Nick Farr-Jones*: "Who the HELL did Farr-Jones think he was, going out every night drinking? Did he think this was some two-bit Sydney University tour, where you could do whatever you liked? Did he think that a rugby tour was no more than just one big party? Did he want to be over here just as a back-up or did he have some ambition to play test rugby and, if so, didn't he think it could be a good idea to start focusing a bit more on football and a lot less on partying? Well didn't he?" Nick had had his bum kicked, and thereafter concentrated on the task at hand.

To no one's surprise after his continuing on-field performances, Farr-Jones was selected to make his debut in the tour's first test, against England. When victory ensued and his ability was obvious for all to see, there was no longer any question as to who should be the test scrum-half. Farr-Jones played in all the subsequent Grand Slam tests. His entry into the test arena was certainly aided by the mercurial play of partner Mark Ella, whose basic instructions to Farr-Jones were simply to throw the ball in his direction.

Mark Ella wrote about Farr-Jones in *Path To Victory*: "Playing the running game, all I wanted from a halfback was to give me the ball. Apart from his size and strength, Nick has a fantastic pass. To vary my game, I sometimes stood a little wider and Nick always found me.

"Nick is a very good runner with the ball, too."

There were significant attitudinal changes towards Farr-Jones after the Grand Slam, as was noted in *Nick Farr-Jones*: "While Farr-Jones had previously noticed the difference in the way people treated him as soon as he had become a Wallaby, it was as nothing compared to the way they now regarded him now that he was a fully fledged test player in a victorious team. The phone seemed never stopped ringing, there was a constant round of celebratory dinners to attend and people even held the lift for him."

Nick, on his return to Australia, took a job with the law firm where his grandfather had been a partner, and thereafter had the unenviable task of balancing his legal duties with his sporting commitment with his club, and the representative demands of Sydney, New South Wales and Australian teams. In 1985, there were two relatively easy tests against a weakened Canadian team, and a single test against the All Blacks, the latter a narrow loss through a simple manoeuvre called 'Shuckey' by the All Blacks and 'Bombay Duck' by the Wallabies. The Wallabies seemed to lose concentration just once, and that was enough for the All Blacks, who took a quick tap and were over the Aussie line. The Fijians were next on the Wallaby calendar and two spiteful games were won by Australia. It was, in actuality, a rather uneventful year after the drama and emotion of the Grand Slam.

Though the world was seemingly Nick's oyster, there were some troublesome undercurrents in 1986 and 1987. One was a continuing vacillation in his relationship with coach Alan Jones, who was, after all, in the driver's seat and was continuingly curbing and correcting real and fancied indiscretions by Farr-Jones. Their temperaments were diametrically opposed, Jones demanding discipline, subservience and agreement and Farr-Jones exploring forever the limits of his own strong personality, in which freedom was a prerequisite since childhood. Jones was most certainly a coach for the golden moment, and had resurrected Australia's flagging prestige, but was fading through excessive exhortations over the passage of time. Put another way, Jones was reaching his 'use-by' date.

As well as one-off tests against Italy and France and a two-match series against Argentina in 1986, there was also a three-test series against the All Blacks. Nick also played in the two games at Cardiff and Twickenham marking the centenary of rugby's controlling body, the IRB. The Wallabies had a glorious year, winning all the tests except one and gaining the Bledisloe Cup in New Zealand. Nick's contribution in the victories was enormous, and Jones nominated him as the 'Player of the Tour' in New Zealand.

The second undercurrent occurred in 1987, and was not of Nick's making but rather neophyte New South Wales coach Paul Dalton, who was convinced that Farr-Jones, and not the incumbent Simon Poidevin, was the captain required to lead the Blues on to bigger and better things under his tenancy. Such a move was against the wishes of the national coach Alan Jones, and caused a worsening of the relationship between the Jones boys. The move was also not a popular one from the viewpoint of many players. It was not that the New South Wales team disliked Farr-Jones in any sense, but rather that Poidevin was both popular and had proven his capabilities. Despite the apparent opposition, Farr-Jones was duly appointed to the captaincy.

The first World Cup was contested in 1987 and particularly because of the Wallaby successes in 1986 there was a high expectation that the Cup would be Australia's. The tragic comedown Australia suffered when bundled out of contention after a superb semi-final against France then became virtual humiliation as they were beaten out of third place by lowly-regarded Wales in the isolated confines of Rotorua.

The bells then tolled inexorably for Alan Jones. 'Winners are grinners', 'tis often said, and all sport psychologists agree that victory rarely elicits recrimination, whereas defeat inevitably brings the rats down the drain-pipes. Defeat always required explanation, and excuse, and much of the pent-up emotion and invective were directed at Alan Jones. The basic arguments were: Jones had required total commitment from his players, yet perplexed his team by continuing with his own radio show and subjected his team to afternoon practices; the team was not supervised well enough through being in their own country, and Jones did not respond well after the defeat by France. The litany went on and on.

After the World Cup Jones alienated most of the players because of his changing position with respect to a South African tour by the Wallabies, and the harsh treatment which was allowed to be meted out by the ARFU to Andrew Slack and David Codey, who took it upon themselves to cement negotiations by flying to South Africa. Jones was seemingly inconsistent and ambivalent in the minds of the players.

When he took the Wallabies to Argentina and they emerged with but a draw and a loss, it was inevitable that Jones had reached the end of his tenure. His position was not enhanced by his selection of a man the other players felt was the 'teacher's pet', Brian Smith, over Farr-Jones for the first test in Argentina. In the opinion of many senior players Smith was unduly and incessantly praised by Jones and to demote Farr-Jones, slight knee injury or not, was deemed to be inexcusable. Jones was deposed on his return to Australia and Bob Dwyer returned to the helm.

With Dwyer, it was different folks, different strokes, and there was a particularly important stroke in so far as Farr-Jones was concerned. Dwyer wanted Farr-Jones as captain, recognising the leadership potential of the scrappy scrum-half. It had been thought that Simon Poidevin would have been the automatic choice, particularly because Poidevin and Dwyer both had Randwick affiliations, but either Dwyer shied off Poidevin because of his support of Alan Jones or his fear after the Roger Gould-Paul McLean fiasco in his initial reign that once more he was being blinded by the green colours of Randwick and did not want to wear that accusation again. There was also Michael Lynagh looming in the wings with tons of captaincy potential. What did Farr-Jones care about the whys and wherefores, he was the captain. As the saying goes, ours is not to wonder why, ours is but to do and die. And Farr-Jones, as always, would go into the valley of death for the green and gold.

Under Farr-Jones and Dwyer the Wallabies prevailed in two tests against England, and Nick revelled in the new man's different personality, his more consultative and laid-back coaching methods and his own overall role as his country's captain. The early success did not continue however in the annual clashes against that old nemesis New Zealand, the Wallabies recording a single draw against two heavy losses.

The subsequent Wallaby tour to England and Scotland started off in a devastating manner as England beat the visitors 28-19, but fortunately

Nick Farr-Jones receives the William Webb Ellis trophy from the Queen.

the Aussies got back on track with an axe job on Scotland to the tune of 32-13. The coach and the captain were not performing sensationally, but they were at least keeping their heads above water and combining well.

In 1989 the British Lions were on hand to test the mettle of the Wallabies. An easy 30-12 opener seemd to foreshadow a 3-0 pasting of the Lions, but they employed biff and bash tactics which unbalanced Australia in the second test, and the Wallabies went down 12-19. In the final game of the series Australia lost 18-19, after an extraordinary gaffe by David Campese when he ran the ball out of his in-goal area and gave a 'Hail Mary' pass to Greg Martin which resulted in a Lions' score. It was one of the classic foul-ups in modern rugby history and Campese and Martin were never allowed to forget it.

There were a few changes to the Wallaby team after that debacle, Simon Poidevin being brought back, and three virtual unknowns were then blooded against the All Blacks: Phil Kearns, Tony Daly and Tim Horan. Kearns was at the time playing second grade for Randwick and Horan was not in the Queensland side. The All Blacks won the single test at Auckland, but the new boys and the veteran all performed admirably. However the losses were mounting, and the critics were already taking aim at Bob Dwyer.

Dwyer was partially rescued by a tour of France, where Australia emerged victorious in the first test only to go down in the next. However, this yo-yo form had Alan Jones on radio and many of the national press calling for the hangman's noose. Dwyer barely survived a challenge for national coach's spot from Alex Evans, the non-official assistant coach of the Grand Slam Wallabies.

A 2-1 series victory over France in 1990 in Australia temporarily restored Australia's rugby prestige, yet a 1-2 loss to the All Blacks in New Zealand sent them backwards again. One step forward, two steps backwards. Inexorably, however, Dwyer was putting the pieces together, marshalling the players and technical experts who could perform at his own level of expectation. Willie Ofahengaue, Phil Kearns, John Eales, Marty Roebuck, Tim Horan, Tony Daly and Jason Little were part of the master plan.

It all started to come together in 1991 with the arrival of the Welsh and English teams, and they were disposed of in a clinical manner. That it was all for real at last became clear when the All Blacks were taken apart at the Sydney Football Stadium by 21-12. Though the New Zealanders emerged as victors two weeks later in Auckland, the 3-6 scoreline emphasised that the difference between the two countries was minute. The All Blacks have ever been the ultimate test of Australia's strength. Dwyer and Farr-Jones were riding high.

The pinnacle of both mens' careers was Australia winning the World Cup in 1991. The Wallabies were now atop the world, and every country fossicked around trying to find out how Australia did it. Sure, there were dietitians, strength trainers, sport psychologists, assistants and assistant to the assistant coaches, biomechanists, coaching advisers and all. All the advice in the world is useless without the right player personnel. It was those on the actual paddock who counted.

As U.S. President Theodore Roosvelt put it: "It's not the critic that counts, not the man who points out how the strong man stumbled, or where the doer of deeds could have done them better. The credit belongs to the man who is actually in the arena; whose face is marred by dust and sweat and blood; who strives valiantly, who errs and comes short again and again; who knows the great enthusiasms, the great devotions, and spends himself in a worthy course; who, at the best, knows in the end the triumph of high achievement; and who, at the worst, if he fails, at best fails while daring greatly, so that his place will never be with those cold and timid souls who know neither victory nor defeat."

The leadership exerted by Nick Farr-Jones was crucial in the Wallabies' drive towards rugby immortality. Despite a narrow let-off as the captain reluctantly departed the field against Ireland and a brilliant Lynagh master-minded an incredible recovery, the indelible portrait of the World Cup, besides the genius of Campese, is of Farr-Jones, prodding, pushing, cajoling, reversing directions, kicking, running. He was the captain's captain. There had been times in his career where he was subjected to criticism for his off-field antics more than his on-field captaincy, but in the World Cup campaign he came into full maturity as a captain, a leader, a player and an inspiration, on and off the field.

Though being crowned world champions was the highlight of every Wallaby's career, there was in actuality a strange mix of feelings when the World Cup was all over and done with. These feelings are described in *Nick Farr-Jones*, and many athletes of the present day who have been subjected to modern multi-media hype will understand them: "'You're happy, of course you are, basically. But really mixed up in the middle of it is all is maybe the sense that in conventional terms a lot of people would regard this as probably the pinnacle of your life – and now it's fifteen minutes behind you and getting further away all the time.'"

Eventually the euphoria departs, to return perhaps in later life with the onset of aching limbs and the realisation of one's mortality. Players come back to ground level again, and this occurred when the Wallabies went to South Africa in 1992. This was a fantastic occasion in any rugby player's career. It had been 23 years since a previous Wallaby visit. A South African tour rated alongside touring New Zealand as the supreme test of rugby manhood, since the All Blacks and Springboks provided that extra measure of toughness and a special sort of fanaticism. Wales used to be spoken of in the same manner, but those days were gone by the early 1990s.

Author Bryce Courtney, quoted in *Nick Farr-Jones*, said: "To the Afrikaaner... rugby is not a game. It is a commitment, a chosen battlefield, a gesture of collective self-assertion against a hostile and unsympathetic world. It is a rally and call to arms. It is the initiation into manhood. It is a sacred covenant."

There were problems that surfaced in South Africa that were associated with their very rugby isolation and yet continuing fanaticism, even to the point of Australia actually and seriously considering abandonment of their tour. Sanity fortunately prevailed, and the Wallabies thereafter overran the Springboks by their greatest defeat in 100 years, 26-3. Farr-Jones, having played his 59th test, felt it was time to retire. In the rugby sense, he had done it all. Now it was time to deal with the real world.

What was for certain was that Nick Farr-Jones was now one of the game's immortals, and he could never escape the inevitability of his own enduring fame. He had come a long way from being a rather brash child, to being an unofficial ambassador for his country. Maybe he was not good enough to play in the First XV at Newington College, but he was sufficiently gifted to captain the Wallabies in glorious victories for the Bledisloe Cup and the William Webb Ellis trophy.

NICK FARR-JONES

CAPTAIN: 49 matches (36 tests) (2 v England 1988, 3 New Zealand 1988, 1 England, Scotland, Italy 1988, 3 British Isles 1988, 1 New Zealand 1989, 2 France 1989, 3 France 1990, 1 USA 1990, 3 New Zealand 1990, 1 Wales, Engand, New Zealand, Argentina, Western Samoa, Wales, Ireland, New Zealand, England 1991, 2 Scotland, 3 New Zealand, 1 South Africa 1992)
BORN: 18 April 1962
SCHOOL: Newington
CLUB: University of Sydney
NEW SOUTH WALES REPRESENTATION: 46 matches (1984-93)
AUSTRALIAN REPRESENTATION: 90 matches (63 tests) (1984-93)

PHIL KEARNS

From Second Grade To Test Rugby

IN A STRANGE TWIST, two of Australia's greatest-ever players could not make the first team at their school, Newington. They were Nick Farr-Jones and Phil Kearns, who both captained Australia, and Kearns played in 67 tests and Farr-Jones 63. Only Kearns went one better. He was plucked from second grade at Randwick to play for Australia. The Kearns case gives considerable hope to those who seem to have not quite made it.

The Newington selectors certainly got it wrong with Kearns and Farr-Jones, but on the other hand they produced some other Wallabies over the years. There was Eric Bardsley (1928), Scott Bowen (1993-96), Jim Brown (1956-58) Dick Roberts (1913), Harry Bryant (1925), Alan Cameron (1951-58), John Carroll (1958-59), Dave Cowper (1931-33), Aub Hodgson (1933-38), Bryan (1913) and Jim Hughes (1907), Peter Jorgensen (1991), Bruce Judd (1925-31), Reg Lane (1921), Dinny Love (1932), Graeme (1961) and Stu MacDougall (1971-76), George Mackay (1926), John Manning (1904), Bill McLaughlin (1936), Ernest Newman (1922), 'Iggy' and Jack O'Donnell (1899), Tom Perrin (1931), Bill Tasker (1913-14), John Taylor (1922) and John Williams (1963). Not a bad line-up, so the school can afford to make a mistake or two over the years. Phil Kearns, Nick Farr-Jones, Alan Cameron and Dave Cowper all captained Australia.

After graduating from Newington, where he showed more flair in the swimming pool than the rugby field, he gravitated to the Randwick club. He spent two years in the Colts team and they made it to two grand finals, one of which was won. He made his way from third grade to a stable position in the second team, and occasionally would play for the first team when its hooker was playing for New South Wales. That hooker was none other than Eddie Jones, who never played for Australia but later became Australia's national coach. Jones was unlucky; Tom Lawton Jr was the Wallaby hooker and played 41 tests, while his back-up was Mark McBain. Both came from Queensland, and they were both world class.

In 1988 'Kearnsey' first came to notice when he played for New South Wales 'B' versus England. There were a few on that team who made it to Wallaby status, including Dwayne

Phil Kearns has a small beer from the Bledisloe Cup.

Vignes, Lloyd Walker, Brad Burke, Mick Murray and Ewen McKenzie. Kearns impressed in a 9-25 loss.

The real breakthrough came in 1989 when Bob Dwyer became the national coach, and understandably he wanted to put his imprint on the game. After Kearns again displayed his abilities for New South Wales against the British Lions, the Blues losing a sensational game by 21-23, Dwyer had made up his mind.

In the single Bledisloe Cup match that year, at Eden Park, Auckland, Dwyer had the rugby pundits shaking their heads in disbelief as Lawton was dropped in favour of the 22-year-old Phil Kearns, who was ensconced in second grade where Dwyer coached. There were a few other bombshells a well. Tony Daly was brought in as a prop, though he had never played a single representative match. Tim Horan was picked at centre. History, of course, has proved Dwyer's selections as spot on, for Kearns eventually played 67 tests, Daly 41 and Horan 80. Horan and Kearns both captained their country. At the time most experts thought that Dwyer had gone crazy.

In the test Australia lost by 12-24, but the Wallaby experiment was deemed as successful.

It was a case of from rags to riches, as suddenly these three young players were off with captain Nick Farr-Jones on a 10-match tour of Canada and France in 1989. 'Kearnsey' displayed his durability by playing in eight of the 10 matches, including the two tests against France.

In the first test, Australia played magnificently and downed the French at Strasbourg by 32-15. It was Australia's biggest-ever score and winning margin in France. Kearns impressed as he picked up three tight heads against a very strong and tough pack. France rebounded and won the following test by 25-19. The tour was a considerable learning experience for Phil, and it allowed him to bond with his fellow Wallabies.

From 1990 onwards Kearns dominated his position. First there were the home tests, against France and the USA. The first test against France was violent, the flanker Benazzi being sent off in his debut, creating some kind of a record. Australia won the first test by 21-9 and the second by 48-31, the latter a sparkling match featuring rugby of the highest order. It was the highest score Australia had registered against an International Rugby Board country. On the other hand, the 31 points France scored was their highest tally in Australia. France rebounded in the third test, but the Wallabies had won the series by 2-1.

The USA team offered no threat to Australia, who coasted to a 67-9 victory. A rugby rarity occurred when within the space of 12 minutes each of the front row, Tony Daly, Ewen McKenzie and Phil Kearns scored tries. Kearns was developing a proclivity for sea-gulling on the short side of rucks, and was highly successful in this manoeuvre over the years.

In 1990 Farr-Jones led a tour to New Zealand, which always brought Australian teams back to earth. There were three new faces in the first test, 'Willie' Ofahengaue, Ewen McKenzie and Rod McCall, who were soon nicknamed 'Willie O', 'Link' and 'Slaughter', respectively. Kearns faced up to Sean Fitzpatrick that day, and their clashes and rivalry became legendary. Australia lost by 21-6, and then the second test by 27-17. The kicking boot of Grant Fox, after a rough first outing, registered 100 percent in the second.

The third test is still implanted in Australian minds. There was only one try scored, and that was by Kearns, who surged over the line and stepped into history as he invited Sean Fitzpatrick to 'two barbecues' with a typically

Churchillian two-fingered gesture. The 21-9 victory ended a 50-match, 23-test unbeaten sequence for the All Blacks. They showed that New Zealand could be beaten by positiveness and determination.

When 1991 came around, Wales was over-run by Australia to the tune of 63-6. It was Australia's greatest score against a founder IRB nation and sparked former Welsh great Gerald Davies to ask: "Was there ever such a fall from grace?"

England was next on the international schedule, and they were disposed of by 40-15, Nick Farr-Jones remarking: "I believe it was close to the best performance since I was involved with the Australian team."

Team spirit was at an all-time high as the Wallabies prepared themselves for two tests against New Zealand, the first at home and the second away. In the first test Australia won convincingly by 21-12. Veteran New Zealand writer Bob Howitt noted: "Most of the day's stars wore gold jerseys – Kearns in the drives, Eales in the lineout, Poidevin in the mauls, Willie Ofahengaue in most things, Lynagh with his kicks, Tim Horan with his tackling, Jason Little with his running and Egerton with his stunning try."

There was general euphoria in the Australian camp, but as had been so often the case, the All Blacks came back at Eden Park to register a close 6-3 victory. Michael Lynagh missed six kicks out of seven in a rare off day.

Australia got its revenge at the 1991 World Cup. The first match was against Argentina which Australia won by 32-19, Kearns scoring a try. However the Wallabies were concerned as Kearns had to leave the field not long after his score, to be replaced by David Nucifora. However he recovered sufficiently to play the next match against Western Samoa. Australia won by 9-3, but they were not convincing.

Wales was next in order, and the Wallabies caned them by 38-3. *The Sunday Telegraph* reporter wrote: "Australia douse feeble dragon's fire."

The next match was the quarter-final against Ireland and late in the game it looked as if Australia would be beaten. Farr-Jones, the captain, had to leave the field, and with time running out Ireland was leading 18-15, and the match looked to be over. Michael Lynagh calmly put a plan in action, scored and Australia had escaped by 19-18.

Revenge came in the semi-final against New Zealand. It was arguably Australia's best game of the tournament as they shocked the All Blacks and ran out 16-6 winners. Sir Nicholas Shehadie commented: "I have never seen an Australian team defend as well as this side... I would say that would be our most significant win ever."

In the final against England, in a tense match, the Wallabies won by 12-6. The William Webb Ellis Trophy was theirs. When a World Cup XV was selected by the *Sydney Morning Herald*, Phil Kearns was selected as a reserve. The boy from Randwick's second XV had come a long way.

The year 1992 saw Scotland in Australia, and there were three new caps in the first test: Richard Tombs as centre, Paul Carozza on the wing and Peter Jorgensen came on as a replacement. Despite the new faces, Australia rolled on to a 27-12 victory in the first test, and a runaway 37-13 victory in the second. One feature of the match was the try by John Eales, which was the last four-point try scored for Australia.

The Wallabies were riding high, and their confidence was shown in two defeats of the All Blacks, 16-15 and 19-17. The latter included

the infamous late tackle on the try-scoring Paul Carozza by Richard Loe. The All Blacks scraped home in the third, but it was too late. The Wallabies had a Bledisloe Cup that sat very well with the World Cup.

South Africa was next and Australia made a four-match tour, the first in 23 years by a Wallaby team. Australia triumphed in the test by 26-3, the biggest defeat in 100 years of South African rugby. There was no doubt that Australia was the world champions. A 13-match tour to Europe under Michael Lynagh followed, and Kearns played in eight of the matches. The test over Ireland was won by 42–17.

The second test against Wales was a significant moment in 'Kearnsey's' life. Lynagh was injured and Phil Kearns was appointed captain. Australia won by 23-6, and Kearns said: "If anything won us the game, it was our big tackles. Wales themselves put in some hard hits and did not slacken off at all – wins over them don't come easy any more." It was a great moment for Kearns.

In the last few months the Wallabies, the world champions, had beaten New Zealand, South Africa, Scotland, Ireland and Wales.

In 1993 Tonga was thrashed by 52-14, but an injury to Lynagh gave Kearns the test captaincy against New Zealand (lost 10-25), and he also led Australia in the three tests against the touring Springboks. The Wallabies won the series 2-1. After the last test, Wallaby skipper Phil Kearns said: "The South Africans have arrived as a world class international outfit. They are a very good side. It was one of the hardest and fastest tests I have played in."

The next tour was to North America and France with Lynagh as captain once more. The

Phil Kearns in a pensive moment.

Wallabies gobbled up Canada by 43-16. But in the first French game, France squeezed home by 16-13. Kearns gave his reaction: "Absolutely shattered. We dominated the game, dominated the lineout. We had enough ball to win 20 games. The score could have been 30-16 our way quite easily. It's pretty demoralising to know you played better than the opposition and still came out far behind." What was obvious about these Wallabies was that they now expected to win, they were a world force. Kearns knew what he was talking about, as Australia ran out clear winners in the final test by 24-3.

Australia won all its test matches in 1994, toppling Ireland twice and then Italy. Kearns was back at captain against Western Samoa, who were run ragged by the Wallabies to the tune of 73-3. It was Australia's highest-ever score and the biggest winning points margin in international rugby.

Another great moment in his career came when he captained Australia in a single match for the Bledisloe Cup. Australia got home by 20-16 at Sydney Football Stadium. In the first fifteen minutes, David Knox put up a high ball for Jason Little to score in the opening seconds, and later from a 5m scrum a rolling maul was set up, allowing Kearns to use his strength and skill to peel off and get over the line. This was as exciting a match as any ever seen, epitomised at the end by the diving tackle, *the* tackle, by George Gregan on Jeff Wilson to dislodge the ball and win the match for the Wallabies. One of Kearns' proudest moments was standing on the podium at the Stadium and hoisting up the Bledisloe Cup for the cheers of the spectators.

Michael Lynagh was back for the two Argentina games in 1995, won easily by Australia, and then the team was off to South Africa to defend the World Cup.

It was a real blow when Australia lost the first match to South Africa, 18-27. Canada was then beaten by 27-11 in none too convincing fashion. Kearns hobbled off the field to be replaced by Michael Foley and was rested for the 42-3 win over Romania. He played the quarter-final, where England won in a 25-22 upset. The world champions had lost their crown. To rub matters in, there were two tests against the All Blacks, and another item of silverware was lost as New Zealand won both matches. Privately, Kearns felt that the team had lost it in 1995, and whether through laziness or arrogance a new broom was needed.

These were turbulent times, as Ross Turnbull was assembling people for his World Rugby Corporation, and secret talks were occurring everywhere as people were signing up or negating advances. The rumour mill disturbed the mind-set of the players.

The game had taken its physical toll on Kearns, and to all appearances he was at the end of his playing career. He hobbled badly, and had to be operated on, the doctors doubtful that he could ever return to the game. The doctors did not bank on the determination of Phil Kearns.

However it would be two years before he was ready to test himself, and then only once in 1997, captaining an Australian Barbarians side to victory over the visiting French by 26-25. It would be another year before he was back in the thick of things, so three years had gone by and he was now 31 years of age.

In 1998 he was in the test team against England. In one of the worst debacles in living memory England was made to look like beginners in a 76-0 thrashing. Australia set all kinds of records:

1. 76 was their highest test score
2. 76-0 was Australia's biggest winning margin

3. Australia's previous highest score against England was 40 in 1981
4. Australia's previous highest margin against England was 25 (40-15) in 1991.

Next up was Scotland and Kearns again took the field, being replaced 10 minutes from the end by Jeremy Paul. The scores were 45-3 in the first test and 33-11 in the second.

Throughout 1998 and 1999 Phil Kearns would start, but would be replaced. One feature of the year 1998 was the winning of the Bledisloe Cup. The victory at Christchurch was particularly enjoyable, as it was Australia's first victory on the ground since 1958. When Australia won the third test, the Wallabies completed the first clean sweep of a three-test series since 1929.

Phil Kearns found himself on the World Cup squad in 1999 and started against Romania (57-9) and Ireland (23-3), but he suffered a recurrence of his old foot injury and was forced to leave the field and returned home. Australia won the World Cup, and Kearns announced his retirement.

His had been a superlative career. He had played 85 matches for his country, 67 of which were tests, and he managed 73 matches for his beloved 'Blues'. He captained Australia ten times.

Soft spoken and articulate, Phil Kearns has always been a role model in his sport. It is interesting that he had stepped into some aspects of a captain's role when Michael Lynagh was appointed. The story is told in Andrew Slack's biography, *Noddy*: "'Noddy knows himself pretty well', agrees Kearns. 'From day one he said to me that he wasn't the type of person to carry on too much in the dressing room. He told me he wanted me to help him get the boys in the right frame of mind.' A bit of strong motivation was necessary from time to time. Lynagh realised that, and he understood it would be more effective coming from Kearns. It was a sensible delegation.'

Sensible or not, it was unusual to say the least. Phil Kearns was, therefore, well practised in the dressing room speech before he was appointed captain.

Greg Growden said of him in *The Wallabies' World Cup*: "Phil Kearns is like all great hookers – ever talkative, sneaky, courageous and zealous. Since he moved into the side in 1989, he has taken over the mantle of the 41-cap Wallaby hooker Tom Lawton and has become a vital member of the Australian team, offering steel up front.

"However, Kearns' role is not just throwing the ball into the lineout or raking the ball back at all scrums. Instead, he regards himself as another backrower, constantly wanting to run with the ball, make the break, and score test tries...

"Despite his fresh-faced features, Kearns can be as unforgiving and determined as anyone else when matches become heated..."

PHIL KEARNS

CAPTAIN: 14 matches (10 tests) (1992 Wales 1, 1993 South Africa 3, New Zealand 1, 1994 Italy 1, Western Samoa 1, New Zealand 1, 1995 New Zealand 2)
BORN: 27 June 1967
SCHOOL: Newington
CLUB: Randwick
NEW SOUTH WALES REPRESENTATION: 73 matches (1989-99)
AUSTRALIAN REPRESENTATION: 85 matches (67 tests) (1989-99)

ROD MCCALL

A Captaincy To Treasure

ROD MCCALL is one of the many unsung heroes of rugby who toil away for the good of the team. They are not flashy, but they are an essential part of the engine room. Rod McCall was a tight forward, unspectacular for the most part, but he would solidify a pack with his strength and effort, he would toil in the lineout and do more than his share at all times, he would never flinch and never allow himself or his team-mates to be muscled out of their game.

Big men like McCall are often quiet and unassuming off the field, but are possessed with an inner but scarcely discernible rage on it. Whether it was for his beloved Brothers Club, the Reds or the Wallabies he was always there, dependable, efficient, refusing to be bowed or beaten. His nick-name was 'Slaughter', and one does not get that from tap-dancing away from trouble. At 1.98m in height and 110kg at his peak, he was a formidable presence.

Rod McCall: They called him 'Slaughter' and he was a hard and loyal player.

Rod McCall learned his trade carefully and slowly. He may not have been an early whiz-bang at school but as he filled out, absorbed advice and hardened up after being cajoled by Tony Shaw at Brothers, he started to come into his own.

His first appearance against a touring team was against Italy for Brisbane, and he packed down that day with Damien Frawley, a second rower of similar talent and capability. Almost all the team, which included Anthony Herbert, Ross Hanley, Michael Cook, Tim Lane, Peter Slattery, Brendan Nasser, David Nucifora and Rob Lawton, would become Wallabies. The captain was the no-nonsense David Codey, who had moved up from New South Wales and who would ever be remembered for being sent off against Wales in the play-off in the World Cup in 1987 in Rotorua. With players like these on the field, it was no wonder that Brisbane won by 38-7.

That same year he went up against France for Queensland, but the Reds were overrun to the tune of 48-9, despite the presence of such players as the captain of Australia, Andrew Slack, exciting winger Brendan Moon and point-scorer extraordinaire Michael Lynagh. McCall partnered Bill Campbell, so Queensland had a formidable second row, and a front row that could play with the best in the world, Andy McIntyre, Tom Lawton and Cameron Lillicrap. They simply could not match it that day with the French.

However the Australian selectors recognised that there was a lot of latent talent in the Brothers' big man and he was rewarded with his first of many Wallaby trips, to New Zealand that year. The locks, or second rowers as Australia called them at the time were, as well as McCall (1.98m), Queensland team-mates Damien Frawley (1.98m), Bill Campbell (2.02m) and Steve Cutler (2.02m). Campbell and Cutler played in the tests, with Frawley and McCall the 'dirt-trackers' or 'Wednesday boys'. Alan Jones was the coach, and after the 1984 Grand Slam he knew the importance of such height in the lineout. So McCall went up against Waikato, Wairarapa-Bush, Wanganui, South Canterbury, Southland and Thames Valley. Despite missing the tests he improved his game and was indeed a worthy Wallaby. In his first appearance, against Waikato, he was flattened by the infamous Richard Loe. Welcome to New Zealand.

Rod McCall, who was not a fan of Alan Jones, clashed with him on the tour and in the next year. It appeared as if his career had taken a nose-dive, as his only appearance in 1987 was in a Queensland 'B' side against South Korea.

Alan Jones' successor was Bob Dwyer, a supporter of McCall, so after some eighteen months on the outer he got a look-in once more. In 1988 he showed his wares once more on the larger stage, playing for Queensland 'B' against England, then Australia 'B' and Queensland against New Zealand. Dwyer realised his value as a solid performer and he was selected on the 1988 tour of England, Scotland and Italy under captain Nick Farr-Jones. Again he found himself a 'dirt-tracker', but Cutler and Campbell were considered the best in the world at this time. So McCall did his thing for the team, playing against Northern Division, South-West Division, Combined English Students, Edinburgh, Scottish North and Midlands, Combined Services and Italy 'B'. It was invaluable experience, and he was seeing a lot of the world.

The tide started to turn his way in 1989, being firmly ensconced in the Queensland side and playing matches against Fiji, the British Isles and Western Samoa. He and Bill Campbell were the Queensland pairing. McCall also made his third tour, to Canada and France with the Wallabies. It turned out to be a 'passing of the guard' tour, as the locks were Peter FitzSimons, Mark McInnes, Tim Kava and David Dix. Campbell and Cutler had retired, so after playing four preliminary games, FitzSimons and McCall ran out in the first test against France. This was a new-look scrum, with a front row of Ewen McKenzie, Phil Kearns and Tony Daly, and there were other exciting youngsters on tour like Tim Horan and Jason Little.

There is nothing quite like putting on the green and gold for the first time in a test, and it was some experience for a Brisbane lad running onto the field following experienced captain Nick Farr-Jones. Not only that, but there was the added exhilaration of a clear victory by 32-15. He had no idea that this would be his first of 40 caps, and that he would have a vital role in the Australian scrum for the next four years.

The fairy-tale ended with a defeat in the second French test. McCall was honoured to be vice-captain of the team, and as such he had the responsibility of calling the line-outs.

In 1990 he played in 11 representative games. He took up where he left off, as France were now touring Australia, and he played three tests against them and one match for Queensland.

Two of the three tests were won, and Queensland toppled the tourists as well. Traditionally, for whatever reason, French teams do not travel well, and they were not quite the force they were on their home territory, particularly in Paris. However there was a tendency towards violence in the tests, the flanker Abdel Benazzi being a particular hatchet man.

In the first test Benazzi was ordered from the field by English referee Tony Spreadbury, for kicking McCall. Benazzi created an unenviable record, as he was the first player to be sent off in his first international. The second test was milder, being won by Australia convincingly in a fine attacking display. In the third test, won by France 28-19, Greg Growden wrote in *The Sun Herald*: "One Australian player who was still upright last night was second-rower Rod McCall, who was close to his team's best, after virtually working solo to ensure Australia won some lineout ball. After the French lineout dominance McCall won eight lineouts to give his backs something to play with."

A walkover 67-9 defeat of the USA followed. In a rugby rarity, each of the front row, Daly, McKenzie and Kearns, scored tries.

McCall's second tour to New Zealand followed and this time he was no longer a 'dirt tracker.' He played against Auckland, Otago and Taranaki, as well as in the three tests. The first two tests were lost, but the Wallabies stormed back to thump the All Blacks in the third by 21-9. The victory for Australia ended a 50-match and 23-test unbeaten sequence for the All Blacks, so there was some consolation.

The 1991 year was particularly busy for the now well-established lock. He played for Queensland against Fiji, Wales and England, and played for the Wallabies against Wales, England and twice against New Zealand.

The Welsh game was phenomenal, as the score was 63-6. Former Welsh great Gerald Davies lamented in *The Times*: "Was there ever such a fall from grace? Was there ever such an improbable plot ever likely to have been imagined and come so terribly to pass?" Rod McCall was now teaming up with a young phenomenon who would leave his mark on the game as few have done before or since, John Eales. This allowed McCall to move to the front of the lineout and provide Australia with more options.

There was one close loss to New Zealand that year, but all thoughts were on the World Cup. Rod played against Argentina, Wales, Ireland, New Zealand and England, as Australia won the World Cup. The Irish game in particular will live among his memories, as Australia got off the hook by the cool head of Michael Lynagh. It was one of the great moments in Australia's long rugby history. *The Mail* reported: "The finest team in the world accepted the trophy they deserved. Australia are worthy champions beyond argument." Campese was the unanimous choice as player of the tournament, but he could not have done it without the possessions that Eales and McCall provided him, and what a combination they were!

In Greg Growden's *The Wallabies' World Cup!*, he had this to say about McCall: "An unassuming Queenslander, Rod McCall is the first to admit that he has not played to his full potential in some internationals. Although he possesses all the necessary attributes to be the world's best second-rower, McCall has sometimes let himself down by 'disappearing' for periods in test matches. However, that proved to be anything but the case during the 1991 World Cup, where he was a revelation at the front of the lineout, taking enormous pressure off his second-row partner, John Eales. McCall's midfield work-rate was exceptional and he was more often than not among the first to the breakdown. McCall was firmly rewarded during the 1991 World Cup campaign, particularly during the Welsh pool match where he and Eales won virtually every lineout."

The year 1992 was another busy one, with two games for Queensland against international teams (Scotland and New Zealand), two tests against Scotland and three against New Zealand. The Bledisloe Cup victory followed that of the World Cup, Australia winning two of the three matches.

A tour to Ireland, Wales and England followed late in 1992, and Rod played in nine of the 13 games, including two tests. Eales was injured and did not play against Wales, so Rod was paired with Garrick Morgan. Against Wales, Rod scored one of his rare tries, and Howell *et al* noted in *The Wallabies*: "Rod McCall was particularly outstanding in the lineout, winning a major share of possession for the Wallabies. McCall muscled his way over from a lineout..."

John Eales was out through injury in 1993 and the Morgan-McCall combination ruled the roost that year. Rod took on the added responsibility without breaking stride, showing an increasing maturity in his play. After playing against Tonga and South Africa at home, he toured North America and France with Michael Lynagh's Wallabies. Not only was he one of the senior men but he was the heart of the pack. He played in seven of the 11 games and all three tests.

The old firm of Eales and McCall was restored in 1994 for tests against South Africa and Italy, who were on tour in Australia. Then he was off again, this time to North America and France, the Wallabies captained by Michael Lynagh. McCall played in seven of the 11 matches, including the test against Canada and two against France.

1995 was his swansong, highlighted by his second World Cup in South Africa. He played in the first match, lost to South Africa by 18-27, and then he was honoured with his first and only captaincy of his country, against Romania, which Australia won by 42-3. He later said: "When you look at those people who have gone before, it's very humbling to be in that company. It was something pretty special, to captain my country."

And so it was, awarded for his considerable service to Australian rugby over the years. No-one deserved it more. Though Australia did not win the World Cup, Rod McCall was honoured as one of Australia's captains. He was right. Some great players had led Australia out on the field.

In total, he had played 72 matches for his country, 40 of them tests. Now 31, it was time to hang up his over-sized boots.

ROD MCCALL

CAPTAIN: 1 match (1 test) (v Romania 1995)
BORN: 20 September 1963
SCHOOL: St Columbans
CLUB: Brothers
QUEENSLAND REPRESENTATION: (1986–96)
AUSTRALIAN REPRESENTATION: 71 matches (40 tests) (1986-95)

JOHN EALES

Another Captain of Captains

When writing the chapter on John Thornett, it was entitled 'The Captain of Captains', mainly because of the great respect and reverence with which he was held. He was modest, self-effacing, a solid but not brilliant performer who embodied everything good about the game. This was in no sense being derogatory about the other captains, it was just that he was legendary, as good an example off the field as on it. He was in the engine room, never complaining, playing to the best of his ability for his country.

Things were very different then. A coach was not allowed on the field of play in a game, so the captain had to figure out the strategies, it was up to him to exhort the players and John Thornett captained his country 16 times, more than any other Australian captain before him. One must remember that there might be only three or four tests in a year.

Now we come to John Eales. He captained his country more than any other player, living or dead. There is something about Eales that sets him apart. He reminds the author in some respects of Thornett. There is no comparison between them on the playing field: Eales jumped better, kicked better, ran better. But there was something about their captaincies that rang a bell. It was in their personality, their demeanour, their modesty, their ethical and philosophical attitudes, the respect with which they were held, their self-effacement, their gentlemanly approach, their respect of others, their communication with others. They transcended the normal captain, there was

John Eales could do anything on a rugby field, including kicking crucial penalties.

something particularly special about them. They were universally respected, role models of what a captain should be like. So this short biographical sketch is called "Another Captain of Captains."

John Eales was Brisbane born and bred, and one only had to meet his parents once to know why he is like he is. He went to Ashgrove Marist Brothers' School, and it may not be a school that is generally thought of as a rugby nursery, like Brisbane Grammar or Nudgee, but the fact is it has produced some outstanding Wallabies as well as John Eales: Mick Barry (1971), 'Paddy' Batch (1975-79), Des Connor (1958-59), Daniel Heenan (2003), Anthony (1987-93) and Daniel Herbert (1994-2002), Barry (1968-69) and Bob Honan (1964), Pat Howard (1993-97), Nigel Kassulke (1985), David L'Estrange (1971-76), Brendan Moon (1978-86), Alex Pope (1968), Sam Scott-Young (also Toowoomba Grammar) (1990-1992), Bob Wood (1972), Garrick Morgan (later Downlands) (1992-97) and 'Mick' Flynn (1971). There are enough for a full team and two reserves, so if rugby is truly played in heaven, Ashgrove Marist Brothers' School would more than hold their own. They produced two captains of Australia, Eales and Connor, who was Australian coach and an All Black. While at school John played rugby, cricket, basketball and athletics, and showed promise in every one of them. His cricket was good enough to keep Matthew Hayden, who was also at the school, out of the First XI, and Eales spent two years in the First XI and one year in the First XV. If anything, he showed more promise at cricket.

The spring-heeled giant from the Brothers started to take the world by storm in 1991. His club debut was against the University of Queensland, where he was a student dabbling in Human Movement Studies, in 1990. He was immediately regarded as a special player and won the Rothmans Medal in his first year as the best and fairest player in Brisbane. He made the Queensland team that year and amazed coach John Connolly with his poise and assurance, particularly in games against some hard-nosed opposing teams. As he filled out physically his game got better and better. In 1991, now a 21-year-old, he made it to the broader field against touring teams. Wales was his first opponent for Queensland, and to the surprise of everyone the state team won by 35-24. It was a tough Queensland team, captained by Michael Lynagh: Anthony Herbert, Ian Williams, Jason Little, Tim Horan, Paul Carozza, Peter Slattery, Sam Scott-Young, Brendan Nasser, Eales, Rod McCall, Jeff Miller, David Nucifora and Cameron Lillicrap all became Wallabies and only Richard Moroney missed out. Eales had a confident introduction to the 'big time.'

On the basis of his performance he was picked on the Wallaby team against the Welshmen. Bill Campbell had retired and Steve Cutler was nearing the end of a remarkable career, so his timing was spot on. He paired in the second row with his running mate at Brothers, Rod ('Slaughter') McCall. Peter FitzSimons in the biography *John Eales*, wrote of his reaction to being selected: "... the instant Templeton read out the last name, John was awash in handshakes and congratulations. Simon Whitehart, who had come along as John's guest, chuckled quietly as he watched John closely. Just about everyone else he knew would have given themselves the luxury of a couple of air-punches or a few cartwheels around the room for joy. Not John. That would have been showing off.

"... John confided... later that at the moment of the announcement... be darned if it didn't feel a bit like an out-of-body experience.

"That is, in some kind of surreal way, John strongly felt like he was watching someone else being so warmly congratulated, not him. Him, John Eales, the Australian test second-rower, in only his second year of senior rugby? It couldn't be right, could it?"

He was different.

Wales was thrashed mercilessly, by 63-6. Gerald Davies, ex-Welsh great, wrote: "Was there ever such a fall from grace?" As Howell, *et al* wrote in *The Wallabies*: "Rookie John Eales showed his influence on a game as Australia won the lineouts 20-5, and Wales did not win a single one in the second half." A star was truly born! A sporting genius had once more appeared on the world's stage.

England was then beaten by Queensland 30-19, Eales being too much of a handful for the visitors, and a test followed, won by Australia, 40-15. John Eales demonstrated once more what a rare talent he was, and David Hinds, in *The Times*, observed that the victory "must rank as one of the outstanding achievements of modern rugby," and concluded that it really emphasised the superiority of southern hemisphere rugby compared with that in the northern hemisphere.

Next on the schedule was New Zealand, and at Sydney Football Stadium, in front of 41,565 fans, Australia enjoyed a stunning victory by 21-12. Eales and McCall had two of the best locks in the world to contend with, Gary Whetton and Ian Jones. In the return test, played at Eden Park, New Zealand won a cliff-hanger by 6-3. Michael Lynagh had a rare off day with the boot, missing six of seven.

The youngster found himself in the British Isles for the World Cup, and the first match was against Argentina, who always seemed to give Australia difficulty. Eales was picked at number eight, with Troy Coker and Rod McCall in the lock positions. Argentina did not offer much resistance on the day, and Australia won out by 32-19. The main concern for coach Bob Dwyer was where Eales should play.

Dwyer continued with the experiment for game two, against Western Samoa. The match was played in atrocious conditions, the field was soft, the ball was greasy and Western Samoa offered more than expected resistance. Australia won narrowly, 9-3.

Eales was back at lock against Wales with Rod McCall, and the exciting 'Willie O', Willie Ofahengaue, was at number eight. Though the match was at Cardiff Arms Park, there was an easy capitulation. Australia won by 38-3, the biggest winning margin for an international team at the home of Welsh rugby. *The Sydney Telegraph* reported: "Wales were totally eclipsed. They were cut to pieces. The repair work will take a decade."

It was now the quarter-finals, and Australia was matched against Ireland, another country that Australia traditionally had trouble with. The Wallabies won 19-18 in a near-miracle finish, masterminded by the ever-cool Michael Lynagh after captain Nick Farr-Jones was forced from the field.

New Zealand was Australia's opponent in the semi-final, and most experts felt that whoever won would win the World Cup. It was a hard, but sensational win for Australia by 16-6. Australia's defence was particularly gritty.

The final was against England, and the Wallabies won a close one by 12-6. There was only one try in the game, to Australia's prop Tony Daly. Australia was World Champion. It had been some year for John Eales, and he was picked in a *Sydney Morning Herald* World XV.

Greg Growden, had this to say in *The Wallabies World Cup!*: "The baby of the

Wallaby pack, John Eales produced one of the quotes of the tour when he confessed after the Cup victory that it would take at least fifty years for the success to sink in. Eales also provided one of the most exciting moments of the tournament when he gave England five-eighth, Rob Andrew, at least a 10-metre start and then mowed him down with a classic tackle late in the final.

"Eales had an extraordinary opening year to what promises to be a long test career. He was repeatedly named 'man of the match' in the domestic tests before establishing himself in Great Britain as one of the best lineout jumpers in the world. Eales also rates as one of the fastest players in the team and can kick penalty goals from anywhere on the field.

"Although he is only twenty-one, there appears little doubt that Eales will develop into one of Australia's greatest players. He is certainly the most versatile player ever to appear in the Wallaby second row."

It was just continuing success from this point to his retirement. In 1992 Scotland came to Australia and lost both tests, then the serious part of the season began with a 3-match series against New Zealand. Australia squeaked by New Zealand 16-15 at Sydney Football Stadium and at Ballymore won the second by 19-17. The latter saw the infamous Richard Loe late-hit on Paul Carozza after the latter had crossed for a vital try. New Zealand turned things around in the third test, winning a close one 26-23. Eales was injured in the game and had to be replaced but Australia had still enjoyed a wonderful run, winning first the World Cup and then the Bledisloe Cup.

Australia had not been to South Africa in 23 years before 1992, when the Wallabies went there for a 4-match tour. Australia won all its games, including the historic one against South Africa (26-3). It was South Africa's biggest defeat in 100 years of international rugby.

There was a tour to Ireland, Wales and England in 1992, captained by Michael Lynagh. There were 13 matches, Eales playing in six and the first international, a win over Ireland. However he suffered a potentially career-ending injury in the Llanelli match, which was subsequently lost by 9-13. It turned out to be a severe shoulder injury. His rotator cuff was completely ruptured, and he was informed by a medical authority that the nerve damage was so extensive that the possibility of playing again was obscure. The repair work required a four-hour operation and he was unable to play in 1993.

The extent of his inner drive showed as he followed every bit of rehabilitative advice to get his shoulder right. It was tested out at the club and state level, and then he resumed his test career against a touring Irish team, with former school-mate Garrick Morgan his partner in the lock position. He was almost back to his own self, dominating the lineouts, and Australia won both the tests (33-13 and 32-18), had two surprisingly hard games against Italy (23-20 and 20-7), then demolished Western Samoa by 73-3, breaking all kinds of Australian records.

The real test came in a single-match test against the All Blacks, the first-ever Bledisloe Cup match under lights, in front of 41,917. Australia won 20-16, and once more had possession of the Bledisloe Cup. Coach Bob Dwyer said after the game: "For tension, pressure and endeavour it lived up to expectations.

John Eales dominated the lineout like no player before or since.

It was a really good test match."

In 1995 Eales went up against Argentina twice (53-7 and 30-13). In the second test Eales, who dominated the lineout again, won the man-of-the-match award. Then he was off to South Africa for his second World Cup.

It turned out to be a disappointing campaign. Australia lost its first match against South Africa 18-27, beat Canada in an uncertain match (27-11), waxed Romania 42-3 and seemed as if they were on the way, but were beaten by England in a cliff-hanger. Bruce Wilson wrote, in *The Courier Mail*: "Some of the Australians covered themselves in glory, none more so than John Eales – who had one of the best forward matches I have ever seen." One item of concern at the time was the threat of professionalism, the World Rugby Corporation led by Ross Turnbull making moves, signing up players. However his move was averted by News Corporation when they signed a pay television deal for $760 million with southern hemisphere rugby unions. But professionalism was there to stay.

Things did not improve psychologically for the Wallabies, as they lost the Bledisloe Cup with two losses, 16-28 and 23-34, Jonah Lomu making the difference in the matches.

In 1995 a new chapter evolved in the life of John Eales. Greg Smith was the new coach, and Eales the new Australian captain. At the instigation of the new chairman of the ARU, Eales was approached. FitzSimons takes up the story in *John Eales*: "'John, I asked you here to talk about the Wallaby captaincy. The board is offering it to you. Will you accept it?'

"At that instant, John had strange thoughts running through his head and was momentarily out-of-kilter. He was, frankly, surprised at the way it was done, having always thought that something like that would not be offered, as he couldn't imagine anyone ever refusing. Surmising that Dick was expecting him to think about it before answering, John proceeded to do just that. "Tick. Tick. Ti...

"Of course, Dick, I'd love to...

"The captaincy settled with a handshake to seal the deal, McGruther then warmed to a couple of other themes he'd thought about in the lead-up to this conversation. He advised John that if he was going to be an effective captain he'd probably have to be more assertive and forceful than his normal easy-going character, with which John readily agreed."

It is an interesting subject, as the board was under the assumption that he had to change his approach, and yet the reason they chose him was because of what he was. There is a general presumption of what a captain should be, when it simply is not so. A team will respond to any captain, quiet or assertive, if that captain is respected and trusted.

So it was a new beginning for Eales, who captained Australia in twelve matches in 1996, ten of them tests. The report card in the tests that year read seven wins and three losses, to New Zealand twice and South Africa once. Eales was also honoured to captain his first overseas tour to Italy and the British Isles.

In 1997 Eales played in ten tests, of which six were won, one drawn and three lost. The losses were to New Zealand twice and Argentina, while the draw was against England.

In 1998 Eales had sufficient captaincy experience, coach Rod Macqueen was in charge and the Wallabies had definite short-term and long-term goals. Thirteen tests were played under his stewardship and only two were lost, both to South Africa. The Cook Cup was Australia's, as was the Bledisloe Cup. Only the Tri-Nations escaped their grasp. John was the dominant lineout forward in the world, everyone astonished at his versatility. In that year there were some massive victories including a 76-0 pasting of an inept English side and a 74-0 demolition of Tonga.

In a phenomenal performance in the third test against New Zealand, John Eales kicked four penalties and a conversion. Against Fiji, he landed a penalty goal and six conversions; against Tonga, two conversions; against Manu Samoa, two penalty goals and two conversions; against France, five penalty goals and a conversion; against England, four penalty goals. While he was taking the duties of captaincy taken in his stride, he also breezed through the kicking responsibilities, showing unbelievable poise under pressure. No other lock in the world could do the things Eales was producing in match after match

Eales was injured in the gymnasium using weights and missed the early tests in 1999, which was another World Cup year. He was encouraged as he received an Order of Australia, then was named in Queensland's 'Team of the Century' and the *Sydney Morning Herald* named him the best forward of the century. Colin Meads had won the comparable combination in New Zealand. Meads and Eales. What a duo that would have been!

After six months of rehabilitation, he was back for the 1999 World Cup, playing in all but the USA game. In his first match, Australia beat Ireland 23-3, Eales kicking two penalties. Then he was back in action against Wales, for a 24-9 victory. South Africa was beaten by 27-21 in the semi-final after extra time and then Australia beat France somewhat easily in the final by 35-12. Rod Macqueen and the freakish captain John Eales had done it. It was his third World Cup, and second win. The William Webb Ellis Trophy was Australia's and Eales proudly held it above his head on the podium.

When the victory was sealed, it was described by Peter FitzSimons in *John Eales*: "Almost as one the Wallabies lifted their arms in triumph before dropping them to embrace each other, and many a tear was shed in the tumultuous scenes that followed and not just on the ground. Up in the Channel Seven broadcast box Chris Handy, his voice breaking, said, 'It doesn't matter if you're a stunned mullet, a young dingo or a vintage red – give them a cheer, Australia, they've done you proud'."

John Eales was now 29 years of age. He had come back from two horrific shoulder injuries, and each time he came back as well as ever. But he decided to play on and captained Australia in ten more tests, only two of which were lost - to New Zealand and England, by close scores. In the first test against New Zealand Australia fell behind by 0-24, but under the leadership of their captain fought back. Australia lost a sensational match by 35-39.

In the second test, with the score 23-21 to New Zealand and a mere 30 seconds remaining on the clock, the captain dragged himself out of a ruck 30 metres from the tryline and some fifteen metres in touch and elected to take the penalty Australia had just been awarded himself. In one of the most dramatic moments in Bledisloe Cup history, the remarkable Eales slotted it over. There was pandemonium in the stands. Everyone understood the immensity of the pressure, and the vision of Eales making that kick will ever be among their most treasured rugby memories. As Rod Macqueen put it: "It was pretty fitting it was John. He's a great captain and it was just another example of the things he can do."

He continued for one more season and led Australia in seven more tests. Then it was time, and he bowed out with a 29-26 win over New Zealand on September 1 2001.

He had an amazing career. The player of the century. The Queensland team of the century and surely the captain of the century.

There had never been anyone quite like him. The last-second kick. The dropped goal from near halfway. The jump to stop the ball going over the cross-bar. On and on it went, memories clouding out memories, of this good-looking young giant up in the air, beating the best of the world.

He played 112 matches for his state and 97 matches for his country, 86 of them tests. He captained Australia in a record 55 tests, an absolutely unbelievable performance.

The records, the feats, they were remarkable. But there was John Eales the man. A gentleman. A man who stood by his ethics. A family man. A nice person. No wonder players followed him, went into battle with him. Because they all knew he was a good man who would never let them down.

So what records did John Eales set?

- The most matches as Australian captain (55) and second on the all-time list behind Will Carling.
- Most capped lock forward in world rugby (86), ahead of Willie John McBride (80) and Ian Jones (79).
- Fifth highest international career points tally for Australia, one of only 12 Australians to score 100 or more career points and the only forward to do so.
- First on the all-time test career points scoring list for forwards. John is one of only two forwards to score 100 test match points.
- Most capped Australian player in internationals against Scotland (7) and equal highest against England (8) and Argentina (7).
- Only one of five players (Dan Crowley, Tim Horan, Phil Kearns and Jason Little) to win the Rugby World Cup on two occasions.
- In twelve international matches at his home ground of Ballymore, from 1991-98, John Eales never played in a losing side.

JOHN EALES

CAPTAIN: 60 matches (55 tests) (1996 Wales 2, Canada 1, South Africa 2, New Zealand 2, Italy 1, Scotland 1, Ireland 1, 1997 France 2, England 2, New Zealand 2, South Africa 1, Argentina 2, Scotland 1, 1998 England 2, Scotland 2, New Zealand 3, South Africa 2, Fiji 1, Tonga1, Manu Samoa 1, France 1, 1999 Romania 1, Ireland 1, Wales 1, South Africa 1, France 1, 2000 Argentina 2, South Africa 3, New Zealand 2, France 1, Scotland 1, England 1, 2001 British & Irish Lions 3, South Africa 2, New Zealand 2)
BORN: 27 June 1970
SCHOOL: Ashgrove Marist Brothers
CLUB: Brothers (44 first grade games)
QUEENSLAND REPRESENTATION: 112 matches (1990-2001)
AUSTRALIAN REPRESENTATION: 97 matches (86 tests) (1991-2001)

TIM HORAN

The Explosive Centre

The names of Tim Horan and Jason Little will be linked forever. Their biographies were written together, they played against each other at school, they played together at Souths, the 'Reds' and the Wallabies, and they seem to have been injured about the same time.

They were one of the truly great centre pairings, like Syd King and Cyril Towers in the 20s, Max Howell and Trevor Allan in the 40s, Jimmy Phipps and Herb Barker in the 50s, Dick Marks and Beres Ellwood in the 60s, Geoff Shaw and Bill McKid in the 70s and Michael Hawker and Michael O'Connor in the 80s. Jason was tall and long-legged, whereas Tim Horan had the perfect inside centre build, solid and reasonably low to the ground. They were a perfect match-up.

Tim had wonderful acceleration, and could make breaks on the inside and outside. He was also very strong, and at times appeared to be held and yet burst through. His defence was sound, his running style quite distinct, with short, sharp steps.

Coach John Connolly said of him in Ian Diehm's *Red! Red! Red!*: "He is a magnificent player, a player who can do almost anything on the field. It's a tremendous asset that he is a great member of the team [Queensland]. He is so important to all of us. Tim makes things happen. He helps other players have great games. That is the true measure of his greatness."

Wallaby great Andrew Slack added his thoughts on the Horan-Little pairing in *Red! Red! Red!*: "Horan and Little are both world-class centres. Little has really come out of Horan's shadow. I think Little's the better athlete and Horan's the more explosive runner."

While Little went to Toowoomba Grammar, Horan was at Downlands, four kilometres away. They were both brought up on farms.

The first XV coach at Downlands was John Elders, who had coached England. In Michael Blucher's *The Perfect Union*, he had this to say of young Horan at school: "He had natural talent, certainly. But the quality that really stood out in my mind was his determination to improve, to learn, to win, to compete... in every sport he played, cricket, athletics, rugby... he was exactly the same."

Both Horan and Little, and other Darling Downs-based Australian Schoolboys, agreed that they would play for Souths in Brisbane.

Tim Horan came into his own in 1989, playing for Australia 'B' and Queensland 'B' against the touring British Lions. In that Australian 'B' team there were many who would make their mark in the game, including David Knox, Brad Girvan, Dominic Maguire, Brad Burke, Steve Tuynman, Scott Gourlay, Peter FitzSimons, Damien Frawley, Ewen McKenzie, Tom Lawton and Mark Harthill. Horan played five-eighth, and though he played most of his career in the centre, there were times when he would play in the pivot slot. The Brits got a shock that day, as they scraped home by a 23-18 score.

Tim Horan: Perhaps Australia's greatest ever inside centre.

Bob Dwyer was the new Australian coach, and he picked the type of player who was capable of playing his way, surprising many with his team to face the All Blacks at Auckland. Tim Horan was picked as a centre outside Randwick's Lloyd Walker, but the real shock was the selection of Tony Daly and Phil Kearns in the front row. Neither had played a representative match, and hooker Tom Lawton in particular felt aggrieved. Greg Martin was also selected in this match. New Zealand won the encounter by 24-12, and the new boys all justified their selections.

On the basis of their performances, they were selected on the Farr-Jones-captained Wallaby team to Canada and France. Tim played in six of the ten matches, including the two French tests, the first won 32-15 and the second lost 19-25. In that first test Horan scored two tries, and the two 19-year-old centres Little and Horan played like veterans. It was obvious that they were both there for the long haul.

The year 1990 started with a tour by France, and in a violent match when the French flanker Benazzi was ordered off the field, Horan had to leave the field with second-degree medial ligament damage. Fortunately, he worked diligently to get his leg back to shape and this was managed so he could tour New Zealand in July and August with the Wallabies. Ironically, Jason Little broke his ankle against the USA and was not available.

Horan played in five of the 12 matches, including the three tests. New Zealand won the first two tests by 21-6 and 27-17, but the Wallabies rebounded and won the third by a 21-9 score. After the match, on a bet if a test was won, Tim Horan and Nick Farr-Jones plunged into the icy-cold water of Wellington Harbour.

The year 1991 was a World Cup year, and everything was geared towards that. But first there were tests against Wales, England and New Zealand. That 1991 tour was a never-to-be forgotten experience, as Australia won the Cup. Horan played against Argentina (won 32-19), Western Samoa (won 9-3), Wales (38-3), had a narrow, Michael Lynagh-inspired victory over Ireland (19-18), then beat New Zealand (16-6) in the semi-final, and England (12-6) in the final.

Michael Blucher describes a critical moment in the final in *The Perfect Union*: "However, if there was one single moment which turned the game, it came in the 28th minute. Australia were leading 3-0 but were on the back pedal, like they had been for the bulk of the first half. England flyhalf Rob Andrew hoisted ahead, in the direction of Horan, who had darted diagonally across field, sensing Australia was badly short on the right. He couldn't have been positioned more perfectly. He soared above Rory Underwood, took the ball and braced himself for Mick Skinner's big hit. But the huge English flanker bounced off, likewise halfback Richard Hill. As Horan spun to his left and set sail for the right hand sideline, English hooker Brian Moore ploughed across in cover but didn't have the speed. Horan's great rival, Will Carling, did. Knowing that that the English skipper had him covered, and unable to position Campese for the pass inside, Horan kicked ahead, a 'banana' kick, which he hoped might turn and bounce into touch close to the English line. The result was better than he could have imagined. The ball bounced right and English fullback Jonathan Webb was still forced to take it across the sideline, giving Australia the lineout throw some 5m out. The rest is history. Kearns threw a perfect throw to Willie O. at No. 5, a rolling maul, and CRASH! Down went Tony Daly and Ewen McKenzie, the ball squashed over the line under 230kg of front row might."

Greg Growden had this to say in *The Wallabies World Cup!*: "Tim Horan surely ranks, with Willie Ofahengaue, as one of the most alluring targets for Sydney Rugby League scouts, their arms loaded with money. A potential representative captain, Horan is the ultimate footballer, combining wisdom with precise ball skills and resolute defence.

"Horan was one of the most consistent Australian players of the 1991 World Cup tour. He was an integral part of a highly productive back line and worked perfectly between Jason Little and Michael Lynagh. The trio were so similar in intent and even looks that one member of the Wallaby management began calling them Huey, Duey and Louie. Yet not even Walt Disney could have dreamt up some of the football fantasies Horan tried to achieve and usually succeeded in realising during the 1991 World Cup campaign."

The rugby schedule did not lessen in 1992. First Scotland visited, Australia winning both tests, and next there were three matches against the All Blacks. The first was won by 16-15, the second by 19-17, and the third was won by New Zealand, 23-26. Either team could have won any game, they were so close. So the Bledisloe Cup was Australia's, on top of the William Webb Ellis trophy. Australian rugby had hit a new all-time high, and Little and Horan were arguably the world's best centres.

But the year was far from over. There was a 4-match tour of South Africa, Australia winning the test 26-3. Terry Smith wrote: "Farr-Jones was in his pomp, Michael Lynagh shrugged off a painful knee injury to keep things under control and centre Tim Horan bounced back to his best."

"One highlight occurred at the 74 minute mark. Tim Horan burst upfield and chipped ahead, but Horan trapped him and flipped him over. The ball went to David Campese, and he scored his 50th test try, the first player to reach the mark."

Following the visit to South Africa, Michael Lynagh captained a tour to Ireland, Wales and England in 1992. Horan played in seven of the 13 games, as well as both tests.

1993 was another full year, with tests against Tonga and three against South Africa, Australia winning the historic series by 2-1. It was in the third test that a writer called David Campese "the Mozart of Rugby." Tim scored Australia's only try in the decider. That same year there was an 11-match tour of North America and France. In the first test against Canada Greg Growden wrote: "Australian inside centre Tim Horan deserved special praise. Even though he was in doubt for several days with a corked thigh, he showed he is still one of the best in international rugby in seizing on the slightest opportunities and making space where no-one else could."

There were two tests against France, Australia narrowly losing the first 13-16 and winning the second comfortably by 24-3. In the latter match, coach Bob Dwyer commented: "I think this was the hardest match I've seen. I just thought it was all very, very well done by our players. France must have had the biggest pack ever assembled. They were giants, but our defence stood up to it... Tim Horan and Jason Little's defence was again outstanding."

The year 1994 was one Tim Horan, or 'Helmet' as he was nick-named, would like to forget. While playing for Queensland against Natal in the Super Ten final he badly injured his knee. He was 23 and had 33 tests under his belt. It looked like the end of his career, but everyone reckoned without that one quality Tim was loaded with, determination. The Australian team physiotherapist Greg Cray even took him into his home in Sydney, and his Brisbane employers gave him all the time off he wanted, at full pay. Even then, because of the horrendous nature of the injury, the doubters felt that even if he recovered it would be the end of his test rugby.

By 1995, through sheer determination and application, he was playing for Queensland 'B' against Argentina. The leg had come right and his skills had not eroded. He made a remarkable recovery to be selected for the World Cup squad, playing against Canada and Romania before Australia lost 22-25 to England. There were also two tests against New Zealand that year; while they were lost, Tim Horan was back and would play four more full years.

In 1996 he was in full swing, with tests against Wales, Canada, South Africa and New Zealand. Horan played his 40th test against Wales, surpassing the Wallaby record for test appearances by a centre previously held by Andrew Slack at 39. In the South African game that was part of the Tri-Nations series, Australia won by 21-16. Spiro Zavos noted: "Occasionally a sports event transcends the actual contest and becomes a symbol for something much greater. The credibility of

Australian rugby was at stake on Saturday night." Greg Growden added: "Australian centre Tim Horan was immaculate in counter-attack and organising the defence line." New Zealand won both the Bledisloe Cup and the inaugural Tri-Nations series that year.

The end-of-the-year tour in 1996 had a new captain, John Eales, and was to Italy and the British Isles. Australia beat Scotland and Ireland, but Eales had to leave the field in his 73rd match. He was unable to play against Wales, and so Tim Horan was accorded the signal honour of captaining his country, for the first and only time in a test. The Wallabies were victorious, writer Evan Whitton writing in *The Australian*: "This was a curious match at the end of a curious tour. Timothy Horan is surely the most adventurous captain in the history of rugby. In the face of an iron rule that the only time you don't take the points is when you are 50 in front or 50 behind, he declined to take 11 kickable penalties, and so established a record that will probably never be surpassed." The fact is, his tactic worked, and it was a 28-9 win. Tim went on to captain Australia in a non-test but important match, a winning one against the Barbarians. So his captaincy record was perfect.

He played nine tests in 1997. In that year Wallaby coach Greg Smith switched Horan and Pat Howard in the inside backs, moving his star centre into five-eighth. Horan broke his thumb playing against New Zealand in July and Stephen Larkham replaced him. He was back into action late in the year, playing twice against Argentina and once versus England and Scotland.

In 1998 there were 11 tests in a busy year, with Australia winning the Cook Cup against England and then playing and winning two tests against Scotland. Although the Tri-Nations was lost to South Africa, Australia achieved a 3-match clean sweep in the Bledisloe Cup series. At the end of the year there were World Cup qualifiers against Fiji (won 66-20), Tonga (74-0) and Manu Samoa (25-13).

The following year, 1999, was a World Cup year. First of all Australia won the Lansdowne Cup against Ireland, the Cook Cup against England, the Bledisloe Cup was retained, although New Zealand regained the Tri-Nations title.

The World Cup of 1999 was the icing on the cake for Tim Horan. He played in five of the six games, against Romania (won 57-9), Ireland (won 23-3), Wales (24-9), South Africa (27-21) and the final against France (won 35-12)

As Howell *et al* summed up the awesome victory: "Tim Horan, as ever, was the man to give Australia the edge in the backs, his incisive running always likely to create a break. He was later recognised as the player of the tournament."

What a way to end an illustrious career, player of the tournament in the prestigious World Cup. However he turned out next season, at home against Argentina, but injured his ankle severely and called it a day. In all he had played 100 matches for his country, 80 of them tests. He had been part of two World Cup-winning teams and he had the honour of captaining his country twice, once in a test against Wales and once against the Barbarians, both in 1996.

TIM HORAN
CAPTAIN: 2 matches (1 test) (v Wales 1996)
BORN: 18 May 1970
SCHOOL: Downlands
CLUB: Souths (Qld)
QUEENSLAND REPRESENTATION: 1990–2000
AUSTRALIAN REPRESENTATION: 100 matches (80 tests) (1989-2000)

DAVID WILSON

The Non-Stop Flanker

David Wilson attended high school at Brisbane State High, which has developed a few Wallabies over the years, such as Mark Bartholomeusz (2002), Eddie Bonis (1929-38), Paul Carozza (1990-93), Paul Kahl (1992), Peter McLean (1978-82), Bill McLean (1946-47), Paul Mooney (1954), Chris Roche (1982-94 and who also attended Downlands), Bernie Schulte (1946), Peter Slattery (1990-95), Tom Barker (1978), Fred Whyatt (1931) and Brian Smith (1987).

While at school Wilson was picked to play in the Australian Under-17 team. He missed three GPS games, and therefore, in a ridiculous decision by narrow-minded individuals, was demoted to the school's second team for the rest of the season.

Incensed, Wilson decided to repeat his final year but transferred to Ipswich Grammar, not overly noted as a Wallaby nursery as only two former students had ever attained test status, Ken Donald (1957-59) and Eric Francis (1914). While there he made the Australian Schoolboy team to tour the United Kingdom. It was captained by Ricky Stuart, who became a Wallaby and then a rugby league great.

A fit, fast and dedicated flanker, David played for Easts Club in Brisbane, and slowly but surely made his presence felt. At 22 years of age he had his first representative appearance against the British Isles in 1989. There were a few others in that team who achieved higher recognition in the game, such as youngsters Jason Little and Tim Horan, Ilie Tabua and Tom Lawton. It was tough to make the State team that year, with back-rowers like Sam Scott-Young, Brendan Nasser and Jeff Miller floating around, each young and highly talented.

Two years passed before Wilson reappeared on the national scene, being selected for an Emerging Wallabies team to play England. It looked as if he would make the 1990 tour of New Zealand because of the unavailability of Simon Poidevin and Jeff Miller, but the possibility ended when he broke an ankle in a game for Easts.

It was another year before he was fully recognised. Now 25 years of age, he provided a perfect example of the value of patience and increasing experience. It had been three years since his Queensland 'B' representation, and he had honed his skills while never giving up on his ambitions.

He was selected in the Queensland side to play Scotland, a match drawn 15-15, due in no small part to his tenacious tackling and speed to

David Wilson was renowned for his non-stop play.

the ruck. Wilson then found himself chosen for the first test. Also making his debut was Paul Carozza, his running mate at Brisbane State High. They both impressed in the 27-12 victory, and were retained for the second test, won by 37-13.

The next three tests represented a tough assignment, as they were against the All Blacks. Australia won the series 2-1, with scores of 16-15, 19-17 and 23-26. No more than three points had separated the teams in any match and, remarkably, both sides had scored and given up the same number of points and both had scored two tries apiece in each test. Wilson teamed up with Troy Coker and Willie Ofahengaue in the series and found himself against Michael Jones, Mike Brewer, Kevin Schuler and Andy Earl at various times.

There were two tours that year including the first to South Africa in 23 years. There was only one test, which Australia won by 26-3. Terry Smith wrote: "The backrowers Tim Gavin, David Wilson and Willie Ofahengaue, John Eales, who proved he is much more than a lineout pylon, and hooker Phil Kearns all did Australia proud..." Wilson played in three of the four matches in South Africa.

Then he was off to Ireland, Wales and England. There were two tests, Australia easily winning each, against Ireland and Wales. Wilson scored a try at Cardiff Arms Park.

From 1993 onwards David Wilson was a vital member of the Wallaby pack, his non-stop play gaining the plaudits of his team-mates. One feature of his play was that he was the ultimate team man, putting his body on the line continuously for his team and his country. Hyper and super-charged, he never stopped coming at his opponents, like a terrier on the loose. Always, however, he played according to the rules.

In 1993 Wilson played tests against Tonga, South Africa and New Zealand, before embarking on another overseas tour, this time to North America and France. Canada was demolished by 43-16, but things immediately stiffened up in the French tests. Australia was shattered in the first test, as the players felt they should have won a match which was lost 13-16. Australia bounced back with a 24-3 victory in the second test, Marty Roebuck playing a fantastic game.

The World Cup defence was slated for 1995 and all eyes were looking ahead, even as 1994 unfolded. Australia had first of all to bond on the field, and then fine-tune its game for the Cup. The Wallabies had a great lead-up a year out and the team seemed to be building nicely as Australia won all its 1994 tests, against Ireland (2), Italy (2), Western Samoa, New Zealand, and Argentina (2).

Everything seemed to be going well, but Australia came apart in the World Cup's first round against South Africa, losing by 18-27. The Springboks played to a high level in the first World Cup match held in their country, but Australia made a plethora of errors and consequently had their backs to the wall. The headlines of the *Cape Times* read: "Campo and co are now world chumps."

Wilson was rested against Canada, Australia unconvincing in its 27-11 victory, but was back against Romania. In this match Daniel Herbert and Wilson bumped into one another like wayward bulls, and both had deep head wounds that needed running repairs as Romania was beaten 42-3.

Australia thus made the quarter-finals against England. Any loss now meant an exit from the tournament. David Campese, he of the loose tongue, infuriated English supporters and players. In a World Cup programme he described the English captain: "[Will] Carling himself epitomises England's lack of skills. He has speed and bulk, but plays like a castrated bull." As for the team, he said: "This is a team which prays for sunshine, but which carries an umbrella." And: "Forget footballs, the only thing you're liable to get on the end of an English backline is chilblains." Ironically, winger Tony Underwood scored England's sole try. Kicking won the game, and Rob Andrew kicked over one more than Michael Lynagh. The 25-22 game could not have been closer and either team could have won, but it was England's day. All the Wallabies could do now was head for home.

David Wilson was always unspectacular, but those on the field knew how vital his role was, so he was virtually an automatic choice in 1996 against Wales (2 tests), Canada, South Africa (2) and New Zealand (2). Much of the zip had gone out of the Wallabies, as they lost both games against New Zealand and broke even against South Africa.

It was almost with a measure of relief that the Wallabies went on tour to Europe under new skipper John Eales, and Wilson played in eight of the 12 games, including the first test. In one mid-week, non-test match, he was appointed captain, and the team won 29-19. He was very honoured by the appointment, but did not envision that in the near future he would captain the Wallabies in a test. Wilson was not in a losing match on this tour and all tests were won: Italy 40-18, Scotland 29-19, Ireland 22-12 and Wales 28-19. Competition was a lot easier in the northern hemisphere. David scored two tries against Italy. There were seven replacement players sent from Australia on this tour, a record, the most serious being because of a fracture to the right eye socket inflicted on John Eales.

Australia seemed on the way back at this point, for in 1997 France came and lost the two tests, meaning Australia had won six in a row. The team came back to earth at Lancaster Park, Christchurch, being taken apart by 13-30. The All Black backrow of Taine Randell, Zinzan Brooke and Josh Kronfeld was simply too strong for the Wallabies. The series resulted in a white-wash, Australia losing the other two tests 18-33 and 24-36. Wilson was captain in that third match.

At least Australia won the Cook Cup that year, beating and then drawing with England. A ray of sunshine suddenly appeared for the Wallabies, as they downed South Africa in Brisbane by 32-20.

Andrew Dawson wrote, in *The Courier Mail*: "The Australian forwards, with Matt Cockbain, John Eales, Owen Finegan and David Wilson inspired contributors, gave halves George Gregan and David Knox the swift, quality possession which the backline had been craving for all season.

"Wilson was to the Australian forwards what Tune was to the backs. He was supreme, absolutely special at the breakdowns..."

That sunshine was only momentary, as Australia was absolutely shellacked in South Africa by the unprecedented score of 61-22. Peter Jenkins wrote in *The Australian*: "It ranks as arguably the darkest day in Australian rugby union. A loss to sit alongside the defeat by Tonga in 1973 as the most embarrassing, most disgraceful, most inept display in Wallaby history." Greg Smith resigned over the pressure and Rod Macqueen took over. David Wilson had the misfortune to be Australian captain in the debacle, and it was a good eighteen months before his opportunity came again.

Ultimately 34 players with the new coach embarked on a 7-match tour of Argentina and the British Isles in 1997. Macqueen, who had been coach of the Brumbies, picked eight of that team in the starting lineup in the first test against Argentina. Wilson was not one of the starting team, the flankers being Brett Robinson and Owen Finegan. He came back as a replacement against England and Scotland. A determined character, he took every opportunity he could, and worked his way into Macqueen's starting team as 1998 opened.

Wilson played in twelve tests that year, proving his worth to the team. When a much-weakened England arrived they were demolished in record-breaking fashion by 76-0. The remaining opponents of the year were Scotland, New Zealand, South Africa, Fiji, Manu Samoa, France and England again. Out of the 12 tests 10 were won and the Wallabies were back on track under Macqueen.

When 1999 came around, John Eales had an early-season injury, and Macqueen called on Wilson to captain the Wallabies in the first seven tests, two against Ireland, one against England and the four Tri-nations matches.

John Eales resumed the captaincy in the 1999 World Cup but Wilson was a vital component of the squad, starting in five of the tests. In the final, Australia beat France 35-12 to win the World Cup and become the first side to win the Cup twice. While Wilson had not been in the 1991 squad, he knew the despair of losing in 1995 and the exhilaration and wonder of victory. It had been a marvellous campaign, and each of the participants became part of history.

David Wilson soldiered on in 2000, but decided to finish his rugby overseas. His determination, single-mindedness and fitness saw the 30-year-old reach the pinnacle of world rugby, where he had gained universal respect. He played 96 matches for Australia, 79 of them tests. He could certainly thumb his nose at the school that dropped him when he made the Australian Under-17s. He backed himself by switching schools, never vacillated in his courage and determination with Easts and Queensland, and made it to the top of the rugby ladder. A resolute character, he had achieved his wildest dreams by captaining his country in nine tests.

DAVID WILSON

CAPTAIN: 12 matches (9 tests) (1997 New Zealand 1, South Africa 1, 1999 Ireland 2, England 1, South Africa 2, New Zealand 2)
BORN: 4 January 1967
SCHOOL: Brisbane State High School/ Ipswich Grammar
CLUB: Easts (Brisbane)
QUEENSLAND REPRESENTATION: (1989-2000)
AUSTRALIAN REPRESENTATION: 96 matches (79 tests) (1992-2000)

JASON LITTLE

The Elegant Centre

JASON LITTLE was a product of the Darling Downs and at Toowoomba Grammar School he showed that he was an exceptional all-round student athlete. He spent two weeks in Los Angeles representing Australia at the World Junior Athletics Championships. He was in the Australian Under 17 Rugby team, and was an outstanding cricketer. Toowoomba had never won the GPS cricket title until Jason was at the school, and then they won it twice.

A teacher at the school, a Mr Bourne, told him at this critical period of his life, as quoted in Michael Blucher's *Perfect Union*: "Well, to be perfectly honest Jason, I think you're a better cricketer than you are a rugby player. I believe you've got a better long-term future in cricket than any other sport." Fortunately he ignored his advice, going on to become one of Australia's greatest ever centres, and his partnership with Tim Horan was respected throughout the world. Australia have had some great centre pairings throughout the years, from the time of Syd King and Cyril Towers. While at school, his friendly rival at Downlands School was Tim Horan.

By 17 years of age Jason was playing rugby for Souths at Brisbane, and his talent was immediately noticed. He made an appearance for Queensland 'B' against the British Isles in 1989, and at 19 years of age was taken on his first Wallaby tour, to Canada and France. Nick Farr-Jones was captain and his mate Horan was also aboard. The other two centres were Dominic Maguire and Anthony Herbert. After matches against the North American Wolverines, Languedoc Regional Selection, a Cote D'Azur Selection and an Alpes Regional XV, he and Horan were pitched in against an experienced and tough French national team. The young centres played like veterans in their first test together, Horan scoring two tries. Both players were beginning illustrious careers.

The French were not so easy in the second test, winning a hard-fought match by 25-19. The two young centres were blooded in a tough cauldron, and showed nothing but class.

The year 1990 was not a good one for the youngsters. The French visited Australia, and Jason played for Queensland against them and the three tests, two of which were won by the Wallabies. In the first test, Horan had a bad medial cartilage injury and that ended his campaign that year. Little was partnered by Paul Cornish, who later on broke his neck, thus ending his career, and Anthony Herbert.

Jason Little was also injured that year, breaking his ankle in the final minutes of a 67-9 romp over USA. 'The Perfect Union' was certainly that, both being wiped out for much of the rest of the year.

In 1991 Jason was back in full flight, playing for Queensland against Wales and England, single tests against Wales and England, and two tests against the All Blacks. Next on the calendar was the 1991 World Cup held in England. Little played against Argentina, Wales, Ireland, New Zealand and England, with Australia winning the Cup. It was a glorious moment for the team, but also for Australian rugby.

The closest match was against Ireland, when it looked like the match was lost as time was almost up. Michael Lynagh took charge, as Farr-Jones was off the field injured. He said: "1. Everybody stay calm. 2. Kick deep into the left corner. 3. Get the ball back and secure possession. 4. The backs will do the rest." Everyone followed orders, Lynagh scored, and Australia won that day.

Michael Blucher describes the aftermath of the final in *Perfect Union*: "On the right side of the foyer, just across from the concierge desk, a bleary-eyed Anthony Herbert was still coming to terms with the ungodly hour. Jug of Cointreau and ice in one hand, passport in the other, Herbert bent down and unzipped the William Webb Ellis Trophy from its bulky foam case.

"He tucked the gold trophy under his arm. 'Come on Bill. We're taking you home.'"

Greg Growden wrote of Jason in *The Wallabies' World Cup*: "The fun-loving prankster of the Australian outfit, Jason Little may take delight in putting carpet snakes in team-mates' bags, but he balances such off-field misbehaviour with moments of grandeur on the football field. Australia's advancement through the semi-final against New Zealand and success against England can be attributed to Little's zealous enthusiasm in ensuring that not one opponent got past him.

"Little's defensive record in earlier tests had been open to criticism, but during the World Cup he was involved in countless telling tackles of repeatedly rounded up opponents who strayed. Similarly, his attacking relationship with close friend Tim Horan was inspiring, producing numerous important midfield breaks and setting up several vital tries."

It was tough to come back to earth after the World Cup, but a heavy schedule awaited the Wallabies.

The rugby year had scarcely got underway when the tests against the All Blacks got going, and there was general euphoria when Australia won two of the three tests and the Bledisloe Cup was back in Australia's hands. The second test featured the despicable act of All Black Richard Loe in hitting Paul Carozza late after he scored. It was Little who set up Carozza for the try that gave the Wallabies an 11-7 halftime lead.

All Black coach Laurie Mains said after the match: "Australia are the world champions, they have just beaten us in a series and they are a great team. They deserve to be called world champions at the moment."

There was a short tour to South Africa, the Wallabies winning the test by 26-3, and then there was a tour led by Michael Lynagh to Ireland, Wales and England. All this was heady stuff for a country boy from the Darling Downs. Jason played in eight of the 13 matches, including the tests against Ireland (won 42-17) and Wales (23-6). The year 1992 was one that Jason Little could never forget.

His test total was mounting now, and in 1993 he played one against Tonga, three against South Africa and one against New Zealand, the latter a 10-25 loss that meant the Bledisloe Cup had changed hands once more.

At the end of the year he was off again, under Michael Lynagh, to North America and France. Little played the most games, eight, and the tests with France were split.

Graceful and elegant, Jason Little was equally at home in the centre or on the wing.

Reebok

The following year, 1994, was another bad one. Queensland played Natal in the final of the Super Ten and both Horan and Little were injured, Horan's injury taking twelve months to heal before he graced the field again while Jason was out for three months. Incredibly, they were operated on the same day in Brisbane, and had hospital beds next to one another. They liked doing things together, but this was carrying things a bit far.

In 1995 Jason was back in the swim, with two tests against Argentina before the Wallabies began their World Cup defence, this time in South Africa. The William Webb Ellis Trophy was lost, Australia losing to both South Africa and England and, on return to Australia, the campaign for the Bledisloe Cup fell apart. It was not the year of years for Jason or Australia.

Jason, and Tim Horan for that matter, were continually subjected to offers to go to rugby league, but both declined.

Jason played eight tests in 1997, nine in 1998 and nine in the 1999 domestic season. Finally, Australia was involved in another World Cup. This was personally important for a number of reasons. First, it was Jason's third World Cup. Second, Australia won and he was more appreciative than he was as a young player eight years earlier, as the realization of all the hard work and the achievement to attain such a goal was more meaningful. Thirdly, he was honoured to be called upon as Australia's test captain. Like many others before him, it was only for a single test but that does not make the magnitude of the occasion any less. A proud Australian, it was a great moment in his life.

He played on in the year 2000, engaging in seven tests, and then he called it a day. He had enjoyed a fabulous, brilliant career in which he played 92 matches for his country, 75 of them tests. Those who saw him in action marvelled at the rhythm of this great athlete, floating around and through opponents in at times a ghost-like manner. In many ways he was the Mark Waugh of rugby, or Victor Trumper, immortalised by cricket writer Neville Cardus. There was an elegance to his game, an effortlessness. He was a natural, playing with fluidity and grace, and what we tend to forget is that he played inside centre, outside centre and wing at the test level, all equally well. He was a gifted athlete, and more's the pity when such players depart the scene.

And he captained his country.

In *The Perfect Union* Tim Horan tells of the other side of Jason Little. He says he is one of the ten worst cooks of all time, he is incredibly modest, and does not like to be known as only a rugby player, and has given away his precious memorabilia to charity or friends.

As Horan describes him: "But I tend to think it's because he is essentially a very private person who feels uncomfortable when other people make a fuss over him He has never been able to understand what the big deal is all about. He plays rugby because he enjoys the game, the friends, and the lifestyle it provides. But that's where it stops. He's not interested in breaking records, or reaching milestones. He couldn't even tell you the score in the World Cup final. Once a game is over, it's history."

JASON LITTLE
CAPTAIN: 1 match (1 test) (v USA 1999)
BORN: 26 August 1970
SCHOOL: Toowoomba Grammar
CLUB: Souths
QUEENSLAND REPRESENTATION: 1989-98
NEW SOUTH WALES REPRESENTATION: 1999-2000
AUSTRALIAN REPRESENTATION: 92 matches (75 tests) (1989-2000)

GEORGE GREGAN

'The Chosen One'

HIS FULL NAME is George Musarurwa Gregan. His middle name means 'The Chosen One' and that is what he appears to be, the chosen one to lead Australia into battle on the rugby field.

George was born in Lusaka, Zambia, Africa, in 1973. His mother, Jenny, was a Zimbabwean nurse and his father John an Australian pharmacist. George, at birth, was registered with the Australian High Commission. At ten months of age, the family moved back to Australia, residing in the Australian Capital Territory.

From the time he was mobile he was interested in sport, and it was in golf and cricket that he shone early on. He had a single-figure handicap in golf and represented ACT in cricket in 1992. George was realistic about his cricket ability, and at an Under-19 tournament at Perth, watching others there like Shane Lee, Ricky Ponting and Jimmy Maher, he came to the realisation that he did not have sufficient talent to compete with players such as these.

He had also been observed on the rugby field and in 1992 he was offered and accepted a rugby scholarship at the Institute of Sport. He pursued studies at the University of Canberra, where he graduated in 1994 with a Bachelor of Secondary Education (Physical Education). In 1993 he came to public notice in two games for ACT, against Tonga (won 29-8) and South Africa (lost 10-57). In his first appearance he scored a fine try.

George was at an invitational Sevens tournament in Fiji in 1994, where ex-Wallaby Greg Cornelsen noticed him and was impressed, informing the Australian Sevens coach Glen Ella about this young dynamo. Before he knew it, George was in a national Sevens tournament. Gregan, who also happened to be halfback for the Australian Under-21s, was named 'Player of the Tournament'.

Two months later, George was in the Wallaby squad, but first went up against Ireland for ACT, who surprisingly downed the tourists by 22-9. Howell *et al* wrote in *They Came To Conquer*: "At halfback George Gregan had a brilliant game for the locals, darting around the rucks and scrums, bringing off some great tackles and generally dictating play."

George warmed the Wallaby bench for the two Irish tests, the Wallaby halfback being Queenslander Peter Slattery.

George's talent was obvious, and so he was pitched into the test against Italy. Though not looked upon as a threat, the Italian team was undefeated at the time of his initial test, having downed a Northern Territory Invitation XV, South Australia, a strong Sydney team, a

Queensland XV and Queensland Country. Some 20,815 were at Ballymore's first test under lights and Australia barely staved off defeat, winning 23-20. At the 60th minute George complained of blurred vision, and had to be replaced by Peter Slattery. The selectors kept faith with the youngster, and he was picked for the second test, held in Melbourne, and Australia was a little more convincing, winning 20-7.

Surely no one would have predicted that by the end of 2004 George Gregan would have played a record 106 tests and would still be going strong.

George held his place against Western Samoa, who was thrashed by 73-3. George Growden wrote in The *Sun-Herald*: "The rapport between halfback George Gregan, five-eighth David Knox and centres Pat Howard and Jason Little was glorious to watch... It was justified that one of the jubilant backline players, Gregan, was named man-of-the-match."

It was in the next match, against New Zealand, that George Gregan left his mark indelibly on Australian rugby. As Howell, *et al* described it in *The Wallabies*: "With four minutes left the All Blacks threw everything at the Wallabies. Jeff Wilson got the ball and beat several defenders. As he went over the line George Gregan made a sensational tackle on him and knocked the ball loose. The game ended at 20-16 in favour of the Wallabies, who once more had possession of the Bledisloe Cup." It was one of the great moments in the history of Australian rugby, and George Gregan's name was on every rugby fan's lips. Was he, indeed, the chosen one?

From 1995 on it was the George Gregan show, and woe betide the poor halfback who sat on the bench expecting a call-up. At a very solid 79kg and 173cm in height he seemed impregnable, able to withstand any player in the world.

In 1995 he played for ACT and then two tests against Argentina, all won, and then it was World Cup time in South Africa. Australia had a poor start, losing to South Africa at Newlands, Cape Town, by 18-27, but they knew they could come back from a loss. Peter Slattery played against the next opponent, Canada, but he was injured during the match and was replaced by Gregan. George started the next game against Romania, easily won by 42-3. But Australia's hopes were dashed when England won a hard-fought match by 25-22 in the quarter-final.

Fame is fleeting, and at the end of the year Steve Merrick took over as halfback in the two Bledisloe Cup tests against New Zealand. Australia lost both matches with Jonah Lomu dominating the proceedings.

A new coach, Greg Smith, was on the scene and Gregan was back in favour in 1996. Wales was thrashed in two encounters, then in turn Canada was beaten and New Zealand administered a 6-43 hiding before Australia got home in a remarkable game against South Africa by 21-16. New Zealand then disposed of Australia again and the dogs were already barking for coach Greg Smith. At the year's end Australia was off to Italy and the British Isles for a 12-match tour under captain John Eales.

On the tour, Gregan played seven of the 12 matches, including the tests against Italy, Ireland and Wales, all won.

The year 1997 was busy, Gregan participating in 12 tests, five of which were won and one drawn. George's best game was against England

George Gregan is extremely fit and has rare tactical ability.

and in the first Cook Cup game he demonstrated to all and sundry the strength of his defensive efforts and his improvement in general play. By the end of the year Greg Smith resigned, and Rod Macqueen became the new steward of the game. In 1998 the tide had turned. Gregan played in 12 tests and 10 of them were won, including the ever-important Bledisloe Cup and, for the first time since 1994, the Cook Cup.

Rod Macqueen showed himself to be a brilliant organiser, and brought Australian rugby to the top echelon. Two of the keys in his success were the freakish John Eales leading the forwards and the team, and a maturing Gregan marshalling the backs.

In 1999 Australia won the Lansdowne Cup in a two-match series with Ireland, the Cook Cup in the Centenary test against England and the Bledisloe Cup was retained, although New Zealand won the Tri-Nations.

Next was the 1999 World Cup. Romania was defeated by 57-9, then a dangerous Ireland side by 23-3. The USA was beaten by 55-19 in a match Gregan missed. In the quarter-final, against Wales, Gregan scored twice to ensure a 24-9 win. His first try was brilliant. As Howell, *et al* described it in *The Wallabies*: "After five minutes George Gregan put Joe Roff away down the left-hand touchline where he eluded Chris Wyatt and in-passed back to Gregan for the try."

In the semi-final, against South Africa, in extra time, Australia emerged victorious by 27 to 21, in front of 72,000 spectators at Twickenham. There were no tries in the game, Australia winning by a first-ever dropped goal by Stephen Larkham and eight penalty goals to Mathew Burke. South Africa recorded a dropped goal and six penalty goals, all by Jannie de Beer.

New Zealand was unexpectedly defeated by France, so France played Australia in the final. The starting lineup that day for the Wallabies was Mathew Burke, Ben Tune, Joe Roff, Daniel Herbert, Tim Horan, Stephen Larkham, George Gregan, Toutai Kefu, David Wilson, Matt Cockbain, John Eales (capt), David Giffin, Andrew Blades, Michael Foley and Richard Harry. The score was Australia 35, France 12.

As Howell *et al* put it: "The early years of the century were very forlorn for Australian rugby, and even with this recent success they were still behind 179-191 in test wins (12 draws).

"Too classy and powerful for the French, Australia's win was a great compliment to coach Rod Macqueen. The winning margin was the most decisive in any of the four finals to date.

"Her Majesty the Queen presented the Cup."

These were certainly heady days for Australian rugby.

The year 2000 was more of the same, with Australia losing only one of seven games.

All of George's aspirations on the rugby pitch were attained in 2001. His captaincy reign began with a 4-test end-of-season tour of Europe. It began on a high note, with Spain going down by 92-10. Burke's 10 conversions was an Australian record, as was the 12 conversions notched by the team. Thirteen tries equalled the record set against South Korea in 1987.

The Wallabies came down to earth in the next match at Twickenham, losing narrowly by 15-21. Then France toppled Australia by 14-13, but Australia handled Wales by 21-13. Ironically Australia won the test in which they failed to score a try, whereas in the previous two tests they had overall scored three tries to one and lost both. Before leaving for home the Wallabies defeated the Barbarians (UK) 49-35 in an entertaining match. It was, however, an inauspicious debut for Australia's new captain.

George captained Australia in ten tests in 2002 and thirteen tests in 2003, with the highlight being the 2003 World Cup. Argentina, Romania, Ireland, Scotland and New Zealand fell to Australian power, but Australia stumbled in the final against England, going down in a tense match, which could have been won, by 17-20.

George Gregan, a remarkable athlete who was 31 years of age in 2004, showed no sign of slowing down or impaired skills, which was a credit to his resoluteness and determination. He captained Australia in eleven tests, winning nine of them under coach Eddie Jones. George's position, as it turned out, was more stable than the coaches he had been under since his test debut in 1994.

At times George Gregan has had to endure the carping critics, but he does not suffer fools gladly and has confidence in his own ability and captaincy. His is a phenomenal record. He has captained Australia in 38 tests, only exceeded by an equally magnificent player, John Eales. He has played more test matches for his country than any Wallaby who has preceded him, 106, and he continues to soldier on. How many will this genius attain?

What has not been developed is his contribution to ACT rugby. He was the first man to play 100 Super 12 matches and has won more than 120 state caps. He has led the Brumbies to two Super 12 competition wins.

George Gregan appears to be 'The Chosen One' by his deeds, but this infers that everything has come naturally for him. Noone hones his skills like George Gregan, no-one has the knowledge and the tactical sense of the master. There is nothing he cannot do on a rugby field, and it is the product of hard work, dedication and application. His is a record that might never be broken. He is the thinking man's captain, who leads his team by what he does.

GEORGE GREGAN

CAPTAIN: 41 matches (38 tests) (2001 Spain 1, England 1, France 1, Wales 1, 2002 France 2, New Zealand 2, South Africa 2, Argentina 1, Ireland 1, England 1, Italy 1, 2003 Ireland 2, Wales 1, England 2, South Africa 2, New Zealand 3, Argentina 1, Romania 1, Ireland 1, Scotland 1, 2004 Scotland 3, England 2, Pacific Islands 1, South Africa 2, New Zealand 1, France 1)
BORN: 19 April 1973 (Zambia, Africa)
SCHOOL: St Edmunds, ACT
CLUB: Randwick/Easts (Canberra)
ACT REPRESENTATION: 1993–2004
AUSTRALIAN REPRESENTATION: 116 matches (106 tests) (1994-2004)

CHRIS WHITAKER

Patience Is A Virtue

Chris Whitaker is patience personified. Who else could maintain his cheerfulness and keep improving his game despite having as Australian captain George Gregan playing the same position? George Gregan is no ordinary individual, as to the end of 2004 he had played in 106 tests, 38 of them as captain. Not only that, he is rarely injured and rarely replaced. In recent years Chris Whitaker has been on the bench, hoping to get into the action. More often than not, he does not make it.

What is inspirational about Whitaker is that whenever he gets his chance he always gives it everything he has got. At various times experts will judge that his game exceeds that of his captain, and most certainly it is not far behind. He has a beautiful long pass, and he throws it from the deck, rarely taking a calamitous step or two, as every step brings the defensive line closer to the attacker. His passing action is nigh on perfect, legs spread and arms right out on the follow through. And he has plenty of guts. He throws his body into the fray, and if there is the slightest opening he has a go. Yet perhaps the best part of his game is his defence. Whatever their size, he brings them down, and often after a relentless cover defence. He is the same when he plays for New South Wales and Randwick. He is, simply, an unlucky player, biding his time, hoping for more opportunities on the rugby fields of the world. He is an example for all those who have toiled and waited for his big break like he has.

Chris Whitaker is a product of Sydney Boys' High, an institution noted for its scholarship as the cream of the state schools, but also for its sportsmen, who have represented Australia over the years. Some of the Wallabies have been John Brass (1966-68), Roy Cawsey (1949), Roy Cooney (1922), John Cremin (1946-47), Charlie Crittle (1962-67), Keith Cross (1949-57), Wal Dawson (1946), Keith Gordon (1950), Peter Johnson (1959-71), Russ Kelly (1936-38), Syd King (1926-32), Tom Pauling (1936-37), Alan Skinner (1969-70), Phil Smith (1967-69), Gordon Stone (1938), Ken Tarleton (1925), John Thornett (1937) and Stan Wickham (1903-05). Only Peter Johnson, John Thornett and Stan Wickham have captained Australia in a test.

It was in 1997 when he first appeared on the national scene, playing for the Australian Barbarians against France, and they had the honour of besting the tourists by 26-25. There were a few others on that team who served notice that they were headed for bigger things, among them Chris Latham, Damian Smith, James Holbeck, Mitch Hardy, Owen Finegan, John Langford, Cameron Blades, Phil Kearns and Andrew Heath. He was in good company.

In 1998 he began his bench-warming regime, with the occasional test replacement. His first

Chris Whitaker releases the ball as well as any halfback in history and is gutsy in defence.

match for Australia was against South Africa on the 22nd August. These days with multiple substitutions we have evidence on when the player got on the field. Unbelievably, it was at the 80 minute mark, in other words just for a few seconds. Surely that is a record for a debut. Whatever, he made it off the bench for his first Wallaby cap. Next match for Chris was against Fiji and he got on at the 48 minute mark, so things were better. What he was learning was that, other than for an injury, he could get on the field when the game was virtually over or when the score was so lop-sided the coach did not want his number one hurt. Much patience was required.

He had his first run-on test against Tonga on 22 September 1998 in a World Cup qualifier. Australia not only won, but the 74-0 hiding was Australia's second biggest-ever test win, only surpassed by the victory against England (76-0) earlier in the year. Chris showed his ability early on, as he dived around the scrum to score a try.

That was all in his first year of action with the Wallabies, and in 1999 he had more of the same. He was on as a replacement against New Zealand (78th minute), and Romania (66th minute). The Romania match was part of the 1999 World Cup, and he had his second run-on against the USA, Australia winning by 55-19, and he scored in that game. To pat him on the back, so to speak, he came on in the final against France, gloriously won by Australia 35-12, at the 79th minute. In some consolation for warming the bench, he could at least say he played in the final.

Sam Cordingley came into the picture in 2000, performing the role that Whitaker had done so well, and Chris only managed one match, replacing the same Cordingley at the 74th minute.

In 2001 he was in the Australia 'A' team beaten narrowly 25-28 by the British and Irish Lions, and was a replacement for George Gregan in the 65th minute in the match against Spain. He was again on as a replacement in the final seconds against Wales later in the same tour.

It was more of the same in 2002, as he made his replacement games against Argentina and Italy. He also captained Australia 'A' that year against Canada.

In 2003 he acted as a replacement against Ireland, Wales and South Africa. Then came his second World Cup, and he acted as a replacement against Argentina. Then came his moment of triumph, his time in the sun, his day of days, as he captained Australia in the World Cup against Namibia. There are many others in the team who might have been recognised that day, but he was selected because he was the ultimate team man. He had accepted his role without anguish or resentment. He had shown that he could and would do everything for Australia, and no more worthy recipient could be chosen. It was a popular choice, and universally welcomed. The score in that match was 142-0, being the highest ever score by an Australian team in its long history. Whatever else might occur, he can surely boast about what happened the day he led his country. His 2003 World Cup playing time ended when he replaced Gregan against Scotland. Chris Whitaker had done what was asked of him, and then some.

In 2004 he was a replacement against the Pacific Islanders and he had another run-on match, against New Zealand in Gregan's absence.

For seven years Chris Whitaker has played his role, and in that time he has played 91 matches for his State, and 23 for his country, 20 of them tests. He has well over 80 Super 12 caps and in early 2005 notched his 100th appearance in the Waratah jersey.

A brilliant player, a clever tactician, in any other time period his name would be on everyone's lips, for his game is at least the equal of all but a few halfbacks who have put on the Wallaby jersey. The true aficionado of the game, the one who digs deeper than normal, knows what a hard role he has had to perform, and appreciates he has done it with dignity, passion and class.

CHRIS WHITAKER

CAPTAIN: 1 match (1 test) (v Namibia 2003)
BORN: 19 October 1974
SCHOOL: Sydney Boys' High School
CLUB: Randwick
NEW SOUTH WALES REPRESENTATION: 91 matches (1997-2004)
AUSTRALIAN REPRESENTATION: 23 matches (20 tests) (1998-2004)

NATHAN SHARPE

A Captain of the Future?

NATHAN SHARPE is a product of Southport School, which has graduated the following Wallabies: Alastair Boys (1958), Eddie Broad (1949), Nathan Grey (1998-2004), Tom Lawton (1983-89), Mark Catchpole (1993), Barry Lea (1993), Vaux Nicholson (1939-40), John Wolfe (1963), Paul Perrin (1962), Matt Rogers (2002-04), Greg Shambrook (1976) and Ross Sheil (1956). He is the only one from that school to captain Australia in a test.

Nathan Sharpe, a lock, is among the heaviest and tallest of the current Wallabies, and is also among the most consistent of the present-day players. In 2003, for example, he played in all 14 tests, and was in every run-on XV of the World Cup campaign. A superb lineout exponent and a destructive runner in the loose, he can ruck with the best of them. He has great leadership potential as well, captaining the Australian Under 19s and Australian Under 21s. He was named the Wallabies' rookie of the year in 2002 despite missing the spring tour of that year with a shoulder injury.

Jim Tucker wrote of him: "His running game is a rarity for a top lock. His hammering charges are always a bankable asset for the Wallabies and work has been put in to extending his value with more off-loads."

Nathan Sharpe: Determined and resolute, he might well be a long-serving Australian captain.

His representative career for Australia began

in 2002, at 24 years of age. His first test was at the Colonial Stadium, Melbourne, where he ran out against the French, who are always a tough and rough opponent. Nathan was in the lock position with Justin Harrison, Toutai Kefu packed in as number eight, George Smith and Owen Finegan were the flankers, and Patricio Noriega, Jeremy Paul and Bill Young were in the front row. George Gregan was the captain and halfback, Stephen Larkham five-eighth, Mathew Burke and Daniel Herbert the centres, Wendell Sailor and Stirling Mortlock the wings, and Chris Latham fullback.

The French team, captained by Raphael Ibanez, was Six Nations champions in 2002. Besides Nathan Sharpe, Wendell Sailor and Matt Rogers (replacement) made their debut, the latter two becoming dual internationals as soon as they ran on the field. Australia won 29-17. Observers felt that all the debutants had fine games and looked like becoming permanent fixtures. The second test was also won by Australia 31-25.

Nathan Sharpe was again a key figure in the opening Tri-Nations match against the All Blacks at Jade Stadium, Christchurch. Despite a continuous steady rain, the closeness of the game kept the 36,500 crowd interested. No tries were scored in the tense match, with 'the boot', Andrew Mehrtens, kicking four penalty goals and Burke two penalty goals, Australia thus losing 6-12. These two kickers held unique records: Mehrtens now had 188 points against Australia, the most by any player against the Wallabies, and Burke's record was its counterpart, with his 153 points against New Zealand standing as the most scored against the All Blacks.

Australia took on South Africa at the 'Gabba as part of the Tri-Nations and prevailed by 38-27, Chris Latham scoring two tries. Matt Cockbain replaced Nathan in the 71st minute.

In the return encounter with New Zealand at Telstra Stadium, Australia won 16-14 in front of 79,543 fans. Locks can remember every time they scored because it is no great memory feat, and Nathan opened the scoring by being driven over by a forward rumble in the New Zealand 22. The Australian lineout game was also superior, which proved to be the match's most decisive advantage.

The advantage of a home ground was becoming obvious when the Wallabies lost narrowly to South Africa by 31-33 at Ellis Park, Johannesburg. Ex-President Nelson Mandela presented the South Africans with the Mandela Cup. George Gregan made his 78th test appearance, thus becoming the most capped halfback of all time.

A shoulder injury then ended Nathan's 2002 campaign.

He was back in the thick of it in 2003, starting against Ireland (won 45-16), which incidentally was Australia's 200th test win. His partner in the lock position was David Giffin, who was playing superbly and putting the pressure on Justin Harrison and Dan Vickerman. In the next match, against Wales, Sharpe was the outstanding forward and rightly won the 'Man-of-the Match' award. For the first time Australian test wins (201), had caught up with their losses. Times had been a'changing.

England was next on the schedule, and they were rated as the best in the world. England won the match and the Cook Cup by 25-14, and Nathan re-injured his knee at the 43 minute mark and had to be replaced by Vickerman.

Jim Tucker told the story in the Australia v England programme in 2004. "It was a night that Sharpe, in particular, has tried to forget. He declared his fitness to play on a dodgy knee, produced only a lukewarm first 40 minutes for a back-pedalling pack and was replaced at half-time. The consequences were immense. He found himself dumped to the bench for the entire Tri-Nations tournament behind first-choice locks David Giffin and Daniel Vickerman. He played just 99 minutes of test rugby in six weeks.

"It was a jolt for a young forward who'd never thought the elevator to the top could stall in such a shuddering way."

Giffin and Vickerman took over in the starting lineup, Nathan warming the bench in the Tri-nations matches, against South Africa (lost 22-26), New Zealand (lost 21-50), South Africa again (won 29-9) and New Zealand again (lost 17-21). He was a replacement in each of them, at the 50 minute mark, the 54 minute mark, the 64 minute mark and the 47 minute mark.

Next in line was the 1993 World Cup, and Nathan Sharpe started in every match. He had learned his lesson. Australia's first opponent was Argentina (won 24-8), followed by Romania (won 90-8), Namibia (won 142-0), Ireland (17-16), Scotland (33-16), New Zealand (22-10) and the loss to England in the final, by 17-20. They had come so close to securing an upset triumph the loss was severely disappointing, but its pain was partly assuaged by the fact that the Wallabies could be considered the second best team in the world that year.

The year 2004 continued on in a similar vein, Nathan playing two tests against Scotland (won 35-15 and 34-13), one against England (won 51-15), and then the Pacific Islands (won 29-14).

With George Gregan injured, Australia had to call on someone to lead Australia against New Zealand for the first test against them that year, and Nathan Sharpe was honoured to be so named. He had shown himself to be a leader, and though only 26 years of age would run out onto the field with his team behind him. He was a proud man, and though he may not have known it he was the 72nd captain of Australia. He was now forever part of history - a captain of his country. The match was unfortunately lost 7-16.

There were three more tests that year, against South Africa (won 30-26), New Zealand (won 23-18), and South Africa (lost 19-23).

In the modern era, Nathan Sharpe had shown himself to be a true professional. As the year 2004 ended, he had played in 28 tests, made over 75 state appearances, with more than 60 in the Super 12. He remains solid and dependable, a vital member of the Wallaby team.

It is difficult to predict, but Nathan Sharpe has the latent ability to lead his country onto the field many more times. There is a lot of luck in the equation. In the meantime, he had his one day of glory. Only 71 others can say the same thing.

NATHAN SHARPE

CAPTAIN: 1 match (1 test) (v New Zealand 2004)
BORN: 26 February 1978
SCHOOL: Southport
CLUB: University of Queensland
QUEENSLAND REPRESENTATION: (1999–2004)
AUSTRALIAN REPRESENTATION: 29 matches (28 tests) (2002-04)

AUSTRALIAN TEST SUMMARY (up to 2004)

			Australia						Opponent							
Test	Year	Opp	T	C	M	DG	PG	Total	T	C	M	DG	PG	Total	Australian Captain	Opposition Captain
1	1899	GB	3	2	–	–	–	13	1	–	–	–	–	3	Frank Row	Matthew Mullineux
2	1899	GB	–	–	–	–	–	0	3	1	–	–	–	11	Bob McCowan	Frank Stout
3	1899	GB	2	2	–	–	–	10	3	1	–	–	–	11	Frank Row	Frank Stout
4	1899	GB	–	–	–	–	–	0	2	2	–	–	1	13	Frank Row	Frank Stout
5	1903	NZ	–	–	–	–	1	3	3	1	2	–	1	22	Stan Wickham	Jim Duncan
6	1904	GB	–	–	–	–	–	0	3	2	–	1	–	17	Frank Nicholson	David Bedell-Sivright
7	1904	GB	1	–	–	–	–	3	3	–	1	1	–	17	Stan Wickham	Teddy Morgan
8	1904	GB	–	–	–	–	–	0	4	2	–	–	–	16	Stan Wickham	Teddy Morgan
9	1905	NZ	1	–	–	–	–	3	4	1	–	–	–	14	Stan Wickham	John Spencer
10	1907	NZ	–	–	1	–	1	6	6	4	–	–	–	26	Peter Burge	Jimmy Hunter
11	1907	NZ	1	1	–	–	–	5	4	1	–	–	–	14	Allen Oxlade	Jimmy Hunter
12	1907	NZ	1	1	–	–	–	5	1	1	–	–	–	5	Peter Burge	Jimmy Hunter
13	1908	Wales	2	–	–	–	–	6	2	–	–	–	1	9	Paddy Moran	Bill Trew
14	1909	Eng	3	–	–	–	–	9	1	–	–	–	–	3	Chris McKivat	George Lyon
15	1910	NZ	–	–	–	–	–	0	2	–	–	–	–	6	Syd Middleton	Fred Roberts
16	1910	NZ	3	1	–	–	–	11	–	–	–	–	–	0	Syd Middleton	Fred Roberts
17	1910	NZ	2	2	–	–	1	13	8	2	–	–	–	28	Syd Middleton	Fred Roberts
18	1912	USA	3	–	–	–	1	12	1	1	–	–	1	8	Ward Prentice	Monti Morris
19	1913	NZ	1	1	–	–	–	5	8	3	–	–	–	30	Ted Fahey	Alex McDonald
20	1913	NZ	3	2	–	–	–	13	5	3	–	1	–	25	Ted Fahey	Joe O'Leary
21	1913	NZ	4	2	–	–	–	16	1	1	–	–	–	5	Larry Dwyer	Joe O'Leary
22	1914	NZ	–	–	–	–	–	0	1	1	–	–	–	5	Fred Wood	Dick Roberts
23	1914	NZ	–	–	–	–	–	0	5	1	–	–	–	17	Jimmy Flynn	Dick Roberts
24	1914	NZ	1	–	–	1	–	7	6	2	–	–	–	22	Fred Wood	Dick Roberts
Pre WW1 totals			**31**	**14**	**1**	**1**	**4**	**140**	**77**	**30**	**3**	**3**	**4**	**327**	**Won 5, Drawn 1, Lost 18**	
25	1920	NZ	3	3	–	–	–	15	6	2	–	1	–	26	Willie Watson	Jim Tilyard
26	1920	NZ	1	–	–	–	1	6	4	1	–	–	–	14	Willie Watson	Jim Tilyard
27	1920	NZ	3	2	–	–	–	13	6	3	–	–	–	24	Willie Watson	Jim Tilyard

Test	Year	Opp	Australia						Opponent						Australian Captain	Opposition Captain
			T	C	M	DG	PG	Total	T	C	M	DG	PG	Total		
28	1921	SA	1	–	–	1	1	10	7	2	–	–	–	25	Arthur Walker	Theo Pienaar
29	1921	SA	3	1	–	–	–	11	4	2	–	–	–	16	Arthur Walker	Theo Pienaar
30	1921	SA	2	–	–	–	1	9	6	3	–	1	–	28	Arthur Walker	Boy Morkel
31	1921	NZ	4	1	–	–	1	17	–	–	–	–	–	0	Arthur Walker	Teddy Roberts
32	1922	NZM	6	2	–	–	–	22	4	2	1	–	2	25	Arthur Walker	Harry Jacob
33	1922	NZM	6	2	–	–	2	28	2	2	–	–	1	13	Darby Loudon	Harry Jacob
34	1922	NZM	4	3	–	1	–	22	6	1	–	–	1	23	Arthur Walker	F.L.Tresize
35	1922	NZ	3	–	–	1	2	19	7	1	–	–	1	26	Arthur Walker	Moke Belliss
36	1922	NZ	1	1	–	–	3	14	2	1	–	–	–	8	Arthur Walker	Moke Belliss
37	1922	NZ	2	1	–	–	–	8	2	–	–	–	–	6	Arthur Walker	Jack Street
38	1923	NZM	4	3	–	–	3	27	5	4	–	–	–	23	Watty Field	Parekura Tureia
39	1923	NZM	5	3	–	–	–	21	4	2	–	–	–	16	Watty Field	Parekura Tureia
40	1923	NZM	4	1	–	–	–	14	3	–	–	–	1	12	Watty Field	Wattie Barclay
41	1923	NZ	3	–	–	–	–	9	3	2	–	–	2	19	Billy Sheehan	Jock Richardson
42	1923	NZ	2	–	–	–	–	6	7	5	–	–	1	34	Billy Sheehan	Jock Richardson
43	1923	NZ	2	1	–	–	1	11	8	4	–	–	2	38	Billy Sheehan	Ginger Nicholls
44	1924	NZ	5	1	–	–	1	20	3	2	–	–	1	16	Arthur Walker	Cecil Badeley
45	1924	NZ	1	1	–	–	–	5	7	–	–	–	–	21	Arthur Walker	Jock Richardson
46	1924	NZ	1	1	–	–	1	8	10	4	–	–	–	38	Ted Thorn	Jock Richardson
47	1925	NZ	1	–	–	–	–	3	7	1	–	–	1	26	Ted Thorn	Jim Donald
48	1925	NZ	–	–	–	–	–	0	–	–	–	1	–	4	Ted Thorn	Jim Donald
49	1925	NZ	–	–	–	–	1	3	3	1	–	–	–	11	Charlie Fox	Jim Donald
50	1925	NZ	2	2	–	–	–	10	8	6	–	–	–	36	Tom Lawton	Cliff Porter
51	1926	NZ	4	1	1	–	3	26	4	1	–	–	2	20	Ted Thorn	Cliff Porter
52	1926	NZ	1	–	–	–	1	6	2	1	–	–	1	11	Ted Thorn	Cliff Porter
53	1926	NZ	–	–	–	–	–	0	2	1	–	–	2	14	Ted Thorn	Cliff Porter
54	1926	NZ	2	–	–	–	5	21	6	5	–	–	–	28	Johnny Wallace	Mark Nicholls
55	1927	Ire	1	1	–	–	–	5	–	–	–	–	1	3	Johnny Wallace	George Stephenson
56	1927	Wales	4	3	–	–	–	18	2	1	–	–	–	8	Johnny Wallace	Ivor Jones
57	1927	Sco	2	1	–	–	–	8	2	2	–	–	–	10	Johnny Wallace	Daniel Drysdale
58	1928	Eng	3	1	–	–	–	11	4	3	–	–	–	18	Johnny Wallace	Ronald Cove-Smith

Test	Year	Opp	Australia T	C	M	DG	PG	Total	Opponent T	C	M	DG	PG	Total	Australian Captain	Opposition Captain
59	1928	Fra	3	1	–	–	–	11	2	1	–	–	–	8	Johnny Wallace	Adolphe Jaureguy
60	1928	NZ	3	–	–	–	1	12	1	–	–	–	4	15	Syd Malcolm	Cliff Porter
61	1928	NZ	4	1	–	–	–	14	3	2	–	–	1	16	Syd Malcolm	Cliff Porter
62	1928	NZ	3	1	–	–	–	11	2	1	–	–	–	8	Bob Loudon	Cliff Porter
63	1928	NZM	2	1	–	–	–	8	–	–	–	–	3	9	Syd Malcolm	George Nepia
NSW totals			101	40	1	3	28	482	154	69	1	3	27	696	**Won 13, Lost 26**	
64	1929	NZ	1	–	–	–	2	9	1	1	–	–	1	8	Tom Lawton	Herb Lilbourne
65	1929	NZ	3	1	–	–	2	17	2	–	–	–	1	9	Tom Lawton	Cliff Porter
66	1929	NZ	2	–	–	–	3	15	3	2	–	–	–	13	Tom Lawton	Cliff Porter
67	1930	GB	2	–	–	–	–	6	1	1	–	–	–	5	Tom Lawton	Doug Prentice
68	1931	NZM	3	1	–	–	1	14	1	–	–	–	–	3	Jimmy Clark	Wampy Bell
69	1931	NZ	3	2	–	–	–	13	2	1	–	–	4	20	Syd Malcolm	Archie Strang
70	1932	NZ	4	2	–	–	2	22	3	3	–	1	–	17	Tom Lawton	Frank Kilby
71	1932	NZ	1	–	–	–	–	3	4	1	–	1	1	21	Tom Lawton	Frank Kilby
72	1932	NZ	3	2	–	–	–	13	5	3	–	–	–	21	Syd Malcolm	Frank Kilby
73	1933	SA	–	–	–	–	1	3	4	1	–	–	1	17	Dave Cowper	Phil Nel
74	1933	SA	4	3	–	–	1	21	1	–	–	–	1	6	Dave Cowper	Bennie Osler
75	1933	SA	1	–	–	–	–	3	2	1	–	1	–	12	Dave Cowper	Phil Nel
76	1933	SA	–	–	–	–	–	0	2	1	–	–	1	11	Syd Malcolm	Phil Nel
77	1933	SA	3	1	–	1	–	15	–	–	–	1	–	4	Alec Ross	Phil Nel
78	1934	NZ	4	2	–	–	3	25	3	1	–	–	–	11	Alec Ross	Rusty Page
79	1934	NZ	1	–	–	–	–	3	1	–	–	–	–	3	Alec Ross	Frank Kilby
80	1936	NZ	1	–	–	–	1	6	3	1	–	–	–	11	Ron Waldren	Jack Griffiths
81	1936	NZ	2	2	–	–	1	13	9	4	–	–	1	38	Ron Waldren	Jack Griffiths
82	1936	NZM	6	5	–	–	1	31	1	–	–	–	1	6	Ron Waldren	Tori Reid
83	1937	SA	1	1	–	–	–	5	2	–	–	–	1	9	Cyril Towers	Phil Nel
84	1937	SA	3	1	–	–	2	17	6	4	–	–	–	26	Cyril Towers	Phil Nel
85	1938	NZ	–	–	–	–	3	9	4	3	–	–	2	24	Vay Wilson	Brushy Mitchell
86	1938	NZ	3	1	–	–	1	14	4	2	–	1	–	20	Vay Wilson	Brushy Mitchell
87	1938	NZ	1	–	–	–	1	6	2	1	–	–	2	14	Vay Wilson	Rod McKenzie
88	1946	NZ	2	1	–	–	–	8	7	5	–	–	–	31	Bill McLean	Fred Allen

			Australia						Opponent							
Test	Year	Opp	T	C	M	DG	PG	Total	T	C	M	DG	PG	Total	Australian Captain	Opposition Captain
89	1946	NZM	–	–	–	–	–	0	5	1	–	–	1	20	Bill McLean	Doc Paewai
90	1946	NZ	2	2	–	–	–	10	1	1	–	–	3	14	Bill McLean	Fred Allen
91	1947	NZ	1	1	–	–	–	5	3	2	–	–	–	13	Phil Hardcastle	Fred Allen
92	1947	NZ	1	1	–	–	3	14	3	3	–	–	4	27	Bill McLean	Fred Allen
93	1947	Sco	4	2	–	–	–	16	–	–	–	1	1	7	Trevor Allan	John Innes
94	1947	Ire	4	2	–	–	–	16	–	–	–	–	1	3	Trevor Allan	Ernie Strathdee
95	1947	Wales	–	–	–	–	–	0	–	–	–	–	2	6	Trevor Allan	Ewart Tamplin
96	1948	Eng	3	1	–	–	–	11	–	–	–	–	–	0	Trevor Allan	Edward Scott
97	1948	Fra	–	–	–	–	2	6	3	2	–	–	–	13	Trevor Allan	Guy Basquet
98	1949	NZM	1	–	–	–	–	3	4	–	–	–	–	12	Trevor Allan	Sonny West
99	1949	NZM	2	1	–	–	–	8	1	1	–	–	1	8	Trevor Allan	Sonny West
100	1949	NZM	4	3	–	–	–	18	–	–	–	–	1	3	Trevor Allan	Sonny West
Sub totals			**208**	**92**	**2**	**5**	**62**	**1020**	**324**	**144**	**4**	**12**	**62**	**1509**	**Won 32, Drawn 3, Lost 65**	
101	1949	NZ	3	1	–	–	–	11	1	–	–	–	1	6	Trevor Allan	Johnnie Smith
102	1949	NZ	3	2	–	–	1	16	1	–	–	1	1	9	Trevor Allan	Johnnie Smith
103	1950	BI	–	–	–	–	2	6	2	2	–	1	2	19	Nev Cottrell	Bleddyn Williams
104	1950	BI	1	–	–	–	–	3	5	3	–	–	1	24	Nev Cottrell	Karl Mullen
105	1951	NZ	–	–	–	–	–	0	1	1	–	–	1	8	Arch Winning	Peter Johnstone
106	1951	NZ	2	1	–	–	1	11	4	1	–	1	–	17	Colin Windon	Peter Johnstone
107	1951	NZ	–	–	–	–	2	6	4	2	–	–	–	16	Colin Windon	Peter Johnstone
108	1952	Fiji	4	–	–	–	1	15	2	–	–	–	1	9	John Solomon	Apakuki Tuitavua
109	1952	Fiji	4	–	–	1	–	15	2	1	–	1	2	17	John Solomon	Apakuki Tuitavua
110	1952	NZ	3	1	–	1	–	14	2	–	–	–	1	9	John Solomon	Kevin Skinner
111	1952	NZ	1	1	–	–	1	8	2	–	–	1	2	15	John Solomon	Kevin Skinner
112	1953	SA	–	–	–	–	1	3	5	2	–	–	2	25	John Solomon	Hennie Muller
113	1953	SA	4	3	–	–	–	18	4	1	–	–	–	14	John Solomon	Hennie Muller
114	1953	SA	1	1	–	–	1	8	4	3	–	–	–	18	John Solomon	Hennie Muller
115	1953	SA	1	–	–	–	2	9	2	2	–	2	2	22	Nick Shehadie	Hennie Muller
116	1954	Fiji	5	2	–	–	1	22	4	2	–	–	1	19	Nick Shehadie	Apakuki Tuitavua
117	1954	Fiji	2	2	–	–	2	16	2	–	–	–	4	18	Nick Shehadie	Apakuki Tuitavua
118	1955	NZ	1	1	–	–	1	8	3	2	–	–	1	16	John Solomon	Ian Clarke

			Australia						Opponent							
Test	Year	Opp	T	C	M	DG	PG	Total	T	C	M	DG	PG	Total	Australian Captain	Opposition Captain
119	1955	NZ	–	–	–	–	–	0	1	1	–	1	–	8	Alan Cameron	Ian Clarke
120	1955	NZ	2	1	–	–	–	8	1	–	–	–	–	3	Alan Cameron	Ian Clarke
121	1956	SA	–	–	–	–	–	0	2	–	–	–	1	9	Alan Cameron	Basie Viviers
122	1956	SA	–	–	–	–	–	0	2	–	–	1	–	9	Alan Cameron	Basie Viviers
123	1957	NZ	1	1	–	–	2	11	4	2	–	–	3	25	Dick Tooth	Ponty Reid
124	1957	NZ	1	–	–	–	2	9	4	2	1	1	–	22	Dick Tooth	Ponty Reid
125	1958	Wales	1	–	–	–	–	3	1	–	–	1	1	9	Bob Davidson	Clem Thomas
126	1958	Ire	2	–	–	–	–	6	2	–	–	–	1	9	Bob Davidson	Noel Henderson
127	1958	Eng	–	–	–	1	1	6	2	–	–	–	1	9	Bob Davidson	Eric Evans
128	1958	Sco	2	1	–	–	–	8	2	–	–	–	2	12	Bob Davidson	Jim Greenwood
129	1958	Fra	–	–	–	–	–	0	3	2	–	2	–	19	Bob Davidson	Michel Celaya
130	1958	NZM	1	–	–	–	4	15	2	1	–	–	2	14	Bob Davidson	Pat Walsh
131	1958	NZM	–	–	–	–	1	3	–	–	–	–	1	3	Des Connor	Pat Walsh
132	1958	NZM	–	–	–	–	2	6	3	2	–	–	–	13	Des Connor	Pat Walsh
133	1958	NZ	1	–	–	–	–	3	7	2	–	–	–	25	Chas Wilson	Wilson Whineray
134	1958	NZ	1	–	–	–	1	6	1	–	–	–	–	3	Chas Wilson	Wilson Whineray
135	1958	NZ	1	1	–	–	1	8	1	1	–	–	4	17	Chas Wilson	Wilson Whineray
136	1959	BI	–	–	–	–	2	6	2	1	–	1	2	17	Peter Fenwicke	Ronnie Dawson
137	1959	BI	–	–	–	–	1	3	5	3	–	–	1	24	Peter Fenwicke	Ronnie Dawson
138	1961	Fiji	6	3	–	–	–	24	–	–	–	–	2	6	Ken Catchpole	Joe Levula
139	1961	Fiji	4	1	–	–	2	20	3	1	–	–	1	14	Ken Catchpole	Orisi Dawai
140	1961	Fiji	1	–	–	–	–	3	1	–	–	–	–	3	Ken Catchpole	Orisi Dawai
141	1961	SA	–	–	–	–	1	3	8	2	–	–	–	28	Ken Catchpole	Johan Claassen
142	1961	SA	1	1	–	–	2	11	3	1	–	1	3	23	Ken Catchpole	Johan Claassen
143	1961	Fra	1	1	–	–	1	8	3	–	–	2	–	15	Ken Catchpole	Francois Moncla
144	1962	NZ	–	–	–	–	2	6	4	1	–	1	1	20	Peter Johnson	Wilson Whineray
145	1962	NZ	1	1	–	–	–	5	2	1	–	–	2	14	Jim Lenehan	Wilson Whineray
146	1962	NZ	–	–	–	–	3	9	1	–	–	–	2	9	John Thornett	Wilson Whineray
147	1962	Nz	–	–	–	–	–	0	–	–	–	–	1	3	John Thornett	Wilson Whineray
148	1962	NZ	1	1	–	–	1	8	3	2	–	1	–	16	John Thornett	Wilson Whineray
149	1963	Eng	4	3	–	–	–	18	3	–	–	–	–	9	John Thornett	Mike Weston

			Australia						Opponent							
Test	**Year**	**Opp**	**T**	**C**	**M**	**DG**	**PG**	**Total**	**T**	**C**	**M**	**DG**	**PG**	**Total**	**Australian Captain**	**Opposition Captain**
150	1963	SA	1	–	–	–	–	**3**	2	1	–	–	2	**14**	John Thornett	Abie Malan
151	1963	SA	1	–	–	1	1	**9**	1	1	–	–	–	**5**	John Thornett	Abie Malan
152	1963	SA	1	1	–	1	1	**11**	–	–	–	–	3	**9**	John Thornett	Avril Malan
153	1963	SA	–	–	–	1	1	**6**	3	2	–	–	3	**22**	John Thornett	Abie Malan
154	1964	NZ	1	–	–	–	2	**9**	1	1	–	1	2	**14**	John Thornett	John Graham
155	1964	NZ	1	–	–	–	–	**3**	4	3	–	–	–	**18**	John Thornett	John Graham
156	1964	NZ	2	1	–	1	3	**20**	1	1	–	–	–	**5**	John Thornett	John Graham
157	1965	SA	2	–	–	–	4	**18**	2	1	–	–	1	**11**	John Thornett	Nelie Smith
158	1965	SA	–	–	–	–	4	**12**	2	1	–	–	–	**8**	John Thornett	Nelie Smith
159	1966	BI	1	1	–	–	1	**8**	2	1	–	–	1	**11**	John Thornett	Mike Campbell-Lamerton
160	1966	BI	–	–	–	–	–	**0**	5	5	–	1	1	**31**	John Thornett	Mike Campbell-Lamerton
161	1966	Wales	2	1	–	1	1	**14**	2	1	–	–	1	**11**	Ken Catchpole	Alun Pask
162	1966	Sco	1	1	–	–	–	**5**	2	1	–	–	1	**11**	Ken Catchpole	Jim Fisher
163	1967	Eng	2	1	–	3	2	**23**	1	1	–	–	2	**11**	Ken Catchpole	Richard Sharp
164	1967	Ire	1	1	–	1	–	**8**	2	–	–	2	1	**15**	Ken Catchpole	Noel Murphy
165	1967	Fra	2	1	–	1	1	**14**	1	1	–	1	4	**20**	John Thornett	Christian Darrouy
166	1967	Ire	1	1	–	–	–	**5**	2	1	–	1	–	**11**	Ken Catchpole	Tom Keirnan
167	1967	NZ	2	–	–	–	1	**9**	4	4	–	1	2	**29**	Ken Catchpole	Brian Lochore
168	1968	NZ	1	1	–	–	2	**11**	6	3	–	–	1	**27**	Ken Catchpole	Brian Lochore
169	1968	NZ	1	–	–	–	5	**18**	3	2	–	–	2	**19**	Peter Johnson	Chris Laidlaw
170	1968	Fra	1	1	–	1	1	**11**	2	2	–	–	–	**10**	Peter Johnson	Christian Carrere
171	1968	Ire	1	–	–	–	–	**3**	2	2	–	–	–	**10**	Peter Johnson	Tom Keirnan
172	1968	Sco	–	–	–	–	1	**3**	1	–	–	–	2	**9**	Peter Johnson	Jim Telfer
173	1969	Wales	2	2	–	–	2	**16**	3	2	–	–	2	**19**	Greg Davis	Brian Price
174	1969	SA	1	1	–	–	2	**11**	5	3	–	–	3	**30**	Greg Davis	Dawie de Villiers
175	1969	SA	–	–	–	–	3	**9**	3	2	–	–	1	**16**	Greg Davis	Tommy Bedford
176	1969	SA	–	–	–	–	1	**3**	2	1	–	–	1	**11**	Greg Davis	Tommy Bedford
177	1969	SA	1	1	–	–	1	**8**	3	2	–	–	2	**19**	Greg Davis	Dawie de Villiers
178	1970	Sco	6	1	–	–	1	**23**	–	–	–	–	1	**3**	Greg Davis	Frankie Laidlaw
179	1971	SA	1	1	–	–	2	**11**	3	2	–	1	1	**19**	Greg Davis	Hannes Marias
180	1971	SA	–	–	–	1	1	**6**	3	1	–	–	1	**14**	Greg Davis	Hannes Marias

Test	Year	Opp	Australia						Opponent						Australian Captain	Opposition Captain
			T	C	M	DG	PG	Total	T	C	M	DG	PG	Total		
181	1971	SA	1	–	–	–	1	6	3	3	–	–	1	18	Greg Davis	Hannes Marias
182	1971	Fra	2	1	–	–	1	13	2	–	–	–	1	11	Greg Davis	Benoit Dauga
183	1971	Fra	–	–	–	–	3	9	1	1	–	–	4	18	Greg Davis	Benoit Dauga
184	1972	Fra	2	–	–	–	2	14	3	1	–	–	–	14	Greg Davis	Walter Spanghero
185	1972	Fra	–	–	–	–	5	15	3	2	–	–	–	16	Greg Davis	Walter Spanghero
186	1972	NZ	–	–	–	–	2	6	5	3	–	1	–	29	Greg Davis	Ian Kirkpatrick
187	1972	NZ	3	1	–	1	–	17	5	2	–	–	2	30	Greg Davis	Ian Kirkpatrick
188	1972	NZ	–	–	–	–	1	3	6	4	–	–	2	38	Greg Davis	Ian Kirkpatrick
189	1972	Fiji	4	1	–	1	–	21	2	1	–	–	3	19	Peter Sullivan	Epi Bolawaqutabu
190	1973	Tonga	5	2	–	2	–	30	2	2	–	–	–	12	Peter Sullivan	Sione Mafi
191	1973	Tonga	2	–	–	–	1	11	4	–	–	–	–	16	Peter Sullivan	Sione Mafi
192	1973	Wales	–	–	–	–	–	0	3	–	–	–	4	24	Peter Sullivan	Gareth Edwards
193	1973	Eng	–	–	–	–	1	3	3	1	–	–	2	20	John Hipwell	John Pullin
194	1974	NZ	1	1	–	–	–	6	2	–	–	–	1	11	John Hipwell	Andy Leslie
195	1974	NZ	2	1	–	–	2	16	2	1	–	–	2	16	John Hipwell	Andy Leslie
196	1974	NZ	–	–	–	–	2	6	3	2	–	–	–	16	John Hipwell	Andy Leslie
197	1975	Eng	1	–	–	2	2	16	1	1	–	–	1	9	John Hipwell	Anthony Neary
198	1975	Eng	5	2	–	–	2	30	2	2	–	–	3	21	John Hipwell	John Pullin
199	1975	Japan	6	5	–	–	1	37	1	–	–	–	1	7	John Hipwell	Ryozo Imazato
200	1975	Japan	8	6	–	–	2	50	5	1	–	–	1	25	Geoff Shaw	Ryozo Imazato
Sub totals			**353**	**159**	**2**	**26**	**179**	**2044**	**581**	**266**	**5**	**40**	**184**	**3032**	**Won 60, Drawn 8, Lost 132**	
201	1975	Sco	–	–	–	–	1	3	2	1	–	–	–	10	John Hipwell	Ian McLauchlan
202	1975	Wales	–	–	–	–	1	3	4	3	–	1	1	28	John Hipwell	Mervyn Davies
203	1976	Eng	–	–	–	–	2	6	3	1	–	–	3	23	Geoff Shaw	Anthony Neary
204	1976	Ire	3	1	–	–	2	20	1	–	–	–	2	10	Geoff Shaw	Mike Gibson
205	1976	USA	3	–	–	–	4	24	–	–	–	–	4	12	Geoff Shaw	Rob Borderley
206	1976	Fiji	4	–	–	–	2	22	1	1	–	–	–	6	Geoff Shaw	Ilaitia Tuisese
207	1976	Fiji	2	2	–	1	2	21	–	–	–	–	3	9	Geoff Shaw	Ilaitia Tuisese
208	1976	Fiji	3	–	–	–	5	27	3	1	–	–	1	17	Geoff Shaw	Wame Gavidi
209	1976	Fra	–	–	–	1	4	15	3	3	–	–	–	18	Geoff Shaw	Jacques Fouroux
210	1976	Fra	–	–	–	–	2	6	6	2	–	1	1	34	Geoff Shaw	Richard Astre

			Australia						Opponent							
Test	Year	Opp	T	C	M	DG	PG	Total	T	C	M	DG	PG	Total	Australian Captain	Opposition Captain
211	1978	Wales	1	1	–	–	4	18	2	–	–	–	–	8	Tony Shaw	Terry Cobner
212	1978	Wales	1	–	–	2	3	19	2	–	–	1	2	17	Tony Shaw	Gerald Davies
213	1978	NZ	1	1	–	–	2	12	1	–	–	–	3	13	Tony Shaw	Frank Oliver
214	1978	NZ	–	–	–	1	1	6	3	2	–	1	1	22	Tony Shaw	Frank Oliver
215	1978	NZ	5	2	–	1	1	30	2	1	–	–	2	16	Tony Shaw	Frank Oliver
216	1979	Ire	1	1	–	–	2	12	2	2	–	1	4	27	Tony Shaw	Fergus Slattery
217	1979	Ire	–	–	–	–	1	3	–	–	–	2	1	9	Tony Shaw	Fergus Slattery
218	1979	NZ	–	–	–	1	3	12	–	–	–	1	1	6	Mark Loane	Graham Mourie
219	1979	Arg	1	–	–	1	2	13	2	2	–	3	1	24	Mark Loane	Hugo Porta
220	1979	Arg	3	1	–	–	1	17	1	1	–	1	1	12	Mark Loane	Hugo Porta
221	1980	Fiji	2	1	–	1	3	22	–	–	–	1	2	9	Paol McLean	Rupeni Qaraniqio
222	1980	NZ	2	1	–	1	–	13	–	–	–	–	3	9	Tony Shaw	Dave Loveridge
223	1980	NZ	1	1	–	–	1	9	1	1	–	–	2	12	Tony Shaw	Dave Loveridge
224	1980	NZ	4	2	–	1	1	26	1	–	–	–	2	10	Tony Shaw	Dave Loveridge
225	1981	Fra	3	1	–	–	1	17	1	1	–	1	2	15	Tony Shaw	Robert Paparemborde
226	1981	Fra	2	2	–	–	4	24	2	–	–	2	–	14	Tony Shaw	Jean-Pierre Rives
227	1981	Ire	1	–	–	1	3	16	–	–	–	–	4	12	Tony Shaw	Fergus Slattery
228	1981	Wales	2	1	–	–	1	13	1	1	–	1	3	18	Tony Shaw	Gareth Davies
229	1981	Sco	3	–	–	–	1	15	1	1	–	1	5	24	Tony Shaw	Andy Irvine
230	1982	Eng	2	–	–	–	1	11	1	1	–	–	3	15	Mark Loane	Bill Beaumont
231	1982	Sco	1	–	–	–	1	7	1	1	–	1	1	12	Mark Loane	Andy Irvine
232	1982	Sco	3	3	–	–	5	33	–	–	–	–	3	9	Mark Loane	Andy Irvine
233	1982	NZ	2	1	–	–	2	16	4	2	–	–	1	23	Mark Ella	Graham Mourie
234	1982	NZ	2	1	–	–	3	19	2	1	–	–	2	16	Mark Ella	Graham Mourie
235	1982	NZ	1	1	–	1	3	18	2	2	–	2	5	33	Mark Ella	Graham Mourie
236	1983	USA	9	5	–	1	–	49	–	–	–	–	1	3	Mark Ella	Ed Burlington
237	1983	Arg	–	–	–	–	1	3	2	2	–	1	1	18	Mark Ella	Hugo Porta
238	1983	Arg	5	3	–	–	1	29	1	–	–	1	2	13	Mark Ella	Hugo Porta
239	1983	NZ	2	–	–	–	–	8	1	1	–	–	4	18	Mark Ella	Andy Dalton
240	1983	Italy	5	3	–	–	1	29	1	–	–	–	1	7	Mark Ella	M Mascioletti
241	1983	Fra	1	1	–	2	1	15	–	–	–	2	3	15	Mark Ella	Jean-Pierre Rives

			Australia						Opponent							
Test	**Year**	**Opp**	**T**	**C**	**M**	**DG**	**PG**	**Total**	**T**	**C**	**M**	**DG**	**PG**	**Total**	**Australian Captain**	**Opposition Captain**
242	1983	Fra	–	–	–	1	1	6	1	1	–	–	3	15	Mark Ella	Jean-Pierre Rives
243	1984	Fiji	1	–	–	1	3	16	–	–	–	–	1	3	Andrew Slack	Esala Teleni
244	1984	NZ	2	1	–	1	1	16	–	–	–	1	2	9	Andrew Slack	Andy Dalton
245	1984	NZ	1	1	–	–	3	15	1	–	–	–	5	19	Andrew Slack	Andy Dalton
246	1984	NZ	1	1	–	–	6	24	2	1	–	–	5		Andrew Slack	Andy Dalton
247	1984	Eng	3	2	–	–	1	19	–	–	–	–	1	3	Andrew Slack	Nigel Melville
248	1984	Ire	1	–	–	3	1	16	–	–	–	–	3	9	Andrew Slack	Ciaran Fitzgerald
249	1984	Wales	4	3	–	–	2	28	1	1	–	–	1	9	Andrew Slack	Mike Watkins
250	1984	Sco	4	3	–	–	5	37	–	–	–	–	4	12	Andrew Slack	Roy Laidlaw
251	1985	Can	9	7	–	–	3	59	–	–	–	1	–	3	Steve Williams	John Phelan
252	1985	Can	7	3	–	1	2	43	1	1	–	–	3	15	Steve Williams	John Phelan
253	1985	NZ	1	1	–	–	1	9	1	–	–	–	2	10	Steve Williams	Andy Dalton
254	1985	Fiji	7	3	–	3	3	52	4	3	–	–	2	28	Steve Williams	Esala Teleni
255	1985	Fiji	5	1	–	–	3	31	–	–	–	1	2	9	Steve Williams	Esala Teleni
256	1986	Italy	6	6	–	–	1	39	2	2	–	–	2	18	Andrew Slack	Marzio Innocenti
257	1986	Fra	1	1	–	1	6	27	3	1	–	–	–	14	Andrew Slack	Daniel Dubroca
258	1986	Arg	4	4	–	–	5	39	3	2	–	–	1	19	Simon Poidevin	Hugo Porta
259	1986	Arg	3	1	–	–	4	26	–	–	–	–	–	0	Simon Poidevin	Rafael Madero
260	1986	NZ	2	1	–	–	1	13	1	1	–	–	2	12	Andrew Slack	David Kirk
261	1986	NZ	–	–	–	1	3	12	1	–	–	1	2	13	Andrew Slack	David Kirk
262	1986	NZ	2	1	–	–	4	22	–	–	–	–	3	9	Andrew Slack	David Kirk
263	1987	S Korea	13	5	–	–	1	65	2	2	–	–	2	18	Andrew Slack	Hycon Kim
264	1987	Eng	2	1	–	–	3	19	1	1	–	–	–	6	Andrew Slack	Michael Harrison
265	1987	USA	8	6	–	–	1	47	1	1	–	1	1	12	Andrew Slack	Fred Paoli
266	1987	Japan	8	5	–	–	–	42	3	1	–	1	2	23	Simon Poidevin	Toshiyuka Hayashi
267	1987	Ire	4	4	–	–	3	33	2	2	–	–	1	15	Andrew Slack	Donal Lenihan
268	1987	Fra	2	2	–	1	3	24	4	4	–	–	2	30	Andrew Slack	Daniel Dubroca
269	1987	Wales	2	2	–	1	2	21	3	2	–	–	2	22	Andrew Slack	Richard Moriarty
270	1987	NZ	1	–	–	1	3	16	4	1	–	1	3	30	David Codey	David Kirk
271	1987	Arg	3	2	–	–	1	19	1	–	–	1	4	19	Simon Poidevin	Hugo Porta
272	1987	Arg	2	1	–	–	3	19	1	1	–	2	5	27	Michael Lynagh	Hugo Porta

			Australia						Opponent							
Test	Year	Opp	T	C	M	DG	PG	Total	T	C	M	DG	PG	Total	Australian Captain	Opposition Captain
273	1988	Eng	1	–	–	–	6	22	2	1	–	–	2	16	Nick Farr-Jones	John Orwin
274	1988	Eng	4	3	–	–	2	28	2	–	–	–	–	8	Nick Farr-Jones	John Orwin
275	1988	NZ	1	–	–	–	1	7	5	3	–	–	2	32	Nick Farr-Jones	Wayne Shelford
276	1988	NZ	2	1	–	–	3	19	3	2	–	–	1	19	Nick Farr-Jones	Wayne Shelford
277	1988	NZ	1	1	–	–	1	9	3	3	–	–	4	30	Nick Farr-Jones	Wayne Shelford
278	1988	Eng	3	2	–	–	1	19	4	3	–	–	2	28	Nick Farr-Jones	Will Carling
279	1988	Sco	5	3	–	–	2	32	2	1	–	–	1	13	Nick Farr-Jones	Gary Callandar
280	1988	Italy	9	8	–	–	1	55	–	–	–	–	2	6	Nick Farr-Jones	Marzio Innocenti
281	1989	BI	4	4	–	1	1	30	–	–	–	1	3	12	Nick Farr-Jones	Finlay Calder
282	1989	BI	1	1	–	–	2	12	2	1	–	1	2	19	Nick Farr-Jones	Finlay Calder
283	1989	BI	1	1	–	–	4	18	1	–	–	–	5	19	Nick Farr-Jones	Finlay Calder
284	1989	NZ	1	1	–	–	2	12	2	2	–	–	4	24	Nick Farr-Jones	Wayne Shelford
285	1989	Fra	4	2	–	–	4	32	–	–	–	1	4	15	Nick Farr-Jones	Pierre Berbizer
286	1989	Fra	2	1	–	–	3	19	2	1	–	–	5	25	Nick Farr-Jones	Henri Sanz
287	1990	Fra	1	1	–	–	5	21	–	–	–	–	3	9	Nick Farr-Jones	Serge Blanco
288	1990	Fra	6	6	–	–	4	48	4	3	–	–	3	31	Nick Farr-Jones	Serge Blanco
289	1990	Fra	2	1	–	1	2	19	2	1	–	3	3	28	Nick Farr-Jones	Serge Blanco
290	1990	USA	12	8	–	1	–	67	1	1	–	–	1	9	Nick Farr-Jones	Brian Vizard
291	1990	NZ	–	–	–	–	2	6	4	1	–	–	1	21	Nick Farr-Jones	Gary Whetton
292	1990	NZ	2	–	–	1	2	17	3	3	–	1	2	27	Nick Farr-Jones	Gary Whetton
293	1990	NZ	1	1	–	–	5	21	–	–	–	1	2	9	Nick Farr-Jones	Gary Whetton
294	1991	Wales	12	6	–	–	1	63	–	–	–	1	1	6	Nick Farr-Jones	Paul Thornburn
295	1991	Eng	5	4	–	–	4	40	1	1	–	–	3	15	Nick Farr-Jones	Will Carling
296	1991	NZ	2	2	–	–	3	21	1	1	–	–	2	12	Nick Farr-Jones	Gary Whetton
297	1991	NZ	–	–	–	–	1	3	–	–	–	–	2	6	Nick Farr-Jones	Gary Whetton
298	1991	Arg	5	3	–	–	2	32	2	1	–	2	1	19	Nick Farr-Jones	Pablo Garreton
299	1991	WSam	–	–	–	–	3	9	–	–	–	–	1	3	Nick Farr-Jones	Peter Fatialofa
300	1991	Wales	6	4	–	–	2	38	–	–	–	–	1	3	Michael Lynagh	Ieuan Evans
Sub totals			636	327	2	61	406	4298	730	357	5	86	394	4578	**Won 118, Drawn 11, Lost 171**	
301	1991	Ire	3	2	–	–	1	19	1	1	–	1	3	18	Nick Farr-Jones	Philip Matthews
302	1991	NZ	2	1	–	–	2	16	–	–	–	–	2	6	Nick Farr-Jones	Gary Whetton

Test	Year	Opp	Australia T	C	M	DG	PG	Total	Opponent T	C	M	DG	PG	Total	Australian Captain	Opposition Captain
303	1991	Eng	1	1	–	–	2	12	–	–	–	–	2	6	Nick Farr-Jones	Will Carling
304	1992	Sco	4	1	–	–	3	27	1	1	–	–	2	12	Nick Farr-Jones	David Sole
305	1992	Sco	5	1	–	–	5	37	2	1	–	–	1	13	Nick Farr-Jones	David Sole
306	1992	NZ	2	–	–	–	2	16	2	1	–	–	1	15	Nick Farr-Jones	Sean Fitzpatrick
307	1992	NZ	2	–	–	–	3	19	2	2	–	–	1	17	Nick Farr-Jones	Sean Fitzpatrick
308	1992	NZ	2	2	–	–	3	23	2	2	–	1	3	26	Nick Farr-Jones	Sean Fitzpatrick
309	1992	SA	3	1	–	–	3	26	–	–	–	–	1	3	Nick Farr-Jones	Naas Botha
310	1992	Ire	5	4	–	–	3	42	1	–	–	–	4	17	Michael Lynagh	Philip Donaher
311	1992	Wales	3	1	–	–	2	23	–	–	–	–	2	6	Phil Kearns	Ieuan Evans
312	1993	Tonga	7	4	–	–	3	52	2	2	–	–	–	14	Michael Lynagh	Martin Manukia
313	1993	NZ	1	1	–	–	1	10	2	–	–	–	5	25	Phil Kearns	Sean Fitzpatrick
314	1993	SA	–	–	–	–	4	12	3	2	–	–	–	19	Phil Kearns	Francois Pienaar
315	1993	SA	3	2	–	–	3	28	2	2	–	–	2	20	Phil Kearns	Francois Pienaar
316	1993	SA	1	1	–	–	4	19	2	1	–	–	–	12	Phil Kearns	Francois Pienaar
317	1993	Can	6	2	–	–	3	43	2	–	–	–	2	16	Michael Lynagh	Ian Stuart
318	1993	Fra	1	1	–	–	2	13	1	1	–	2	1	16	Michael Lynagh	Olivier Roumat
319	1993	Fra	2	1	–	–	4	24	–	–	–	–	1	3	Michael Lynagh	Olivier Roumat
320	1994	Ire	5	1	–	–	2	33	1	1	–	–	2	13	Michael Lynagh	Michael Bradley
321	1994	Ire	3	1	–	–	5	32	2	1	–	1	1	18	Michael Lynagh	Michael Bradley
322	1994	Italy	2	2	–	–	3	23	1	–	–	–	5	20	Michael Lynagh	Massimo Giovanelli
323	1994	Italy	1	–	–	–	5	20	1	1	–	–	–	7	Phil Kearns	Massimo Giovanelli
324	1994	WSam	11	6	–	–	2	73	–	–	–	–	1	3	Phil Kearns	Peter Fatialofa
325	1994	NZ	2	2	–	–	2	20	1	1	–	–	3	16	Phil Kearns	Sean Fitzpatrick
326	1995	Arg	7	3	–	–	4	53	1	1	–	–	–	7	Michael Lynagh	Sebastian Salvat
327	1995	Arg	3	–	–	–	5	30	1	1	–	–	2	13	Michael Lynagh	Sebastian Salvat
328	1995	SA	2	1	–	–	2	18	2	1	–	1	4	27	Michael Lynagh	Francois Pienaar
329	1995	Can	3	3	–	–	2	27	1	–	–	–	2	11	Michael Lynagh	Gareth Rees
330	1995	Rom	6	6	–	–	–	42	–	–	–	1	–	3	Rod McCall	Tiberiu Brinza
331	1995	Eng	1	1	–	–	5	22	1	1	–	1	5	25	Michael Lynagh	Will Carling
332	1995	NZ	1	1	–	–	3	16	1	1	–	2	5	28	Phil Kearns	Sean Fitzpatrick
333	1995	NZ	2	2	–	–	3	23	5	3	–	–	1	34	Phil Kearns	Sean Fitzpatrick

			Australia						Opponent							
Test	Year	Opp	T	C	M	DG	PG	Total	T	C	M	DG	PG	Total	Australian Captain	Opposition Captain
334	1996	Wales	7	6	–	–	3	56	3	2	–	–	2	25	John Eales	Jonathon Humphries
335	1996	Wales	6	3	–	–	2	42	–	–	–	–	1	3	John Eales	Jonathon Humphries
336	1996	Can	10	9	–	–	2	74	–	–	–	–	3	9	John Eales	John Graf
337	1996	NZ	–	–	–	–	2	6	6	2	–	–	3	43	John Eales	Sean Fitzpatrick
338	1996	SA	2	1	–	–	3	21	1	1	–	–	3	16	John Eales	Francois Pienaar
339	1996	NZ	2	–	–	–	5	25	2	2	–	–	6	32	John Eales	Sean Fitzpatrick
340	1996	SA	1	1	–	–	4	19	1	1	–	–	6	25	John Eales	Francois Pienaar
341	1996	Italy	4	4	–	–	4	40	2	1	–	1	1	18	John Eales	Massimo Giovanelli
342	1996	Sco	2	2	–	–	5	29	2	–	–	–	3	19	John Eales	Gregor Townsend
343	1996	Ire	1	1	–	–	5	22	–	–	–	–	4	12	John Eales	Keith Wood
344	1996	Wales	3	2	–	–	3	28	1	1	–	–	4	19	Tim Horan	Jonathon Humphries
345	1997	Fra	2	2	–	–	5	29	2	1	–	–	1	15	John Eales	Abdelatif Benazzi
346	1997	Fra	3	1	–	–	3	26	1	1	–	–	4	19	John Eales	Abdelatif Benazzi
347	1997	NZ	1	1	–	–	2	13	4	2	–	–	2	30	John Eales	Sean Fitzpatrick
348	1997	Eng	4	1	–	–	1	25	–	–	–	1	1	6	John Eales	Phil de Glanville
349	1997	NZ	2	1	–	–	2	18	3	3	–	–	4	33	John Eales	Sean Fitzpatrick
350	1997	SA	4	3	–	–	2	32	3	1	–	–	1	20	John Eales	Gary Teichmann
351	1997	NZ	4	2	–	–	–	24	3	3	–	–	5	36	John Eales	Sean Fitzpatrick
352	1997	SA	3	2	–	–	1	22	8	6	–	–	3	61	David Wilson	Gary Teichmann
353	1997	Arg	1	–	–	–	6	23	–	–	–	–	5	15	John Eales	Pedro Sporleder
354	1997	Arg	2	–	–	–	2	16	2	1	–	–	2	18	John Eales	Pedro Sporleder
355	1997	Eng	2	1	–	–	1	15	–	–	–	–	5	15	John Eales	Lawrence Dallaghio
356	1997	Sco	5	3	–	–	2	37	1	–	–	–	1	8	John Eales	Andy Nicol
357	1998	Eng	11	6	–	–	3	76	–	–	–	–	–	0	John Eales	Tony Diprose
358	1998	Sco	5	4	–	–	4	45	–	–	–	–	1	3	John Eales	Rob Wainwright
359	1998	Sco	4	2	–	–	3	33	1	–	–	–	2	11	John Eales	Rob Wainwright
360	1998	NZ	2	1	–	–	4	24	2	–	–	–	2	16	John Eales	Taine Randell
361	1998	SA	2	–	–	–	1	13	1	–	–	–	4	14	John Eales	Gary Teichmann
362	1998	NZ	4	2	–	–	1	27	2	2	–	–	3	23	John Eales	Taine Randell
363	1998	SA	–	–	–	–	5	15	2	2	–	–	5	29	John Eales	Gary Teichmann
364	1998	NZ	1	1	–	–	4	19	1	–	–	1	2	14	John Eales	Taine Randell

Test	Year	Opp	Australia T	C	M	DG	PG	Total	Opponent T	C	M	DG	PG	Total	Australian Captain	Opposition Captain
365	1998	Fiji	9	9	–	–	1	66	2	2	–	–	2	20	John Eales	Setareki Taiwake
366	1998	Tonga	12	7	–	–	–	74	–	–	–	–	–	0	John Eales	Semi Taupeaafe
367	1998	WSam	3	2	–	–	2	25	2	–	–	–	1	13	John Eales	Pat Lam
368	1998	Fra	3	1	–	–	5	32	2	1	–	–	3	21	John Eales	Raphael Ibanez
369	1998	Eng	–	–	–	–	4	12	1	–	–	–	2	11	John Eales	Lawrence Dallaghio
370	1999	Ire	6	5	–	–	2	46	1	1	–	–	1	10	David Wilson	Dion O'Cuinneagain
371	1999	Ire	2	2	–	–	6	32	3	1	–	–	3	26	David Wilson	Dion O'Cuinneagain
372	1999	Eng	4	1	–	–	–	22	2	1	–	–	1	15	David Wilson	Martin Johnson
373	1999	SA	4	3	–	–	2	32	–	–	–	–	2	6	David Wilson	Rassie Erasmus
374	1999	NZ	2	1	–	–	1	15	1	1	–	–	9	34	David Wilson	Taine Randell
375	1999	SA	–	–	–	–	3	9	1	1	–	–	1	10	David Wilson	Joost van der Westhuizen
376	1999	NZ	1	1	–	–	7	28	1	1	–	–	–	7	David Wilson	Taine Randell
377	1999	Rom	9	6	–	–	–	57	–	–	–	–	3	9	John Eales	Romeo Gontineac
378	1999	Ire	2	2	–	–	3	23	–	–	–	–	1	3	John Eales	Dion O'Cuinneagain
379	1999	USA	8	6	–	–	1	55	1	1	–	1	3	19	Jason Little	Kevin Dalzell
380	1999	Wales	3	3	–	–	1	24	–	–	–	–	3	9	John Eales	Robert Howley
381	1999	SA	–	–	–	1	8	27	–	–	–	1	6	21	John Eales	Joost van der Westhuizen
382	1999	Fra	2	2	–	–	7	35	–	–	–	–	4	12	John Eales	Raphael Ibanez
383	2000	Arg	9	4	–	–	–	53	–	–	–	–	2	6	John Eales	Lisandro Arbizu
384	2000	Arg	3	1	–	–	5	32	2	–	–	–	5	25	John Eales	Lisandro Arbizu
385	2000	SA	5	2	–	–	5	44	3	1	–	–	2	23	John Eales	Andre Vos
386	2000	NZ	5	2	–	–	2	35	5	4	–	–	2	39	John Eales	Todd Blackadder
387	2000	SA	2	2	–	–	4	26	–	–	–	–	2	6	John Eales	Andre Vos
388	2000	NZ	2	1	–	–	4	24	2	2	–	–	3	23	John Eales	Todd Blackadder
389	2000	SA	1	1	–	–	4	19	–	–	–	–	6	18	John Eales	Andre Vos
390	2000	Fra	–	–	–	–	6	18	1	1	–	–	2	13	John Eales	Fabien Pelous
391	2000	Sco	3	3	–	–	3	30	–	–	–	–	3	9	John Eales	Budge Poutney
392	2000	Eng	1	1	–	–	4	19	1	1	–	1	4	22	John Eales	Martin Johnson
393	2001	GB	2	–	–	–	1	13	4	3	–	–	1	29	John Eales	Martin Johnson
394	2001	GB	3	1	–	–	6	35	1	–	–	–	3	14	John Eales	Martin Johnson
395	2001	GB	2	2	–	–	5	29	2	2	–	–	3	23	John Eales	Martin Johnson

Test	Year	Opp	Australia						Opponent							
			T	C	M	DG	PG	Total	T	C	M	DG	PG	Total	Australian Captain	Opposition Captain
396	2001	SA	–	–	–	–	5	15	1	–	–	–	5	20	John Eales	Bobby Skinstad
397	2001	NZ	2	2	–	–	3	23	2	1	–	–	1	15	John Eales	Anton Oliver
398	2001	SA	1	–	–	–	3	14	1	–	–	–	3	14	John Eales	Bobby Skinstad
399	2001	NZ	2	2	–	–	5	29	2	2	–	–	4	26	John Eales	Anton Oliver
400	2001	Spa	13	12	–	–	1	92	1	1	–	–	1	10	George Gregan	Antonio Leon
Sub totals			**964**	**530**	**2**	**62**	**711**	**7249**	**872**	**445**	**5**	**102**	**744**	**6256**	**Won 191 , Drawn 13, Lost 196**	
401	2001	Fra	2	1	–	–	1	15	–	–	–	2	5	21	George Gregan	Neil Back
402	2001	Fra	1	1	–	–	2	13	1	–	–	–	3	14	George Gregan	Fabien Galthie
403	2001	Wales	–	–	–	–	7	21	1	1	–	–	2	13	George Gregan	Scott Quinnell
404	2002	Fra	2	2	–	–	5	29	1	–	–	–	4	17	George Gregan	Fabien Pelous
405	2002	Fra	4	1	–	1	2	31	3	2	–	–	2	25	George Gregan	Raphael Ibanez
406	2002	NZ	–	–	–	–	2	6	–	–	–	–	4	12	George Gregan	Rueben Thorne
407	2002	SA	4	3	–	–	4	38	4	2	–	–	1	27	George Gregan	Corne Krige
408	2002	NZ	2	–	–	–	2	16	1	–	–	–	3	14	George Gregan	Rueben Thorne
409	2002	SA	3	–	–	1	3	31	5	4	–	–	–	33	George Gregan	Corne Krige
410	2002	Arg	1	–	–	–	4	17	–	–	–	–	2	6	George Gregan	Lisandro Arbizu
411	2002	Ire	–	–	–	–	3	9	–	–	–	–	6	18	George Gregan	Brian O'Driscoll
412	2002	Eng	3	2	–	–	4	31	2	2	–	–	6	32	George Gregan	Martin Johnson
413	2002	Italy	5	3	–	–	1	34	–	–	–	–	1	3	George Gregan	Marco Borolami
414	2003	Ire	6	6	–	–	1	45	1	1	–	–	3	16	George Gregan	David Humphrey
415	2003	Wales	5	1	–	–	1	30	1	1	–	–	1	10	George Gregan	Martyn Williams
416	2003	Eng	1		–	–	3	14	3	2	–	–	2	22	George Gregan	Lawrence Dallaglio
417	2003	Ire	6	1	–	–	6	45	1	1	–	–	3	16	George Gregan	David Humphreys
418	2003	Wales	5	1	–	–	1	30	1	1	–	–	1	10	George Gregan	Martyn Williams
419	2003	Eng	1	–	–	–	3	14	3	2	–	–	2	25	George Gregan	Martin Johnson
420	2003	SA	3	2	–	1	–	22	2	2	–	–	4	26	George Gregan	Corne Krige
421	2003	NZ	3	2	–	1	2	21	7	4	–	–	3	50	George Gregan	Rueben Thorne
422	2003	SA	2	2	–	–	5	29	–	–	–	–	3	9	George Gregan	Corne Krige
423	2003	NZ	1	–	–	–	4	17	2	1	–	–	3	21	George Gregan	Rueben Thorne
424	2003	Arg	2	1	–	–	4	24	1	–	–	–	1	8	George Gregan	Augustin Pichot
425	2003	Rom	13	11	–	–	1	90	1	–	–	–	1	8	George Gregan	Romeo Gontineac

			Australia						Opponent							
Test	Year	Opp	T	C	M	DG	PG	Total	T	C	M	DG	PG	Total	Australian Captain	Opposition Captain
426	2003	Namibia	21	16	–	–	4	142	–	–	–	–	–	0	Chris Whitaker	Hakkies Husselman
427	2003	Ire	1	–	–	1	3	17	1	1	–	1	2	16	George Gregan	Keith Wood
428	2003	Sco	3	3	–	–	4	33	1	1	–	1	2	16	George Gregan	Bryan Redpath
429	2003	NZ	1	1	–	–	5	22	1	1	–	–	1	10	George Gregan	Rueben Thorne
430	2003	Eng	1	–	–	–	4	17	1	–	–	1	4	20	George Gregan	Martin Johnson
431	2004	Sco	4	3	–	–	3	35	–	–	–	–	5	15	George Gregan	Scott Murray
432	2004	Sco	5	3	–	–	1	34	2	1	–	–	1	13	George Gregan	Scott Murray
433	2004	Eng	6	3	–	–	5	51	2	1	–	–	1	15	George Gregan	Lawrence Dallaglio
434	2004	Pac.Is.	5	2	–	–	–	29	2	2	–	–	–	14	George Gregan	Inoke Afeaki
435	2004	NZ	1	1	–	–	–	7	1	1	–	–	3	16	Nathan Sharpe	Tana Umaga
436	2004	SA	4	2	–	–	2	30	3	1	–	–	3	26	George Gregan	John Smit
437	2004	NZ	1	–	–	–	6	23	–	–	–	–	6	18	George Gregan	Tana Umanga
438	2004	SA	3	2	–	–	–	19	2	2	–	–	3	23	George Gregan	John Smit
439	2004	Sco	4	4	–	–	1	31	2	2	–	–	–	14	George Gregan	Gordon Bulloch
440	2004	Fra	1	–	–	–	3	14	2	1	–	–	5	27	George Gregan	Fabien Pelous
441	2004	Sco	4	4	–	–	1	31	1	–	–	–	4	17	George Gregan	Gordon Bulloch
442	2004	Eng	2	1	–	–	3	21	3	2	–	–	–	19	George Gregan	Jason Robinson
Sub totals			1106	615	2	67	827	8477	937	487	5	107	750	6991	Won 216, Drawn 13, Lost 213